Decoding the IRA

Without the Army Ireland cannot gain her freedom
Frank Aiken referring to the IRA, 1925

TOM MAHON & JAMES J. GILLOGLY

DECODING THE IRA

MERCIER PRESS
WHAT YOU NEED TO READ

Mercier Press

Cork

www.mercierpress.ie

Trade enquiries to:

Columba Mercier Distribution,

55a Spruce Avenue, Stillorgan Industrial Park, Blackrock,

County Dublin

ISBN: 978 1 85635 604 6

10 9 8 7 6 5 4 3 2 1

Mercier Press receives financial assistance from
the Arts Council/An Chomhairle Ealaíon

Printed and bound in the EU

Contents

This book is dedicated to my sister Rosemary and mother Mary
In memory of Tom Crofts and his comrades of Cork 1 Brigade

Tom Mahon

To the late William G. Sutton, my long-time cryptographic collaborator
and friend, who was always ready to test and suggest new approaches as
I developed the cryptanalytic tools I used to break these ciphers.

Jim Gillogly

Key Characters

Aiken, Frank: IRA chief of staff, April 1923 to November 1925. He supported Éamon de Valera and was a founder member of Fianna Fáil in 1926.

Cooney, Andy: also known as 'Mr Smith'. IRA chief of staff from November 1925 to spring 1926, and chairman of the Army Council from November 1925 to January 1927.

de Valera, Éamon: president of Sinn Féin and of the shadow republican 'government'. In early 1926 he resigned from both positions and founded Fianna Fáil.

Devoy, John: veteran Irish-American 'Fenian' leader, who supported the Free State and opposed both de Valera and the IRA.

George: also known as 'HS'. IRA Officer Commanding in Britain from the autumn of 1926 through 1927. Worked closely with the Soviet agent 'James'. He was likely George Power, an IRA intelligence officer originally from Cork.

James: pseudonym for a Red Army intelligence agent in London. The IRA supplied him with information in return for payment.

Jones, Mr: pseudonym, also known as JB. An IRA secret agent in New York, who worked for Soviet intelligence.

Lynch, Liam: IRA chief of staff during the Civil War, from 1922 until his death in April 1923. Moss Twomey's mentor.

MacBride, Seán: also known as 'Mr Ambrose'. An IRA leader closely allied with Moss Twomey. He travelled extensively on the continent, where he was in contact with Soviet agents.

McGarrity, Joseph (Joe): chairman of Clan na Gael. The most important IRA supporter in America.

Neenan, Connie: also known as An Timthire. The official IRA representative in the US.

O'Donnell, Peadar: member of the Army Council and editor of the IRA's paper, *An Phoblacht*. He was the leading IRA republican socialist intellectual and also a distinguished novelist.

Russell, Seán: IRA quartermaster general, in charge of weapons and explosives. He was the leading militarist in the organisation and was dismissive of any political involvement by the IRA.

Sheehy, John Joe: captain of the Kerry football team and commander of the Kerry IRA.

Stephen: pseudonym for the Red Army intelligence agent in America who was in contact with the IRA.

Twomey, Maurice (Moss): also known as 'Mr Browne'. Succeeded Andy Cooney as chief of staff in the spring of 1926 and in January 1927 was also appointed chairman of the Army Council. He remained chief of staff until 1936 and was one of the most influential of the IRA's leaders.

NOTE:

The text which was originally in the IRA's secret code or cipher, is printed in a typewriter type font. For example: Let me know [the] names of [the] prison officials against whom action should be taken.

Introduction

Tom Mahon

Try and get formulae for these tear gases and mustard gases and [an] idea of [the]
plant necessary [for production].

IRA chief of staff to agent in America

Could you get some mines or incendiary bombs put on ships or put ships on fire
with petrol or other inflammables?

Moss Twomey, IRA chief of staff, to the IRA in Liverpool

In 2001 I was researching a (still unfinished) project at the University
College, Dublin (UCD) Archives when I came across a number of IRA
documents from the 1920s that were written in a secret cipher or code.
At the time, I didn't think much about them and continued with my
research, but every now and then I'd find another such document and
slowly my curiosity grew. Eventually, three years later I started to gather
them together (with the help of the principal archivist Seamus Helferty
and his staff) and set out to have them decrypted. I eventually met up
with James Gillogly, one of the leading civilian cryptologists in the world,
and this book is the result of James' decryptions of these documents – a
world of espionage and intrigue never before described.

This is the IRA for the first time, in its own uncensored words – no
topic is omitted and there is no attempt to present a sanitised image
for public consumption. This is the complete IRA network – operations,
arms smuggling, disputes and retaliation. A story with spies, Russian
agents, clandestine meetings and poison gas – it is part James Bond and
part Walter Mitty. The tenor of the documents ranges from ruthlessness
to pathos and often with a dash of humour. The strength and ingenuity
of the IRA is revealed alongside its incompetence and the widespread
demoralisation of its members.

In all James decrypted 312 documents written in cipher. The IRA
encrypted them so they would remain secret to all except the intended

recipients and they were concerned about seizure by the police. To the best of my knowledge, they have never before been decrypted for publication.

I found the documents among the tens of thousands of papers donated to UCD by the family of Moss Twomey, IRA chief of staff from 1926 to 1936. The encrypted documents represent the most highly classified correspondence between the IRA's General Headquarters (GHQ) in Dublin and its units and operatives. These include units throughout Ireland and Britain, prisoners in jail in Ireland and agents in Britain and America. Some of them contain only a name or address in cipher, others have several pages of densely typed secret text. The despatches to America are the longest, as Moss Twomey had no other way to keep in contact with his representatives there. The vast majority of these documents were dated 1926 or 1927, with a few from either 1925 or 1928.

The cipher is easy to distinguish from ordinary English (or plain text) – frequently consisting of blocks of five letters with no overt meaning. For example, Moss Twomey sent a message to the IRA in Liverpool: UEIRS, NRFCO, OBISE, IOMRO, POTNE, NANRT, HLYME, PPROM, TERSI, HEELT, NBOFO, LUMDT, TWOAO, ENUUE, RMDIO, SRILA, SSYHP, PRSGI, IOSIT, B. When decrypted this read: Could you get some mines or incendiary bombs put on ships or put ships on fire with petrol or other inflammables?[1]

This order was written in 1927, but was dated 1924. This was deliberately done to confuse the police in the event of capture of the document.

THE MAJORITY OF THE documents were written in a transposition cipher, meaning that the individual letters of the original (plain text) message were rearranged. A significant minority of the documents used a substitution cipher, where letters were replaced by assigned letters or symbols. A cipher is different from a true code where the original text is replaced by assigned words, phrases or sentences rather than by individual letters.[2]

When I first rounded up samples of the documents and brought them back to my home in Hawaii, there were two questions on my mind. Could they be decrypted? What story would they tell? It seemed to me that a cipher dating from before the time of the German Enigma cipher

C. S.

Y. I8. 24th. February '24

DESTROY WHEN READ.

To/
O.C. No3 Area, Britain.

I. II3: UHTAO, EUESI, YSOIO, OMTOG, OSHNY, DMHRS, OSRAS, NOEEO, MRYUR, TRRRF, CNTYR, NIRIH, IUSNR, TNENF, UMYOA, SRUEO, TOIME, IPEPR, WIAOT, TRHDT, AOTNP, TOCOA, NMB.

96: UEIMS, NRFCO, OBISE, IOMRO, POTNE, NANRT, HLYME, PPROM, TERSI, HEELT, NBOFO, LUMDT, TWOAO, ENUUE, RMDIC, SRILA, SSYHP, PRSGI, IOSIT, B.

84: ETNEU, OIKLD, IYTTE, UOTOI, HBRUA, EYTHY, DHHOA, SESRR, NIPEO, ITNNS, ESROS, OISIE, ERBTL, TTTSG, OTSRA, OTACC, CPAU.

2. Bearer of this despatch will bring back the £ 20 which you are to refund. This is the cash which was advanced in connection with sailors.

3. I was very sorry I could not go over last week. I hoped to, but could not get away.

CHIEF OF STAFF.

Figure 1. Moss Twomey wrote to the OC of the IRA's Liverpool company: Your intelligence officer reports shipments from there for China. If you can do your utmost to destroy any ammunition or other armament or stores being sent. Could you get some time mines or incendiary bombs put on ships or put ships on fire with petrol or other inflammables? Keep this absolutely secret. Do not discuss it. Either carry out the operations or say nothing about it.

machines of the 1930s and 1940s could be broken. But at the time I had no appreciation of the challenges that decryption would present.

When the ciphers were composed, they were encrypted by the sender and then decrypted by the recipient, both of whom possessed a common secret word or keyword (also known as the key). The keyword was any agreed word of moderate length such as 'imprisonment' or 'determination'. In most cases, the keywords were no longer known and even if I had the original keyword, I did not know how the cipher was constructed around the key.

In my quest to decipher the documents, I started with a search on Google, which did not turn up much of promise. I then talked to a colleague at work who was a reserve officer in the US army, and he made some inquiries of fellow officers who worked in intelligence. Understandably they were reluctant to use government computers, and time, for any unauthorised project. Next, I contacted a professor in the department of mathematics at the University of Hawaii. He had spent some time as a post-graduate student studying cryptology and instantly recognised them as a form of cipher called columnar transposition. However, even with this insight I was no closer to unlocking the secrets.

Hoping for a lucky break I continued to surf the web. Among the sites I looked at was that of the CIA; then late one evening I came across the National Security Agency (NSA) website. The NSA is one of the most secret and important security agencies in the United States. It is the main centre for cryptanalysis in the country, with responsibility for collecting and analysing signals intelligence from around the world.[3] The website included a section on the history of cryptology; I sent an e-mail titled 'history', explaining my dilemma.

A little later the NSA replied that they couldn't help but recommended I contact the American Cryptogram Association. I sent the association a sample of six brief ciphers, which Dave Smith kindly shared with the association's membership by e-mail. Exactly two hours later (to the minute) the solutions came back to me courtesy of Dr James Gillogly. One was a message on importing explosives to Ireland from Britain, while others talked of secret meetings. At last, I was on to something – or rather James was!

James became my new partner and together over the next three years we tried to reveal the secrets of the IRA. I corresponded with him by e-mail for a few years before we actually met face to face. In the meantime, I discovered that I had stumbled across one of the most brilliant cryptologists in the US. A quiet-spoken man, he approached each new cipher as a complex but logical word puzzle.

James had been fascinated with ciphers since his days as a cub scout, when his father challenged him and his brother with simple letter substitution ciphers. At university he majored in computer science, and in 1978 received a PhD from Carnegie-Mellon University. At that time he wrote TECH – one of the early computer chess programmes – with the aim of pushing forward the frontier of computer technology in the realm of artificial intelligence. TECH went on to take second place in a world computer chess championship and pioneered some of the search techniques used by Deep Blue, which in 1997 became the first computer programme to defeat a world chess champion, Garry Kasparov.

In 1977, James made his first break of a previously unsolved cipher — a vellum page with odd symbols from the reign of King Henry VI (1421–1471) of England. It turned out to be an alchemical formula beginning 'take 1 ounse of your gold tat is desoluid and chaue 22 …' To the best of my knowledge neither James nor his family have since made gold from base metal! Many other successes followed. The most famous of these was his decryption in 1999 of most of the cipher embedded in sheets of copper on the *kryptos* sculpture in a courtyard at the CIA headquarters in Langley, Virginia. *Kryptos* is a Greek word that appropriately means 'hidden'. James also worked on German codes from the Second World War which had been encoded by the Enigma machine and his method was used to break a number of previously unbroken messages from the war.

Over the years, he went on to found a software company with his wife Marrietta and to develop network security programmes for computer operating systems. Since his retirement in 1999, he has acted as a consultant to the FBI and designed software to support law enforcement cryptanalysts combating criminals and gangs who use cipher, including gang members communicating with their imprisoned colleagues.

Working on the IRA documents, James delighted in beating the IRA cryptographers, without having the need for the original keywords. He performed the decryptions by loading the cipher text onto his computer and then analysing it with highly sophisticated decryption software that he had developed himself. Several times, he deciphered messages that the original recipient had complained could not be decoded — messages where the wrong keyword was used or the numbering of the encrypted letters was incorrect. On occasion, he was able to decrypt messages where a part of the document had been damaged or torn. This is possible with transposition ciphers as the letters for each word are distributed throughout the text, whereas in plain text all the letters of a word are together in sequential order. Thus if the corner of a cipher document is torn off and a block of letters missing, there may still be most of the letters of each word available, allowing one to deduce the actual message. However, with plain text if a word is missing there are no components of it in the remaining portion of the document.

While I was interested in the contents of the cipher, James revelled in this great puzzle and the variety of encryption and security techniques used by the IRA.

Over the course of several trips back to Ireland, I was able to accumulate the 300 or so documents with cipher, in addition to a large number of papers containing supporting or background information. This work was largely done at UCD Archives in Belfield, Dublin, one of the premier repositories of documents covering twentieth-century Irish history. The Twomey Papers and the Ernie O'Malley Papers, both housed in the UCD Archives, are among the most important primary sources relating to the IRA. These, and other, collections make the IRA perhaps the most comprehensively documented revolutionary group of the twentieth century.

Copies of the documents arrived at my home in Honolulu, Hawaii, where I copied them again, sorted them and forwarded them to James in Los Angeles. On receiving the decryptions back from James I tried to assemble the cryptic messages into a coherent narrative within the appropriate historical context.

The world described by the papers was difficult to comprehend at first. We were getting seemingly unrelated snippets of information. Few of the messages were understandable on their own without reference to other documents or without knowledge of the background in which the events described were taking place. It was rather like assembling a large jigsaw without a picture on the box. And at the beginning it seemed like all we had were a few blue pieces that could have been either sky or ocean!

For security purposes the IRA were deliberately indirect and cryptic, even in cipher. For instance, only rarely were IRA leaders or key agents referred to by their real names; instead they were assigned a pseudonym or referred to by rank. So we were left with a list of fictitious names – Mr Brown, Mr Smith, Mr Ambrose and Jack Jones. By cross referencing with multiple documents and correlating the movements of the characters with those of known IRA leaders I was eventually able to find out the real name behind many of the pseudonyms and make a probable guess at some of the others. In the case of unsigned letters, it was often possible to credit them to a particular author by their reference number, cross-referencing to other papers or by looking at subsequent letters acknowledging receipt of the original letter.

'Mr Brown' (or Browne) and 'Mr Smith' at GHQ oversaw most of the correspondence with the IRA's agents in America. So it seemed likely that they represented Moss Twomey and Andy Cooney, the IRA's two key leaders. From the cipher, we learned that 'Mr Smith' had recently returned from a visit to America and later went to England to complete his studies. This fitted the profile of Cooney, who visited America in the summer of 1926 and resigned as chief of staff so he could complete his medical studies and qualify as a doctor. The proof finally came in a security lapse by Moss Twomey when he wrote to Connie Neenan in America: 'send Cooney [a] copy of the addresses he had [in the US]'. But then in the précis (or plain text summary of the cipher that was kept on file at GHQ) he made the error of writing: 'send address to Smith'. Twomey should have written 'Smith' in both cipher and the précis. This slip-up confirmed that 'Mr Smith' was a cover for Andy Cooney.[4]

Twomey was appointed chairman of the Army Council in January 1927 and the following month 'the chairman' (Twomey) sent a despatch to 'Mr Jones' in New York in which he acknowledged receiving two prior letters, which in turn had been addressed to 'Mr Brown'. This is some of the evidence that supports the contention that 'Mr Brown' was Moss Twomey.[5]

Later in this book we present evidence that 'Mr Ambrose' was Seán MacBride; that 'HS' the IRA's commander in Britain was likely George Power, an IRA intelligence officer from north Cork and that 'Mr Jones' (or 'JB') an espionage agent in America was most probably Dan 'Sandow' Donovan from Cork. There are also a number of despatches to and from 'Jack Jones' a senior IRA leader based in the Portlaoise area. I suspect 'Jones' was really Jim Killeen from Westmeath (who was appointed IRA adjutant general in 1927), but in this case the evidence is insufficient to be certain.[6]

Two other interesting characters were 'James' and 'Stephen'. 'James' was a frequent visitor or resident of London, while 'Stephen' was in contact with the IRA in America. In a later chapter, we show that these were the cover names for two Soviet Red Army intelligence officers working with the IRA. Despite some research, I am (as of yet) unable to find their real names. Indeed Soviet agents frequently had so many pseudonyms that their true identity often remains unknown to this day.

Ref.No.7 HS/30.

(Urgent)

To/
C.S.   6th. May, 1927.

1.   (238)   ¤¤¤O¤. DDTTT. NRK¤U. HMLSS. FSOMY. ¤¤AIO. ACO¤L. AY¤HA.
                ASTHG. DXCIP. ILGTE. THIOI. RILYT. FITSU. TAWC¤. SHBA¤.
                ¤OITO. POBI¤. AOSPH. OWL¤A. MMMUI. XAO¤R. V¤¤TT. ¤NCTT.
                SWN¤U. AULOS. MATYI. HI¤¤L. MCOAW. UIASR. NS¤OW. T¤NWH.
                ON¤OH. ISYDR. IHL¤T. 3AAND. JO¤TN. ¤NUC¤. ¤ADP¤. NDKWR.
                ITRRB. HHHOT. INRRW. BBTTH. HFVLN. S¤N¤¤. CHOCI. LSK.

I await acknowledgments of my HS/28 & HS/29.

Figure 2. Despatch from George (alias 'HS'), the IRA's commander in Britain, to Moss Twomey. This letter includes the only direct reference to Moscow in the documents. George reported that 'James', the Soviet intelligence officer, had written to inform him that the Soviets would improve their funding of the IRA: I had a letter from 'James'. He is in Moscow. He told me to inform you, that everything would be fixed up and he is anxious that you cable this decision to our representative in America. He also acknowledges the receipt of your letter, which was sent to him by hand. He will be back in less than two weeks.

It was also challenging trying to identify IRA operatives when they were referred to by rank rather than name. I frequently found it difficult to find out who held a specific appointment at a particular time – this was due not only to the organisation's secrecy but also to the high turnover in staff due to arrests and resignations. As soon as one officer became unavailable, a substitute was quickly appointed in his place. Andy Cooney was appointed chief of staff in November 1925 and Moss Twomey took over the position in the spring of the following year. However, the exact date for the change in command is uncertain and in the case of letters signed 'chief of staff' in May 1926 it is unclear whether the sender was Twomey or Cooney. Similarly during the period of Moss Twomey's imprisonment in November 1926, it is uncertain who was the author of letters signed 'chief of staff' – though Andy Cooney most likely stepped back temporarily into the role. Hopefully this gives an idea of some of the challenges James and I faced.

James was scrupulous in his attention to detail and accuracy. The copies we worked on were sometimes of poor quality, due to the age and state of the originals, and individual letters could be unclear or a portion of the text missing. An 'I' could be mistaken for a 'T' or an 'O' for a 'D'. Additionally words were sometimes misspelled or abbreviated. James' decryption produced a long string of text and he manually entered word breaks and punctuation based on the context. This could be challenging in the case of misspellings or where colloquial Irish expressions were used. One decryption, without the word breaks, was as follows: 'avolunteerwasapproachedbycidwhoofferedhimtwopoundperweekforanyinformationhecouldgivethemconcerningduuhsalsoonepoundforeachrifleflego'.

After James entered the appropriate word breaks, symbols and numerals this became: 'a volunteer was approached by cid who offered him £2 per week for any information he could give them concerning duuhs also £1 for each rifle go'. James and I then worked together on this and realised that 'duuhs' was a misspelling of 'dumps' and that a 't' had been dropped from 'go'. Thus the corrected text became the much more understandable: 'a volunteer was approached by [the] CID [detectives] who offered him £2 per week for any information he could give them concerning [IRA arms] dumps, also £1 for each rifle got'.[7] Many times James went back and forth over the interpretation of a single word or sentence. In this book simple spelling mistakes have been corrected, but where there remained any ambiguity in the text or the cipher was uninterpretable we left it uncorrected without making any assumptions.

On rare occasions, words in Irish (which the IRA virtually never spelled correctly) or colloquial Irish expressions posed a temporary challenge to James – who was raised in America. The most memorable incident was when Moss Twomey recommended that an IRA volunteer visit a 'call house' to meet a young lady. Now the American Merriam-Webster dictionary defines a call house as 'a house or apartment where call girls may be procured' and James feared the worst.[8] However, shortly afterwards I received an e-mail back from him after he realised that the IRA's meaning of a call house was a place where contact could be secretly made with an IRA representative.

It was only after almost three years that the papers' full significance became apparent as they revealed activities and facets of the IRA that have never been openly known before. They expose the full extent and nature of the organisation's relationship with the Soviet Union; military espionage in America; the IRA's interest in acquiring chemical weapons; methods and routes for importing arms and explosives; infiltration of the Gaelic Athletic Association in America; IRA security and intelligence techniques; new insight into the reaction of the IRA's leadership to the founding of Fianna Fáil; personality clashes, indiscipline and the state of readiness of the IRA.

Some of this information was truly bizarre, and when I came across the following message from Moss Twomey to the IRA's commander in Glasgow 'could a ship or ships for China be burned or destroyed by scuttling or other means?' I thought that 'China' was a code word. But no, the IRA actually wanted to attack British ships sailing to China.[9] References to republican support for Chiang Kai-shek and the Chinese nationalists can be found in Brian Hanley's *The IRA: 1926–1936* and in contemporary issues of the IRA's newspaper, *An Phoblacht*. However, the ciphered documents add significantly to our knowledge of this unusual episode.

I have attempted to tell the story of the IRA in the context of the times. The IRA, like any other revolutionary group, can't be fully understood without reference to the interplay of contemporary factors such as ideology, the role of personalities, local and international political developments, financial and military resources, strategy and morale and discipline. The personalities of the leadership played an important part in the IRA, particularly as the organisation lacked a single unifying ideology. Additionally, knowledge of the many failed or aborted military attacks tells us as much about the organisation as the odd successful attack does. A history that emphasised one particular aspect of the IRA, such as the socialist ideology of some of its leaders, or concentrated on military activity would give a very incomplete and misleading picture of the organisation. I wanted to avoid this compartmentalisation and to give 'a feel' as to what the IRA was really like and how its members saw themselves.

Researching this book has been an extremely enjoyable adventure and I frequently allowed myself be distracted when reading old newspapers and documents. Trying to piece together the section on chemical weapons was quite a challenge given the (understandable) reticence of experts to talk in this post-September 11 world. At one time I contacted an employee of the US army's chemical corps and asked him about getting a copy of a book containing poison gas formulae which the IRA had given to the Soviets in 1927. When he refused, I told him I could get it on the internet or through an inter-library loan. He politely replied that if I did so I could be monitored and even visited by an unnamed government agency. So far, I haven't seen anyone searching my bin at night! Ironically, all the experts in chemical warfare I talked to gave me at least one piece of helpful information, though communication was frequently abruptly terminated on their part. I suppose most people who inquire about chemical warfare are either crazy or potentially dangerous – or both!

The only topic more difficult to get information on than chemical warfare was the covert activities of the IRA and republicans in America. Not surprisingly for a clandestine organisation, there is a lack of documentation and material. However, much of the discussion in the Irish-American community is still rooted in stereotypes of English perfidy and IRA freedom fighters, which has stifled healthy debate and balanced research. When I contacted the Gaelic Athletic Association in New York with questions about the IRA the door was quickly shut – though I was able to get the information I needed at the New York Public Library. However, the process of creating 'history' to satisfy the needs of the present, results in us forgetting the complexity of the struggles of the past and the sacrifices of ordinary men and women. History is about remembering in context, rather than inventing an imaginary past.

The value of these documents is that they are the nearest we can come to having an open and collegial conversation with IRA leaders such as Moss Twomey and Andy Cooney. Especially in the letters sent to America, Twomey and Cooney give their opinion on a whole range of topics – from the state of the IRA to distrust of Éamon de Valera. There are also detailed descriptions of IRA techniques and security procedures. However, at times the IRA deliberately communicated in an indirect manner or attempted to mislead the recipient. For instance, Twomey presented an overly upbeat assessment of the readiness of the IRA in a letter to America in early

1927 – to encourage fundraising in the US. Overall, the documents give a unique insight into what the IRA was actually like at the time.

This is a world of moral ambiguity: even a generally sympathetic figure such as Moss Twomey had a ruthless streak. And though the greatly respected George Gilmore endured considerable hardship in prison for the cause, the documents raise some suspicion that IRA money under his control went missing.

There were a number of pieces of information that James and I found to be particularly repugnant. One was a document written by the IRA in Offaly attempting to justify the execution of a group of local citizens, whom the writer claimed were 'notorious spies'.[10] Other documents reveal IRA efforts to intimidate witnesses and jurors by threatening them or their families, while another sordid episode was the IRA's torture and killing of one of their own, Dan Turley, who was suspected of informing.

These papers can be compared to other sources of information on the IRA, such as the interviews IRA leaders gave in their old age to writers and journalists. Many of the interviews took place in the 1960s and 1970s and the IRA men were carefully preparing their legacy with a sanitised version of events. Their recollections were also subconsciously influenced by events that occurred in subsequent years. Though important books such as Uinseann MacEoin's *Survivors* and *The IRA in the Twilight Years* make fascinating reading, much is missing from them. In MacEoin's books, the Russian connection is largely missing and Connie Neenan in his interview does not mention his involvement in the IRA's espionage activities in America. There is no discussion of operational techniques that, even in the 1970s, might have compromised the IRA. As for the memoirs written by IRA veterans, Twomey himself dismissed many of them as 'myths and legends'.[11] Ernie O'Malley's *On Another Man's Wound* is a classic of the genre and well worth the read. When Bowyer Bell's *The Secret Army* was first published in 1970, it was ground-breaking; however, it tells the story from the IRA's perspective and lacks sufficient critical assessment. Brian Hanley's recently published *The IRA: 1926 to 1936* is an excellent and invaluable history and particularly strong on the political background of the organisation.

Police and intelligence sources are a valuable adjunct to any study;

however, their information is often fragmentary, alarmist and even inaccurate. Police informants were frequently of dubious nature, while the police themselves had their own biases, coupled with a desire to satisfy their superiors. The primary obligation for the police and intelligence agencies was to curtail or destroy the IRA, not to understand it.

The source that comes nearest to these documents are the interviews Ernie O'Malley held with IRA veterans in the 1930s and recorded in the O'Malley Papers. These are refreshingly direct and honest, though again they avoid certain incidents and details.

I have tried to treat all those mentioned in this book (whether IRA members or not) with a mixture of sympathy and scepticism, which I believe produces the most balanced picture.

Throughout the papers, the names and addresses of many individuals and businesses are mentioned and are reproduced in this book. James and I are of the opinion that it is historically important to publish the uncensored contents of the papers. It conveys a full picture of the extent of the IRA's network throughout the Irish community at home and abroad, illustrates the IRA's *modus operandi* and is a way to remember the many people who contributed to a cause they believed in. However, in some cases the IRA may have been mistaken in their opinion of these people and businesses and any activities that occurred in businesses may have been unknown to the owners. Furthermore, the businesses described in this book relate to the period 1926–7 and not to any establishment currently operating with the same or similar name.

Aside from information that was incomplete, repetitious or inconsequential, James and I have omitted nothing we deemed to be of significance.

CHAPTER I

Breaking the Ciphers

James J. Gillogly

Did courier at Xmas give you copy of Woolworth edition of novel *The Scarlet Letter*,
which was to be used for keys for cipher?

Moss Twomey to Connie Neenan, 24 February 1927, using the old key

Re: Yours of 16th inst. I cannot decipher your code. Has the keyword been
changed? If so I have not received the new keyword.

Staff Captain Wilson to chief of staff, 29 April 1926

Many challenge ciphers float into my office over the transom, but this was
my favourite sort: an unsolved cipher in an unknown system, whose content was a mystery to everyone now living.[1] One of the greatest intellectual thrills is experienced at the moment you break an old cipher and
realise that you are the only person in the world who knows this particular bit of history. The first six ciphers arrived on the mailing list of the
American Cryptogram Association, forwarded by a cryptanalyst who had
tried unsuccessfully to break them using many of the standard methods.[2]
This seemed promising: the ciphers were clearly going to be challenging but ultimately quite likely solvable, since effective attacks have been
developed for many of the ciphers used in the first few decades of the
twentieth century.

One key to solving an unknown cipher is a positive attitude: if you
believe you have a good chance of breaking it, you may well be correct.
If you believe you will not be able to crack it, you are almost certainly
correct. Another key is persistence: cryptanalysis often involves many
false leads, and if you allow those to discourage you, the game is lost. As
an example, I first encountered in 1968 a mysterious vellum document
called the Voynich Manuscript[3] in David Kahn's classic, *The Codebreakers*.[4]
This small book is written in an unknown script with fancifully obscure
illustrations, dates back to the early seventeenth century or earlier, and
has successfully resisted all attempts to extract clear meaning from it.[5]

Over this forty-year period I have tried dozens of approaches, started an international mailing list discussing the manuscript's history and potential attacks on it, and coordinated efforts to transcribe it into a form suitable for computer analysis. None of these efforts has produced a solution, but we now know a good deal more about it than when we started, and there's a good chance that if meaning is found in the manuscript, our spade-work will have helped unearth it.

Like many cryptanalysts I am much less interested in the actual content of cipher messages than in the process of decrypting them. For me the challenge comes from discovering the method used and inventing attacks to decrypt them. Although I am originally of Irish descent, my ancestors emigrated from Ireland in 1803, so any necessary historical and geographical context had to come from my co-author. Little of this context was needed for the actual solution of these messages, though, since for the most part the decryption process was unambiguous.

Diagnosing the first cipher

The first cipher in the set of six messages sent to the mailing list was the upper cipher shown in Figure 3, with 151 letters.[6]

No. 84.

16th June 1927.

Dear Sir,

To formally acknowledge yours No. 38 which I had already informed you verbally I had received.
Yours No. 40 of the 10th reached me on the 14th with enclosures. The White Paper you sent was the correct one. Thanks very much.

Your No. 39 undated did not reach me until today, as you sent it to an address which had b en cancelled and is not being used now.

(151) ALOOA IIIEO ABAEW LWUO ELBAP HAEKA EIIIE AAAHO IPWWTN COUMA FSOSG MEGHS YPITT AUSYA OMDOO EKHNQ EKEVR TTMDI SOSEN PEIEE ISUTI ERRAS TTKAH LPSUG MDLKP WEYDM EMGEO HULDC MEWTB ICHIA T.

I herewith send you a reply for Ted, also a note with regard to Jim's clothes. This Note should be sent on to W2.

(97) WAIGA OITYA MMAAB CEECA OIEEN JPAOD OURGE MANNH AMSIT NTOMD ONTIK TTOEE MMAPW OITGA OTFWM IWGME HPWYI CIIHR SMIRS UI.

I came away without taking the address of our friend to whom I promised to send the book. Please send this address in your next note.

I am sending you in clear a list of persons supplied by Clare and who are reported as being friendly. The person who is taking this note will let you know when she is returning. If you should have the adaptors she will bring them along.

c/s.

Figure 3. The first cipher, 16 June 1927.

23

I needed to determine which of the two basic cipher types was used to encrypt this message: transposition or substitution.[7] Cryptograms found in newspaper puzzles use substitution: one letter substitutes for another but the letters remain in their original order. For example, LETTER might become OHWWHU by advancing each letter three places in the alphabet – the system used by Julius Caesar.[8] Transposition ciphers leave each letter's identity intact, but shuffle the letters around so that the message becomes unreadable. One common method used for this shuffling process is columnar transposition. The sender and receiver agree on a key – for example, a single word like MONARCHY.

The sender writes the message under the **key** in rows:

Key:

M	O	N	A	R	C	H	Y
D	E	M	O	C	R	A	C
Y	I	S	T	H	E	B	E
S	T	R	E	V	E	N	G
E	B	E	N	A	Z	I	R
B	H	U	T	T	O		

The sender then *alphabetises the key*, keeping the columns intact.

Key:

A	C	H	M	N	O	R	Y
O	R	A	D	M	E	C	C
T	E	B	Y	S	I	H	E
E	E	N	S	R	T	V	G
N	Z	I	E	E	B	A	R
T	O		B	U	H	T	

The sender completes the shuffling by reading the message out by columns, using the alphabetical order of the key. If the key contains two or more of the same letter, the leftmost one is used first. The encrypted message starts here with the A of MONARCHY, then the C and so on, so the final encryption is OTENT REEZO ABNI DYSEB MSREU EITBH CHVAT CEGR. Usually the message will be presented in five-letter groups to conceal any hints to a would-be codebreaker concerning column length or order. The receiver counts the letters in the message, sets up a frame with the correct number of letters in the last row and enters the encrypted message under the key, again in alphabetical order, finally reading the original plain text message in rows.

Counting letter frequencies quickly distinguishes between the two types: with transposition ciphers the most and least common letters of the cipher will be the most and least common letters of the underlying language. I assumed English was used for this set of six messages, since the surrounding text ('Dear Sir', 'Yours Faithfully') is in English. The most common letters of the cipher, EARIOST, are common letters in English. The least common letters of the cipher, BQVKP, are uncommon letters in English. The proportion of vowels in standard English text is about 40 per cent, and in this cipher is 47 per cent – rather high, but within normal variation. I was quite confident I was looking at a transposition cipher.

Solving the first cipher

The cipher may use any of scores of types of transposition: for example, the columnar transposition shown [p. 24] with the columns shuffled according to a secret key; pattern-based systems such as route transposition or rail-fence; the turning grille, using a square with cut-outs in which to write the message, turning it to each of four positions; nihilist transposition, where both the rows and columns of an array are shuffled; and many other variations on these themes. Each system uses a key: a secret piece of information intended to keep the message private even if the general system is known to the attacker, assuming the underlying cipher system is strong enough. The number of letters in this cipher serves to eliminate some of the possible systems: the 151 letters will not fill a square or rectangle evenly, so many of the common rectangle-based systems need not be considered.

I chose for my first attempts the columnar transposition system: it is simple to explain to a correspondent who may not be an experienced cipher clerk, it can be used for messages that do not fit in a complete rectangle, and it had been used rather widely before the 1920s, when these ciphers were composed. A cryptanalyst can solve normal columnar transpositions using only pencil and paper, depending on the length of the cipher, the length of the key, and in some cases the content of the message. The analysis can become more difficult if the encryption method is varied, if the key is very long, or if the message is short compared to the key length.

A message using a ten-letter key, meaning the message block will have ten columns, would be relatively straightforward to solve if it were, say, 75 or more letters long and used no tricks. A typical manual attack would be to write the cipher message in a ten-column block and then cut it apart in vertical strips. Since the order of columns is not known, the cryptanalyst would not know in advance which columns were short and which were long in an incompletely-filled block, so extra letters would be added to the top and bottom of each column to allow for that difference. The cryptanalyst would then shuffle these columns around on a table, finding where they can be aligned to form the hidden message.

This process can be tedious to execute with pencil, paper and scissors, especially if many ciphers are to be attacked. Over the past forty years I have developed a wide array of computer programmes to help in my analysis and in many cases to solve common types of ciphers automatically. One of the most effective general-purpose automatic methods I call Shotgun Hillclimbing. This method picks a key length in what I consider a reasonable range, creates a key of that length with randomly chosen letters, 'decrypts' the message using this key, then progressively changes the key to try to get a decryption that looks more English-like. When it reaches a plateau where simple changes to the key no longer improve the result, it compares the result with the best found so far, then goes back to try a new random starting point. The efficacy of the process depends on a number of factors, including the difficulty of the cipher itself, the length of the key, the methods used to modify each successive key, and the method used to score a decryption on the English-like scale. The process itself is, in principle, much like the pencil, paper and scissors method described above, trying the columns in different combinations until words and phrases begin to appear.

I unleashed my Shotgun Hillclimbing programme on this cipher, treating it as a columnar transposition with a partially-filled block of between eight and fifteen columns, and it returned the following, successively better, trial solutions, each using twelve columns:

theafrdahaisteweshceohsuwyloooneeiilotudfosqraffsismragewe ...
theraeaassictoyhewheousewidnollestorufmqoffagiswsmeearse ...
theshaeachsuwoyoneweelotuidsqolerfsisfmgeofawsdeymeneare ...
theaaddaresstowhecieh**youwill**oe**sendstufffor**oaqmg**ismrs**awse ...

The process stopped with the last of these – no better solutions were found using a few hundred more starting keys. The programme produced the key 'fdbjalhcgkei': these letters give the conjectured order of the twelve columns of the cipher, with the 'a' of the key indicating that the beginning of the cipher text (AEOOA IIIEO ...) goes down the fifth column.

This attempted solution looks rather close: we see some clear words such as 'send stuff for' that must be part of the original message. To see why the text is imperfect I set the message in a partially-filled block with twelve columns, yielding twelve rows of twelve letters and one row of seven, and used the programme's proposed key:

Key:	f	d	b	j	a	l	h	c	g	k	e	i
1												
2												
3												
4												
5												
6												
7												
8												
9												
10												
11												
12												
13												

The cipher begins AEOOA IIIEO AEAEW, andstarts down column A, then continues to column B:

Key:	f	d	b	j	a	l	h	c	g	k	e	i
1			E		A							
2			W		E							
3					O							
4					O							
5					A							
6					I							
7					I							
8					I							
9					E							
10					O							
11					A							
12					E							
13					A							

The next few groups are LFRRD ELBAP RAEEA EIIIE AAAHO IFMFN, and these are filled in the same way, continuing after the EW in column b and going on to columns c and d.

Key:	f	d	b	j	a	l	h	c	g	k	e	i
1		H	E		A			A				
2		O	W		E			E				
3		I	L		O			E				
4		F	F		O			A				
5		M	R		A			E				
6		F	R		I			I				
7		N	D		I			I				
8			E		I			I				
9			L		E			E				
10			B		O			A				
11			A		A			A				
12			P		E			A				
13			R		A							

As I filled these in I noted that all the letters in columns **a** and **c** are vowels. This would not happen by chance: since only 40 per cent of English letters are vowels, the odds against having this many in a row appear by chance are astronomical. This means that the person encrypting the message put the vowels in independent of the plain text, and we will soon see the result. Filling in the rest of the cipher text in order gives the following result:

Key:	f	d	b	j	a	l	h	c	g	k	e	i
1	T	H	E	A	A	D	D	A	R	E	S	S
2	T	O	W	H	E	C	I	E	H	Y	O	U
3	W	I	L	L	O	E	S	E	N	D	S	T
4	U	F	F	F	O	R	O	A	Q	M	G	I
5	S	M	R	S	A	W	S	E	E	E	N	E
6	Y	F	R	U	I	T	D	I	E	R	E	R
7	A	N	D	G	I	E	R	I	E	N	G	R
8	O	C	E	R	I	I	F	I	V	E	H	A
9	R	O	L	D	E	C	S	E	R	O	S	S
10	D	U	B	L	O	N	I	A	T	R	Y	T
11	O	M	A	K	A	I	E	A	T	U	E	T
12	O	A	P	P	E	A	E	A	R	L	L	K
13	E	F	R	H	A	T	I					

The meaning of the two columns of vowels is now clear: they were added to obfuscate the message. The sender and receiver would have arranged in advance on two columns of 'duds' (letters to be ignored), the sender could fill them in at random with vowels, and the receiver would know to ignore them. This also explains why the initial frequency count during the diagnosis showed more vowels than usual for English: the excess vowels were in the columns of duds. Removing these duds we see the result:

Key:	f	d	b	j	a	l	h	c	g	k	e	i
1	T	H	E	A		D	D		R	E	S	S
2	T	O	W	H		C	I		H	Y	O	U
3	W	I	L	L		E	S		N	D	S	T
4	U	F	F	F		R	O		Q	M	G	I
5	S	M	R	S		W	S		E	E	N	E
6	Y	F	R	U		T	D		E	R	E	R
7	A	N	D	G		E	R		E	N	G	R
8	O	C	E	R		I	F		V	E	H	A
9	R	O	L	D		C	S		R	O	S	S
10	D	U	B	L		N	I		T	R	Y	T
11	O	M	A	K		I	E		T	U	E	T
12	O	A	P	P		A	E		R	L	L	K
13	E	F	R	H		T	I					

The programme has made an error in recovering the key: columns **l** and **h** have been switched. The result so far:

The address to which you will send stuff for QMG is Mrs Sweeney, Frudterer and Greengrocer, Five Harold's Cross, Dublin. Try to make it ue to appear llke frhit.

The text is now clear, and there are four obvious errors: in Fruiterer, up, like and fruit. Referring back to the original document, we see the first error resulted from the sender overstriking the original **D** with an **I** on their typewriter, and the transcriber (me) reading the **D** instead. The second error is a result of the poor quality of the copy: the **P** in the typescript copy has a smudge on the bottom that I read as the bottom of an **E**. The next letter is clear on the typescript as an **I**, and was simply a transcription error. The final error, in frhit, results from another over-strike on the typescript – the correct **U** can be seen in retrospect, but is not obvious when transcribing it.

I solved the remaining five ciphers from this initial set the same way. The second in the set was from the same document and used the same key, again with two columns of duds. The next three used a different twelve-letter key, AHCKEDJLBFGI, but were simpler than the first two in that they did not use the columns of duds.[9] The final cipher was relatively short – only fifty-eight letters:[10]

```
c/s.
  C.12.                                    5th April 1927.

To:
    O/C South Dublin Batt.

      Please let me know immediately why you have not
(58) NESAW.DNNNR.TADDS.UIESP.TASYN.THEAO.GEATA.TBSOK.
NREEO.UUEIC.TLPCA.IIN.
      I want this pressed on at once.


                             CHIEF OF STAFF.
```

Figure 4. Short message from Twomey, 5 April 1927.

Although short messages can be difficult to decrypt, my programme had no trouble with this one, producing key LIAHKFDJBCGE (again with no duds) and plain text:

> continued to take action against the undesirable Sunday news-papers.

I returned these solutions the same day by e-mail to Tom Mahon, who offered to send the rest of his papers for decryption.

The game was on!

Decrypting the Columnar Transposition Ciphers

When the ciphers began arriving, it became clear that the project was to be very extensive. In all, the corpus consists of about 1,300 individual cryptograms. Most of them are typed and clearly legible, but in many cases the quality of the copies – either too faint[11] or too dark[12] – led to challenges in transcription. In some cases the typewriter used had mis-aligned[13] or dirty[14] typebars, so that certain letters were obscured or ambiguous. Some of the messages are torn or stained in ways that obliterate a group of adjacent letters.[15] The copying process itself led to other problems: in some cases the flimsy copy was folded or crumpled as it was photographed for the microfilm, making separation of the lines of text quite challenging,[16] and in other cases the reproduction process cut cipher letters off one side or the other.[17] Some of the messages are hand-written in various writing styles, and without the cues of connected English text it can be difficult even to identify the different letters of random-looking connected cursive text.[18]

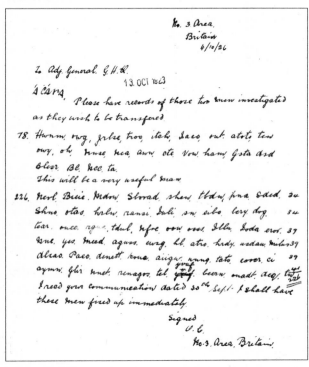

Figure 5. Penmanship challenge, 4 October 1926.

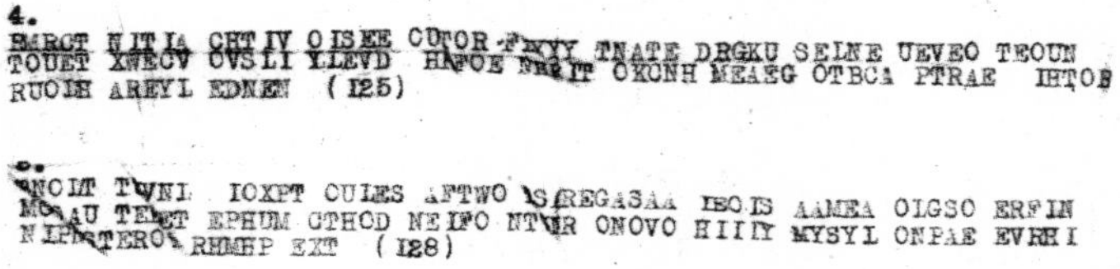

Figure 6. Creases through cipher text, 25 October 1926.

Columnar transposition resists mutilation rather well – even adjacent missing letters in the cipher text come from different places in the plain text, so there is still a good chance to read through the garbles. For example, consider the final cryptogram shown in Figure 6, which appears to be a photostat of a crushed and creased onion-skin copy. Replacing the damaged letters with a hyphen, the cipher to be solved is:

-NOLT T-VNL IOXPT OULES AFTWO –S-RE GASAA IEOIS AAMEA OLGSO ERFLN
MO-AU TE-ET EPHUM CTHOD NEIFO NT-—R ONOVO HIIIY MYSYL ONPAE EVRHI
NIP—- TERO- RHMHP EXT

Decrypting and adding word divisions, we see:

I may have –o go to californ-a next month for st-phen I will ha-e to appoint ma- to
do a- -imthire unle-s yo- people get – m-ve on he is very anxious for results

We can read this quite easily from the context, since the gaps did not happen to fall in places that would make the decryption ambiguous.

In some cases we were able to read messages that could not be deciphered by the recipient. In some cases the senders had used incorrect keys: either the wrong day's key, or an obsolete key. In some cases they used the correct key, but used it incorrectly, not quite taking the columns in alphabetical order. They occasionally botched the encryption by leaving out a letter or by combining two letters in a single cell of the cipher frame, either of which would make the decipherment much more difficult. We see several testy exchanges in the message traffic, exhorting one correspondent or another to take more care with their key protocol and encryption process, or criticising the length or volume of encrypted messages.

Since my decryption methods do not require me to know the intended key, I was more or less immune to the problem of senders using the wrong key. But for some of the botched encryption attempts I needed to resort to the same procedures that the original recipients would have needed to try, laying it out carefully on quadrille paper and sliding the columns up and down until the text came into alignment.

We eventually worked through the complete set of transposition ciphers, producing good decryptions of all but one:

(52) GTHOO KOSNM EOTDE TAEDI NKAIIE EBFNS INSGD AILLA
YTTSE AOITDE.

Figure 7. The unsolved transposition cipher, 16 November 1926.

This message is identified as having fifty-two letters but only fifty-one appear in the cryptogram itself.[19] I tried a number of approaches, including assuming the missing letter was in each of the fifty-two possible positions in turn (or in none of them, leaving fifty-one letters as shown), but none of my attacks succeeded. If you crack this one please let us know.

Recovering Transposition Keys

The process I used to break the transposition ciphers was very effective: a message of sixty or more letters typically falls in a matter of seconds to a completely automated programme with no human intervention required beyond supplying word breaks. Shorter messages presented more challenges: I sometimes needed to inspect the best results and intervene in various ways, such as telling the programme to keep a particular phrase and continue making changes with that phrase held constant. Several factors worked in my favour. A document frequently consists of a number of encrypted messages, and each message within the document was encrypted with the same key. This means I needed to break only one of these messages, and this would give me a key that would break the rest. Many of the keys were re-used across documents: the IRA used standard transposition keys for different brigades and battalions and even individuals, and these were used whenever a transmission was sent to or from these recipients. Particularly for foreign agents the IRA implemented a system for producing different daily keys based on a book and once even on a list of phrases sent in the clear. These frequent key changes improved the security but still allowed me to try recovered keys against other traffic sent on the same day to different recipients.

My procedure for breaking each cipher gave me a key that would allow me to read that cipher and others that used the same key, but it did not tell me the key that had actually been used to encrypt the message. The recovered 'equivalent key' simply gives the order for reading off the columns. If the keyword were MONARCHY, for example, an equivalent key showing the column order could be DFEAGBCH:

MONARCHY

DFEAGBCH

That is, column four ('A' in both cases) would be the first column to be read out of the message array, then column six ('C' in MONARCHY, 'B' in DFEAGBCH) and so on, retaining the order of the original word. Either of these keys will allow us to read the cipher, but if we deduce that MONARCHY was used, it can give us more insight into the way keys were chosen, and perhaps allow us to guess other keys to try on messages that continue to elude us. In this case several other words would match the alphabetical pattern, including MONARCHS, INLANDER and OUT-BULLY, and the key that was actually intended might become obvious once we had a list of other recovered keys to compare with it.

Having broken the fifty-eight-letter message from the first set that I described above, I wanted to find out what actual key had been used to encrypt it.[20] The recovered 'equivalent key' is LIAHKFDJBCGE, and the order of the letters determines which column of the message array must be read first. That is, column three (the 'A') is the first to be copied out, then column nine ('B') and so on. I assumed this column order was determined by a keyword or keyphrase. I assumed also that the keys were in English, since all the messages are in English. The third letter in the key must be the lowest letter in the alphabet that this key uses, and if that letter is used more than once, it would appear again as the 'B' in ninth place in LIAHK-FDJBCGE. The 'C' after the 'B' will be a letter at least as far along in the alphabet as that represented by the 'B'. Finally, the L must represent the highest letter in the alphabet used in this key, and since there is no higher letter to its right, it must be the only occurrence of that letter.

Using these restrictions on the keyword, we can write the alphabet repeatedly on a series of twelve vertical strips of paper and slide them accordingly, keeping these restrictions in mind — that is, column two must start no higher than column one, and so on — until a word begins to appear across several lines of the strips. During the period when these ciphers were used this was the standard way to recover the key. Now, however, we have more efficient methods: we can programme a computer to check each word or phrase in a list in turn to see whether it matches this pattern. For a key this long, very few words and phrases will match the restrictions forced by the pattern. I used a wordlist from an unabridged dictionary of 308,081 English words, and of these only one matched the pattern for this key: TRANSFERABLE.

This procedure allowed me to find many of the one-word keys used by the IRA, but many others did not appear in my unabridged dictionary list. I postulated that short phrases were being used. It is much more difficult to find adequate lists of phrases on the internet, so I produced my own, making lists of phrases of a specified length from digital books. This time-honoured process has been used to good effect by generations of cryptographers, who would painstakingly count hundreds of thousands of letters to get good statistical distributions and find common phrases. I downloaded books from Project Gutenberg, a public service effort that distributes digital copies of books in the public domain.[21] Their first set of twenty complete books was made available to the public in 1990 and 1991, and the three million words in them would make a fairly good start on any statistical project. However, my feeling is that if a thing is worth doing, it is worth overdoing. I downloaded Gutenberg's production from 1990 through 2006 to run my statistics: 10,607 books in all, comprising over 89 million lines, 730 million words, and 4.4 billion letters.

When I ran my key-finding programme on twelve-letter words and phrases from this collection, again the only matching key it found was TRANSFERABLE. To identify the source of more keys I wrote to Bill Mason, another member of the American Cryptogram Association and one of our top cryptographic programmers. He reminded me that Google has made available for purchase a huge list of words and phrases gleaned from the World Wide Web. I bought this collection and wrote programmes to extract more potential keys from all this data. The collection is derived from over one trillion phrases, and is distributed on data DVDs as 24 gigabytes of compressed data. This made me very glad that I use a fast computer![22]

With these tools in hand I was able to find likely English keys for nearly all of the recovered keys. As we read more of the archived messages and broken ciphers we found clues to the way keys were chosen. In a message on 5 May 1926 the IRA's Department of Intelligence sent the unencrypted message shown in Figure 8, a list of key phrases to be used from 6 May through 14 May.[23]

Just to make the keys crystal clear to anyone who might obtain this page, a line was drawn through this list indicating the first twelve letters of each phrase: 'Isms go in wave', 'Speak of the co', and so on. These phrases

óglaig na n-éireann.
(IRISH REPUBLICAN ARMY)

Áro oifis, át cliat.

Department __Intelligence.__

Reference No. { Yours _____
{ Mine __DA/90.__

(Please Quote my Number and Date)

GENERAL HEADQUARTERS,
DUBLIN.

5/5/26.

TO:- C/S,

4 MAY 1926

I.   To acknowledge yours CD/5 & CD/6 of the 3rd. also your CD/7
of the 4th. Inst.the latter with Boyne Communication attached.
I have also received your copy of your comm.nication to
S/Capt W. with communication from him to D/I attached.

2.   Your CD/5 re Boyne report.. Your instructions noted.

3.   Re your CD/6. The following <u>headings</u> should meet the case.
I presume you have been supplied up to the 6th. You can therefoee
safely proceed as follows:-

            6th.-'Isms'go in waves you notice
            7th.-Speak of the consolation religion
            8th.-Is capable of absorbing
            9th.-I decided to visit India
            I0th.-And the wonder-worker was sent
            IIth.-I placed a private mark on the glass
            I2th.-And the swallowing capacity of the man was known
            I3th.-They were just ordinary folk and had the
            I4th.-Stalest tricks.

4.   Your CD/7. A detailed report on the various items con-
        tained therein will be sent to you as soon as possible.

                                        _____ S/Commdt.
                        for D/Intelligence.

Figure 8. Sending keys in clear text, 5 May 1926.

---

may be from newspapers or magazines of the period. I was unable to find
any of the sources in open literature. However, they were indeed used for
some of the messages we decrypted: P69/48(50), sent on 6 May, used
'ISMSGOINWAVE' and P69/48(23), sent on 14 May, used 'STALEST-
TRICK'. This represents a serious blunder in communication security,
and cryptanalysts always welcome entries of this sort. It also broadened
my search for keys from complete words and phrases to checking for
keys starting at a word boundary but going for as many letters as needed,
without paying attention to whether the key ends on a word boundary.

One partially encrypted document included lists of keys used to communicate with each battalion and brigade, and with individuals.[24] Even
without decryption this kind of information can be very valuable to an opponent: it allows the analyst to see the extent and command structure of the

army. Another partially encrypted message gave keys that had changed.[25] Again, intercepting this message would be a great boon to the cryptanalyst, who might have lost contact with the keys but can continue reading the message traffic if this one is encrypted in a known key. To emphasise the importance of this message, the sender said in clear English 'The following Key-words are now in use' before giving the keywords in encrypted form.

As I broke more messages and found more keys using the Project Gutenberg book list, I found several keys that clearly came from Nathaniel Hawthorne's *The Scarlet Letter*, including one dated 2 March 1927 with key 'Surveyor Pue e'.[26] The header of this message includes the notation '(Cipher – New formula)'. Looking further, we found and broke a message dated 24th February 1927 saying:[27]

> Did courier at Xmas give you copy of Woolworth edition of novel The Scarlet Letter which was to be used for keys for cipher?

Using this clue I tried each possible starting point for keys in the Project Gutenberg online edition of *The Scarlet Letter* and found a number of keys that appeared in this book – many of them common phrases such as 'however had be' and 'on this side of', but some as distinctive as 'the scarlet le' and 'a writhing hor'.

However, a message dated 14 December 1926 detailed the method completely:[28]

> Herewith method for using a different keyword for each.
> Dispatch bearer will give you book to be used for this purpose.
> Take the date of dispatch you are about to send.
> Multiply the month by ten and add the date.
> This gives you a number.
> Take the page in the book corresponding with this number.
> The first twelve letters in the fourth line on this page will be your keyword for that date.
> For example take the date of this dispatch.
> The number found is one hundred and thirty four.
> The first twelve letters in the fourth line on page one hundred and thirty four are lampandsomet.
> This would be the key word for this dispatch.
> Verify this with book.
> Name of book is The Scarlet Letter by Hawthorne.

As the sender suggested, I did indeed verify this with the book. I was unable to find the correct edition, but by comparing the position of the phrase in the digitised book with the page number derived from the above method using the date of the message I found that the key locations did indeed line up very well. We attempted to find an edition of *The Scarlet Letter* that appeared with these keys in exactly the right place, but without success – for example, none of the dozen or so editions in the University of California at Los Angeles (UCLA) library came close to matching the data. If we could find the correct edition, then the keys for these messages could be found the same way the original recipient would have found them: by finding the page number from the date of the message and going directly to the fourth line of the text to read off the key.

I wrote to Jude Patterson, a fellow cryptanalyst who is good at finding 'hats' (the original English of the equivalent key) for transposition keys. Jude had spent many years as a typesetter, and she had an interesting thought: that by testing different fonts we might be able to reconstruct the Woolworth edition closely enough to find precisely where the keys should fit. I sent seventeen recovered keys with their associated page numbers, as well as photocopies of some pages from cheap editions of various books from Britain and America from that period to give an idea of contemporary standards, fonts and conventions, and she went to work. Six months later, near the end of 2007 the breakthrough appeared in my inbox: Jude found that using eleven-point type with Garamond font produced results that almost exactly matched our data points for the Woolworth edition, suggesting that this may indeed have been the type face and size used in the original. She had needed to reconstruct by trial and error esoteric typographical conventions such as standards for dealing with widows (the last line of a paragraph at the top of a page) and orphans (the first line of a paragraph at the bottom of a page).

Jude Patterson wrote:[29]

> 11 pt Garamond by 19¼ picas is the only trial where most keys fell spot on or with minimal adjustments in hyphenation.
>
> Having found this so-called ideal setting, I proceeded to trials for page depth, and having established page depth, I took the whole slice of *The Scarlet Letter* from pages 29 to 134 and ran the final trial. It was amazing how little twiddling was needed to get the pages to fall beautifully. I put myself in the shoes of the typesetter, trying to keep all pages the same length, allowing orphans but disallowing widows, inserting hyphens to reduce big spaces between words, 'feathering' the type with extra letter-spacing where needed to gain a line to avoid a widow.

We now had a best-guess equivalent of the Woolworth edition used to produce many of the keys for this period! For example, here is the beginning of page fifty-six with these settings:

> external matters are of little value and import, unless
> they bear relation to something within his mind. Very
> soon, however, his look became keen and penetrative
> *A writhing hor*ror twisted itself across his features,

The key on the fourth line was used to encrypt a message dated 6 May.[30] May is the fifth month, so we multiply it by ten and add the date: 50+6= 56, the correct page number.

Decrypting the substitution ciphers

Nearly all the ciphers we encountered in these sets proved to use columnar transposition, either with or without the columns of dud letters. However, a substantial number of messages between GHQ and the outlying Irish battalions used a different system: mostly short fragments of cipher to encrypt the most sensitive parts of a message that was otherwise sent in clear English. We see a typical example of this in Figure 9:[31]

> Have you yet got X&OYC&UIJO&MN? Did you look up that man FX&WA HKGKH/ whom I spoke to you about. I am most anxious that this case be followed up. I would suggest that if necessary you put your Staff Officer entirely on it until it is carried through.

```
        C/S
        CD/7                                May 4th. 1923

To:
D/Intelligence.

1.      Have you yet got X&OYC&UIJO&MN?  Did you look up that man
FX&WA HKGKH/ whom I spoke to you about.  I am most anxious that
this case be followed up.  I would suggest that if necessary you put
your Staff Officer entirely on it until it is carried through.

2.      Has O/C B. replied to your regarding PJACQ UXOVY XKT/  If he
has not you should remind him about it, that is, if there is any post
these days.
```

Figure 9. Short Vigenère-style substitution ciphers, 4 May 1926.

These ciphers are strikingly different from the columnar transposition ciphers that form the bulk of the encrypted traffic. They're very short, they are not broken up in five-letter groups, they include the symbol '&',

and they are mixed freely with plain English text. Most importantly to a cryptanalyst, their statistics are quite different from normal English: a count of the individual letters shows no obvious correlation between the high and low frequency letters in the messages and the high and low frequency letters in English. This indicates that the cipher used for these messages is a substitution cipher.

An easy and commonly used substitution cipher is called, appropriately enough, 'simple substitution'. In this system a keyword may be chosen to mix the alphabet by any of a large variety of methods, and each letter of the plain text is substituted with the corresponding letter of the keyed alphabet. For example, with the key MONARCHY placed in a prearranged position within the alphabet, we could have a cipher alphabet that looks like this:

Plain: A B C D E F G H I J K L M N O P Q R S T U V W X Y Z
Cipher: Q S T U V W X Z M O N A R C H Y B D E F G I J K LP

A message is encrypted by finding each letter of the message on the 'plain' line and substituting for it the letter below on the 'cipher' line:

On a monkey's day to die all trees become slippery.
HC Q RHCNVL'E UQL FH UMV QAA FDVVE SVTHRV EAMYYVDL.

With enough cipher text we can solve a simple substitution rather easily by looking at frequencies (e.g. the very common 'E', 'T', 'A') and pattern words (e.g. 'trees' with its double 'E' or 'become' with 'E's in the second and sixth positions). Analysing the messages this way got me nowhere. My chief roadblock was the length: most of the messages were too short to allow productive analysis. I set these substitution ciphers aside for several months while continuing to work on the outstanding transposition ciphers.

Having finished most of the columnar transpositions I returned to an intriguing set of substitution cipher messages from an IRA communications logbook, shown in Figure 10.[32] The reward for solving these pages was clear: it is a list of encrypted keywords used to communicate in cipher with each of the IRA units, from Antrim ('No code yet') through Wicklow, as well as additional keys for correspondents out of Ireland. In all, the list contains keywords or contact information for fifty-seven recipients. Although most of these are short words or phrases, I hoped to combine them in a way that would give me some leverage into their solution. I resolved to try each likely common substitution method in turn.

After simple substitution, the next most common substitution cipher is known as Vigenère, named for sixteenth-century cryptographer Blaise de Vigenère.[33] This method uses a key to choose among a number of different cipher alphabets to encrypt each letter of the cipher in turn. Using multiple alphabets increases the security of the cipher by evening out the frequencies of the letters and by eliminating the patterns of the letters within words. In its most basic form, for each alphabet Vigenère uses the Caesar cipher described earlier, counting down the alphabet one letter for key-letter 'A', two for key-letter 'B' and so on, using the key in order and repeating it as needed. As an example using keyword FACE:

```
Key:          FACEFACEFACEFACEFACEFACEFACEFACEF

Message:      Itisnotthepantsthatmakeyoulookfat

Encryption:   ITISNOTTHEPANTSTHATMAKEYOULOOKFAT

              J JTO UUI QBO TUI UNB FZP MPP GBU

              K KUP VVJ RCP UVJ VOC GAQ NQQ HCV

              L VQ  WK  DQ  WK  PD  BR  RR  DW

              M WR  XL  ER  XL  QE  CS  SS  EX

              N S   M   S   M   F   T   T   Y

Cipher:       NTKWSOVXMERESTUXMAVQFKGCTUNSTKHEY
```

Some writers, including Lewis Carroll, called the cipher 'undecipherable', but cryptographers of the sixteenth century had already broken it on occasion.[34] The Confederate States of America trusted it implicitly, and used it throughout the American Civil War with only three keys. The northern side (the Union) had no trouble reading their message traffic.[35] The cipher may be executed entirely by hand, as shown above, or with a twenty-six by twenty-six table showing each alphabet, or using a cipher disk or slide that can be moved to indicate the correspondence between plain and cipher letters.

2 Armagh Batt.	No. 2 Area	SDRDPX also Capt W's Keyword 2
1 Belfast Batt.	No. 1. Area	VVQDTYG I (OISOCTGOHYYG
Boyne Batt		WXGKTXB
Carlow Batt	(IJMPWGMMQDTUT)	~~HMMKXK TO~~ GMNWL&OX
Carrick/Shannon ~~Bde~~ Batt	(IJLWTYSS) ~~NXDQJ~~ JDLEWQ GIDYFYKT)	SJMCEKX (LJQCLXJ)DCP)
Cavan Batt		V&SB&R
Clare Bde		LPMOCGR
Claremorris Bde	(DDMCEXAKSS)	MVLLWK (HVKVTTGHNBP)
Connemara Batt	(HVQDSURJLOH)	~~QSS~~. BPKMLT (15/3/16)
Cork 1. Bde		HMNMLJK (YPADDXX VMOLTD
Cork 2. Bde		IVQL&ROX
~~Cork 3 Bde~~ now Bantry Batt	(OISOC XAKSS)	~~MS WOT~~ VD BDFXK
3 Derry Batt	No. 3. Area	UMDMWOT& N (IJQBPYVJMNPPG
Dublin Bde	25 copies	GGCOCSGRI (SVFXTLOXD
Dundalk Batt		XVMC&S
N Kerry 1. Bde		S VQM&TO (FXNWAKTN DTU
Kerry 2. Bde		J&&M&T (DOGKYQ Y&HFFTMS
Kildare Batt		MMNEYJ (N MMPLUMVKCJ
Leix Bde " '''		KHAKCQ (HOBJSUILOY
Limerick Bde		J&&DS. (DXNXWKTOQKEKJL
Midland Batt	(DXNXEOTJTCWE)	UM&XRK (DXNXEOTPWE
Nth Kilkenny Batt	(IJL PTYVSS T)	&VQKTYN
Nth Mayo Bde	(IJL&BYOOHYY)	VM8 KN K VM&XVX
Nth Wexford Batt	(IJLWPSUM DTUT)	DW VWGYOW
Offaly Bde	(X&BVLX&QHYX)	IM&FPT (UMFKYOYVSS
Sligo Bde	(IJNBOOTYSS T)	S&&N&C (I&BVLXGOHYY
Sth Dublin Batt		IM&WA
Sth Galway Bde		LPQXLIK
Sth Kilkenny Batt	(IJN PXGOHYY)	L&QDTRK
Sth Wexford Batt	(OIREAKXVAVP)	HVQ MUT& HVQ UT
Tipperary Bde		HMHQLTJ (EYD PXSD
Tuomond Batt		SVF&TK (JQ R PXGOHYY
4 Tyrone Batt	No. 4 Area	VVQC&T (X QYXSKICKEOU
No (X QBYXSKICKEOU)		

Figure 10. Encrypted cipher keywords, communications logbook, no date.

The cryptanalyst's leverage in Vigenère-like ciphers comes from the periodic nature of the cipher. All letters encrypted with 'F' above are from the same alphabet, so that if we look at every fourth letter we will be seeing only letters encrypted with the same key letter. If we have enough material to work with, this alone will be enough to break that particular alphabet, because the equivalent of 'E', 'T', 'A' and so on will have the highest frequency in the cipher alphabet, and they will be in the same position relative to each other because the cipher alphabet is a simple Caesar shift of the standard A–Z alphabet. For example, the cipher equivalent of 'E' will appear four letters after the cipher equivalent of 'A'. This process may be repeated for the other assumed alphabets, finding the best Caesar shift for each.

To test for a Vigenère-style cipher, then, we need enough material encrypted in the same key to find a statistical pattern in the letter distributions. Although most of the words encrypted in Figure 10 are short, I postulated that each could be encrypted with a polyalphabetic cipher such as Vigenère with the key beginning anew with each entry.

I selected the first six letters of all the ciphers in this group with at least six letters and that did not include the nonalphabetic character '&' within those six letters. This gave a depth of twenty-two encrypted words all (by assumption) starting at the same place in the key:

```
SDRDPX VVQDTY WXGKTX SJMCEK LPMOCG MVLLWK HMNMLJ VDBDFX
UMDMWO GGCOCS MMNEYJ KHAKCQ LPQXLI HMHQLT IJMPWG DDMCEX
HVQDSU OISOCX DXNXEO IJLWPS IJNBOO OIREAK
```

I presented this to my Shotgun Hillclimbing programme and told it to try it as period six Vigenère and it immediately returned mostly reasonable text with key GVZKLG:

```
mister partis qchair monste funera famble brocad pictur orecli alderm ground
embark furnac brigan confla xinstr bartho interr xconti commem coordi insupe
```

These beginning fragments plainly show that the method used was equivalent to Vigenère, using a keyword of at least five letters: the repeated 'G' in the key could mean that the key has begun to repeat, or that the keyword used has a repeated letter in that position. Further experimentation with the longer words and passages in this document showed that the latter is true: the full Vigenère keyword is GVZKLG, and it repeats as long as necessary to finish the section it encrypts. The '&' could now be determined from context: if it is replaced with 'Z' in the cipher text, it encrypts to the right letter using standard Vigenère decryption.

Why GVZKLG? After some experimentation, I found that it is derived from a reversal of the alphabet:

```
A B C  D E F G  H I J K L  M N O P Q R S T U V W X Y Z
Z Y X W V U T  S R Q P O N M  L K J I  H G F  E D C  B A
```

If each letter in the Vigenère key is replaced with the corresponding letter in the reversed alphabet, we get G=T, V=E, and so on, so that the actual key used in 'IRA Vigenère' is TEAPOT. A reversed encryption alphabet of this sort is called Atbash, and the technique was used in the Bible. David Kahn points out that in Jeremiah 25:26 and 51:41 the word Sheshach appears in place of Babel (Babylon).[36] The repeated Hebrew 'beth' of Babel becomes the repeated 'shin' of Sheshach: beth is the second letter of the Hebrew alphabet, and shin is the penultimate. Kahn cites an Aramaic paraphrase of the passage using Babel in place of Sheshach to prove they mean the same thing. Using Atbash for the IRA substitution keys may have been chosen to give a little more security against someone who suspects a Vigenère cipher system and has captured an English key to try.

Some of the keywords in this table include letters at beginning and/or end that are not part of the actual keyword. For example, the encrypted key for Boyne Batt is WXGKTXB, which decrypted with keyword TEAPOT becomes QCHAIRV. The longer encrypted key for Claremorris Bde is DDMCEXAXSS&T, which becomes XINSTRUCTION. In the course of later decryptions it became clear that these include nulls: the key for Boyne is actually CHAIR, and the key for Claremorris is INSTRUCTION. In the substitution examples throughout the corpus we found that nulls were frequently used at the beginning and/or end, especially 'Q', 'X', 'Y' and 'Z'.

We can now address the message in Figure 9 that began this section:[37]

Have you yet got X&OYC&UIJO&MN? Did you look up that man FX&WA HKGKH/ whom I spoke to you about.

The message is an internal GHQ communication from the chief of staff to the director of intelligence, so the key used is the same as the one used to encrypt all the keys for internal consumption: TEAPOT. The solution is unambiguous:

Have you yet got report on Keogh? Did you look up that man z Campbell x whom I spoke to you about.

The second encrypted bit includes the nulls 'Z' and 'X' in an attempt to disguise the name further. Repeated uses of the name encrypted the same way with the same key would be a security problem: even if a person intercepting the messages could not solve the cipher, they could tell that the same person was being discussed because the encrypted version would be the same. Adding a letter to the front (z Campbell x) is enough to make it different, but unless different numbers of letters are used each time the name is sent in the future, CAMPBELL will be encrypted with the same part of the key and will appear the same when encrypted.

The particularly interesting message shown in Figure 11 from Seán Lemass, the republican Minister for Defence to Seán Russell, the quartermaster general, was one of the most cryptic and one of the shortest.[38]

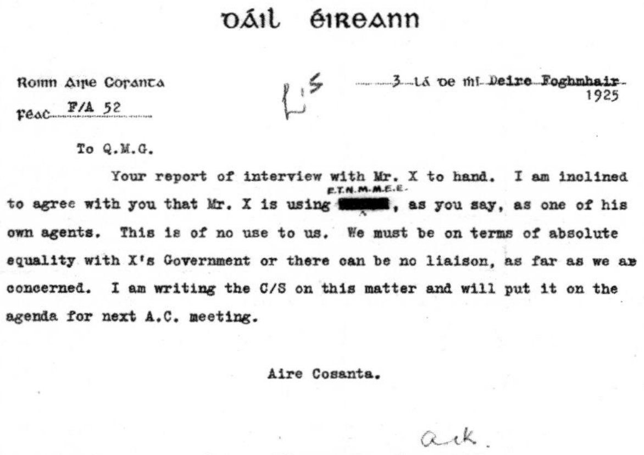

DÁIL ÉIREANN

Roinn Aire Cosanta — 3 Lá de mí Deire Foghmhair 1925

Feac. F/A 52

To Q.M.G.

Your report of interview with Mr. X to hand. I am inclined to agree with you that Mr. X is using [redacted], as you say, as one of his own agents. This is of no use to us. We must be on terms of absolute equality with X's Government or there can be no liaison, as far as we ae concerned. I am writing the C/S on this matter and will put it on the agenda for next A.C. meeting.

Aire Cosanta.

ack.

Figure 11. Soviet use of IRA officer, 3 October 1925.

We knew from other messages that 'Mr. X' was a Soviet agent. The encrypted part is ETNMMEE. Decrypting this with the GHQ substitution keyword TEAPOT gives us the plain text: YY OCB YY. As we've seen above, the 'Y's are nulls used for padding around the three-letter message. OCB (or OC.B) stands for Officer Commanding, Britain.[39]

Choosing the correct keyword to decrypt the substitution ciphers in this collection was sometimes challenging. Not all the messages had obvious senders and recipients, so it was not simply a matter of pulling the keyword off the master list for those correspondents. In addition, not all of the keywords were on any list: some had been superseded, and others were assigned after the lists in our possession were compiled.

For the longer ciphers I used my Shotgun Hillclimbing programme to recover the keyword, modifying it to deal directly with the IRA Vigenère style of Atbash-encrypted keywords. For shorter ciphers I prepared a new programme which would try a list of keywords on the cipher, then compare the results on how English-like the decryption looked by assigning a weighted score based on how common words and fragments of words are in English. I used this method to solve the list of keywords in a message from the director of intelligence to the chief of staff, shown in Figure 12.[40]

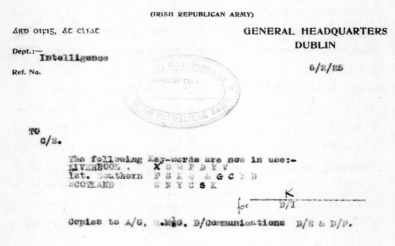

Figure 12. Keywords encrypted with Vigenère-style substitution cipher, 6 February 1925.

None of the recovered keywords solved these encrypted words, so I used this programme to try everything in a list of 14,611 common words of eight or fewer letters, and then sorted them according to the 'English-like' criterion. The best few results for the longest cipher, FGKQ&GCYD, were:

360 beadle hllullede
360 potash vversosnx
360 reptile xlakishqi
360 volcano bvwtaurus
360 wardrobe chcurveda
360 wattage chekanhve
360 where copiedkdv
450 maxwell shinesole

```
450 upstair awdkaputt
490 bedlam hlocatedh
490 flange lsleglike
```

Of these choices, 'bedlam' looked most promising, with the word 'located' embedded between nulls. I tried 'bedlam' on the other two encrypted words with complete success, getting 'z label x' for LIVERPOOL and 'y scot x' for Scotland – the latter a rather uninspired choice of keyword.

Communication security practices

Any organisation with important secrets must pay serious and continual attention to its methods of protecting those secrets. The IRA from 1925 to 1928 monitored and modified their procedures in an attempt to maintain and improve their communication security. They maintained separate networks with distinct cipher keys, and used several different methods of secret communication, including at least two main types of ciphers, a code system for cables, and invisible ink. They gradually changed their cipher systems and key distribution methods over this period, apparently expecting that the newer system offered more security. Leaders transmitted messages in several different ways: by courier, by post, by cable, and even by writing them on silk and dropping them in a predetermined spot on the prison grounds.

In principle, this diversity of methods and networks and their attention to communication security should have provided strong protection against the compromise of part of the network, resulting in unravelling the whole system. However, in practice their ciphers provided much less security than some other ciphers of the day – armies in the First World War used much stronger versions of both of the IRA's basic cipher types, and their enemies broke them readily at the time. If the British had access to the IRA's cipher communications, they probably read them. Our attacks on these messages capitalised on weaknesses in the cipher systems themselves.

In addition, in many cases the IRA correspondents used poor practices, including sending the same message in more than one system; sending messages in clear asking about another specific message that they could not read; mixing encrypted messages with clear text giving hints about the subject matter; sending messages that were too long or too short for the security of the system being used; sending many messages in the same key that could be 'stacked' to simplify the solution; sending cipher keys in clear; and using a weak cipher and key to encrypt pages of keys for the (assumed) stronger system. Each of these 'cipher clerk weaknesses' occurs regularly in military organisations, especially where those in charge of communications have other responsibilities. However, each of these errors offers a crack in the cipher system's armour that a cryptanalyst can enter and expand, and I took advantage of all of them in cracking these IRA ciphers.

Working with Tom on this cipher set turned out to be a massive and exciting project for me. I was able to draw on experience from having solved the Zendian Problem,[41] a large training exercise developed in the 1950s by Lambros D. Callimahos for the National Security Agency, the American code-breaking service. Both the IRA ciphers and the Zendian ciphers allowed the cryptanalyst to develop an understanding of the communication network and hierarchy while breaking the individual ciphers. I modified several of my existing programmes and wrote dozens more to deal with the eccentricities of these ciphers, and to crunch the data I used to attack the ciphers and their keys.

IN THE END WE were very successful. We broke nearly all of the transposition and substitution ciphers, and were able to read more of them than the original correspondents had been able to manage because of mistakes in key selection or encryption. A few messages remain undeciphered, including a transatlantic cable using a code system that cannot be solved without much more material and a munitions' list using a substitution system for the digits that we have been unable to break from the context. However, we can now read the vast majority of the encrypted material, and it has given us a rare look into the inner workings of the IRA.

Definitions

Cryptogram or cipher: An encrypted message.

Plain text: The letters of an original clear message that are to be encrypted for transmission.

Cipher text: The encrypted letters comprising the concealed parts of a cipher.

Clear or clear text: A message or part of a message sent without using encryption.

Encrypt: To convert plain text into cipher text using processes and keys agreed on by the sender and recipient.

Cipher system: A method for concealing plain text using individual letters of the clear message.

Key: A piece of information shared between sender and recipient and used as part of the encryption process.

Decipher: To convert cipher text to plain text with full knowledge of the cipher system and key.

Cryptanalysis: The process of converting cipher text to plain text without knowing the key in advance.

Substitution: A cipher system that replaces each letter with another.

Transposition: A cipher system that shuffles letters without changing their values.

Hat: A key used in a transposition cipher to shuffle the order of columns.

Caesar cipher: A substitution cipher system that replaces each letter with the one three positions further along the alphabet, wrapping at the end so that W goes to Z, X goes to A, Y goes to B and so on. By extension, a cipher system that replaces each letter with one any fixed number of letters further along in the alphabet.

Vigenère cipher: A substitution cipher system that uses a keyword or key phrase to encrypt each letter of plain text in turn using a Caesar cipher whose distance along the alphabet depends on the corresponding letter of the key. The key restarts repeatedly until all the plain text has been encrypted.

Atbash: Substitution that reverses the alphabet: A for Z, B for Y and so on. Used in IRA keyword substitution for Vigenère-style cipher.

Null: An extra letter added to the plain text in an attempt to improve the security.

Dud: In the IRA columnar transposition cipher system, a column of nulls used to improve the security.

Code: A cryptographic system for concealing plain text using complete words, phrases or sentences of the clear message.

CHAPTER 2

The IRA's system of communications

Send gelignite and detonators at once to ... Mrs Coady, 5 Glegg Street, off Great
Howard Street, Liverpool. Messenger will say stuff is for Mr Kucas.

IRA chief of staff to the IRA in Scotland

Mr Cowan, Catholic Young Men's Society, 9 and 10 Harrington Street, Dublin.

Covering address for the delivery of IRA despatches

The IRA had a sophisticated communications system enabling it to safely
send messages and orders, not only throughout Ireland, but also to Britain,
the continent and America. In addition, it was able to keep in contact with
IRA volunteers in prison. In each circumstance, the mode of communication depended on an appropriate balance between security, and speed
and ease of communication. The most highly confidential despatches were
encrypted.

There were three key components to the communications network:
the message itself, the method or courier used to transmit the information, and the recipient or the address designated to accept the information.
The director of communications at GHQ had overall responsibility for the
system.

IRA despatches

The organisation took great care to guard its communications and ad-
hered to Earl Long's famous dictum: don't write anything you can talk,
don't talk anything you can whisper, and don't whisper anything you can
wink.[1] The result is that the decryption of these documents is of significance – they are one of the few sources of contemporaneous uncensored
and secret IRA communications.

The most secure way to send a message was verbally. And in the majority of situations Moss Twomey and his officers would have passed on

their orders in this way. As the IRA's director of intelligence reminded the intelligence officer in Waterford: 'Highly confidential reports must be sent verbally, not even in cipher.'[2] Connie Neenan in New York wrote to Moss Twomey in cipher saying he would send him a report by way of Art O'Connor, the leader of Sinn Féin, who was on his way back to Ireland: '[I] have such a large report to make on [our] position [that I] will give all to Art O'Connor verbally for transmittance [to you]. He will be able to describe more explicitly.'[3] The drawback in using O'Connor was that he wasn't a member of the IRA and couldn't have been trusted with the most confidential information.

Right from its inception the IRA created a vast amount of documentation – covering topics ranging from meeting minutes to reports on attacks, along with myriad administrative issues. During the Anglo-Irish War and the Civil War there were several large seizures of papers, resulting in numerous arrests of IRA men named in the documents. Indeed in the Anglo-Irish War the British forces' two best sources of information on the IRA were captured documents and the interrogation of prisoners.[4]

Over time, the IRA became more cautious. They stopped using their members' real names in despatches, referring to them only by rank or by using initials or a pseudonym, while sensitive matters were discussed in an indirect or cryptic manner. On occasion this could be so successful that even the intended recipient didn't know what the message meant. In 1927 the IRA's commander in Britain, George, wrote to Moss Twomey: 'K. clothes has arrived safely in Dublin' and Twomey replied 're. K. clothes: I do not understand the note'.[5] Later George sent another cryptic note to Twomey, this time also in cipher: '[the] printer [is] not available at present. [His] assistant printed and gave me 1,000 copies today'.[6] Luckily for us (or we would never have come to know what it meant), Twomey sought clarification: '[I] presume "copies" stand for pounds and "printer" is James'. To which George replied: 'sorry for not making [the] message clearer in my last letter. Cash is correct'.[7] By corroborating and referencing with other documents, I was able to deduct that 'James' was a Soviet intelligence officer in Britain. And therefore George was giving Twomey news that the Soviets had just handed him £1,000 for the IRA.

Of the thousands of IRA papers that I've looked at, only a small percentage were in secret cipher or code. And these are predominately from 1926 and 1927, with a small number from 1925 and 1928. In the papers dated 1925 the IRA used a less sophisticated form of cipher and tended to only encrypt a few critical words in the document, whereas by 1926 they regularly wrote all the text in cipher. Why are the documents mainly from these years?

Ref.No. HS/37.

To/
C.S.   27th., May, 1927.

1. (159) PASTA. SDLHL. NN▼TT. PTNHS. UOAWL. LRV▼N. GUOAT. D▼I▼O.
   TBAN▼. CISW▼. ADAAR. ADOTC. RNHLS. HR▼S▼. NPLNI. N▼WYO. TSAT▼.
   OF▼WA. LUNAT. IMDWR. ▼MUNU. ▼LSTO. OL▼RK. RITRI. ▼PVAA. L▼▼YG.
   Y▼NAI. D▼IYD. TOCIO. ILNR▼. NYOST. OAOL.

Figure 13. The IRA's commander in Britain, 'HS', wrote to Moss Twomey informing him that a Soviet officer in London had given him £1,000 for the IRA. This is an example of a highly cryptic communication.

> [The] printer [is] not available at present. [His] assistant printed and gave me 1,000 copies today. Will you call, or send for these? Write and let me know, when you are calling and I will see you at your hotel.

The printer was the Soviet agent 'James', while copies stood for pounds.

There are a number of possible explanations. Firstly, in July 1925 the gardaí in Dublin captured the IRA's director of intelligence, Michael Carolan, along with a large haul of intelligence files.[8] This debacle may have spurred his successor Frank Kerlin to improve security procedures and to place greater reliance on cipher. Secondly, also in the summer of 1925, the IRA reached an agreement with the Soviet Union to carry out espionage in Britain and America in return for payment. This work was one of the most highly classified of all IRA operations and necessitated the use of cipher. Furthermore, Soviet intelligence officers may have trained IRA officers in cryptography, as the Soviets had more to lose than the IRA from public exposure of the connection. It's likely that the alliance with the Soviets was terminated or downgraded after a few years and this would in turn have decreased the IRA's need to rely on cipher. Thirdly, the IRA elected a new leadership in November 1925 and, being anxious to revive the organisation, they may have seen a greater need for secrecy. Finally, there is evidence that there are other IRA documents in cipher in private hands, but that the papers James Gillogly and I worked on just happen to be those that made it into a collection open to researchers.

The IRA is known to have had experience with cipher and code before 1925. This originated with its forerunner, the Irish Republican Brother-hood (IRB), which together with its sister organisation in America, Clan na Gael, revelled in cloak and dagger work. In 1893 when Joseph Mc-Garrity was inducted into Clan na Gael in Philadelphia he swore that he would 'defend a Republican form of government in Jsfmboe'. 'Jsfmboe' is a simple form of substitution cipher, which can be deciphered by re-placing each letter with the letter that comes before it in the alphabet – giving the word 'Ireland'.[9] During the Anglo-Irish War the IRA in Cork and Kerry was familiar with the use of cipher by the police.[10] And in 1920, after the IRA in Cork city obtained the keywords for the police's ciphers, it decrypted a police despatch, leading to the capture of a British spy by the name of Quinlisk, who was shot and his body dumped in a ditch.

By 1926, the IRA had trained officers throughout Ireland and Britain, as well as key agents abroad in the use of cipher. IRA units were assigned a secret keyword which they used to both encrypt messages they sent and to decrypt those they received. So as to maintain security, the director of intelligence in Dublin could change the keyword as needed. Examples of keywords include: 'teapot' for GHQ, 'dry-the-teapot' for the IRA unit in Manchester, and the unfortunate 'insignificant' for the Armagh battalion.[11] On the other hand, the IRA's agents in America used keywords selected from a copy of the novel *The Scarlet Letter* they carried with them, while another copy was kept back at GHQ (see Chapter 1).

Considering that most of the IRA's officers lacked formal military training and hadn't gone beyond a secondary education, their ability to develop a communications system based on cipher was quite an achievement. However, by conventional military standards of the time these ciphers were relatively unsophisticated, and the British government's cipher division undoubtedly would have been able to break them. In Ireland the intelligence section of the Free State army had some experience of cryptanalysis, though I'm uncertain as to whether it had the capability to decrypt these messages without having the keywords.[12] On several occasions the Free State authorities allowed the Irish newspapers to print the contents of seized despatches to discredit the IRA. But I've no evidence to suggest that the Free State government ever learned the contents of these encrypted documents; if they had, there would have been a major propaganda value in publicising them. Alternatively, it may be argued, that if the gardaí were intercepting and decrypting IRA communications, it was in their interest to hide this from the IRA.

The use of cipher alone did not make IRA despatches secure, and the sender was expected to adhere to a whole set of precautions. Twomey reminded Connie Neenan in New York to 'be very careful even in sending cipher messages, things which you may assume I will know, can be referred to in an obscure way'.[13] There are very few direct references to Moscow in cipher; rather it was referred to as 'Stephen's headquarters', etc., 'Stephen' being a Soviet intelligence officer.[14]

However, there are many instances in these papers where the IRA operatives made serious security blunders. The OC in Britain wrote to Twomey that he was concerned that the IRA's agents in America were careless with their communications regarding the Soviet connection: 'Is there [too] much writing regarding this affair? I am sure you have no idea, what kind of precautions, are being taken by your people at the US end'.[15] Twomey replied: 'In my last communication to America, I strongly urged the necessity for secrecy and caution, and to avoid any unnecessary reference to the matter on paper'.[16]

In January 1925 the then director of intelligence, Michael Carolan, made a major mistake when he issued a memo listing the keywords for several units in plain text rather than in cipher.[17] Had the Special Branch seized this document they could have gone on to decrypt subsequent despatches they intercepted from these units.

In particular the IRA encrypted the names and addresses of members and supporters. And Moss Twomey wrote: 'never mention an address, even when coming by hand [i.e. carried by a courier] except in cipher'.[18] In October 1926 Twomey sent a message in cipher to the OC of the Scotland battalion ordering him to send 'gelignite and detonators ... to Mrs Coady, 5 Glegg Street, off Great Howard Street, Liverpool'.[19] However, two weeks later the adjutant of the Liverpool unit tripped up by listing her name and address in plain text in a despatch sent to GHQ.[20]

Another security feature was that all documents had a unique identifier. For instance, letters from the OC in Britain carried the letters 'HS' followed by the number of the despatch in sequence. Thus, if Twomey received HS 10 and the next letter from Britain was HS 12, he'd know that a despatch was either delayed or possibly captured. This would allow the IRA to consider that the contents and the method of transport may have been compromised. Frank Kerlin explained this in a letter, 'Dw 99 – Despatch 1', which he had smuggled into Mountjoy prison for Donal O'Donoghue: 'The despatch number on this despatch will be used in sequence in all despatches sent to you, to enable you to know if all despatches sent are received.' Kerlin told him to acknowledge this despatch by way of a cryptic question to one of his visitors: 'When you receive this despatch, ask Mary Mc or Kathleen how their sister Madge is.'[21] More commonly the recipient was expected to acknowledge each letter in writing. And O'Donoghue wrote to Kerlin: '[I] wrote last week [and] received no reply. Always acknowledge [my letters] otherwise [I'm] uneasy.'[22]

Like any other organisation, the IRA needed ready access to its files to effectively manage and administer its affairs. This posed a problem when documents were encrypted. The letters to America often contained long policy discussions and for these documents a short summary of the document in plain text or précis was kept. The précis was usually cryptic and omitted sensitive information such as names and addresses, but at the same time enabled officers at GHQ to refresh their memory of a despatch without having to decode the original again.

It's usually extremely difficult to understand the meaning of a despatch by reading the précis unless one is already familiar with the full decryption. As an example, in March 1927 Twomey wrote to an IRA agent,

'Mr Jones', in New York: 'Try and get formulae for these tear gases and mustard gases and [an] idea of [the] plant [or facility] necessary [for production].' The précis for this sentence merely states: 'Try and get formulae. Plant'.[23] Twomey himself removed the précis on a highly sensitive document that listed American military intelligence provided to the Soviets in America. The document (dated 10 May 1927) is in cipher, and written at the top of the page in handwriting is 'précis taken by C/S [chief of staff] 6/7/27'.[24] The IRA also frequently backdated letters to potentially mislead an unauthorised reader. Usually only the year was changed, so that 1926 was written as 1923 and 1927 as 1924.[25]

Telegrams (or cable) were another useful method of communication. As these messages needed to be brief, they could only contain a limited amount of information. Additionally, since they were sent by the post office they were in a sense always intercepted by the authorities and therefore had to be cryptic. Usually they contained a prearranged sentence that signified the sender's assent or disagreement to a proposal. For instance, Twomey asked the OC in Britain to wire a Mrs Plunkett 'examination papers correct' if he had cash for him, and 'examination papers inaccurate' if he didn't. The telegram was to be signed 'Armstrong'.[26] On another occasion Twomey told 'Mr Jones' to demand $25,000 from 'Stephen' (the Soviet intelligence agent) in return for American military secrets which the IRA was obtaining. Twomey added: 'If 'Stephen' agrees to conditions cable as follows: 'quotation accepted', if partially agreed to: 'can you quote lower', if he rejects and breaks [the connection with us]: 'quotation unacceptable' ... You may add any other message which may be intelligible.'[27] Occasionally telegrams were sent in cipher, though these would have appeared suspicious to any vigilant employee of the post office. In 1926 Seán MacBride complained that he was unable to decipher two telegrams sent to him in Paris and that 'it appears to me as if they were interfered with in transmission'.[28] Given MacBride's penchant for espionage and his evident abilities, his suspicion was likely warranted.

The IRA used invisible ink, though it's difficult to know how frequently. Naturally one can't keep on file a collection of documents in invisible ink! In April 1927 'Mr Jones' obtained secret ink, possibly from 'Stephen', and passed it on to Moss Twomey by way of Art O'Connor: 'Gave Art invisible ink. You can use it to a great extent safely. I also showed him how to send communications on picture postcards.'[29] Twomey replied: 'I made a few experiments here and they are quite satisfactory'.[30] However, at least for the period 1926/1927, cipher was the primary technique used by the IRA to keep its correspondence secret.

In the latter half of 1926 three senior IRA leaders, Mick Price, Donal O'Donoghue and George Gilmore were imprisoned in Mountjoy prison. Frank Kerlin and GHQ, however, managed to keep in contact with all three by a variety of methods. The driver of a truck who brought coal to the prison delivered encrypted messages 'bound in silk paper stuck to the outside of [the] despatch and sealed' to the prisoners by placing them on the ground at a pre-arranged site. The IRA also likely availed of the services of corrupt warders. The prisoners used any paper they had to send messages out, including toilet paper, which was extremely thin and easy to conceal.[31] This is reminiscent of the Provisional IRA's use in the 1970s of cigarette paper (along with toilet paper) for messages smuggled out of Long Kesh prison. However, to provide Gilmore and his comrades with more writing paper, Kerlin told him: 'I am getting white paper sent around parcels in future.'[32]

Gilmore appears to have suggested to Kerlin to send written notes inside 'sugar sticks' and barm brack. Presumably by 'sugar sticks' he meant the hard sugar 'rock', which to this day is sold in souvenir shops and contains little hidden notes with messages such as 'A greeting from Ireland'. While traditionally messages or predictions are hidden in barm brack at Halloween, Kerlin replied to Gilmore: '[I] will try your suggestion re sugar sticks as soon as I can get some made, but I am sending barm brack or cake at once.'[33]

Kerlin also told Gilmore and Price to soak certain letters in water to make a 'watermark' visible. It's unclear what exactly he meant by 'watermark'. He doesn't appear to have meant a form of invisible ink, as water usually has to be acidic, alkaline or coloured to reveal an invisible ink. It's also unlikely to be a reference to a true watermark which is produced with a wire during the manufacturing process of the paper itself. However, if one scratches a message onto paper with a sharp instrument and then soaks the paper in water the message becomes visible and this rather crude method may have been Kerlin's technique.[34] He wrote to Gilmore: 'Wet in water any letters from your mother, in which there is any reference to your cousin Mary and look for [the] watermark' and told Price to do the same with 'any letter from your brother Charlie, in which there is [a] reference to Peg'.[35]

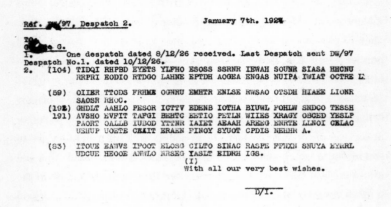

Figure 14. Letter from Frank Kerlin, the director of intelligence, to George Gilmore, in Mountjoy prison. It was smuggled in by a man delivering coal to the prison.

> [The] bearer of this despatch is prepared to do anything required. He goes in with coal lorries and says h[e] saw you in [the] hospital grounds. Three or four other lorries go in with him and also some horses and carts. Can you suggest a way by which, this could b[e] availed of? Leave reply to this despatch at the exact place on [the] ground, where [the] bearer is leaving this note for you, and pin it to a piece of the blue hospital cloth to enable [the] bearer to find it easily.
>
> When writing [g]ive full details of your location and hours of exercise, also any suggestions re. [an] escape [plan].

Couriers and the communication network

Once a message had been prepared, the IRA needed to have it delivered to a secure address. Many letters were sent in the post, while the most sensitive communications, including deliveries of money, were hand carried by a courier.

As Moss Twomey wrote: 'Except [for] very secret [letters] the post is quickest and surest.'[36] Letters for the post were usually placed inside an inner envelope on which was written the name of the intended recipient, or more likely their pseudonym. This was then placed inside an outer envelope, which was sent to a covering address. The covering address was frequently that of a woman, whom the IRA believed was not under surveillance by the Garda Special Branch. She then passed the inner envelope on to whomever it was intended for. There were also covering addresses designated specifically for receiving telegrams, newspapers, money orders, etc.

The list of names and addresses of these covering addresses gives an idea of the extent of support for the IRA throughout all sections of Irish society at the time. Some had Anglo-Irish names, which was likely a deliberate ploy on the part of the IRA, but also reflected that it wasn't purely a Catholic movement. Letters intended for the IRA's intelligence officer in Tipperary could be sent to 'Joyce, [the] Royal Hotel', Tipperary town,[37] while those for the OC in Britain to 'Miss Lena McCormack, 33 St George's Court, Gloucester Rd, Kensington, SW 7'.[38] And at the other end of the globe, letters for New Zealand were to be sent to: 'Mr C Bray, 26 Pipitea Street, Wellington'.[39] One of the covering addresses for GHQ was: 'Mr Cowan, C.Y.M.S. [Catholic Young Men's Society], 9 and 10 Harrington Street, Dublin'. The inner envelope or enclosure was to be addressed to 'Miss Kearney'.[40]

The IRA used multiple covering addresses and changed them whenever there was any suspicion they had been compromised. 'Jones' in New York complained to Twomey that: 'I have only one covering address for mail. I would want at least three and a cable address.'[41] The North Mayo brigade wrote to GHQ concerned about the safety of letters after the woman at one of its covering addresses moved and had no relatives nearby to take care of her post.[42]

Twomey sent a letter to Connie Neenan reminding him what covering addresses were appropriate for what types of communications. 'Send cables to [the] Sweetman brothers, 28 South Frederick Street, Dublin. For newspapers: Miss Una Garvey, 6 Morehampton Road, Donnybrook, Dublin. For parcels, magazines or books: Fitzpatrick Newsagents, Wexford Street, Dublin. For occasional letters: Nurse B Monley, Meath Hospital, Dublin. For dispatches: Miss Alice O'Grady, Clarence Hotel, Wellington Quay, Dublin.'[43] Twomey wanted funds raised for the IRA in America to be sent as a money draft to Miss O'Connor: 'I have already informed you that for the present drafts can be sent to Miss O'Connor [in Leitrim].'[44]

He reprimanded Neenan for sending a telegram 'to [an] address which should only be used only for dispatches. I told you several times – cables to be sent through [the] Sweetmans'.[45] The Sweetmans were a prominent nationalist family. The patriarch, John, had been a Home Rule MP and in 1906 helped fund Arthur Griffith's new party, Sinn Féin. Fr Sweetman ran a school in County Wexford and was also well known for his efforts to cultivate tobacco in Ireland. He was a life-long republican and was associated with the Anti-Imperialist League, which was both an IRA and Soviet front organisation. Another republican in the family, Malachy Sweetman, was arrested by the Free State in 1922 and later escaped from Kilmainham Gaol, while Roger Sweetman had been elected a Sinn Féin MP for Wexford in 1918.[46]

The most sensitive correspondence was entrusted to couriers to hand carry. The couriers travelled around Ireland by train, bicycle, bus, motorcar, and even pony and trap, and took the boat to Britain and occasionally to the US. They were predominately women from Cumann na mBan (the women's republican organisation) or relatives of IRA volunteers. Some of the crew members on transatlantic liners also acted as couriers and, at least during the Anglo-Irish War, teenage members of Na Fianna (the IRA's version of the boy scouts) carried messages.[47] An influential IRA officer, Todd Andrews, wrote that this 'wonderfully reliable system of communication ... was the only really efficient part of the IRA operation during the Civil War', adding a well intended compliment (but one which nowadays would be taken as patronising): 'It never failed, thanks to the devotion of these women.'[48]

While most IRA couriers were Irish, in March 1926 'a Jewish engineer' on the transatlantic ship the *SS American Farmer*, by the name of Cohen, delivered despatches to London. He dropped them off at a designated house where he 'met only the old woman, who met him at the door, [and] took the stuff'. He later received $10 (£2) for his expenses, which included tram and taxi fares. The IRA's American representative was critical of the OC in Britain for not having met the courier, and showing his appreciation for his services.[49] Money, in the form of cash or bank drafts, was also carried by courier. Andy Cooney once asked Jones for funding from America: 'If you can, send cash by hand without delay. Do so in preference to post.'[50]

Couriers frequently delivered despatches to call houses. A call house was a home or business where a visitor could be put in contact with an IRA representative, or which would accept a delivery for the IRA. Call houses were located throughout Ireland and Britain, as well as in New York. Twomey even reported: 'We have a call house in Montreal.'[51] Crew members who smuggled messages or munitions across the Atlantic could hand them in to the Rob Roy pub in Cobh, to be picked up by Mick Burke (a well known local IRA man).[52]

When a caller wasn't known, they would identify themselves by using an agreed code word. Twomey arranged for an officer to travel to Glasgow to make contact with the IRA battalion there, telling him: 'You will call to Patrick Morin, 10 Robson Street, Aikenhead Road, Glasgow. You will give the name Moore and ask for Bob.'[53]

In 1927 the director of intelligence reported to an IRA officer in Portlaoise: 'We can arrange a line of communication by bus between Maryboro [Portlaoise] and Dublin. Can you let me have a call house for our busman in Maryboro near [the] bus stopping place if possible?'[54] To which the officer replied: 'The busman can call for [the] first time to myself and I will then make arrangements with him.'[55] A well known IRA haunt and call house in Dublin was the Exchange hotel. Another correspondence from the director of intelligence to the officer from Portlaoise instructed that: 'Our friend can call to Miss Fuller, Exchange hotel, Parliament Street on Friday at 3 p.m. He can ask for Kelly.'[56]

Requiring couriers to go to a call house rather than making direct contact with the IRA was a useful security precaution, which prevented the courier from having to know the name or address of local IRA members. In 1927 the OC in Britain, George, dismissed a courier codenamed 'W2' and warned Twomey: 'W2 has given a lot of trouble since I finished with him. Now he wants his fare home, which I suppose I will have to give him. I used him as a courier so he knows nothing about [my] offices or hardly anything about my work, so if you should see him be careful not to give him any particulars re the addresses etc. that we were using. Please inform the D/I. [director of intelligence] or any others that he may meet.'[57] Throughout these documents George comes across as one of the most careful and security conscious of all the IRA's officers. Indeed it's a credit to him that he avoided arrest, despite the intense police activity in London at the time.

During and after the Civil War the gardaí had success in arresting IRA officers by following the trail of despatches or couriers to them, a technique that was also popular with the British police. Therefore, the more intermediary steps the IRA inserted in the delivery of despatches, the safer were their operatives. Even when Moss Twomey visited London he notified George: 'I will call to your usual call house', rather than going directly to his office or digs.[58] In June 1927 Moss Twomey again took the boat to Britain and travelled to London to collect money. George warned him: '[I] will call at [the] hotel where you stayed last time, at 11 o'clock next Saturday morning. Please try and come yourself. Be careful you are not followed to your hotel.'[59] On other occasions officers made contact with George by meeting him in a pub at an agreed time.

In addition to covering addresses and call houses, the IRA had addresses which they designated safe houses. Safe houses, weren't directly related to the communications network, but were places where the IRA could hold meetings, store supplies and documents, or where a volunteer could safely spend the night. There was the constant risk of raids by the gardaí and in September 1927 the director of intelligence reported a Special Branch raid on a safe house: 'Ward's, Glenmalure House, Rialto was raided last week and a very thorough searching made. This house was used by [the] 4th Battalion [of the Dublin Brigade] up to recently.'

WHATEVER BECAME OF THE IRA's military prowess and discipline in the years following the Civil War, it still retained a complex and efficient communications system, which rivalled that of any other revolutionary organisation at the time. The network had an elaborate set of security procedures and precautions, enabling it to function efficiently despite the best efforts of the Special Branch and a number of blunders by the IRA. Most importantly, it allowed the IRA to successfully shield its activities from the security services in Britain and America.

List of alleged IRA covering addresses

Cooper, Mrs Mary Anne, Cobh, County Cork.[60]

Bray, Mr C, 26 Pipitea Street, Wellington, New Zealand.[61]

Brown, C/O Schwab Piano House, 148 East 34th Street, New York – for telegrams.[62]

Cowan, Mr, Catholic Young Men's Society, 9 and 10 Harrington Street, Dublin – enclosed envelope to be addressed to Miss Kearney.[63]

Crehan, Michael, Menlough, Ballinasloe – letters for the South Galway brigade to be sent to Crehan, and then forwarded to Packie Ruane.[64]

Cremin, Miss Mary, 84 Bridge Lane, Golders Green, London NW.[65]

Downey, Molly, 65 Webb Street, Smithdown Road, Liverpool.[66]

Elie [*sic*], 4 Rue de la Terrasse, Paris 17 – for telegrams to Seán Mac-Bride.[67]

Fitzpatrick's Newsagents, Wexford Street, Dublin – for parcels, magazines and books.[68]

Garvey, Miss Una, 6 Morehampton Road, Donnybrook, Dublin – for newspapers.[69]

Kelly, The Poplars, Merryvale Av, Stockton.[70]

Kelly, Mrs Andrew, 242 Windsor Place, Brooklyn, New York.[71]

Lynch, Miss Florrie, 112 South Circular Road, Dolphin's Barn, Dublin – enclosed envelope to be addressed to Mr Tom R Cleary.[72]

Lynch, 20 Rue de la Paix, Paris – for letters to Seán MacBride, the enclosure was to be marked 'Ambrose'.[73]

Lynch, Nurse B SRN and CMB, 104 Cazenove Road, Stamford Hill, London N 16 – State Registered Nurse and midwife, letters to be delivered on Tuesdays and Fridays, those marked urgent were forwarded to the OC. Britain.[74]

McCormack, Mrs Lena, 33 St George's Court, Gloucester Rd, Kensington, SW 7 – for communications to the OC. Britain.[75]

MacDarby, Miss, 22 Northbrook Terrace, North Strand Road, Dublin – enclosed envelope to be marked for Miss Kearney.[76]

McDonnell, Tom, Collinstown, County Westmeath – copies of the IRA journal *An tÓglach* to be sent to him.[77]

MacHale, Miss, 8 Bessborough Parade, Rathmines, Dublin.[78]

Masterson, Miss E, 44 Acacia Road, Johnswood, London NW.[79]

Monley, Nurse B, Meath Hospital, Dublin – 'for occasional letters'.[80]

Nolan, Michael Junior, 3 Hospital Lane, Enniscorthy, County Wexford – for letters only.[81]

O'Leary, Con, Beaufort Street, off Northumberland Street, Liverpool.[82]

Plunkett, Mrs, 17 Marlborough Road, Dublin – telegram to be sent here.[83]

Price, Miss, 29 South Anne Street, Dublin – envelope to be marked 'personal'.[84]

Rafferty, John, The Stores, Katesbridge, Belfast – pseudonym 'Mr Johnson'.[85]

Sweetman, brothers, 28 South Frederick Street, Dublin – telegrams.[86]

Toner, John, 264 West 118th Street, New York.[87]

Watters, Miss May, 117 Butler Street, Belfast.[88]

White, Miss H, 505 West 40th Street, New York.[89]

List of alleged IRA calling houses

Coady Mrs, 5 Glegg Street, off Great Howard Street, Liverpool – for delivery of gelignite and detonators, caller to 'say stuff is for Mr Kucas [*sic*]'.[90]

Cooley, Mrs, 74 Cavendish Street, Clonard, Belfast – call house for the Belfast battalion, not for comms [letters or despatches].[91]

Fuller, Miss, Exchange hotel, Parliament Street – caller to ask for Kelly.[92]

Lagan, Miss, 353 East 31st Street, New York and Astor Court Building, 18 West 34th Street, Room 207, New York – call house for Connie Neenan, the IRA's representative in America.[93]

McCarthy, Miss, 21 Dawson Street, Dublin.[94]

McLoughlin, Miss, Sinn Féin Offices, 23 Suffolk Street, Dublin.[95]

Magee, Mr H, Motor and Cycle Agent, Edward Street, Lurgan – address for delivery of a motorcycle for the Armagh battalion.[96]

Morin, Patrick, 10 Robson Street, Aikenhead Road, Glasgow – caller to give name 'Moore' and ask for 'Bob'.[97]

O'Grady, Miss Alice, Clarence hotel, Wellington Quay, Dublin – for despatches.[98]

Rob Roy pub, Cobh, County Cork – received despatches and weapons smuggled from America.[99]

Sweeney, Mrs, Fruiterer and Greengrocer, 5 Harold's Cross, Dublin
— consignment of explosives, disguised as fruit, to be sent here.[100]

Turley's [pub], Newbridge, County Galway.[101]

Miscellaneous names and addresses

Cadden, Phil, Connolly St, Fermoy — ex-British soldier who told the
IRA about a secret tunnel leading into Fermoy army barracks.[102]

Cohen, Second Engineer on the *American Farmer*—trans-Atlantic courier for the IRA.[103]

Delahunty, Fr, Kilkenny — in contact with the IRA.[104]

Irwin, Henry P and Williams, John F., care of Thomas Cook and Son,
Grafton Street, Dublin — false American passports for Moss Twomey
and Seán Russell to be posted to them from the US.[105]

Lalor, JJ, 63 Middle Abbey St, Dublin — printer.[106]

McKenna, Father Martin, C/O Parish Priest's House, Ballymackey,
Carrickmacross, County Monaghan — priest in England whose name
was used by IRA volunteers as a referee. He was also associated with
an IRA passport scheme.[107]

Murphy, William, Chief Engineer on the *Tuscor*, which sailed between
Liverpool and Waterford — IRA courier.[108]

O'Shea, Miss Winnie, 8 Loraine Road, Holloway, London — £50 cheque
from Dublin for the IRA commander in Britain to be made payable
to her.[109]

Shanahan, Martin, 1900 Lexington Avenue, New York (c/o Dan O'Brien)
— ex-OC of the Clare brigade, who emigrated to America.[110]

Sloan, Todd, 2 Crown Street, Tidal Basin, London E 16 — English communist organiser who offered to give the IRA information on British
government ammunition stores.[111]

Ward's, Glenmalure House, Rialto, Dublin — safe house for the 4th battalion, Dublin brigade.[112]

CHAPTER 3

A New Leadership: 1926–1927

I would suggest kidnapping and giving him a good hammering, tarring and feathering, or heaving him over the quay.

IRA chief of staff

We will be closed for [the Christmas] Holidays.

IRA chief of staff

At an IRA army convention in November 1925 the delegates rejected the moderate leadership of Frank Aiken and asserted the organisation's autonomy from Éamon de Valera and the politicians of Sinn Féin. They elected a new generation of leaders who were more militant than their predecessors. Andy Cooney succeeded Aiken as chief of staff but was soon replaced by Moss Twomey. Twomey remained in that position for ten years and was to become one of the most influential of the IRA's leaders. At a time of great division within the republican movement, Twomey attempted to hold the IRA together, as well as to reorganise militarily and develop social and economic policies that would resonate with the Irish people. During his tenure the greatest threat to the IRA was not the Free State and the gardaí, but the growth of de Valera's new political party, Fianna Fáil.

Historical background

In April 1923 on a windswept Tipperary hillside, a rifle shot from a Free State soldier mortally wounded the IRA's chief of staff, Liam Lynch, and effectively ended the Civil War. Lynch was a noble brave man, but his incompetent leadership had doomed the IRA to certain defeat and his obstinacy had prevented a timely end to the conflict. In his stead Frank Aiken was elected chief of staff and in May Aiken issued the order 'to cease fire and dump arms'.[1]

The IRA's defeat in the Civil War had been absolute. Throughout the conflict the IRA possessed no coherent or consistent military strategy, it had let the Free State's national army take the initiative and had failed to develop a supporting political programme. By the end of the struggle, considerably more IRA volunteers had been killed than in the Anglo-Irish War (though the exact number is unknown), seventy-seven had been executed and there were 12,000 in jail.[2]

Over the course of 1924 the vast majority of the prisoners were released. However, they and the other IRA veterans had little prospect of employment in the Free State. This was due to a combination of factors: the economic slump that followed the First World War, the considerable hostility to the IRA that existed throughout the country and frequently the volunteers' lack of job skills. Republicans were also barred from state jobs unless they took a pledge of allegiance.[3] Frank Aiken himself wrote that '80% of the Volunteers living in towns, I am sure, are unemployed'.[4] Pax Ó Faoláin of Waterford, who was both an IRA brigadier-general and a plumber, spoke for many when he said: 'Life was a struggle when I came home. You were trying to get a job, to pay a load of debts, to get going again. Yet everybody was boycotting you.' And he added: 'The few people I could get work from here were the Protestants.'[5] Connie Neenan of Cork said that there was a 'campaign of economic tyranny' against republicans.[6] The IRA managed to provide a small number of grants to disabled men and the Sinn Féin Reconstruction Committee made loans to help volunteers start up their own businesses – though these efforts failed to significantly alleviate much of the hardship.[7]

During the course of the Anglo-Irish War and the Civil War the IRA had prohibited the emigration of volunteers. However, as veterans were forced by economic circumstances to seek opportunity in the United States and Britain, the organisation needed to face up to the economic reality and in July 1925 reversed its ban.[8] Though the number of IRA veterans who emigrated was likely in the thousands, a little over 300 formally notified the organisation of their plan to emigrate and registered with its so-called 'foreign reserves'. Of these, 200 went to America, 100 to Britain and a handful to other countries such as Canada and Australia.[9]

In the aftermath of the Civil War, GHQ still expected IRA units to maintain a state of readiness. Officers were instructed to hold parades and training sessions, gather intelligence in their locality, regularly report to headquarters, maintain arms dumps and recruit new members. However, relatively few officers were carrying out their duties – either finding them pointless or prevented by their need to work. Many volunteers and officers were profoundly demoralised and disillusioned with the organisation following the war. A senior officer who was also a member of the Army Executive typified the prevalent apathy: 'He [admitted he] could not be regarded as an active Volunteer' and went on to make a half-hearted commitment that 'he was willing to perform any duties assigned to him provided he had sufficient spare time'.[10] The only area in which the IRA was stronger than ever was in its number of top brass! In 1924 there were at least twenty-one generals in the organisation and by 1927 OCs of the thirteen brigades had been given the rank of brigadier-general – and that was in addition to the generals back at headquarters.[11]

Throughout 1924 and 1925 Aiken reorganised and attempted to revive the organisation; he toured the country (speaking to officers and inspecting units) and disbanded the major units such as divisions. With the decline of the IRA the divisions were no longer effectively functioning and their dissolution removed a redundant layer of bureaucracy, freeing up their staff officers to work with their local units. The thirty-seven local units – brigades, battalions and in the smaller areas companies – now reported directly to GHQ in Dublin and were referred to as 'independent units'. Aiken hoped to decrease the duties of the officers, thereby enabling those 'who have civil work to carry on their Volunteer work at the same time'.[12] The priority for now was to hold the organisation together and await more propitious times. However, despite Aiken's efforts it is estimated that membership declined from 14,500 in August 1924 to 5,000 in November 1926.[13]

Aiken was a dour, brusque northerner, a man of few words, who held his council. During the years of fighting he had shown 'plenty of guts'. He was a stern disciplinarian, who could be short with his men. In a characteristic exchange he wrote to the intelligence officer in Tipperary, who had wanted to set up a meeting to discuss the state of the IRA: 'I cannot conceive what suggestions you can have for curing apathy and disorganisation and maintaining unity, that could not have been ... brought up at the [army] Convention.'[14] And he wrote to Liam Pedlar in America

that 'there is no excuse really for my delay in replying but a general dis-
inclination to deal with [your correspondence]'.[15] Aiken's letters and the
minutes of Army Executive meetings also display an irrational sense of
optimism, though this may have been a *façade* he effected in the hope of
improving morale. In 1924 he reported to America: 'Things are going
pretty well here: in spite of everything – unemployment and bad weather
– we are gaining ground. We are consolidating our forces and the [Free]
Staters are disintegrating rapidly.'[16] Though the Free State government
had to weather the Army Mutiny crisis in March of that year it was the
IRA and not the government that was disintegrating. Aiken was very close
to de Valera whom he 'adored' and regarded almost as 'a holy symbol'.[17]

Meanwhile, developments on the political front were to have significant consequences for the IRA. Back in November 1922 the organisation
had given allegiance to the (largely imaginary) republican 'government'
presided over by Éamon de Valera, who was also the president of Sinn
Féin. This 'government' claimed its legitimacy derived from the Second
Dáil which had been elected in 1921. Following elections in June 1922
to what was to be called the Third or Free State Dáil, Michael Collins
and William Cosgrave dissolved the Second Dáil, and the Third Dáil became the functioning parliament of the new state. However, the legal
basis for the dissolution remained at best unclear. And de Valera, with his
supporters in Sinn Féin and the IRA, was to claim that the Second Dáil
remained the country's legitimate parliament.[18] Sinn Féin thus boycotted
the Free State Dáil and refused to recognise the institutions of the state.
The republican 'government' however was a government in name only
and provided no functioning alternative to the Free State administration.

During the Civil War the IRA, under the control of Liam Lynch and
the IRA Army Executive, largely ignored de Valera and Sinn Féin. In effect it was a military dictatorship, which claimed to act on behalf of the
Irish people, but without their mandate.[19] It was only following the defeat of the IRA and Aiken's appointment as chief of staff that de Valera
and the republican 'government' were able to assert control over the organisation. De Valera's position was strengthened in February 1925 when
another one of his supporters, Seán Lemass, was appointed republican

Minister for Defence. In addition the republican Minister for Finance controlled the IRA's budget and paid the salaries of the headquarters staff. With these developments, de Valera – in the words of Seán Mac-Bride – 'assumed more power [over the IRA] than had been intended'.[20]

By 1925 rumours began to spread that de Valera was exploring the option of entering the Free State Dáil – provided this could be done without taking the oath of allegiance to the king – and that Lemass and Aiken were sympathetic to this strategy. With de Valera in a dominant position over the IRA, this became a source of disquiet to the more militant officers, such as Andy Cooney, Moss Twomey and Seán Russell. They feared that de Valera and Aiken would compromise on the IRA's goal of a thirty-two county republic and corrupt the organisation by entangling it further in the political process. In the autumn of 1925 Cooney approached Aiken and directly asked him if he would support Sinn Féin's entry into the Free State Dáil, but Aiken was evasive and refused to give a straight answer.[21]

In May 1925 the Army Executive called for the convening of a general army convention that November.[22] Aiken, as sanguine as ever, wrote about the upcoming convention: 'I believe there is no cause for the slightest worry in the matter.'[23]

1925 IRA army convention

On 14 and 15 November, IRA delegates from across the country attended the general army convention at the (inconveniently namely) Queen's hotel, Dalkey, County Dublin. This crucial meeting was to determine the direction of the IRA for many years.

The convention approved a new IRA constitution that asserted the organisation's primary aim as the establishment of a thirty-two county republic through the use of force. It also decreed that the general army convention was 'the supreme army authority', but that the Army Council fulfilled this role when the convention was not in session. The convention would elect the twelve members of the Army Executive, which in turn selected the seven members of the Army Council. However, aside from selecting the Army Council, the Executive (which had been such a powerful body during the Civil War) was now largely powerless and was rarely convened. Even in early 1925 all Aiken could say of it was that: '[The] Army Executive is still in existence.'[24] In practice the IRA was governed by the chief of staff working with the Army Council and the senior officers at General Headquarters.

The second major development at the convention was the passage of Peadar O'Donnell's resolution that: 'The army of the Republic severs its connection with the [Second] Dáil and act [sic] under an independent executive, such executive to be given the power to declare war when, in its opinion, a suitable opportunity arises to rid the Republic of its enemies'. This signalled the IRA's formal split with de Valera and Sinn Féin, and was additionally a vote of no confidence in Aiken's leadership. O'Donnell wanted to break away from the legalistic and socially conservative attitude of Sinn Féin and for the IRA instead to develop its own radical social and economic policies, leading to a revolution that would be both nationalist and socialist.

The atmosphere became acrimonious when Aiken admitted that he had been involved in discussions about entering the Dáil. The delegates then elected the members of the Army Exectuive, with those that opposed Aiken – such as Andy Cooney, Moss Twomey and Peadar O'Donnell – topping the poll, while Aiken himself was barely re-elected. The Army Council soon afterwards selected Andy Cooney as chief of staff.[25]

The historian Richard English has described the army convention as marking the 'birth of a new, autonomous IRA'. However, it was those that were to soon resign and join with de Valera, such as Aiken and Lemass, who had tried to change the IRA, while Andy Cooney and his associates wanted a return to its traditional autonomy.[26] The convention's assertion that the IRA was primarily committed to physical force was certainly not a new departure, and aside from the period of Aiken's tenure, political control of the organisation was tenuous at best. For instance, during the Anglo-Irish War Cathal Brugha, the republican Minister for Defence, was largely ignored and sidelined by the leadership of Richard Mulcahy and Michael Collins.

A few days after the convention, Frank Aiken wrote a prescient letter to Cooney laying out his (evolving) position. In it he implied that the new leadership lacked 'foresight and common-sense' as it pinned its hopes on 'the extremely remote possibility of a successful *coup d'etat*' and argued that the IRA needed to retain both a military and political strategy: 'I think the fight before our country should appear difficult enough ... without seeking to limit our tactics [to a purely military solution].' Aiken warned the leadership of the danger of withdrawing from political participation and becoming 'a society of select brethren who will admire one another'. He continued to support the existence of the IRA: 'Without the Army, Ireland cannot gain her freedom', and ended with an appeal for the Army Council to tolerate volunteers who supported republicans entering the Dáil, once they could do so without taking the oath.[27] Rather ironically (in the light of subsequent events) he proclaimed: 'I haven't the slightest sympathy in the world with the people who would ... take the oaths or declarations [of] allegience [*sic*].'

The IRA's new leadership

The appointment of Cooney heralded a virtual complete change in the IRA's senior leadership. Unlike Aiken and his supporters, who were looking at alternatives to armed action, the incoming leadership envisaged the IRA seizing power at an opportune moment. Many were also inspired by the Russian Bolsheviks and saw the IRA as the vanguard of a social revolution. Though not significantly younger in years, these Young Turks represented a new generation. With the exception of Seán Russell, few of them had held senior positions during the Anglo-Irish War. The IRA's legendary leaders who fought the British had now largely left: Michael Collins had gone Free State and was shot dead in an IRA ambush in the Civil War, Tom Barry was no longer actively involved and wasn't to return until the 1930s, Seán Moylan supported de Valera and Seán MacEoin was now a senior officer in the Free State army.

Andy Cooney as chief of staff was 'supreme in all military matters'. He chaired the Army Council and oversaw the staff at GHQ.[28] The Army Council decided on policy and strategy, while the headquarters staff were responsible for the day to day running of the IRA. As has already been noted, the Army Council had subsumed most of the responsibilities previously accorded to the Army Executive. This occurred during Frank Aiken's tenure and was likely due to his disagreement with several of its members, particularly over the circumstances of the ending of the Civil War. In turn Cooney had no reason to resurrect the power of the Executive as several members remained loyal to Aiken and de Valera, whereas the Army Council fully backed Cooney and his allies.

After the chief of staff, the second most senior officer was the adjutant general, who was responsible for discipline and administrative matters, including the keeping of records and communications with local units. The quartermaster general (QMG) oversaw the importation, supply and distribution of arms, equipment and explosives. Other headquarters officers included the director of intelligence and the finance and accounts officer.

Cooney voluntarily relinquished his position as chief of staff to Moss Twomey in the first half of 1926. Tom Daly of Kerry was adjutant general in 1926 and was likely replaced by Donal O'Donoghue the following year.[29] Seán Russell was QMG.[30] Peadar O'Donnell was editor of the IRA's newspaper, An Phoblacht (The Republic) and a member of the Army Council. Frank Kerlin was director of intelligence. Mick Price was OC of the Dublin brigade and also a member of the Army Council. Other senior leaders included Donal O'Donoghue, George Gilmore, Jim Killeen and Seán MacBride.

In some ways work at headquarters resembled that at any other office (aside from the constant risk of a raid by the gardaí!). Moss Twomey wrote to George Gilmore telling him of the difficulties caused by resignations and the lack of money: '[Staff captain] Wilson is now with me here. You see we are pretty short handed. Bridie left suddenly a few weeks ago and has a job. Wilson tries to type',[31] while Andy Cooney sent a secret communication to the OC in Britain telling him not to visit over Christmas: 'We will be closed for [the] Holidays from the 22nd [of December], but you can come before that date.'[32] Even revolutionaries need a break!

During this time there was a significant decline in the organisation's income, due to the drying up of funds from America, the break with de Valera and the decrease in Soviet funding. The IRA was perennially strapped for cash and had difficulty paying its full-time officers at headquarters. Due to the (illegal) nature of its business, financial records were often inadequate and there were frequent allegations of misappropiation of funds by officers. Moss Twomey was continually asking officers to account for their use of IRA monies. He wrote to the finance officer telling him not to 'certify any other account without receipts' but was forced to qualify his statement: 'that is in cases where it is possible to get them'.[33] There still remained money that had been dispersed during the Civil War to prevent its seizure by the Free State. Twomey wrote to the OC of the Dublin brigade: 'See Donal O'Donoghue's mother who has some brigade funds. I do not know exact amount.'[34]

An inner circle existed within the leadership composed of Andy Cooney, Moss Twomey and Seán Russell. Cooney and Twomey were staunch allies and worked closely together, while Peadar O'Donnell gave Twomey advice and assistance on political initiatives and was influential in this regard — though he was unable to persuade the Army Council to adopt his more revolutionary Marxist ideas. Seán MacBride, who was close to Twomey, was also a key player.

Additionally the leadership could be broken into three groups, each with a broadly different outlook. Twomey and Cooney represented the centrists, who felt that the IRA needed to have a social and political policy to support its military strategy. The socialist republicans, as exemplified by Peadar O'Donnell, advocated both a nationalist and social revolution. Militarists like Russell, on the other hand, were committed to the IRA as purely a physical force movement; they regarded any political entanglement or alliance as likely to compromise the organisation and corrupt the membership.

Andy Cooney was originally from Nenagh, County Tipperary. During the Anglo-Irish War, while still a medical student at University College, Dublin, he was active in the Dublin IRA. He was a member of Michael Collins' hand-picked unit, the 'Squad', and in November 1920 participated in the assassinations of British intelligence agents on Bloody Sunday. In 1921 he strongly opposed the Anglo-Irish Treaty and wanted to have Collins and the other negotiators arrested on their return to Ireland. In the months leading up to the Civil War, while many of the IRA officers (who were to go on to fight against the Free State) desperately tried to avert war, Cooney was one of the few who advocated the IRA go on the offensive and attack Beggar's Bush barracks in the capital. During the conflict he was appointed OC of the grandiosely sounding 1st Eastern division. Following the war he disapproved of Aiken's drift towards politics and at the 1925 army convention topped the poll for the Army Executive.[35]

Cooney, at six foot two, towered over most of his comrades. He was a strict disciplinarian, not renowned for his charisma. A colleague described him as 'withdrawn, definitely not the sort you would crack jokes with', though his friend, Todd Andrews, painted a more sympathetic picture: 'All women, young or old, liked Cooney.'[36] Cooney's stint as chief of staff was to prove brief, as in April 1926 he received permission from the Army Council to visit America for the purpose of meeting with representatives of the IRA's main support group there – Clan na Gael. He planned to bring them up to date on developments in Ireland and to ensure their continued financial backing. Moss Twomey was appointed interim chief of staff, and was confirmed in that position later in October.[37] Cooney was happy to relinquish the post to Twomey who was the 'overwhelming choice' of the Army Council as his replacement.[38] On Cooney's return from the US he resumed his medical studies in Dublin. He retained the chairmanship of the Army Council until January 1927 when that too was assumed by Twomey.[39] As Twomey wrote in cipher: 'The late chairman asked to be relieved temporarily of [the] chairmanship, to give him [a] chance of getting [his] exam. He should either go for it now, or abandon [the] idea of [the] profession.'[40]

The exact date of the handover of the chief of staff's position in 1926 is uncertain. There is some evidence it may have occurred in April before Cooney's departure in late May or early June.[41] One piece of evidence that supports an April handover is a letter written on 12 April by the 'Chief of Staff' to the 'Chairman of the Army Council'.[42] Unless Cooney was writing to himself, or was deliberately trying to be deceptive (which was possible) then Twomey had already become chief of staff. Also in April the IRA's representative in America wrote to Cooney: 'tell M. I can supply him with gold braid should he need it in his new office'. Given that 'M' likely stands for Moss, this appears to be a reference to Twomey's appointment.[43] Additionally, the encrypted documents (on which James

Gillogly and I have based this book) were from Moss Twomey's personal collection and the papers signed 'chief of staff' start in April 1926, not in November 1925 or June 1926, further suggesting that the handover occurred in April. Therefore it's likely that letters signed 'chief of staff' from 12 April on were written by Moss Twomey. This is of relevance as a number of important orders were sent to Britain from the chief of staff in May 1926 (see Chapter 6). In confidential correspondence Cooney was frequently referred to as 'Mr Smith' and in the minutes of the Army Council as 'A'.[44]

Maurice (or Moss) Twomey was chief of staff from 1926 to 1936. His ten-year tenure was the longest of any IRA chief of staff, by virtue of which he had a very significant influence on the organisation. Twomey was from Fermoy, County Cork and during the Anglo-Irish War he served under Liam Lynch with the North Cork brigade. In the Civil War he followed Lynch to GHQ, where he was a staff officer, eventually rising to the rank of adjutant general. He was very closely associated with Lynch and was with him when he was shot dead in 1923.[45]

In contrast to both his predecessors, his leadership style was one of encouragement and positive reinforcement and he generally avoided confrontation. It was said that he 'had the smooth diplomacy of a Cork man'. On one occasion he wrote to the adjutant of the North Mayo brigade: 'We have not been hearing from you very frequently for some time, I hope it is not due to the fact that you are unwell. I hope you are keeping in good health.'[46] This is a letter that any professional manager would be proud of.

His principal goal was to hold the organisation together and to reign in the 'wild horses' chomping for action.[47] He believed that the IRA had to wait for the opportune moment to stage a *coup d'etat*, leading to the establishment of a thirty-two county republic. In the meantime the organisation had to tread water. It's likely that many of the military operations he approved in the late 1920s (with the exception of the 1926 barrack raids) were with a view to maintaining both unity and a degree of readiness, while at the same time avoiding any significant confrontation with the forces of the Free State.

Twomey regarded the IRA as primarily a physical force organisation, though he promoted the development of social and economic policies, which he saw as necessary for the maintenance and development of support among the civilian population. He felt the absence of such polices had contributed to the Civil War defeat.[48] Much of the IRA's stance on economic and social policy during this period was socialist. However, Twomey avoided the more confrontational and revolutionary Marxist approach of Peadar O'Donnell, realising that a lurch too far to the left would alienate many of the IRA's volunteers and the population in general. Years later he noted: 'GHQ was ahead of the Army [IRA] on questions of socialism, while the Army was ahead of the people.'[49]

The well liked and moderate Twomey is remembered as an effective and capable leader. He was highly regarded by all (the warring) factions within the IRA and was seen as 'reasonable and capable of seeing another's viewpoint'.[50] The historian Bowyer Bell described him as 'a tower of strength in the Fenian tradition, an excellent organiser with an almost faultless intuition'.[51] However, the period of his leadership was one of decline – during which de Valera and Fianna Fáil outmanoeuvred the IRA at every step and took the republican mantle for themselves. Twomey was incapable of developing effective policies to counter those of Fianna Fáil, he failed to organise the IRA as a disciplined fighting force and never came up with an achievable plan for the establishment of a republic. Maybe he was cut out to be a staff officer rather than chief of staff – better at carrying out orders than at formulating them. As he read books on grand strategy and generalship, he jumped from one idea to the next without ever having a coherent strategy.[52] Even in the unlikely event that the many attacks and campaigns he contemplated had been successful, they wouldn't have advanced the country one iota along the road to a republic.

Some of the outlandish ideas he promoted included a plan to set off stink bombs at a meeting in Manchester attended by the president of the Free State government, William Cosgrave.[53] It seems hard to understand how he could have expected IRA volunteers to risk imprisonment for such a farcical idea. On another occasion he wanted the boy scouts and their pernicious influence investigated. He ordered the burning of corrupting English Sunday newspapers, and in early 1926 even proposed that the IRA expend its limited resources on making a propaganda film, with the irresistible box office draw of genuine IRA film stars! 'Though it may at the moment appear too ambitious, the idea of getting out a good film dealing with [the] phases of the struggle since 1916, should be borne in mind. A film, something on the line of "America" or [the] one got out by Montenegro ... would be one of the very best forms of publicity. There should be no reason why a syndicate in the USA could not be got to finance it as a business proposition ... Our men in the USA, I am sure, would take part in the filming for little payment.'[54]

Twomey's 'great mentor', Liam Lynch, had also been prone to flights of fancy, particularly towards the end of the Civil War. With the IRA facing certain defeat in 1923 Lynch pinned all his hopes on acquiring mountain artillery in Germany, and shortly before he died he spent time considering the design for an IRA uniform.[55] In 1923 P. A. Murray, the IRA's commander in Britain, received totally impractical orders from Lynch to carry out major sabotage operations there. The IRA in Britian simply wasn't equipped or organised to undertake these attacks. Murray placed some of the responsibility on Twomey: 'I blamed Moss Twomey for these rediculous [sic] orders, for he was a green Staff Officer who had no sense of reality.'[56]

Perhaps Twomey's greatest success was that during his tenure the IRA overall acted with restraint and didn't commit some awful atrocity or folly – something that would have been well within the capability of militants like Seán Russell. In confidential correspondence – especially to and from America – Twomey was known by the pseudonym 'Mr Brown' or 'Mr Browne', while in the minutes of the Army Council meetings he was given the designation 'C'. In these documents Twomey frequently comes across as almost fatherly; he expressed concern for his men's health and was sympathetic to their plight and in turn they felt comfortable enough with him to occasionally exchange a caustic remark. Though Twomey could show a tough and ruthless side, his correspondence is altogether different from that of the more intimidating and less empathetic Frank Aiken. The degree of respect Twomey commanded within the IRA and the longevity of his leadership was due in large part to his personality, which the following few examples from the documents help illustrate.

The OC in Liverpool wrote to him about an IRA prisoner, Patrick

Walshe, who was due for release from an English jail, having served five years for possessing arms, and was now seeking financial assistance. The IRA in Liverpool believed that at the time of his arrest 'he had mentioned some names'.[57] Despite this cloud of suspicion Twomey was sympathetic to his plight and replied to the OC: 'Of course if he is badly off, and if money is available, I think he should certainly get some.'[58] Twomey's letters to his comrades George Gilmore and Mick Price in Mountjoy prison seem genuinely warm and affectionate (see Chapter 5). When he learned that Connie Neenan in New York had the flu, Twomey replied in characteristic fashion: 'I sincerely hope you are in good health again and was very sorry to hear you were not well.'[59] On another occasion the IRA OC in Britain, having received a large amount of encrypted documentation from Twomey, sarcastically commented: 'You must think that I like deciphering.'[60] This was not the sort of comment a subordinate would send to a feared commander. On the other hand Twomey reminded the OC of the South Dublin battalion: 'I wrote [to] you re. action to be taken against a man named Bollard of Bray. Have these instructions carried out without further delay.'[61] And when another person crossed him he wrote: 'I wish I had my hands on him.'[62]

One of the most colourful of the IRA's leaders was Peadar O'Donnell, the leading member of a group called the republican socialists. In addition to being editor of *An Phoblacht*, he was a distinguished author and novelist in his own right. The three formative influences on his life were: the nationalist struggle against England, the poverty of the west of Ireland and Marxism. Following the Anglo-Irish War O'Donnell was primarily involved in the political aspects of the republican movement, and he himself later said that he 'was not the military type', though this may have been somewhat of an overstatement.[63]

O'Donnell was born in 1893 in Dungloe, County Donegal.[64] One of nine children, his family eked out an existence on a five-acre farm on the western seaboard. Having received a scholarship to teacher training college in Dublin he returned to Donegal in 1913, where both the poverty of the people and the community spirit that helped sustain them made a lasting impression on him.[65] Later he spent time in Glasgow where he was introduced to the 'exciting world of the working class struggle' and thereafter became a lifelong Marxist. Back in Ireland he abandoned teaching to become a full-time organiser for the Irish Transport and General Workers Union (ITGWU). And during the Anglo-Irish War he joined the IRA full time, becoming OC of the 2nd brigade of the northern division.[66] During the Civil War he was a member of the IRA's Army Executive, and in 1923 he was elected a Sinn Féin TD for Donegal.[67]

Rather ironically, the 1925 army convention passed his motion to sever the IRA's allegiance to the Second Dáil and the republican 'government'.[68] O'Donnell's intent (at least in part) was to break with Sinn Féin – which lacked a commitment to social activism – and to enable the IRA to facilitate a combined nationalist and socialist revolution. However, in doing so he inadvertently handed the IRA back to the militarists and their allies – 'the cult of armed men' – who had little interest in social and economic policies and were to effectively block many of his proposals, while many of the socially progressive members of the republican movement, such as Seán Lemass and P. J. Rutledge, aligned themselves with Éamon de Valera.[69]

Though a self-professed Marxist, O'Donnell (in common with the other republican socialists) lacked a rigid adherence to communist orthodoxy, and 'displayed considerable flexibility in his interpretation of socialism', which was influenced by his own observations and experiences.[70] He saw the IRA as the 'spearpoint of a mass movement' and believed that a successful nationalist revolution was dependent on the IRA's mobilisation of the working-class.[71] In his mind, England was the oppressor whose subjugation of Ireland included economic exploitation, and this situation was mirrored within Ireland by the struggle between the oppressor and the oppressed classes.[72] Under his editorship, *An Phoblacht* became a 'radical revolutionary organ', promoting a socially progressive agenda with energy and clarity.[73] He was actively involved in Soviet-sponsored organisations, including the League Against Imperialism and the Workers' International Relief.[74] O'Donnell was close to Moss Twomey and he played an important role in preparing the IRA's case for a republican alliance (of Sinn Féin and Fianna Fáil along with the IRA) to contest the June 1927 general election.[75]

There were many contradictions and weaknesses in O'Donnell's polemic. In reality the IRA was a *petite bourgeoisie* conspiratorial organisation, rather than a workers' and peasants' army. It was firmly routed in the nineteenth-century concept of a nationalist revolution, and its few socialists were largely peripheral to the organisation. Kevin O'Higgins, a leading Sinn Féin activist during the Anglo-Irish War, famously said: 'We were probably the most conservative minded revolutionaries that ever put through a successful revolution.'[76] Additionally O'Donnell failed to justify the IRA's refusal to acknowledge the wishes of the majority of the southern Irish population who supported the Free State. Most glaring of all, he had no satisfactory explanation of what was to be done with the Protestant working-class in Northern Ireland who were prepared to take up arms to prevent their 'liberation' by the IRA. Despite the many flaws in his argument, he has received much serious attention from historians and biographers.[77]

Due to his skill as a writer and propagandist, the extent of Peadar O'Donnell's influence within the IRA has been exaggerated.[78] However, he was likely more tolerated than listened to. In 1927, he was unsuccessful in trying to persuade the Army Council to support his campaign to encourage farmers to withhold payment of the land annuities due to Britain.[79] He later recalled that 'there was endless argument on the Army Council between the claims of armed struggle and agitation' and despite his best efforts the former consistently triumphed.[80] One republican related: 'I liked Peadar. I did not pay great attention to some of his theories but I loved his droll humour.'[81] To Tom Maguire (a senior IRA leader from Mayo and a member of Sinn Féin), 'Peadar was more a socialist leader than a national leader'.[82] Seán MacBride, who was 'a close friend', wrote: 'He was always bubbling over with energy and different schemes. The real trouble was that he used to forget his schemes and plans from one week to another.'[83] And in a similar vein Connie Neenan stated: 'Peadar had a brilliant new idea every week.'[84] In 1929 MacBride travelled with O'Donnell to a meeting of the League Against Imperialism in Frankfurt, and he later dismissed it as 'one of those high-sounding organisations that we felt we had to support'.[85]

O'Donnell's fellow travellers among the senior leadership included well respected men like Mick Fitzpatrick, Dave Fitzgerald, Mick Price and especially George Gilmore. But with Twomey and the centrists in a tacit alliance with the militarists, there was little significant progress towards a people's revolution that these republican socialists could make. While there were pockets of radicalism within the IRA, in the words of one officer from Dublin: 'We were not revolutionaries.'[86] Presumably he meant to put the word 'socialist' in front of revolutionaries! The legendary fighter Ernie O'Malley worded it stronger when he referred to the attitude of the average IRA man: 'The Volunteer spirit in essentials was hostile to Labour'.[87]

From the late 1920s on, the IRA adopted left wing policies (ranging from the nationalisation of the banks to free secondary education and support for trade unions) and publicly associated itself with organisations aligned with the Soviet Union. However, the encrypted documents in this book show that the IRA's clandestine relationship with the Soviet Union was utilitarian and not ideologically based.[88] This relationship was overseen by Twomey and Cooney and based on the financial and military needs of the IRA. There is no evidence that the republican socialists played any significant role in the alliance. In 1927, when Twomey proposed that he should go to Moscow to negotiate improved funding, he recommended that Seán Russell and not Peadar O'Donnell accompany him. In the encrypted correspondence, Twomey and Cooney fail to express any left-wing sympathy, aside for some anti-imperialist sentiment. The only (rather unimportant) references to O'Donnell in cipher are in connection with contacts with the Chinese nationalist representative in London. On the other hand, the apolitical Seán Russell figures relatively prominently. To a certain extent, O'Donnell's role in the IRA could be viewed as that of an ideological fig leaf – plus he happened to be a good newspaper editor to boot!

Peadar O'Donnell was most likely a member of the Army Council during this period.[89] However, it's difficult to be sure what letter from the alphabet was his alias, though review of the council's minutes presents considerable circumstantial evidence that he was likely 'D'. Some of the evidence is as follows. Just as O'Donnell was known to play a leading part in the Army Council's political initiatives, 'D' proposed the formation of a 'civilian Revolutionary Movement' and along with Twomey developed a draft constitution for the movement.[90] On 17 February 1927 the Army Council asked 'D' to look into arrangements for IRA men to volunteer to fight in China, and the following day Twomey reported that 'Peadar O'D' had a letter for the Chinese representative in London.[91] It is also known that O'Donnell helped draw up and promote the plan for a republican election pact in 1927, and similarly 'D' is reported in the minutes to have been prominently involved, along with Moss Twomey and Andy Cooney.[92]

Seán Russell was the archetypical IRA militarist and admitted 'he had no liking for political parties'.[93] A Dubliner, he joined the Irish Volunteers on their inception in 1913 and, rising through the ranks, he was appointed the IRA's director of munitions in 1920. By 1927 he was quartermaster general and continued in that position until 1936.[94]

One veteran remembered him as 'very sincere, but not so easy to get on with. You would not open up to him readily, nor he to you'.[95] Tony Woods of Dublin alluded to similar characteristics but was more critical: 'I never liked him very much. I don't know why. I had no reason not to like him except that I though he was a devious person, quiet and absolutely ruthless.'[96] Seán MacBride disliked Russell and accused him of being overly secretive and of controlling 'an organisation within an organisation'.[97] George Gilmore claimed that Twomey kept a firm hand on him and didn't seem to take him seriously.[98] Some of these reminiscences may have been influenced by Russell's subsequent disastrous takeover of the IRA in 1938.

It's clear from these papers and from other evidence that Russell was a powerful and influential figure within the IRA. In June of 1925 he was a member of the delegation that travelled to Moscow to solicit support and weaponry. In 1927 Twomey proposed that he should again accompany him to Moscow, and the same year Cooney suggested that he should visit America with him as part of a fundraising tour. Russell's responsibilities were key to the military plans of the organisation, and he ran an efficient network for the importation of explosives from Britain. His contacts were such that he felt that he could retrieve a cache of explosives captured by the customs in Dublin 'without trouble'.[99]

Russell appears to have been given the designation 'E' in the Army

Council minutes. In 1926 'E' advocated attacks in Britain as a way to focus international attention on the IRA's struggle, rather than have the Irish question relegated to that of a 'domestic wrangle'.[100] This is similar to the position adopted by Russell in 1939 when he organised a bombing campaign in England. In 1927, 'E' was the sole member of the Council who objected to the formation of 'a civilian Revolutionary Movement' to promote public support of the IRA.[101] This was also consistent with Russell's viewpoint.

Another militarist was George Plunkett, the brother of the executed 1916 leader, Joseph Mary Plunkett and the son of the Sinn Féin politician, Count Plunkett. He was a member of the GHQ staff and held similar views to Russell, whom he supported.[102]

Seán MacBride was also attached to the headquarters staff. Like Twomey he was a 'centrist' and was to become one of his closest collaborators. He was likely appointed adjutant general in the late 1920s and in 1936 he was briefly chief of staff following Twomey's arrest.[103]

MacBride was born in Paris in 1904, and despite his relative youth (he was almost ten years younger than most of the other senior IRA leaders) he commanded respect and authority.[104] He was intelligent, educated, well spoken and of an impeccable republican pedigree; his (alcoholic and abusive) father, John, an IRB man, had been one of the martyrs of 1916 and his mother, Maud Gonne MacBride (the beauty who inspired Yeats), worked tirelessly on behalf of republican prisoners throughout the 1920s. In January 1926, he married 'Kid' Bulfin and they moved to Paris, where as a freelance journalist he wrote a number of articles for the *Herald Tribune*.

In Paris he was subjected to British secret service surveillance and he became aware that they were opening his correspondence. Additionally the IRA OC in Britain warned Twomey: 'I have received information from two different sources that Seán is under close observation over there.'[105] Living abroad, he continued to work for the IRA and was in regular communication with GHQ. In September 1926 he sent back papers for Art O'Connor of Sinn Féin along with '1,000 rounds of .45 ammunition'.[106] Such was MacBride's stature within the IRA, that following Moss Twomey's arrest in November 1926, Andy Cooney sent him a telegram requesting his return to Ireland.[107] On his return he went on to resume his law studies, write for *An Phoblacht* and helped manage the jam factory that his mother and her companion Charlotte Despard had founded.[108]

MacBride travelled extensively throughout Europe – sometimes on the pretext of purchasing supplies and equipment for the jam factory – with his own selection of false passports.[109] He was fluent in French and even spoke English with a French accent. He seemed to have a natural affinity for undercover work and 'Peadar O'Donnell considered that Mac-Bride shone in liaison with continental revolutionaries. He enjoyed being abroad and gave a good impression of the Irish movement.'[110] Interestingly, he failed to mention his clandestine Soviet contacts in his posthumously published memoirs.

In his encrypted correspondence MacBride used a fifteen-letter key-word (or keyphrase), the longest used in these documents. This would have made decryption without the keyword more difficult. The keywords used by other IRA officers averaged twelve letters (ranging from six to thirteen letters, with one of fourteen letters). The documents show Mac-Bride to have had a sophisticated understanding of communications security. Aside from using a long and obscure keyword, he used a key that was not shared with other IRA communications networks, the key was not listed on any of the master lists that James and I reviewed, and MacBride also on occasion took the precaution of asking Twomey and Frank Kerlin to destroy his message after they had read it.[111]

In these documents there's considerable evidence that MacBride was known by the pseudonym 'Mr Ambrose'. Some of the evidence is as follows. In 1924–5 Seán MacBride was asked to investigate the whereabouts of a substantial sum of IRA money that had been set aside for arms purchases in Germany and had 'disappeared' – possibly into the personal bank account of Robert Briscoe, who purchased weapons for the IRA in the Anglo-Irish and Civil Wars.[112] Coincidentally in early 1926 'Ambrose' wrote a letter to the chief of staff detailing the loss of several thousand pounds in transactions involving Briscoe.[113] Just as MacBride was known to be living in Paris in 1926, the contact addresses for 'Ambrose' in the IRA's communication log book were in Paris.[114] In September 1927 the

IRA OC in Britain asked that 'Ambrose' go over to Amsterdam to meet a Russian agent; however, Moss Twomey wrote back: 'Ambrose is not available.' And at this time Seán MacBride was one of the few IRA senior officers in jail, aside from George Gilmore (who doesn't fit the profile for 'Ambrose').[115]

The IRA and republican women

The IRA's attitude to women reflected the beliefs of Irish society at the time. Though the IRA was heavily dependent on women in auxiliary roles – as nurses, couriers, informants, running call houses and safe houses, and providing support for prisoners – women were barred from becoming members. At its best the republican attitude was paternalistic and there was a reluctance to accept women as leaders – even in the political arena. For instance, in 1922 Joe McGarrity, the leading IRA supporter in America, requested that a 'really competent' man and specifically not a woman, be sent over from Ireland as a republican representative.[116] In contrast, the many socialist and communist groupings in Ireland were more ready to accept women in leadership roles. Maud Gonne, Charlotte Despard and Hanna Sheehy Skeffington (along with Peadar O'Donnell) were all on the executive committee of the Irish section of the Soviet-sponsored Workers' International Relief.[117]

However, there were a significant number of talented (and even extra-ordinary) women who were staunch republicans, many of whom were also socialists. Countess Markievicz was a prominent member of the socialist Irish Citizen Army, fought in the 1916 Easter Rising and in 1918 was the first woman elected to the British House of Commons. In 1926 she was one of the few republican women who went on to join Fianna Fáil. Mary MacSwiney was a leading member of Sinn Féin and was elected to the Second Dáil; she distinguished herself as one of the most intransigent of all republicans, refusing to recognise the Free State in any way. In 1927, Sighle Humphreys and a number of female comrades started a campaign to intimidate jurors in trials involving IRA volunteers. It was only with reluctance that Twomey and the IRA supported what was to become one of the most serious threats to the state in the late 1920s.[118]

Though prevented from joining the IRA, women could participate in

Cumann na mBan (Society of Women), which was essentially a women's IRA auxiliary – pledged to organise and train the women of Ireland to take part in 'the military, political and economic movements towards the enthronement of the Irish Republic'. The leadership of Cumann na mBan showed itself to be independent of the IRA and at times not afraid to criticise IRA policy. In 1926, Eithne Coyle replaced Countess Markievicz as president, and Mary MacSwiney was vice-president. It was a small organisation and by 1928 had only fifty members in Dublin; its main centre of activity.[119]

A despatch sent by a member of the Army Council, Donal O'Donoghue, illustrates the attitude of many men towards women republicans. At the time O'Donoghue, himself a prisoner in Mountjoy (the 'Joy), suggested that a protest should be staged in support of the IRA prisoners. He wrote to Frank Kerlin, the director of intelligence: '[I] suggest [that there be a] daily picket [by the] girls, [of the] 'Joy and [the] Gov't [Government] Buildings.'[120] The 'girls' likely included the octogenarian Charlotte Despard!

IRA prisoners were often incarcerated in deplorable conditions and during the Civil War had been subject to torture and execution (judicial or otherwise). Maud Gonne and Charlotte Despard were the two most prominent and indefatigable champions for the rights and welfare of republican prisoners. In 1922 they formed the Women's Prisoners' Defence League (WPDL), with Gonne as the driving force and Despard as her right-hand woman.[121] The group, though tiny, with only about twenty members, held vigils outside prisons, organised public protests and wrote to the papers, all of which managed to achieve considerable publicity and helped keep the government frequently on the defensive.[122] The two women were also associated with the Political Prisoners Committee and the Irish Republican Dependents Fund.

Maud Gonne MacBride, known as 'Ireland's Joan of Arc', was a romantic Irish nationalist, a tall striking woman who became the centre of attention whenever she entered a room.[123] Yeats wrote of her: 'I have spread my dreams under your feet; Tread softly because you tread on my dreams'.[124] She was a fervent advocate for republican prisoners. On one occasion, after she was told about a republican family living in poverty in Donegal whose son had been a prisoner, she drove to the family's home and left them her car so that they could start a taxi business.[125] Another time Moss Twomey reported that a republican defendant, Mrs Maher from Cork, 'was found here [in Dublin] after her trial by Madam Mc'Bride [*sic*] without a penny, nowhere to go in Dublin, and no money to take her home. Madam is paying her hotel expenses and gave her £1. 13. 0 for her train and car fares.'[126]

At eighty-two, Charlotte Despard was twenty-two years Maud Gonne's senior. She was born in Kent, England in 1844. Her brother, John, joined the British army, becoming commander of the British Expeditionary Force on the western front in the First World War and in 1921 was appointed lord lieutenant in Ireland. Charlotte initially occupied her time as a romantic novelist, writing *Chaste as ice, pure as snow*, but following the death of her husband dedicated her life to the cause of the poor. She went on to involve herself in a wide variety of causes, and became a socialist, communist, suffragette, theosophist, Catholic and vegetarian.[127] In 1909 she met Gandhi and, impressed with his theory of passive resistance, she later campaigned against the First World War as an 'uncompromising pacifist'.[128] Following the war she was a member of a Labour party delegation that toured Ireland and in 1921 she moved permanently to Ireland, becoming in the process both Irish and a 'Sinn Féiner'.[129]

In 1922 Despard bought Roebuck House in the Dublin suburbs, a large Victorian house surrounded by gardens and several outhouses. There she lived with her close friend Maud Gonne and among those they shared the house with was Gonne's son, Seán MacBride. It was said that 'any person could walk in and ask for dinner or asylum for life' and the ladies played host to a varied assortment of guests: IRA gunmen, homeless ex-prisoners and refugees from Belfast – all were welcome.[130] The house became an important meeting place and centre for IRA activity and not surprisingly was frequently raided by the gardaí.[131] During this time, though 'only half understanding the cryptic references to IRA activities' around her, she was said to have come to a 'tacit acceptance' of IRA violence.[132]

In December 1926 Andy Cooney wrote to the IRA's representative in New York to send on a bank draft for $1,000: 'send [the] draft to [the] covering address. Make it payable to Mrs Despard, Roebuck House,

Clonskea, Co. Dublin. Send with it a note to Mrs Despard saying you are sending her [the] draft for [the] relief of [IRA] dependents.' The IRA has a long history of disguising army funds as monies for the welfare of prisoners' dependants and it's clear from Cooney's correspondence that the money was meant for the IRA's own coffers.[133] Charlotte Despard would have needed to be terribly out of touch to be unaware that the considerable sum of £1,000 was not ultimately going to the prisoners' dependants' fund.

Despard set up a jam factory in 1924 to support unemployed republicans, though it never employed more than fifteen people. The enterprise continuously lost money, until she closed in down in 1926. It was a sad and disillusioning experience for her, as the republicans proved unco-operative and a number of people she trusted stole from the business.[134] During her time in Ireland she was most comfortable in the company of socialist republicans such as Peadar O'Donnell rather than the more conservative nationalists. After her shock at the killing of the Free State minister, Kevin O'Higgins in 1927, she increasingly turned to communism and away from Gonne's pure nationalism.[135] In 1933 she left Roebuck House, eventually moving to Belfast where she died bankrupt in 1939.[136]

Throughout the encrypted documents there are many women mentioned, the vast majority of whom were couriers or who ran safe houses or call houses (see Chapter 2). While some were from well-known republican families, the names of others are no longer remembered. The following are a few examples.

When the IRA's OC in Britain received money from the Soviets, he sent £100 to Dublin to Peadar O'Donnell's wife, Lile, for GHQ.[137] Money for the OC in Britain was sent as a cheque for £50 payable to 'Miss Winnie O'Shea, 8 Loraine Road, Holloway, London'.[138] IRA despatches to London were to be sent to: 'Nurse B Lynch SRN [State Registered Nurse] and CMB [Central Midwife's Board], 104 Cazenove Road, Stanford Hill, London'. The IRA's OC in Britain told Twomey to 'try and arrange that letters arrive on Tuesdays and Fridays. Any letters marked urgent will be delivered to me. On other days make your letters as few as possible' and he helpfully added 'the six letters after "Lynch" stand for degrees of some kind'.[139]

The IRA simply couldn't have functioned without these dedicated and unacknowledged women. It's ironic that they showed much more competence and carried out their duties far more efficiently than many of their male counterparts.

The IRA and anti-imperialism

Under the leadership of Moss Twomey the IRA engaged in a series of attacks (mainly in Dublin) against what they perceived to be symbols of British imperialism. These ranged from tirades in *An Phoblacht* to public protests and street brawling and even armed attacks, and formed a major focus of IRA activity into the 1930s. The majority of the targets now seem rather innocuous, and included the boy scouts, Poppy Day, English newspapers and war films and the display of the Union Jack.[140] However, there could be deadly consequences; in 1929 Albert Armstrong was shot dead after he gave evidence in court against IRA men who had removed a Union Jack from outside his offices.[141]

In 1926 the IRA also launched a campaign against moneylenders which had many similarities with the anti-imperialist activities and will therefore be discussed in this section. The anti-imperialism campaigns were as successful as anything the organisation undertook in these years and benefited the IRA in a number of ways. The activities allowed units to organise and maintain a degree of military readiness, but were not provocative enough to merit a major crackdown by the state. Blowing up the statues of British generals and nobility in Dublin gave the impression of military prowess and had a useful propaganda value – though the IRA often had difficulty successfully demolishing the intended victim. The IRA's targets were frequently unpopular and these activities generated public support and recruits. For example, there were few among the nationalist majority in the Free State who had much sympathy for Trinity College students halting traffic in College Green and singing 'God Save the King' during Poppy Day! The activities also kept the hotheads in the Dublin IRA occupied, acting as a safety valve, and helped Twomey keep the organisation together until the time was right for a major assault on the Free State.[142]

In addition to the trappings of imperialism, the IRA had a concern about the influence of 'imperialists' who formed an imaginary fifth column in the country. The term is rather imprecise and could be interpreted as a substitute for 'wealthy Protestant'. Certainly there were far greater threats to the IRA in the Free State than the remnants of the nineteenth-century elite. In May 1926 Moss Twomey wrote to the director of intelligence asking him 'Have you yet made a list of the principal imperialists in Dub [sic]?'[143]

Aside from political considerations, part of the IRA's objection to these British symbols was cultural, as ostensibly they wanted to promote the re-Gaelicisation of the country. The new IRA constitution adopted at the 1925 convention included as one of its primary objectives the goals of reviving the Irish language for daily use and of promoting 'the development of the best mental and physical characteristics' of the Irish race.[144] Twomey felt that republicans should be committed to building 'a distinctly Gaelic nation, which will cherish Gaelic traditions and ideals'.[145]

However, in general members of the IRA were not noted for their proficiency in Irish and the extent of many volunteers' commitment to the language was to translate their names into Irish and this they often achieved with a high degree of originality. In these documents even the name *An Phoblacht* is frequently misspelled. Moss Twomey for instance referred to it as *An Poblacht*.[146] The adjutant of the Limerick brigade couldn't spell the IRA's name in Irish and wrote a letter with '*Oglaig na hÉireann*' typed on the top of the paper; unfortunately '*Oglaigh*', the Irish word for soldier, was misspelled.[147]

Irish nationalists saw British books, periodicals, cinema and newspapers as a form of cultural imperialism, while Catholic activists saw them as a source of all vice and immorality. The offending papers included the *News of the World* – a purveyor of shock and titillation. The majority of the IRA's members, though angry with the hierarchy's excommunication of them during the Civil War, were observant Catholics and a campaign against the English media resonated with many on both political and religious grounds. The archbishop of Tuam called on Catholics to 'shun ... as you would a pestilence' all imported literature, while the local Sinn Féin cumann passed a resolution against newspapers from London which were 'injurious to our National virtue'.[148]

The Catholic Church's concern with this threat predated that of the IRA's, and organisations such as the Catholic Truth Society urged newsagents to refuse to stock offending papers and were alleged to have been involved in the seizing and burning of papers from trains.[149]

In November 1926 the IRA inaugurated a campaign against the English Sunday papers. GHQ wrote to the Dublin OC: 'You are hereby granted permission to seize papers at Dun Laoghaire ... This operation is not of sufficient magnitude to warrant the use of arms and they, therefore, should not be used in its execution.'[150]

The following March Moss Twomey issued orders to IRA units throughout the country, including Dublin, Cork, Waterford, Mayo and Limerick: 'Arrange to seize and destroy objectionable English Sunday papers on Sunday 13th March. They should be seized on trains or at stations [and] if offered for sale outside churches and in shops. Arms are not to be used in these operations. You will continue this action weekly until the nuisance ceases.'[151]

```
                 C/S                              March 3rd. 1924.
                 N/16
       To:
       O/C. Limerick.

       (77)  OTNSO TAZOE ANMAN EGAYC IYLDU NNDCL PTHEO BNSER AJNPA RGDTI EHREB
             EYDAT SOHSR EEISR ISRAU NE.

       (81)  RTFDD ADSSI AUHTZ APOHS BNNSH SOETF UEAEI ORCNN IROEC POOSE TSRUE
             OFLRO TTAEI NSENT RSAMS AIOEI R.

       You will continue weekly action until the nuisance ceases.


                                         ─────────────────
                                            CHIEF OF STAFF
```

Figure 15. A similar despatch from Moss Twomey to the OC of the Limerick brigade ordering him to destroy the English Sunday newspapers.

Arrange to seize and destroy objectionable English Sunday papers on Sunday 13th March. Seize [the papers] on trains or at [the] station, [or] if offered for sale outside churches and in shops. Arms are not to be used.

This despatch was written in 1927, but was dated 1924. This was deliberately done so as to confuse the gardaí in the event of capture of the document.

The South Dublin battalion (whose operational area included Dun Laoghaire where many of the papers were unloaded from the mailboat arriving from Britain) responded with great enthusiasm and on the Sunday destroyed thousands of newspapers valued at about £80. After the papers had been loaded into a delivery van, a group of IRA men seized the van and burned the papers in a laneway. Mrs Dixon, a widow who was the owner of the newspaper distributors, alleged that one of the men produced a revolver during the operation.[152] This attack was warmly received by the Irish-American newspaper the *Irish World*, which reported that 'a truckload of 30 bales of English Sunday newspapers were seized and burned by an armed body of masked men on its arrival at Kingstown [Dun Laoghaire]' and in April it ran the headline 'Filthy English newspapers burned in Dun Laoghaire'.[153] Later Charlie Gilmore (the brother of the better-known George), one of the battalion's officers, wrote to Twomey proposing that 'papers be dumped overboard on arrival [at Dun Laoghaire on] Sunday 10th April. This means holding [the] pier [for] ten minutes.'[154] Twomey cautioned the unit not to carry arms during the operations and 'you must avoid any damage to the pier or railway or ship property. Otherwise you may go ahead.'[155]

The Dublin brigade was less active – though on Sunday 20 March half a dozen men stopped a newspaper delivery lorry in Parnell Street, unloaded the papers, doused them in petrol and lit a bonfire in the street.[156] Twomey wrote to the brigade's OC in early April asking why he had 'not continued to take action against the undesirable Sunday newspapers'.[157]

In Cork, however, it was the Catholic Church and not the IRA which took the lead. In March the Church, with the full approval of Bishop Daniel Cohalan, helped organise a public meeting which drew thousands of supporters, including much of the city's political establishment. The lord mayor presided and the Free State's Minister for Posts and Telegraphs, J. J. Walsh, shared his concern about 'the moral well being' of the country. The dean of Cork, Monsignor Sexton, said that 'the movement against immoral literature was not intended to interfere with the liberty of the press'. The meeting passed resolutions, including a proposal that the (more wholesome) *Cork Examiner* should publish a Sunday edition.[158]

Fr Barrett of St Mary's church said there was a 'declaration of war for a high purpose – to save the beautiful soul of holy Ireland'. He admitted he took Sunday papers from a newsboy and threw them into the River Lee, though he did let him keep copies of the *Sunday Independent*. It's unknown if the clerical bully ever compensated the boy for the stolen papers.[159]

Monsignor Sexton, along with several priests, supported a group that was described as the Cork Angelic Warfare Association. In February four Angelic warriors seized newspapers from a newsvendor, John Courtney, including copies of the *News of the World* and the *Sunday Pictorial*. Courtney was later refunded the cost of the papers. When one of the gang, Percy Kelly, was brought to trial, the proceedings were so farcical that it was the witnesses who were effectively put on trial. Before a large audience of priests and other supporters, the prosecuting state solicitor agreed that Kelly's actions were 'meritorious' though against the law, while garda superintendent Butler denied that he had threatened 'that the priests of Cork would be brought to their knees'. Courtney was asked whether he was a married man and whether he'd allow the offending papers into his home. To loud cheers the judge applied the probation act to Kelly, who walked free.[160]

Bishop Cohalan despised the IRA, having excommunicated volunteers in 1920 during the Anglo-Irish War, and wouldn't have welcomed IRA support for the activities of the Cork Angelic Warfare Association. However, the IRA's campaign clearly coincided with that of the Church, and Twomey may have hoped to benefit from public support for the issue. Charlie Gilmore's involvement is ironic, as he was both a socialist and a Protestant and would have been expected to resist attacks which gave conservative Catholic nationalists greater influence over the press.

The Irish people continued to read the English Sunday papers and other corrupting filth – despite legislative actions such as the 1929 Censorship Act and the imposition of a tax on foreign newspapers in 1933. In 1938 the Fianna Fáil Minister for Justice, P. J. Rutledge, reported that 1,048 books and twenty periodicals had been permanently banned. The offending authors included such well-known pornographers as Aldous Huxley, Herman Hesse and Seán Ó Faoláin.[161] In one way or another many in power in the state allowed themselves to be drawn into this crusade, which was largely orchestrated by elements associated with the Catholic Church.

In the 1920s, British studios made a number of propaganda films about the Great War, which didn't accord with IRA sensibilities. In November 1925 a group of three armed men exploded a mine inside the Masterpiece cinema in Dublin during a showing of the film *Ypres* (having warned the cinema beforehand against showing the film). Following the explosion, two pursuing gardaí were fired upon; a few days later two of the men were arrested.[162]

The following year the *Battle of Mons*, which was officially sanctioned by the British Army Council, was released. It told the story of the British army's retreat from Belgium in the early months of the First World War and depicted acts of heroism, such as that of the soldier who rescued his wounded comrade in a wheelbarrow. A critic at the time called the film 'inspiring' as it showed 'the gallant fighting', and in one scene where two officers played the 'The British Grenadiers' on a tin whistle and toy drum, he reported that it brought a lump to his throat.[163] Obviously this film posed a major threat to the gullible Irish public and Twomey wrote to the OC of the Dublin brigade: 'Seize ... [the] picture "Mons" to be shown in [the] Corinthian [cinema] tomorrow and next week. Do not destroy [it] but hold [it] safely pending instructions.'[164] He then sent similar orders to IRA units in Tipperary and Cork.[165] The OC in Dublin promptly sent a missive off to the Corinthian's owner objecting to the film, partially on the grounds that it glorified war (and who better to know about glorifying war):

Sir,
I note that a British war-propaganda film entitled 'Mons' is being shown in your Theatre this week. This picture, as is admitted even by the English Press, is not a true representation of the horrors of the European War, but has for its aim the glorification of the British army.

British propaganda pictures cannot be tolerated in Ireland. You will remember that I have had to take drastic action against another Dublin Cinema [a reference to the Masterpiece Cinema] which persisted in showing a companion picture to 'Mons'.

I now request you to discontinue this film within twenty-four hours from date [*sic*]. Should you refuse, I will be obliged to take drastic action against you.

You will note also that such drastic action shall be delayed only so long as suits my convenience.

(Signed)
Brigadier-General
Commanding Officer Dublin 1 Brigade.[166]

The proprietor of the Corinthian doesn't seem to have been cowed into submission as twelve days later the cinema was still showing the film.[167]

Another perceived threat emanated from the boy scouts, including the sea scouts, which the IRA saw as 'British reservists'.[168] However, there was some rational (though largely misguided) basis to the IRA's fears about the scouts. General Baden Powell, who had distinguished himself in South Africa fighting the independent-minded Boers, founded the scouting movement. Powell has been described as an 'Empire propagandist' and he promoted an essentially English concept of boyhood and citizenship.[169] The organisation had many military trappings – with uniformed boys parading in formation. In Ireland they inspired Na Fianna Éireann, the youth wing of the IRA, which unlike the scouts, had a very definite military function.

In early 1926 the IRA chief of staff wrote to the OC in Britain:

> At your convenience I would like you to pick up as much information as possible as to the inner working, and purpose of the Baden Powell Boy Scouts. If some of the speeches and confidential communications could be got they would be of much use here. These B.P. Scouts are so strong here that they are a positive menace. They can do as they please while Fianna Éireann are prosecuted. We mean to give publicity to the fact that the B.P. Scouts are much more a Military Organisation than the Fianna. If the reports from Ireland to London could be got they would be invaluable for the purpose in view. I am sure they make reference to Ireland in their general reports, but the confidential ones would be much better.[170]

The OC wrote back that he was unable to get any information, as 'at present I have no connection whatever with that organisation'.[171] In 1928 the IRA burned down and fired shots into a number of scout huts and the following year reportedly planned to bomb Elvery's sports shop in Dublin for having a window display promoting the World Scout Jamboree.[172]

Every November unionists and British army veterans celebrated Poppy Day or Remembrance Day (in honour of those that had died in the First World War) by displaying the Union Jack and wearing poppies. Beginning in the mid 1920s, the IRA in Dublin attempted to prevent these displays and obstruct the British Legion's parade. They organised public demonstrations which attracted speakers from across the republican spectrum, ranging from Éamon de Valera to communists and feminists. These rallies were usually held in College Green and were attended by a substantial number of people; in 1932 some 15,000 attended. They degenerated into disorder and fighting as IRA supporters attempted to snatch flags from members of the Legion and engaged in running battles with the gardaí.[173] The protests were supported by many outside of the IRA and continued until the early 1930s when the IRA adopted a more tolerant approach.[174]

By engaging in these activities the IRA left itself open to the accusation of bigotry and religious intolerance, and its response that it supported the right of the veterans to honour their dead but opposed the glorification of the Great War was unconvincing.[175] In October 1927 Moss Twomey tried to gather information showing that Poppy Day was more than an occasion of remembrance and he wrote to the IRA's OC in Britain: 'Get some literature or any official stuff you can, showing [the] imperialistic nature of Poppy Day and post it. Get into [the] headquarters of [the] British Legion.'[176]

Seán Russell, however, had more exciting plans for the day. He recommended to Twomey that the IRA should blow up the equestrian statues of King William III in College Green and that of Lord Gough in the Phoenix Park.[177] An attempt was made to blow up King William's statue on Remembrance Day in 1928, though the job wasn't finished until 1946. Gough's statue was eventually destroyed in 1957.[178]

Though most anti-imperialist activities were carried out on Remembrance Day, IRA volunteers and members of Cumann na mBan also sporadically removed flags from largely Protestant-owned businesses in the fashionable area around College Green and Grafton Street. Though the perpetrators were on occasion arrested, they were frequently not convicted due to intimidation of the jury or due to the jurors' sympathetic attitude.[179] In 1927 Twomey reminded the OC of the Dublin brigade to have his unit on stand-by for British Empire Day, 24 May: 'Have your plans ready for 24th inst. [May] Empire Day, in case of imperialist displays.'[180]

For a few months in the summer of 1926 the IRA conducted a campaign against the unsavoury practice of moneylending. Like the anti-imperialist activities, this had the potential to generate popular support for the IRA by targeting a group outside the mainstream of Catholic nationalist society. Many of the moneylenders were Jewish and these attacks had a taint of anti-Semitism, though this was denied by the IRA and particularly by the republican activist Robert Briscoe, who was Jewish himself. Interestingly, there is some anecdotal evidence that Jewish moneylenders were regarded as more scrupulous than non-Jewish moneylenders.[181] Twomey later said that he and many others disagreed with the raids, which were initiated by Mick Price – the OC of the Dublin brigade and a leading republican socialist.[182]

From July to August IRA raiding parties seized the account books and records of moneylenders in Dublin and Limerick. The gardaí, however, successfully responded by arresting several IRA members including Price and Donal O'Donoghue, along with George Plunkett's sister Fiona, which soon put an end to the attacks.[183] Though the moneylenders (wisely) failed to identify Price and O'Donoghue in court, the two remained incarcerated until 1927, while Fiona Plunkett was released in December 1926. By February 1927 Peadar O'Donnell had negotiated a deal, under which the moneylenders agreed not to pursue debts in the 'Free State Courts' and that 'where in conscience a borrower admits liability ... this re-payment will be made through a committee without the moneylenders being allowed to call himself [sic] to make collections'. Both O'Donnell and Briscoe were to monitor compliance with the agreement.[184] As Twomey noted: 'This undertaking was signed only by the moneylenders' and so in theory wasn't binding on the IRA, though they were unlikely to restart this abortive campaign.[185] Twomey wrote to O'Donoghue in prison: '[It is] considered advisable to tacitly agree, as activities on our part had ceased.'[186] The arrangement allowed the IRA to save face and explain away its ending of the campaign.

While these actions kept many members in Dublin busy and enabled the IRA to keep a high profile, Éamon de Valera was moving steadily ahead with his own plans.

Éamon de Valera and Fianna Fáil
Éamon de Valera was the dominant personality of the republican movement. He was a natural authority figure and within the egalitarian republican fraternity was the one leader who was not addressed by his first name, but rather was called 'Mister de Valera', 'Sir', or by those close to him 'Chief'.[187]

He was a highly polarising figure and the very mention of his name could elicit passionate debate. While many members of the IRA and the public were devoted to him, others accused him of either causing the Civil War or alternatively of betraying the 'republic'. The extent to which many volunteers and officers admired him is not fully appreciated nowadays, when he is commonly unfavourably compared to Michael Collins. Todd Andrews, who had been a staff officer at GHQ, considered him 'extraordinarily friendly and informal', and that 'his capacity to charm affected me ... all during his long life'.[188] On the other hand, the veteran Fenian John Devoy was not alone when he opined that he was 'the most malignant man in all Irish history'.[189]

De Valera had long realised that by refusing to participate in the political life of the *de facto* state, republicans had marginalised themselves and were becoming increasingly irrelevant to the lives of its citizens. In the words of Robert Briscoe: 'De Valera was still President of the Irish Republic, a shadow government which governed nothing. He was president of Sinn Féin, a shadow political party which took no part in practical politics. He decided the situation must end.'[190] Given the IRA's failure to overthrow the government during the Civil War, the only option left open was that of political engagement.

There remained a significant republican constituency in the country, which de Valera could endeavour to harness – unless the IRA beat him to it. In the August 1923 general election, despite formidable challenges, Sinn Féin won a respectable 28 per cent of the vote against 39 per cent for the ruling Cumann na nGaedheal, while a low turnout of 59 per cent reflected considerable lack of enthusiasm among the electorate for the existing parties.[191]

In March 1926, at a special Sinn Féin árd fheis, de Valera put forward a motion that, in the absence of the oath of allegiance, abstention from the (Free State) Dáil was a matter of policy, not principle. With his proposal narrowly rejected, he resigned as president of both the party and the republican 'government'.[192] On 16 May at the La Scala theatre in Dublin he and his supporters launched a new political party, Fianna Fáil.[193]

Fianna Fáil planned to put forward candidates to run for election, and (unlike the Sinn Féin TDs who refused to take their seat) on being elected they would enter the Dáil and assert their right to represent their constituents without taking the oath.[194] De Valera contended that this didn't imply recognition of the Dáil as a legitimate parliament, but that participation was the only way to 'untreaty' the state and ultimately bring about an Irish republic.[195]

From its inception Fianna Fáil emphasised its economic policies which, though decidedly capitalist, were committed to a multi-class harmony. There was something in it for everybody – economic development to appeal to the bourgeoisie, social welfare for the working-class and policies to protect the small farmers. The goals included the development of 'a social system in which, as far as possible, equal opportunity will be afforded to every Irish citizen to live a noble and useful Christian life', 'to get the greatest number possible of Irish families rooted in the soil of Ireland' and to make the country 'an economic unit, as self-contained and self-sufficient as possible – with a proper balance between agriculture and the other essential industries'.[196] This approach was decidedly different from the social and economic policies adopted by the IRA, which were largely based on Peadar O'Donnell's socialist theories of 'class conflict' and included the nationalisation of the state's resources, though Fianna Fáil successfully borrowed (and modified) the anti-annuity campaign from O'Donnell.[197]

Many members of the IRA and the electorate had great difficulty discerning where de Valera's approach was in conflict with the aims of the IRA. Fianna Fáil politicians continued to use strong republican rhetoric and they shared platforms with the IRA, particularly on issues related to the republican prisoners. By 1927 Fianna Fáil TDs were lobbying the Free State ministers and the prison authorities on behalf of the prisoners and reporting back to the IRA. The IRA's director of intelligence reported that on one occasion a Fianna Fáil deputation received a surprise when they pleaded the case of a prisoner at Portlaoise prison with the Minister for Justice: 'One of the deputation told the C.S. [chief of staff, Moss Twomey] that when he was making a great case on Cavanagh's [sic] case, the Minister produced two letters from Cavanagh offering if released to join the Free State army, and twitted them with fighting about such a man.'[198]

Indeed a significant number, if not most, of the IRA's members supported Fianna Fáil and it was only over a number of years that de Valera's supporters left the organisation. The Army Executive elected in November 1925 was referred to as a 'composite executive' as it contained a number of his supporters, including Frank Aiken and Tom Derrig (who were both later Fianna Fáil cabinet ministers).[199] Up until mid 1927 many officers (including Aiken) held joint membership of both organisations, while a number of volunteers held joint membership into the 1930s.[200] The Fianna Fáil organisation was frequently based on existing IRA units, with IRA companies simply transformed into Fianna Fáil cumainn (branches).[201] As late as 1932 the IRA commander in east Clare was also secretary of the local Fianna Fáil cumann.[202] Members of the leadership of the IRA and Fianna Fáil remained firm friends until the 1930s. Seán MacBride said: 'There was this kind of bond of friendship which existed, for those who were working in the republican movement.'[203] Twomey said he remained 'very friendly' with Frank Aiken until the 1930s.[204]

Not surprisingly, the gardaí were unsure as to who was a member of what organisation, and Fianna Fáil members were frequently arrested for the crimes of an organisation they no longer gave allegiance to. According to Moss Twomey, even by 1928 '[the Special Branch] did not rightly know who was FF and who was still IRA'.[205] In November 1927 the IRA intelligence officer in Armagh reported that the police in Britain were making enquires about a member of Fianna Fáil: 'Enquiries have been sent to Armagh police barracks re. Tommy Donnelly, who is working in Fianna Fáil interests in Glasgow.'[206]

Peadar O'Donnell later argued that the republican socialists should have joined with de Valera, saying that '[Fianna Fáil] took all the radical and worthwhile elements from Sinn Féin ... there was more radical content in Fianna Fáil than there was in any other organisation.'[207] Throughout 1926 *An Phoblacht* ran a column titled 'Fianna Fáil (Republican Party) Organisation Notes', which listed Fianna Fáil activities and meetings, while in the US the *Irish World* supported both Fianna Fáil and the IRA. George Gilmore said that by 1932 he 'considered that at that time the broad policies of the two organisations hardly differed'.[208] Indeed for many years Aiken and de Valera consistently tried to absorb as much of the IRA into Fianna Fáil as possible, thereby garnering support for Fianna Fáil and at the same time undermining the IRA.

However, the IRA's senior leadership (who after all had ejected Frank

Aiken) were aware that Fianna Fáil was diverging from the IRA's path. In February 1927 Moss Twomey wrote: 'Recently [the] Fianna Fáil party in public speeches, and by their general policy, have been getting away more and more from [a] revolutionary attitude, and in fact have pronounced it a constitutional party, which will use only constitutional methods.'[209] De Valera's ability to win over members from the IRA was dramatically brought home to Twomey during the former's tour of America in 1927 (see Chapter 7).

While the IRA was able to survive the birth of Fianna Fáil, Sinn Féin was effectively annihilated by the loss of its more talented and certainly more pragmatic members, and ceased to be a credible political opposition. The dynamism of Fianna Fáil stood in marked contrast to the intellectual bankruptcy of Sinn Féin. Many members of Sinn Féin were furious with de Valera for having 'compromised his principles'. A leading member, Brian O'Higgins, was reported to have been so bitter towards de Valera that he left his own wife's funeral when de Valera arrived to attend.[210] Though the leadership of the IRA and Sinn Féin continued to maintain contact with one another, the relationship became acrimonious, and the IRA tended to be dismissive of the party. In 1927 *An Phoblacht* stated 'not much can come out of Sinn Féin'.[211]

The case of Patrick Garland

While all of these developments were taking place, a relatively minor incident occurred in Cork in April 1926 which illustrates some of the IRA's abilities and attitudes. An IRA courier, Patrick Garland, having disembarked from a transatlantic liner, was arrested in Cobh.

Garland, aged forty-four, was originally from Dundalk and had emigrated to New York in 1914, where he worked as a boiler operator at a hotel on Fifth Avenue. Aside from having contributed to the Friends of Irish Freedom before the founding of the Free State, he wasn't known to have any involvement in Irish politics. In April 1926, he received a telegram telling him that his mother in Ireland had 'double pneumonia and was not expected to live'. His sister, with whom he lived, helped him pack his two suitcases, and she 'was sure he did not have any papers in his possession to warrant his detention on the other side'.

Garland sailed from New York on the *Adriatic*, and on his arrival at Cobh was allegedly found by customs to be attempting to smuggle in a gold watch. The officer then searched him and found a concealed package suspended by string under his shirt. Inside the package were IRA despatches, which contained the names of several well-known republicans. One letter appeared to refer to IRA attempts to sell some of their cache of Thompson submachine guns in New York, though the Free State authorities misinterpreted this as an attempt by the IRA to purchase the weapons. Garland was also found to be in possession of £800 in bank drafts, which was meant for the IRA.

On his arrest, he said that wrongdoing 'was the furthest thing from his mind' and that if he had known what was in the documents he would have burned them. He gave the improbable story that a man, whom he didn't know, had asked him to deliver the letters to another person at a railway station in Dublin. As for the money, he claimed this was his own, and even produced evidence that he had a bank account containing the very considerable sum of $35,000 (£7,000).

The capture of the documents and money along with the possibility that Garland might speak freely to the gardaí was of serious concern to the IRA, and the chief of staff contacted Seán MacSwiney in Cork (who held the interesting title of assistant adjutant Cork 1 brigade). The chief of staff at this time was probably Moss Twomey, though there's a possibility it remained Andy Cooney. He wrote: 'I presume [Garland] is in Cork Prison. It is very important that he be visited and treated well whilst there by our friends. See to this. **Is there any possible chance of rescuing him?** I would be very keen on this and meant to send an Officer specially [*sic*] about it were it not that I was expecting the O/C. [of Cork 1 brigade] up. I was hoping this would have been done immediately after his capture. You will recognise it **would have a great effect** ... Action against [the] Customs Officer [who searched him] depends on yourselves locally. What can you do? I would suggest **kidnapping and giving him a good hammering, tarring and feathering, or heaving him over the quay.** If anything is to be done it should be done immediately.'

Garland was held without bail before his trial in Dublin. Though a naturalised American citizen, he was charged under the Treasonable Offences Act of 'conspiring for the overthrow' of the government and of 'conspiracy to spread sedition throughout the Free State'. He pleaded guilty to having the documents but maintained he was an 'innocent messenger'. As often happened with IRA men convicted around this time, he got off rather lightly, with the judge appearing to accept his explanation. He was fined £50 and ordered to post bail to be on good behaviour for the remainder of his time in the country.

From the chief of staff's remarks it doesn't appear that the customs service was held in great fear by the IRA. It is ironic that, while the majority of IRA couriers were women, one of the few to be caught with money and incriminating documents should be a man.[212]

The barrack raids

In November 1926 the IRA raided garda barracks throughout the country, the nearest the organisation came in the second half of the 1920s to a co-ordinated military action. What was the purpose of these attacks? Did they mark a resurgent IRA?

In *The Secret Army* Bowyer Bell wrote that Twomey, having been impressed by the 'growing confidence and efficiency' of the IRA, came up with the idea and told Andy Cooney the objectives were to gather intelligence and capture weapons. GHQ devised a general outline of the campaign, but individual units were to draw up specific plans for their own area.[213]

However, in early November the planning was disrupted with the arrest of Twomey. On his way to a staff meeting he travelled to Mullingar and then took a taxi to the venue at the remote townland of Crooked-wood (seven miles away). There he was arrested by waiting Special Branch officers.[214] *An Phoblacht* reported: 'A young man named Maurice Twomey of Fermoy Co. Cork was charged' under the Treason Act with 'taking part in the organisation and maintenance of a military force not established by law'. He made no reply to the charges and was remanded in custody to Mountjoy prison.[215]

The IRA immediately suspected treachery. Twomey later said that Seán Harling, who was a garda informer, had handled a despatch concerning the meeting and that the letter had been tampered with.[216] But initially the main suspect was the OC of the IRA's Midland battalion. Following an internal investigation the IRA's director of intelligence wrote in December: '[I] have since found out [the] OC [of the] Midland [battalion] to be all right [*sic*] and I now know who gave Moss away.'[217]

Despite Twomey's arrest the raids went ahead, with most attacks occurring on Sunday 14 November. Groups of up to thirty men, armed with rifles and handguns, attacked twelve barracks in Cork, Kerry and Meath; in Waterford twenty-four were attacked and raids were also carried out in Tipperary. Garda documents were destroyed or taken away. Two gardaí were killed during the operation: Sergeant Fitzsimons in Cork city and Garda Hugh Ward in Tipperary, fatally shot in the neck. In addition to the barrack raids, two yacht clubs in (the Anglo-Irish bastion of) Dun Laoghaire were broken into and searched for poppies.[218]

The raids were a disaster. Aside from the killings, which elicited a swift response from the gardaí – and met with disapproval from the public and even from within the IRA's own ranks – little information or weapons were acquired, while many IRA units were either unable or unwilling to participate.[219]

Cooney confided to a colleague: 'From reports to hand many areas refused to carry out the raids.'[220] Even the diehard republican, Tom Maguire of Mayo, disobeyed orders: 'Tom McGuire [*sic*] conveyed [the] order to [his] adj. [adjutant] but cancelled it at the last moment.'[221] The Offaly brigade's excuse for its inactivity was that a supervising staff officer hadn't arrived from GHQ as promised: '[The chief of staff] was to send down a staff officer to this area, to make final arrangements for the executions [*sic*] of the operations, which were to be brought off in this area on Sunday last. I and [the] staff here, very closely scrutinised the details necessary for the bringing off of the well planned raids on the Tullamore and Birr barracks, but were badly disappointed by no staff officer turning up. What a pity it was, that this area was not included in the lists of last Sunday's activities. I presume the arrest of Moss would account for the mix-up.'[222] Cooney (rather magnanimously) replied to this lack of initiative: 'I regret very much that final instructions were not sent [to] you. Everyone at GHQ were convinced that your area was already informed of the date. Arrest of [the] C.S. [chief of staff] was responsible for the hitch.'[223]

There was also dissent in Tipperary, and GHQ wrote to the brigade OC: 'Re. refusal of units to carry out raids, it is advisable that no undue haste be shown in dealing with those units. Our main efforts should be devoted to keeping the organisation intact against the present enemy offensive. That areas were not prepared for immediate operations is evident, but for future work I am convinced that these areas will not be caught napping. The moral to be impressed on all officers, is that they should be prepared and ready for all eventualities in a military organisation such as ours.'[224]

Within days the government proclaimed a state of emergency and the police rounded up over 110 republicans across the country.[225] 'Flying squads of armed detectives carried out numerous raids.'[226] In Dublin Special Branch officers searched well-known IRA haunts such as the Clarence and Exchange hotels looking for Cooney and other GHQ officers.[227] *An Phoblacht*'s offices were raided and the printing press was smashed, preventing the production of the 3 December issue.[228] Cooney reported: 'Men and women are being arrested daily. Raiding is as intensive as in the old days.'[229] He even managed to strike a note of defiance: 'Most leaders arrested and will be interned. [There is a] big offensive by the enemy to crush the army. They will not succeed, but our task will be tremendous.'[230]

In pre-dawn raids Frank Kerlin and George Plunkett were among twelve leading IRA members arrested in Dublin. They were remanded in custody for a week and though discharged on 24 November, the court had them immediately re-arrested under the Public Safety Act.[231] Others arrested included John Joe Sheehy, OC of the Kerry 1 brigade, and Michael Kilroy and Dr J. A. Madden, both of the North Mayo brigade.[232]

However, it was the arrests in Cork city that proved the most problematic for the IRA's leadership. Initially forty republicans were arrested there, but the majority were released and just ten were remanded in custody for a week. This latter group comprised some of the city's leading IRA gunmen from the time of the Anglo-Irish War, many of whom were either in the process of resigning or had already left the IRA and were supporters of Fianna Fáil. They included P. A. Murray, who was on the Army Executive and had recently been adjutant general, Mick Murphy, who was also a member of the Army Executive, and Tom Crofts, who had been OC of the

November 25th. 1926.

A Chara dhil,

Yours of the 6th. inst. received.

You will, I trust, understand delay in replying when I explain that a telegram to A. asking him to return was sent on the 6th. inst. I was awaiting his arrival before writing you. For some, as yet unexplained, reason this telegram was not received, and a subsequent one was sent on the 13th. which achieved the desirable result. Re the question of your returning; I want you to understand thoroughly that on no account will it be considered. You will remain away until you receive notification from here to return. We will be able to carry on alright here for the present and it is advisable always to have someone on reserve.

```
(186)  EAAAN YDNGI WRNUY MSEEL IEMDT ERNNS CFTTA SHEIE HELLA RERTW
       SOECH DEEEU BDOLE EIAOT XDLRW OTHNR OAEDH ANNDE REOIA AEADN
       DETFA ERERN CEERN IAEFY ESNSA LUREK RFEDT RGOUE ELEMT ELRRA
       RHHEA RESDS DGCHO HSCSI PDSKN TCENI NGEIH I.

(168)  ODSHP ATNEI OOTSY CNFSW SNIIH EUMGV EIECA NRNUT RNOIT YIYHA
       ERYDE OTGWG OROKE ITRDE TOSAR IOREE SNLTO ACDSU AHPLH TIERM
       DORVE OIAEN TAMPR RHAIA MMEEH MMCNN HRRRA SSRRA RCMSF AFTUA
       EDTNT RFYOX OOSKE LTN.

(126)  ERNGI ROALT AMKIA NLREE MNSLI ISHUO NFONG SEEMT EIWNT HVAAI
       LDLRD HRNOM AACOA HERNH TPEDA ANRTL IPRUT CNIEE DDESL KTRAR
       NHRKO SOFTN DODWY MTLSC HOGTS O.

 (85)  METLI GOADT IEVJT EGFOY UTRAR COASL RHDIN NDCOE NEKIE EOILE
       TLEBO GRMTL LMDCR EERRL MSOTE BADEO UDCMY Y.

(120)  AATHW FNEEO TOWPR WLAIG ORTLI EEETE DOBSE IPASR NUSHT UHAAI
       DTLRA EEEAI ILYTA HLNGU MSRPR CGFUR NTDCI RDOEA OAMNN CTAPO
       EOWBM HLEIL SOFLM OHTHO

 (52)  URREA SMOYE OEUTD NWSCS LTEOU DABER EDYGN ILIOR GDMAC VOTOA
       NS.

 (52)  OAETT DBRNA YOWEN AAEEA RHIEA NCEGK LTGHN EAECH UDENE TBTTA
       TE.
                      E
 (94)  MHENN MTURL OOEMO ETHAT SOUAN SCMYR OMSON HNEFT LSMSS HSVPS
       REEIU ROWHA OGEIO XXXXXXXXXXXXXXXXXXXXXX.         EEDLD GORHW
       EETOJ DIWHH IASSI DNR
```

(Note that the 1st line 3rd. group should read OOEEMO)

Hope you are getting on alright and I would again impress on you the necessity for taking extreme care to avoid colds, draughts, etc

Mise do Chara,

Figure 16. In the aftermath of the barrack raids Andy Cooney wrote to a colleague, warning him not to return to Ireland for the time being. He addressed his comrade as 'A Chara dhil' or 'dear friend' and may have been writing to Seán Russell.

[John Joe] Sheehy, [Michael] Kilroy and [Dr J. A.] Madden are among latest arrests. Clarence, and Exchange [Hotels] searched for you, and me. All the Dublin men [have been] interned under new Act. George [Gilmore] and Moss [Twomey] will be tried this week. I fear the former has been identified for rescue.

From reports to hand, many areas refused to carry out the raids. Mick Murphy, Moss Donegan, and four or five others, arrested in Cork have written [to] the press, denying all connection with [a] military organisation. They deplored the murders [of the two gardaí] and have done much harm amongst the rank and file. Cork No. 1 is working normally, nothwithstanding arrest of all its late officers.

Tom McGuire [sic] conveyed [the] order to [his] adj. [adjutant] but cancelled it at last moment. Ned Rielly [sic] is being eagerly looked for.

1st Southern division during the Civil War. Disappointed with the pointless killing of Garda Sergeant Fitzsimons and wishing to distance themselves from the organisation, they recognised the court, obtained legal representation and were granted bail. All of this was against the IRA's General Order 24, which barred recognition of Free State courts. The lawyer for Tom Crofts and one of the other defendants stated that 'he wished to say that his clients had not hand, act or part in the occurrences of that Sunday night, which they all so deplored and regretted',[233] while Mick Murphy referred to the raids as 'regrettable happenings' and that he had 'severed my connection with all political military organisations over twelve months ago'.[234]

So public a break with the IRA – by men who had fought a hard battle against the British – provoked an angry response from within the organisation. In particular Mick Murphy's comments were singled out for criticism. Cooney reported: 'Mick Murphy, Moss Donegan, and four or five others, arrested in Cork have written [to] the press, denying all connection with [a] military organisation. They deplored the murders and have done much harm amongst the rank and file. Cork No. 1 [brigade] is working normally, notwithstanding [the] arrest of all its late officers.'[235] He accused them of having 'done much harm by surrendering completely to enemy aggression'.[236] Interestingly, Cooney himself was likely disturbed by the killing of the two gardaí and used the term 'murder'.

As Murphy planned to emigrate to America, Cooney sent word across to the IRA's agent there, 'Mr Jones': 'Mick Murphy's attitude is [by] far the most serious, as his statements are untrue and every[body] knows so. He is a member of the Executive and of Cork 1 Bde [brigade]. He never resigned from either. As he is reported to be going to America, I consider it essential that ye have these facts.'[237] 'Jones' who was a fellow Corkonian, replied: '[I] am aware of [the] action of [the] Cork people. If any one of them come to this country they will be treated as they deserve.'[238] Connie Neenan, who was also from Cork and based in New York, wrote: 'The action of [the] Cork officers who surrendered was condemned by all. It was a deplorable step by men who should at least remain loyal [even] if [they're] otherwise inactive.'[239] He added that, embarrassed by their ex-comrades' betrayal, the Liam Lynch IRA Club in New York, which was composed of veterans from Cork, contributed to a special IRA emergency appeal: '[The] Liam Lynch Club [of] New York contributed [the] largest sum, as proof of their repudiation of [the] Cork officers.'[240]

The arrest of Twomey and other senior officers thrust Cooney into the centre of the action. To add to his worries, a financial crisis occurred on 17 November when the Soviets abruptly announced that they would drastically decrease their funding of the IRA (see Chapter 8). This forced Cooney to travel to London the following week to meet 'James', the Soviet intelligence officer there – but to no avail.[241] The only other potential source of significant revenue was Clan na Gael in America and he wrote asking for an urgent fund drive. Cooney was so desperate that he even threatened to disband the IRA unless adequate support was forthcoming from the Clan (see Chapter 7).[242] And to save money GHQ sent a letter to the OC in Britain telling him to close up his operation there.[243]

The Free State government, having made its point, soon relaxed the pressure. On 17 December *An Phoblacht* reported that the charges against Moss Twomey were dropped by the Circuit Criminal Court in Dublin, though the paper was indignant that the president of the government, William Cosgrave, had attempted 'to prejudice his case, while he was on remand, by describing him as Chief of Staff of the IRA'. On his discharge Twomey was immediately rearrested and interned again in Mountjoy, only to be finally released very soon afterwards, along with the other internees.[244]

On 17 December Frank Kerlin wrote to one of the IRA's convicted prisoners, Mick Price, in Mountjoy: '[The] internees are all released.'[245] Moss Twomey also wrote to Price on the same day: 'You must have been as surprised as ourselves to hear that we had been released. We were sure when called out that we were to be sent to some other prison. We were only hoping that all political prisoners in the place would be cleared out as well. It would not in the least surprise me if yourself and Donal [O'Donoghue] were released before Xmas. I am not saying this in any way to cheer you up … [I] got [a] note in prison from yourself and Donal. [I] had [a] reply written and smokes ready when [I was] released … [I] cannot yet form [a] judgement on [the] situation [following the raids]. Things are not so upset as I expected.'[246]

Within the IRA the verdict on the raids was decidedly mixed. The 4th battalion of the Dublin brigade wrote that the battalion council 'was unanimous in their demand that an explanation is due from H.Q. re. the above [barrack raids]. Isolated Raids as in our opinion shuch [sic] activities have been instrumental in creating an atmosphere that facilitated the Free State Government in declaring a State of War, resulting in the Safety of the Army [IRA] in general been [sic] seriously jeopardised … [the raids have] proven detrimental to the [republican] movement in general.'[247] At the other end of the spectrum, Connie Neenan reported: 'The recent attacks at home by the army gave rise to great enthusiasm and admiration here amongst all our fellows. We should gain considerably in membership and finance', though he did admit that 'the army has an enormous task [ahead of it]'.[248] Also in New York, the *Irish World* led with a triumphant front-page headline: 'Spy lists seized by Irish Republicans'.[249]

Moss Twomey alluded to these differences of opinion when he wrote: 'There appears to be a very emphatic demand that the army decide what the policy is to be, as regards the question of armed activity.'[250] Andy Cooney expressed a somewhat similar concern: 'We are going to have a difficult time to pull through. The army, as a whole, was not prepared for the operation, and there will be much local dissension.'[251] The failure of officers and men to carry out orders and the inability of the leadership to discipline them are ominous signs in any military organisation. Without discipline and cohesion the IRA was incapable of carrying on any sustained or determined campaign. The organisation was now split into at least two major camps: one supporting Twomey and GHQ and the other supporting de Valera and Fianna Fáil. One solution that Twomey suggested, and if it had been implemented would have greatly strengthened the IRA, was of forming a smaller, more clandestine and better-trained army: '[The] feeling is growing in favour of a smaller and more secret active organisation and for organising other volunteers and ex-volunteers in an open organisation.'[252]

In contrast to Twomey and Cooney, Seán Russell felt that the raids presented an opportunity for republican unity. He wrote to Twomey in May 1927: 'You will remember, following the barrack raids last November, how Dev, believing that a National crisis had arisen, requested a meeting of SF, FF and army representatives (as nominated by the army). The Free Staters by their action in arresting army Officers of both sides made such a meeting possible. The army at that time, I believe, failed to take advantage of a favourable opportunity to bring about the unity we work so hard to make today. The Staters, realising that the arrests had the opposite effect to that which they desired, ordered the release of all the internees.' This spurred on Russell to propose a joint anti-imperialist platform with Fianna Fáil and Sinn Féin – with the IRA blowing up statues and symbols of British imperialism.[253]

While GHQ had learned its lesson and the raids weren't repeated, it was important to propagate the notion that they had achieved some degree of success. Twomey wrote in early February 1927 to Connie Neenan: 'Explain barrack attacks were for intelligence purposes. [I] heard there was disappointment [over] there, when [they were] not followed up.'[254]

As for the Cork officers, in April 1927 the Army Executive urged that the Army Council take steps to see that both Mick Murphy and P. A. Murray were brought before a court martial 'without further delay'.[255]

Overall the raids had a detrimental effect on the organisation and likely precipitated the resignation of many members. In 1970 Bowyer Bell wrote about 'practically everyone's desire for a second round' of raids.[256] From the information now available, this statement is clearly inaccurate. Bowyer Bell doesn't reference this statement but it's likely that he got it from Andy Cooney whom he interviewed in the 1960s. This and the other comments by Bowyer Bell on the raids appear to be Cooney's later explanation and justification for the raids, rather than an accurate representation of the events.

It's also noteworthy that despite the killing of two unarmed gardaí the

IRA internees were all soon released. This was part of a pattern of largely lenient treatment by the authorities at the time. Though the Special Branch could still badly mistreat prisoners and regularly harassed known IRA operatives, under the circumstances the Free State was rather benign in its treatment of the IRA. This policy was probably as successful at undermining the organisation as repression would have been. The gardaí and courts were often successful in persuading defendants to recognise the courts, apply for bail, etc. – all of which was against IRA rules (and specifically General Order 24). And a frustrated Twomey reported: 'The enemy do not want to have political prisoners, if he can get them to leave the Organisation or trick them into doing something for which he knows he will be dismissed.'[257] Even senior officers laid themselves open to the accusation of cooperating with the enemy, and in December 1926 the director of intelligence, Frank Kerlin, had to send a letter to Donal O'Donoghue in Mountjoy: 'Re. [your] attitude towards [the] appeal tribunal. It is to be considered as [a] Free State court and no appeal [is to be made]. [I] am sending [you a] copy of GO [General Order] 24 for reference.'[258]

The republican election pact

By 1927 many in the Free State looked forward to the possibility of a change of government in the upcoming summer's general election. The ruling Cumann na nGaedheal party was unpopular among many sections of the public and in particular the Intoxicating Liquor Bill was badly received. In addition, those republicans who had reluctantly supported the Anglo-Irish Treaty and the Free State were very dissatisfied with the outcome of the Boundary Commission and the resultant accommodation the government reached with Britain and the Northern Ireland state.[259] Far from emasculating Northern Ireland (as many in southern Ireland had hoped it would), the commission had the opposite effect of helping to bolster the new state. This disquiet began to express itself in calls for the IRA to broker an alliance of Fianna Fáil and Sinn Féin to contest the election. In the words of Moss Twomey: 'Efforts [for an alliance] are chiefly by Treatyite opponents of [the] present government.'[260]

Many felt a unified republican platform could win a majority at the election, enabling the republican deputies to form a government, renege on the Treaty and establish a republic. Such a plan was doubly attractive to the IRA in that it would both help to maintain the unity of the organisation and allow it to seize power.[261] After the dismal performance of the IRA during the barrack raids it should have been clear to GHQ that it was incapable of a conventional fight against the Free State army and needed the assistance of some such stratagem. Twomey wrote: 'We felt justified in making the effort for several reasons; chiefly because of hope we entertained of getting [a] majority [in the Dáil] and if we did not, to prevent an acute division in the Army over [the] elections.'[262]

Peadar O'Donnell, Moss Twomey and Seán MacBride worked together to draw up a detailed proposal to be put before representatives of the three key republican groups: the IRA, Sinn Féin and Fianna Fáil.[263] The plan called for events to unfold in the following sequence: representatives of Fianna Fáil, Sinn Féin and the Army Council would meet and constitute themselves as a National Board. The board would approve a panel of republican candidates for the election and would also approve the campaign and election literature of the candidates. Before the election it would select the members of the future republican cabinet. On winning the election, the republican TDs were to refuse to attend the (Free State) Dáil, and to instead form an Assembly, which included representatives from the six counties of Northern Ireland. The Assembly would declare itself the 'sovereign Assembly of the country' and annul the Free State Constitution and the Anglo-Irish Treaty or 'all Imperial commitments'. This Assembly and its cabinet now became the 'lawful' legislature and government of the Irish Republic, with the 'Second Dáil' and its 'Republican Government' transferring over its 'powers and functions'. So as not to alarm Britain, the actual declaration of an Irish Republic could be delayed! Then, moving carefully, the new government would disband the Free State army and replace it with the IRA.

This plan contains so many improbabilities and assumptions that one would be forgiven for thinking that it had been drawn up by Hans Christian Andersen. What on earth drove O'Donnell (who was, most likely, the principal author) to think that the Free State army could be somehow peacefully disbanded? And why would de Valera submit again to the vagaries of the IRA? What would be the reaction of the unionists of Northern Ireland? How would the IRA defend itself against a British attack?

Though Twomey promoted the plan in public, in private he was less sanguine. He admitted he was prepared to back down in the face of opposition within the IRA: 'If [there is] any opposition [within the IRA] we will not pursue the matter.'[264] And even before formal meetings were held with representatives of Sinn Féin and Fianna Fáil he wrote: 'We are doubtful if either political party as such will accept our basis [for the discussions]. Sinn Féin may absolutely refuse to cooperate with Fianna Fáil on any basis and Fianna Fáil [are] likely to regard [the] proposals as too revolutionary ... We believe coordination [is] most difficult, but intend that a decision shall be arrived at without delay.' His hope was that influential 'Individuals in each party may force acceptance' on their more reluctant colleagues.[265]

On 5 April the Army Council formally gave its backing to the proposal, provided it was also approved by a specially convened meeting of the senior officers along with representatives of the local units.[266] This meeting was held on 9 April. Following the administration of an 'oath of secrecy', Moss Twomey made an opening speech in which he stated that the proposal 'was an effort to keep the Army [IRA] together' and that 'an opportunity exists for overthrowing the present Colonial administration'. He was concerned that 'if the present Government is re-elected it would be difficult to maintain the Organisation [IRA] for another six years.' But to reach an agreement the parties would have to make concessions: 'Sinn Féin [must] agree not to insist on an immediate proclamation of the Republic should a [republican] majority be secured and Fianna Fáil [must] agree not to enter the Free State legislature as a minority party.'

In particular, Twomey and the delegates discussed the thorny problem of what to do with the Free State army. Officially the proposals called for 'the abolition of a standing army and the organisation of the defence forces on a territorial basis', the 'territorial basis' meaning, in effect, the IRA. The process would begin with 'the removal from Dublin and vicinity of all enemy military forces, and this being done, that they be disarmed and demobilised. All armament be placed under the control of Oglaigh na h-Éireann [IRA]'. Finally, the Army Council would act as an advisory body to the new Minister for Defence.

Peadar O'Donnell suggested that: 'The Free State Army might fight against disbandment but we could meet and beat them on the grounds of economic necessity.' If successful, this would have been an event unparalleled in history! An army defeated by a discussion of economic theory. Twomey and Russell were, however, more realistic. Twomey 'believed a military situation would ensue in which the Army [IRA] could use a strong hand', and to meet this threat the Dublin brigade would need to be strengthened. After the Free State army was neutralised, the IRA would be 'in a position to meet the English'. Russell, though against the proposals, concurred with Twomey that 'a military situation would probably arise from which the Army would benefit.'

As Twomey and Russell envisaged fighting in Dublin, how would the IRA have had a realistic chance of defeating the army? Either by using a masterly surprise attack or with the use of weapons which the army couldn't defend against. Twomey didn't answer the question. But it may be more than coincidence that around this time he was writing to the IRA representatives in America inquiring about both tear gas weapons and poisonous mustard gas (see Chapter 7). 'Mr Jones' wrote to Twomey in late April that the IRA could capture Dublin by using tear gas weapons and at the same time avoid civilian casualties.[267]

While an overwhelming majority of delegates supported the proposals, a number of the more militant members voted against them on the basis that they would end up merely ensnaring the organisation in party politics. This was Russell's position, though he said he wouldn't work against the proposals if they were approved. The OC of Cork 1 brigade said that the IRA 'should have nothing to do with present day politics' and George Plunkett 'was against anything that savoured of going near Leinster House'.

Before the meeting ended, Peadar O'Donnell was able to come up with another idea – that in the newly declared republic the role of the gardaí might become superfluous: 'If you have the high moral Volunteer spirit there would be no need for the police.'[268]

The Army Council next moved quickly to get the approval of both Sinn Féin and Fianna Fáil, by meeting with senior members from each party – many of whom were also IRA members.[269] These meetings were held while de Valera was in America. Given that Twomey regarded him as the 'chief obstacle in Fianna Fáil', this was at the very least a fortunate coincidence.[270] However, Twomey greatly under-estimated de Valera if he thought the other members of Fianna Fáil could (or would try to) force him to accept an agreement. Twomey wrote: 'De Valera we believe [is] an obstacle to such an agreement [that would be] satisfactory to Sinn Féin and us. Many of his followers [are] anxious to get [an] agreement in his absence and force it on him. Seán T [Ó Ceallaigh, vice-president of Fianna Fáil] is most anxious for this.'[271]

Twomey also used the possibility of the pact to try and get desperately needed funding for the IRA, from both the Russians and Irish-Americans. In these attempts he pretended to be far more optimistic of the chances of success. Knowing that the Soviets dearly wanted to see the collapse of the British empire, he asked them for £5,000 and suggested that a republican victory would result in the newly declared Irish Republic withdrawing from the British Commonwealth, which would ultimately undermine the empire through a domino effect (see Chapter 8). In a letter marked 'secret and urgent' he wrote to Connie Neenan discussing a possible fundraising trip to Moscow with Seán Russell: 'I am keen on this trip ... [to Moscow] in view of [the] great probability of coordination between Sinn Féin and Fianna Fáil, and their winning of the election.' The upbeat tone of this letter is in marked contrast to his more realistic assessment in other correspondence. In May when it was clear that there was to be no agreement, Twomey wrote to the OC in Britain telling him not to inform the Soviet intelligence officer 'James', in case it would dissuade the Soviets from providing money: 'Our effort to secure coordination between [the] republican bodies for the election failed. Do not mention anything about this to 'James' should you see him.'[272]

Twomey urged Neenan to raise as much money as possible in the US: 'We must have all [the] cash possible from you. Do your utmost, even borrow if you possibly can. If we secure coordination, in addition to military expenditure, we may under certain conditions expend money on [the] election.'[273] It's also evident from this statement that Twomey felt that if the plan succeeded there would likely be fighting in Dublin.

The insurmountable obstacle was that Sinn Féin wanted an assurance that Fianna Fáil wouldn't enter the Dáil in the event that only a minority of republican deputies were returned, while Fianna Fáil were prepared to take their seats provided there was a way to avoid taking the oath of allegiance.[274] Twomey implied that the members of Fianna Fáil with whom he had met (including Seán T Ó Ceallaigh, P. J. Ruttledge and Tom Derrig) had agreed in principle to the plan – which amounted to a form of quasi-legitimate *coup d'etat* – but that the sticking point was what to do if the republican bloc didn't gain a majority: 'The proposals for setting up of [the] machinery for coordination during [the] election, the creation of a panel [of candidates] and the line of policy to be pursued if majority were got were acceptable The difficulty, of course, arose on the question if only a [republican] minority being secured. Sinn Féin would not cooperate with Fianna Fáil, while they [Fianna Fáil] [were] prepared to enter parliament on conditions. Fianna Fáil would not forgo this portion of their policy. The effort failed on this point.'[275]

By late April the National Executive of Fianna Fáil replied to the Army Council that 'it was unanimously decided that the proposals were not acceptable' and the Council accepted that 'the efforts of the Council had failed, and that no fresh attempt in the same direction should be undertaken'.[276] Twomey wrote: 'We tried our utmost to secure coordination between both political organisations for the election. We failed up to this and I can see no hope now ... we feel [that] with coordination, enthusiasm could be aroused [among the electorate] and a majority got and that to get it was worth taking big risks ... We found Fianna Fáil would be afraid to do anything in the way of meeting the situation in de Valera's absence.'[277] He added: 'We found Sinn Féin very difficult to deal with and at times insulting.'[278]

But in fact one last attempt was made to secure agreement. On de Valera's return to Ireland the Army Council sent a letter directly to him, which was most likely written by O'Donnell, in which he explained that he was writing to him as 'the [Fianna Fáil] Executive may have felt reluctant to take such steps in your absence', adding 'Trusting you are very well after your tour abroad'.[279] De Valera in a terse note rebuffed O'Donnell: 'I am in complete agreement with the view expressed by the Executive.'[280]

And so ended O'Donnell and Twomey's plan. The IRA moved quickly to remind volunteers of General Order 28 (GO 28) which forbade members from accepting nomination as a candidate for election to the Dáil.[281] Twomey reported: 'We are insisting on the rigid enforcement of GO 28 forbidding Volunteers from being [Dáil] candidates since [there are] no hopes of [a republican] majority with [the present] disunion.'[282] However, the order hastened the resignation of many Fianna Fáil supporters.

The results of the June election largely vindicated de Valera's strategy. Fianna Fáil won an impressive 26 per cent of the vote and forty-four seats, as against 27.4 per cent and forty-seven seats for Cumann na nGaedheal, while Sinn Féin imploded and only managed to win five seats. Among those elected was Frank Aiken.[283] De Valera then led his deputies to the Dáil but had to withdraw when the clerk of the Dáil blocked their way – unless they complied with the 'little formality' of the oath.[284] Over the summer de Valera tried to devise a manoeuvre to enter the Dáil without taking the oath, while Cosgrave for his part was determined to prevent him. Then on Sunday 10 July a shooting occurred which was to have a profound impact on Irish politics.

The killing of Kevin O'Higgins

Kevin O'Higgins was the most able parliamentarian in the Dáil and as vice-president of the Executive Council, Minister for Justice and Minister for External Affairs one of the most powerful members of Cumann na nGaedheal. Seán MacBride described him at the time as 'the brains of the government'.[285] Though he dealt firmly with the IRA, he was committed to a civil society based on law and order and had been instrumental in bringing the army under effective civilian control and was strongly critical of garda abuse of IRA prisoners. Seán MacBride later wrote: 'I was not aware of any particular antagonism to Kevin O'Higgins on the republican side at that period … it was generally felt that he was trying to restore law and that he disapproved of … acts of violence undertaken by the CID or the military. The CID had become a little law unto its own at the time.'[286] However, by the time MacBride wrote this in his memoir, his opinion had likely mellowed. But to some republicans O'Higgins was a much hated figure who (as Minister for Home Affairs) was held responsible for the execution of IRA prisoners during the Civil War, including that of Rory O'Connor, who had been the best man at his wedding. In 1923 Éamon de Valera had referred to him as a 'scoundrel'.[287]

On that Sunday in July, as O'Higgins was walking to church in the south Dublin suburb of Booterstown, a hijacked car happened to pass by with three IRA volunteers on their way to a football match in Wexford. Recognising O'Higgins they jumped out of the car and, firing at him with their revolvers, mortally wounded him. He died five hours later at home.[288] The three IRA men – Bill Gannon, Archie Doyle and Tim Coughlan – were never caught and their involvement only became known to the public in the 1980s.[289]

GHQ immediately denied responsibility for the attack and it's unclear when it became aware of the identity of the perpetrators. Not surprisingly, the gardaí launched the most intensive investigation in the history of the Free State, which, however, produced nothing. Senior IRA leaders and associates were arrested, including Michael Fitzpatrick, George Plunkett and Frank Kerlin.[290] Tom Merrigan was arrested but freed after priests at the Capuchin friary in Church Street stated that they had been talking to him at the time of the shooting. Merrigan was an IRA company captain, who in 1925 had helped place the bomb in the Masterpiece cinema and went on to become a member of the Dublin brigade staff.[291] Jimmie Brennan, a Dublin quartermaster, was questioned by 'about a dozen CID men [who] were around him all throwing questions & using filthy language. When he said he believed the IRA did not shoot O'Higgins he was told that is what the rank and file are told. They informed him to tell his intelligence [officer] there will be shooting over it.'[292] As part of their investigation the Special Branch ordered IRA captain Michael Clark to put on 'the clothes he wears on Sundays' after they arrested him.[293] Detectives also took away Tom Merrigan's Sunday clothes.[294]

The gardaí, along with members of the IRA, also suspected ex-members of the Free State army – bitter about their treatment following the failed 1924 army mutiny.[295] As late as September 1927 GHQ must still not have known who killed O'Higgins, for the director of intelligence told the OC in Waterford that it was 'most important' that he should investigate a report that 'a doctor named McGuinness was in Waterford and was entertained by Dr Coughlin. McGuinness is reported as stating he attended O'Higgins after being shot [and] that O'Higgins recognised one of those who shot him and that they were Free Staters.'[296]

In late August Seán MacBride was arrested, even though he had a watertight alibi of being on the continent at the time and had bumped into a Cumann na nGaedheal TD with whom he was on friendly terms.[297] He was 'charged with conspiracy to murder' but was eventually released in October.[298] On his release, Andy Cooney warned the IRA that MacBride was likely being followed by police agents trying to capture other IRA leaders or discover safe houses: 'Smith [Cooney] has an idea that they had a reason for letting Seán out and thinks that he will be closely watched for some time. [He] suggests that he remain very quiet.'[299] In December the gardaí unsuccessfully tried to link Mick Price to the killing.[300]

Meanwhile the government's immediate reaction was to pass an emergency Public Safety Act, but more importantly they enacted a law requiring every candidate for election to the Dáil on nomination to swear to take the oath. This forced de Valera's hand, and on 11 August he led his deputies into Leinster House. There he pushed the bible to the side, covered the words of the oath and signed his name to the ledger. He later said he took no oath but merely put his name down on the ledger to gain admittance to the Dáil.[301] Whatever the semantics, the significance of this occasion was that it marked the beginning of the 'untreatying' of the Free State, and it was de Valera and Fianna Fáil, not Moss Twomey and the IRA, who were to achieve this.

The entry of Fianna Fáil into the Dáil resulted in a vote of no confidence in the government which the government barely survived – forcing Cosgrave to dissolve the Dáil and call for an election in September. In the year's second general election Fianna Fáil increased its share of the vote to 35 per cent and won fifty-seven seats. However, Cumann na nGaedheal also improved its position – winning 39 per cent and sixty-two seats – at the expense of the smaller parties.[302] Fianna Fáil, in the words of Seán Lemass 'a slightly constitutional party', now entered a period of spirited opposition in the Dáil. Outwardly their rhetoric continued to be strongly republican but de Valera was firmly in control and committed to the 'constitutional' path. Though he was interested in subsuming the IRA's membership into the ranks of Fianna Fáil, he wasn't going to share power with them.

For the IRA, 1927 ended on a relatively quiet note. In November eighty delegates attended an army convention in Dublin and passed a motion pledging support for Russia in the event of war with Britain.

WHILE, 1926 AND 1927 have been described as a time of reorganisation and stabilisation for the IRA, they were, in reality, a period of decline and marginalisation. The initiative had clearly passed to de Valera and Fianna Fáil. Though the IRA's newly installed leadership – with the likes of Moss Twomey, Peadar O'Donnell and Seán MacBride – contained ample talent, it failed to show any real aptitude in guiding and developing the paramilitary organisation. At no time did it develop a coherent strategy or achievable goal, instead rushing from one dream to another.

The failure of the barrack raids should have alerted Twomey to the critical weaknesses of the IRA. Command authority – which is essential to the functioning of every army – had collapsed. Officers and men ran little risk of punishment for failure to obey orders (aside from the offence of informing) and most units lacked cohesion, being divided between supporters of GHQ and de Valera. Few volunteers had shown themselves prepared to kill (or be killed by the) gardaí or Free State soldiers. In short this was a force no longer capable of overthrowing the Free State or of fighting the British.[303]

Twomey was unable to reconstitute the IRA as a smaller, more disciplined and better trained clandestine organisation. The organisation failed to develop effective social and economic politics attuned to the Irish electorate and to the IRA's own membership. Time was to vindicate Frank Aiken's warning in the autumn of 1925 that 'faith alone is no good for national salvation [the leadership] must use foresight and common sense'.[304]

CHAPTER 4

The IRA's local units

There are ten men in this area – who come under the category of spies, bailiffs, sheriff and judiciary – to be shot here.

IRA officer in County Offaly

Are you able to carry out the annihilation of all known spies? If so, is your brigade in a position to look after the men, who may have to go on the run

IRA chief of staff

During the period 1926–7, the country at times resembled the 'wild west'. Gangs of armed men staged raids and robberies and threatened their opponents. In Dublin young men went around with loaded revolvers in their pockets, and were accustomed to hijacking a car when the need arose, while in court, witnesses were too frightened to identify accused IRA men. GHQ was not in full control of the IRA arsenal and it was often difficult to distinguish official IRA actions from those of criminals.

However, following the turmoil of the Civil War, Ireland was returning to a state of relative normalcy. The only killings publicly attributed to the IRA were those of the two gardaí shot during the barrack raids and that of Kevin O'Higgins, while no IRA volunteer was killed.[1] Overall the organisation was badly split between supporters of GHQ and Fianna Fáil, with the result that many local units were inactive.

In November 1926, the IRA had an estimated membership of only 5,042, compared with 112,650 at the end of the Anglo-Irish War in July 1921.[2] With the exception of Dublin, some of the areas where the IRA had been most active during the Anglo-Irish War and the Civil War saw the greatest decline in membership and organisation. This paralleled the defection of the most capable commanders to Fianna Fáil, who frequently took with them many of their men. In addition, members left the IRA due to disillusionment and disagreement with its policies (or lack or policies) while many other volunteers emigrated. Of the 5,042 documented members, 583 (12 per cent) were from Dublin, whereas only 280 (6 per cent) were from Cork and a mere 80 (2 per cent) from Tipperary. On the other hand, localities which had seen much less fighting were becoming relatively more important. Mayo had 747 (15 per cent) members and even in Kilkenny there were 235 (5 per cent). At the most only half of these volunteers actively participated in the organisation.[3]

A holdover from the Civil War was that much of the IRA's weapons remained in the possession of units in Munster. Even as late as 1930, sixteen of the organisation's twenty-nine machine guns were in Cork, and the three counties of Cork, Kerry and Tipperary possessed 588 (68 per cent) of its 859 rifles.[4]

During the second half of the 1920s the organisation lost much of its weaponry, due to the success of the gardaí and the defection of IRA volunteers to Fianna Fáil or their emigration abroad. In 1926–7 alone the gardaí seized 385 rifles, five machine guns, 609 bombs, 6,644 lbs of explosives and almost 80,000 rounds of ammunition.[5] Their success in uncovering weapons may in part have been due to intrepid police work, but they were also facilitated by two other factors. Firstly, many of the Special Branch had themselves been IRA members in the recent past and were familiar with the volunteers and the location of hiding places, while, secondly, the gardaí regularly offered IRA volunteers money for each weapon or arms dump located. Indeed one of the largest seizures of the period, that of the arms dump found in the basement of St Enda's college in Dublin, occurred after a member of a gang associated with the IRA sold its location to the gardaí.[6] The IRA's inability to safeguard its weapons was even reported to Joseph Stalin in Moscow, who in 1925 provided an IRA representative with precise details of the seizures and commented that he was reluctant to supply the IRA for fear that the weapons would be captured and traced back to the Soviets.[7]

By the late 1920s many arms dumps were under the control of men who had jumped ship to Fianna Fáil, while the whereabouts of others became unknown following the emigration of the local IRA quartermaster. In 1927, Connie Neenan wrote to GHQ with information on an arms dump in Cork: '[I] met Collins re. [the] dumping of arms in Cork 1 Brigade. Guns and [a] matchless motorcycle were dumped near White's Cross, Coole. Mick Kenny, Saint Lukes, Cork city is aware of [the] exact location.' He added: ' I did not see Murphy, who sold guns before he left.'[8]

The arms seizures, together with the poor morale, dissension and weak leadership of the IRA rendered it more an irritant to the Free State and the state of Northern Ireland than a mortal threat. It was capable of causing outrages but not of overthrowing either state.[9] Most IRA activity was of a low level as typified by incidents such as the shooting and wounding of Garda Hanly in the village of Ballinakill, County Laois after he tried to stop two cyclists for not having a light on their bikes.[10] Indeed many incidents had an element of thuggery and the IRA was used as a cover to settle personal disputes.

Following an inspection tour in early 1927, Moss Twomey reported to the Army Executive and to his imprisoned comrade, George Gilmore, that he was 'quite pleased'.[11] Based on the actual state of the organisation and the reports reaching him at GHQ, this was not an accurate assessment. On the other hand he had already badly over-estimated the capability of the IRA when he authorised the barrack raids in 1926.

The following sections help illustrate the state of the army in various localities.

Dublin

Dublin was a major focus of IRA activity, with GHQ and most of the leadership based in the city. Leaders like George Gilmore and Mick Price who were passionately committed to the organisation were an inspiration to the local volunteers, whereas elsewhere there was a dearth of such commanders. There were two independent units in the county: the Dublin brigade which was the IRA's largest unit and the South Dublin battalion in the Dun Laoghaire area with fifty members.[12] Both units played a leading role in the anti-imperialist campaigns. In November 1925 George Gilmore helped lead the spectacular rescue of nineteen IRA prisoners from Mountjoy prison. However, most IRA activity in the city lacked the drama and 'wholesomeness' of the rescue.

In October 1926 an IRA volunteer, Patrick Morrissey, who worked as a chauffeur, was part of a gang that held up a horse and trap at the South Circular Road. After a revolver was pointed at the driver, Morrissey pistol-whipped the passenger, Maurice Boland, on the head and arms. The gang then escaped with the horse and trap. Later that afternoon Detective-Sergeant Mark Byrne of the Special Branch questioned Morrissey and noted that the radiator of his car was warm, and he found traces of blood on a wheel of the vehicle. Morrissey claimed that he had been held up by armed men who had taken the car. He was arrested and brought before court in Dublin a week later. Maurice Boland wasn't well enough to attend but a witness, George Browne, testified that he saw Boland scream in pain as the IRA men held him on the ground and beat him.[13] The purpose of this brutal assault is not clear – were the IRA men merely trying to seize the horse and trap, or were they out to punish Boland? Twomey, however, wanted to teach Browne, and anybody who would testify against the IRA, a lesson, and in a letter titled 'case of P Morrissey in enemy custody' wrote to the OC of the Dublin brigade: 'If no action [has] already [been] taken against Brown [sic], have him visited in his home, interrogated, threatened, and a few shots fired over his head, or even wound him.'[14]

The following March an IRA party of twenty-five carried out one of the largest ambushes of the time. On a Sunday morning a group of nine Free State soldiers and two non-commissioned officers were returning by bicycle to Portobello barracks, having been relieved of guard duty at Tallaght camp. The advance party of four, rounding a bend in the road near Terenure, ran into a roadblock of two cars. A group of armed and masked men then sprang upon them and disarmed them, while a second group pointed revolvers from the walls overlooking the road. However, a fifth soldier, Private Thomas O'Shaughnessy, came around the corner and, seeing what was happening, reached for his rifle. One of the attackers shot him in the ankle, which alerted the other soldiers and in the ensuing fire fight the soldiers fired forty rounds as the IRA beat a retreat with the four captured rifles. One IRA volunteer on the wall fell after he was shot near the mouth and a bloodstained handkerchief was later found at the scene. Soldiers from Portobello barracks and Special Branch officers soon arrived and arrested three men in a car, after a loaded Colt revolver was found under the seat. The three arrested volunteers were Benjamin Cole (21), his brother, Francis (17) (both grocers' assistants) and a medical student, Michael Keohane (20).[15] Twomey reported to Connie Neenan: '[The] disarming of Free State troops recently near Dublin was [an] official [action], [though] not quite successful.'[16]

Another action that occurred in November 1925 illustrates the difficulty of distinguishing IRA operations from criminal activities. In what was at the very least an 'unauthorised operation' a gang of ten, including seven bakers, attempted to blow up Landy's bakery in Rathfarnham. There was an ongoing industrial dispute at the bakery and a number of employees had been fired. The gang decided to make a bomb and first raided Thom's pharmacy in Kimmage to acquire potassium chlorate. Armed with revolvers, they demanded the explosive 'for the cause', but were only able to get half a pound, instead of the needed seven pounds. As they left they handed Mrs Thom a receipt signed by the OC of C company of the Dublin IRA. With insufficient explosives the plan was changed to burning down the bakery, and that evening they seized a Chevrolet motorcar 'in the name of the IRA'. They loaded the car with petrol and drove to the bakery, but when they arrived, Arthur Kelly, the gang leader, decided that the bakery wall was too high to scale and aborted the operation. The car was abandoned that evening in the Dublin Mountains.

A few months later, in March 1927, a fire broke out in the bakery causing 'considerable damage' to the value of £1,757. The fire was deemed to be arson. The following month eight of the original gang were charged in Dublin District Court with conspiracy to blow up the bakery. The driver of the seized car and his passenger (not surprisingly) were unable to identify the defendants. A Special Branch officer produced confessions from two of the defendants who had incriminated their comrades; one of these was Thomas Gerrard. During the Civil War Gerrard served as a medical orderly in the Free State army. While stationed at Portobello barracks he smuggled out a letter for the badly wounded IRA leader, Ernie O'Malley, who was under arrest in the infirmary. Gerrard was discharged from the army in 1924. Following his attempt to blow up the bakery, he ironically landed a job at Landy's, and having heard there was a £100 reward for information on those involved in attacking the bakery he went to the gardaí. In court he admitted that it was the reward that prompted him to come forward. He also confessed under cross-examination that he was prepared to 'stick up' a motor car as part of a robbery. There were a number of inconsistencies in Gerrard's evidence and the only defendant convicted was Patrick Hogan, who was identified by the two women in the pharmacy. Hogan was sentenced to six months in prison.[17]

While this attack largely appears criminal, the gang were possibly associated with the IRA. They had a number of revolvers and ammunition in their possession, knew how to make a bomb, used the name of the IRA and handed over a receipt signed by the IRA. Arthur Kelly was also the name of an IRA operative in Dublin. Alternatively, they could have been men who left the IRA following the Anglo-Irish War. Whatever they were, this was not the type of publicity the IRA needed.

Munster

There's a certain truism to the words of the song 'the boys who beat the Black and Tans were the boys from County Cork'. During the Anglo-Irish War one-third of all British army and police casualties occurred in Cork.[18] However, the Cork IRA's enthusiasm and performance in the Civil War was decidedly mixed. And in the years following the conflict the majority of its most admired leaders, who hadn't already resigned, joined Fianna Fáil. One exception was Tom Barry, who in 1924 became inactive and didn't fully rejoin the IRA until 1932.[19] Without Barry's participation there was little IRA organisation in the west of the county in the late 1920s.

The result was that in 1926 IRA strength was down to 200 members in Cork 1 brigade, which was centred in the city, sixty members in Cork 2 brigade in the north of the county and twenty members of the Clonakilty battalion in the west.[20]

Seán MacSwiney (Cork 1's assistant adjutant) was one of the few senior leaders from the Civil War era who remained active in Cork 1 brigade.[21] MacSwiney was a brother of Terence who, as brigade OC and lord mayor of Cork, had died on hunger strike in an English jail in October 1920. His sister Mary was a leader of Sinn Féin. At this time Seán was described as 'drinking and jobless … [and] a drain both emotionally and financially' on Mary, who wanted him to emigrate to Canada.[22] In April 1926 he reported to GHQ that 'at present things are not working to our satisfaction' in the brigade and that the OCs of the two city battalions hadn't bothered to turn up at the recent IRA commemoration for the 1916 Easter Rising. The volunteers retained a distrust of GHQ which dated back to the Anglo-Irish War when the IRA in Cork felt that the Dublin leadership provided insufficient support and weaponry to the county that was doing the lion's share of the fighting.[23]

The chief of staff urged the brigade's OC to remove all arms from dumps in the vicinity of the village of Ballyvourney, due to recent captures in the area, adding that 'it should be possible to lay hands on the machine guns'.[24] Ballyvourney had been one of the last republican strongholds during the Civil War and considerable arms and munitions were hidden there, some of which likely came under the control of supporters of Fianna Fáil.

In 1927 Twomey wrote to the OC that he had 'great apprehensions [sic] with regard to the general spirit prevailing in your Unit. There is too much of the politician amongst a number [of the officers and men].' He blamed the poor morale on the 'defeatist influence ... [and] insidious intrigue and propaganda' of officers like P. A. Murray, Mick Murphy and Tom Crofts, who had distanced themselves from the organisation following the barrack raids.[25]

At the IRA officers' meeting in April 1927, which was called to discuss the proposed republican election pact, Cork 2 brigade and the Clonakilty battalion didn't even send a representative, suggesting that they were largely inactive, while the OC of Cork 1 took a hard line, saying that the IRA 'should have nothing to do with present politics' and voted against the pact.[26]

The Limerick brigade, which had a paper strength of a mere sixty volunteers, reported that 'everything [is] in a state of disorganisation, communications scattered etc.'[27] The IRA cast a greedy eye on the estimated 200 tons of industrial explosives stored locally for use in the construction of the hydroelectric power plant at Ardnacrusha on the River Shannon, known as the Shannon Scheme. The brigade adjutant sent an indignant note to Twomey: 'Reports have reached me that there are men taking explosives from [the] Shannon Scheme who are not in our organisation and as far as we know are ex-Free State soldiers.'[28]

Seán Carroll had been OC of the Mid-Limerick brigade during the Civil War but, finding his fellow Limerick officers uncooperative, had

Figure 17. Report from the IRA's department of intelligence to the chief of staff:

Sean Carroll informs m[e] that he has several rifles, revolvers, and lots of ammunition badly hidden, and wants to have it handed over to the Tipp Brigade. He asked the local officers to take it away, long ago. They did not.

He says there is about 200 tons of explosives at Doonass House, Clonlara, [County] Clare, for the Shannon work. There is a guard of about 20 minding it. Almost half of the guard are in Castleconnell each night up to 10 o'clock. He thinks it a handy wee job.

His nephew, a very good lad, lives at 25 Lower Mount St, and attends some wireless class in Dublin. [He] is not linked up with the [Dublin] brigade. This ought to be seen to at once to at once. I think his name [is] Willie Edmons [sic].

linked up with the Tipperary brigade.[29] The director of intelligence's office reported to Twomey that: 'Seán Carroll informs me that he has several rifles, revolvers, and lots of ammunition badly hidden and wants to have it handed over to the Tipp. Brigade. He asked the local officers to take it away, long ago. They did not.'[30]

Waterford was the only Munster county which had seen little fighting during the Anglo-Irish War. In 1926 Twomey wrote to the local battalion OC: 'I am indeed extremely disappointed at the report on your area sent by the officer [from GHQ] who recently attempted to inspect it. So far as I can learn from him, you had no arrangements made for the holding of parades and he made many fruitless journeys. Did I not give you ample notice of the inspection? I cannot accept any excuse as to why proper arrangements were not made. This officer had other work to do, besides wasting his time in your unit. I feel that this matter is so important that I have instructed another officer to report to you in the near future. You must see to it that this officer is able to inspect every single area. You will facilitate him in every way. See that he is billeted in friendly houses as he has very little cash.' Twomey added that the inspecting officer 'will report to (the) Metropole Hotel and give the name of "Whitmore". Leave word, as to how he will get in touch with you, at once.'[31]

Offaly

County Offaly failed to distinguish itself during the war against the British. Richard Mulcahy, IRA chief of staff at the time, was highly critical of the brigade's inactivity and an inspector from GHQ reported that: '[The] enemy has contempt for the [Offaly 2] Brigade in general.'[32]

By 1926 the Offaly brigade claimed a membership of 216 (making it one of the largest of the IRA units).[33] At the April 1927 officers' meeting in Dublin its OC sided with the IRA militants, stating that 'he had no faith in politicians' and that republicans who stood for election were 'deserters of principle'. Not surprisingly he was one of the minority who voted against the proposed republican election pact.[34]

During the barrack raids of November 1926 the brigade again managed to avoid action but the unit's first staff officer came up with an alternative proposal to GHQ. Writing in an awkward style, he suggested: 'In this area's case, however, I have certain incumbent action otherwise, to be executed here [sic]. Action, which if carried out, universally will strike terror into the hearts of our opponents. There are ten men in this area – who come under the category of spies, baillifs [sic], sheriff, and judiciary – to be shot here. Will you acquiesce in making a General Order in this direction, for Friday night the 3rd [of December] [ap]prox. between the hours of 7 and 10 o'clock? Signed, 1st Staff Officer, Offaly Area.'[35]

Two weeks later the staff officer sent details to the chief of staff of some of these 'notorious spies'. A national school teacher from Daingean, by the name of McInerney, showed his British sympathies by wearing a poppy on Remembrance Day and selling poppies at the school. He was reported to carry a revolver and to regularly drop into the local garda barracks. At the time of the barrack raids he was quoted as saying that if the IRA attacked the barracks, they should be let in and then murdered by the gardaí, though the IRA staff officer didn't elaborate as to how the unarmed gardaí would accomplish this.

John Lennon from Tullamore was an IRA officer arrested by the gardaí for selling poteen. To be treated leniently, he and his brother allegedly offered to inform for the gardaí and to give information on the whereabouts of IRA weapons. The staff officer said that Lennon's brother then asked to meet him. Knowing it was a trap, the officer didn't attend the proposed rendezvous and Special Branch officers were later seen at the meeting place searching for him.

John Campbell of Rahan had been dismissed from the IRA during the Civil War for signing a written undertaking not to engage in future armed activities against the state. He went on to work as a paid informer for the Special Branch and tried to recruit other IRA members. On one occasion the gardaí raided an IRA house looking for a secret room which was used to store weapons. Campbell was suspected of having given the information to the gardaí, as he was said to be the only one outside of the household who knew of the existence of the room. The gardaí also uncovered some weapons in the area and for this Campbell received £30. In this case the IRA's informant was reported to have been a brother in a religious order who was related to a garda chief superintendent.

John Rigney was a 'scoundrel' and an officer in the Free State army whose family betrayed two IRA men who sought refuge at their home during the Civil War. The men were soon arrested and later executed. It was said that 'Rigney and a party of military feasted the evening of the arrest at his house in apparent jubilation for the capture.'

The final 'spy' listed was Major General Prout, who had been a senior

December 13th. 192?

To:
1st. S/Officer, Offaly

To acknowledge yours of the 15th. inst.

1. (51) TDGSP OOOSE NINFM TNEWI MOAII NROTL ODRIS AFAIT IHOSF
         TFIRD R.

2. (195) RPACN FEBSA HOCYH VTNOY IKSAO RYHOI VAUAR OAOIR OKWGQ
         MWAYA IERIL IETTM NNSTN ATAUA OIETH ARGTR YLMRA NASRI
         FOOAA AIALL TINYN LMENV NOOYG EEHOS OAOET GECTN RCBTT
         WSIOE VUIAN MORAT ENPUP ONOHA EHESS YRHLF GIEAT NSEGP
         OUOLN ODNTH ETSEN

3. (152) VBSSP ICNOW ESHAK OUIIS IPREP SEONT YTIAT SHSTS TTSOE
         OTHLU SETNE NECLG LNUEE ETIRC UDCII ALOGG CTNCH AELWT
         NAEIN SEETR NOIAA INOAT GDLSH TINTO PSMET ERTAH PMSUY
         ALSSS CESBN NPNEE FI.

4. (61) ORNBI ONIKE JEIOH PTCTB TCNND RSAES URAAN MNTSS EIEWH
         OADAT TRATA EUDOE N.

CHIEF OF STAFF

Figure 18. The chief of staff wrote to the Offaly brigade seeking to thwart the unit's plan to shoot several suspected 'spies'. Moss Twomey was in prison at the time and therefore Andy Cooney may have been the author. It was written in 1926, and not 1923.

List of spies [you sent] noted. Am forwarding it to DI [Director of Intelligence] for his information. Your last paragraph is not clear. Are you able to carry out the annihilation of all known spies? If so, is your Brigade in a position to look after the men, who may have to go on the run? GHQ cannot give any assistance whatever, not having any money

The best action to be taken against those agents is publicity. [Placing] prominent notices in conspicuous places, and tying them to chapel gates will render their usefulness as spies worthless.

[Regarding] Major [General] Prout, I understand, certain action was to be taken. Has this been done?

divisional commander of the Free State's national army during the Civil War. He fought in the Tipperary/Waterford region where his troops were regarded as undisciplined and frequently drunk and he himself was accused of being weak and incompetent. Towards the end of the war in April 1923 his soldiers killed Liam Lynch and arrested several leading IRA officers.

The IRA staff officer sought to justify these intended killings by disingenuously comparing them to Michael Collins' execution of (actual)

British intelligence agents during the Anglo-Irish War: 'I am sure you will agree with me when I state that it was the annihilation of the spies which brought about the consolidation of our position in the old days. Similar action to my mind is again incumbent on our part.'[36]

Fortunately GHQ didn't share the Offaly officer's enthusiasm and a despatch was sent from headquarters (likely written by Andy Cooney): 'The operation you suggest requires more consideration, before sanction for its execution could be granted. Permission cannot at present be given.'[37] Headquarters followed this up with a letter asking: 'Are you able to carry out the annihilation of all known spies? If so, is your brigade in a position to look after the men, who may have to go on the run? GHQ cannot give any assistance whatever, not having any money.' GHQ offered a much more practical solution: 'The best action to be taken against those agents is publicity. [Placing] prominent notices in conspicuous places and tying them to chapel gates will render their usefulness as spies worthless.'[38] This despatch appears to have finally put the matter to rest.

Connaught

Overall the IRA in Connaught was weak and largely inactive. Nominally Mayo had a large IRA contingent, though it went into rapid decline and from 1926 to 1930 the membership of the Claremorris brigade declined from 227 to 40.[39]

In September 1926 the OC of the Connemara battalion spent three days inspecting the South Galway brigade and reported: '[I] found the area so badly disorganised that I could not find a single officer who could exactly tell me what rank he held.' He was unable to find any member of the brigade staff. But eventually 'after much trouble and searching' came across one of the 'old veterans', 'Packie Ruane' of Menlough who agreed to summon a meeting of the officers (if required) and to reply to despatches from GHQ. Letters for Ruane were to be sent via a covering address – 'Michael Crehan, Menlough, Ballinasloe' – from where they'd be forwarded to Ruane.[40] When Moss Twomey later visited the area he arranged to meet the brigade's officers at Turley's pub in Newbridge, where 'everybody in it [is] alright'.[41] Unfortunately for the IRA

Packie Ruane eventually went the way of many other IRA veterans and was appointed chairman of the local Fianna Fáil cumann.[42]

There were two IRA brigades in Mayo, the North Mayo brigade with a reported 520 members and in the south the Claremorris brigade with 227.[43] As with all IRA units these numbers were largely imaginary. Both brigades were badly demoralised by the exodus of volunteers, many of whom either emigrated or joined Fianna Fáil. In June 1927 a grand total of seven members defied GHQ by standing as candidates in the general election, and four were elected – three for Fianna Fáil and one for Sinn Féin. Michael Kilroy, who was the most prominent IRA commander from the county and was a member of the Army Executive, was among those elected for Fianna Fáil.[44] Kilroy was later 'dismissed' from the brigade.[45] Needless to say it was unlikely that those who remained were the cream of the crop.

The plight of Michael Kitterick illustrates the situation many volunteers, particularly those from the poorer counties of the west, now found themselves in. The North Mayo brigade headquarters recommended to GHQ that the IRA should employ him as a weapons instructor. This offer seemed primarily motivated by a desire to help out an unemployed comrade. Kitterick was an 'unattached' officer, meaning that he was no longer active. He was 'very intelligent and extremely enthusiastic about Army affairs'. Following his release from prison in 1924 (and due to his association with the IRA) he was unable to find 'casual employment' locally and emigrated to Liverpool, but not finding a job there either he soon returned to Mayo. Kitterick had fought for the IRA in both the Anglo-Irish War and the Civil War and had no civilian vocational skills, though he was able to instruct in 'general organisation and advanced infantry training' and was a 'qualified trainer ... [for the] Vickers [and] Lewis [machine guns] and [the] Stokes trench mortar'.[46] While the IRA was known to possess a number of these machine guns, they had few if any Stokes mortars. However, being a relatively portable weapon, capable of firing an eleven-pound shell 800 yards every two seconds, it had the potential to be devastatingly effective if used by a properly trained and equipped IRA.[47] This was the sort of weapon that Twomey, as chief of staff, should have tried to acquire!

In 1926 the IRA had 517 members in the six counties of Northern Ireland, with 242 volunteers attached to the Belfast battalion alone. Remarkably this number remained stable in 1930, though the total membership of the IRA declined significantly.[48] This was likely a testament to the *de facto* disenfranchisement and marginalisation of the Catholic nationalist minority in the north rather than any organisational skills of the IRA.

The predicament of the nationalists in the north however remained of peripheral concern to the IRA's leadership in Dublin. Moss Twomey and his colleagues were more focused on dealing with the Free State and minimising the threat posed by Fianna Fáil.

The despatches show that the IRA was relatively powerless, isolated and weak in the north. The twenty-three volunteers in Antrim (outside of Belfast) were so cut off that the chief of staff wondered how he could remain in contact with them.[49] The IRA didn't appear to have any significant intelligence sources in the state. The only exception was some low-level information obtained on the police in Armagh, which suggested that the IRA had an informant either in the barracks or one who had access to the post sent to the barracks.[50]

GHQ sent an organiser, Staff Captain Wilson, to work in the north.[51] There he set up a joint IRA–Sinn Féin committee to organise commemorations for the anniversary of the eighteenth-century United Irishman, Wolfe Tone. Wilson, however, found the committee 'very slow' and had 'to quicken them up'.[52]

Wilson also appointed 'Dan Turley' as OC of the Belfast battalion. He regarded Turley as 'the only member of the [battalion's] staff one could consider' for the position.[53] The chief of staff, however, wrote: 'I am not quite sure that the appointment you have will work out satisfactorily as I think he is an officer who is rather hard to get on with, though I have no doubt he is one of the best otherwise.'[54] Unfortunately for Turley's sake he was to find a place in the history of the IRA. He was a longstanding Belfast republican, having acted as an election agent for Sinn Féin in the city in 1918 and since then had served numerous terms of imprisonment. In the 1930s he was the battalion's intelligence officer; however, following a number of successful police raids and arrests, he came under suspicion of being an informer. The

IRA brought him across the border to a house, where he was beaten and tortured with a pliers and a poker. A subsequent court martial in Dublin found him guilty of spying and sentenced him to death, though this was commuted to banishment from Ireland. He agreed to the sentence and went to live in Britain. However, lonely and unable to support his family, he returned to Belfast after six months. There he spent most of his time in a secret room in his house, only venturing out at night. Friends warned him that the IRA would kill him, but he stayed and continued to protest his innocence. Finally in December 1937 he was shot dead on his way to mass. Twomey later refused to comment directly on the killing, merely saying: 'He would not have been shot had he followed my advice which was to remain in Scotland.' Turley's family remained staunch republicans (with both of his sons members of the IRA) and they put considerable effort into trying to prove his innocence.[55]

Aside from sending despatches by courier, GHQ had difficulty communicating with its northern units. Wilson noted that: 'The post is not safe for any length of time as the censorship is still pretty active here.'[56] At least two addresses were used for sending letters – 'John Rafferty, The Stores, Katesbridge, Belfast' (the cover name for Rafferty was 'Mr Johnson')[57] and 'Miss May Watters, 117 Butler Street, Belfast'.[58] Miss Watters was presumably related to Tommy Watters who later became general secretary of the Communist Party of Ireland in 1941.[59] The officers of the Belfast battalion could be contacted by calling on 'Mrs Cooley, 74 Cavendish Street, Clonard, Belfast'.[60]

Attempts were also made to smuggle in copies of *An Phoblacht* and the chief of staff wrote to Wilson: 'You never reported how you would suggest *An Phoblacht* can be got over the border. Would you get it in at a few places? Hegarty's of Derry have a place just outside the border and run a car across every day – without much searching.'[61] In 1930 a man from Tyrone was reported to have received a month in prison for possessing a single copy of the paper.[62]

Two volunteers from the village of Leitrim, in County Down, 'Eddie Toman and Barney Cunningham', were reported as anxious to become involved again with the IRA following their release from prison in 1924.[63]

The IRA's representative in New York reported to Twomey that a number of veterans there were critical of GHQ's efforts in the north: 'There is a group of Six County men, very active here, [and] they think you are neglecting their area. They say there is no [IRA] organization in the north, and it is only [a] waste of time to send a man from the FS [Free State] area to reorganize them. He will not be listened to. One of them have [sic] volunteered to go over and reorganize that area, if you give him the necessary authorization. His name is Frank Donnelly, of County Tyrone. He is an exceptionally good man, and is willing to report at once. In doing this, he is making a great sacrifice, as he has a good business [here].'[64] Andy Cooney sent a rather indignant reply denying that the IRA were 'neglecting the place' and defended Captain Wilson. 'I have only to say that a GHQ Officer has been permanently stationed in the Six Counties, since December last, on organisation work. They also have a representative on the [Army] Executive and on the Army Council.'[65] Jones further pressed his case and finally Twomey sent a more diplomatic reply than Cooney's rebuttal. 'Personally I consider it unnecessary at this stage for [the] Six Counties man [Frank Donnelly] to come over. He will not be able to do much and may only become a financial responsibility. Of course if he is anxious it would be wrong to prevent him. It is really the spirit, as you state, that we should encourage and we should not do anything which might give the impression that this is not the spirit we wish to prevail.' This exchange highlights the difference in personality between Moss Twomey and Andy Cooney, and is a reminder of the skills that made Twomey such a popular leader.

WHILE THESE REPORTS AND despatches don't constitute a comprehensive overview of all the IRA's units, they all support the same conclusion. The IRA was disorganised, unprepared, split and disintegrating.

CHAPTER 5

Intelligence

Seán Hogan has offered his services to [Chief Superintendent] Neligan for money.

IRA chief of staff

Warder Bailey ... is always prepared to work for money.

IRA Department of Intelligence

Frank Kerlin, the IRA's director of intelligence, oversaw a clandestine network that extended throughout the country. He received reports and tips from sympathisers and IRA men, along with a small number of key informants. This chapter provides a rare glimpse into that network.

Historical background

The Anglo-Irish War has been called 'overwhelmingly an intelligence war' and on the intelligence front the IRA was the clear victor.[1] It was Michael Collins, the IRA's director of intelligence at the time, who established a highly effective intelligence system throughout the country. Intelligence officers were appointed to local IRA units and oversaw the gathering of information on the British police and army, as well as suspected sympathisers. Countless men and women were prepared to pass information to the IRA. Especially valuable were those employed in transport and communications, such as railway porters and post office clerks, along with hotel staff. This information was supplemented by frequent raiding of the mail by the IRA. A number of members of the police also communicated with the organisation, either out of a sense of nationalist sympathy or fear of the IRA. In Dublin, Collins controlled a group of high-value agents within the police and the British administration at Dublin Castle. One of the most important of his sources was David Neligan, a Dublin Metropolitan Police (DMP) detective.[2]

With the aid of a small group of gunmen, known as the 'Squad', Collins used targeted assassination to eliminate British intelligence capability in Dublin. These efforts culminated in November 1920 in the 'Bloody Sunday' killing of fourteen British officers and ended British covert intelligence for the remainder of the struggle.[3]

Soon after the Treaty of 1922 Collins set up an armed 'police' force based in Oriel House, Dublin, which became know as the Criminal Investigation Department (CID) or simply 'Oriel House'. It was staffed largely by ex-IRA men, including intelligence officers and members of the 'Squad'. The CID protected the government in Dublin and assisted the army in the Civil War fight against the IRA.[4] Members lacked discipline and organisation and the force became notorious for the brutal treatment and killing of prisoners.[5] In November 1923, with the ending of the Civil War, the CID was disbanded.[6]

Meanwhile, in February 1922, an unarmed Civic Guard was formed, which was soon renamed the Garda Síochána (Guardians of the Peace). In 1925 the Garda Special Branch, under the command of David Neligan, took over responsibility from the army for combating the IRA. The Special Branch was the only armed section of the Garda Síochána. While the gardaí became well accepted by the community, the Special Branch, though considerably less brutal than the CID, was unpopular and known for its rough treatment of republicans.[7] As a mark of its disdain the IRA continued to refer to the Special Branch as the 'CID'.

In July 1925 the Special Branch raided a house in Adelaide Road, Dublin and captured the IRA's director of intelligence, Michael Carolan, along with a considerable file of intelligence papers. Carolan was sentenced to a year in jail and his assistant, Frank Kerlin, succeeded him.[8]

The Special Branch

Special Branch detectives, being frequently ex-IRA men, were at a considerable advantage in tackling the IRA, having intimate knowledge of the organisation's members, their haunts and hiding places. They engaged in a policy of continued harassment, arrest and interrogation of suspects, along with inducements to inform or reveal the location of arms dumps. Their task was made easier by the desperate economic straits of republicans and by the drift of many men away from the IRA. As one volunteer remembered: 'We were continuously being lifted by the Special Branch and being released again.'[9]

In August 1927 the Dundalk IRA reported that: 'A volunteer was approached by [the] "CID", who offered him £2 per week for any information he could give them concerning [arms] dumps, [they] also [offered him] £1 for each rifle got.'[10] John Kelly, a Dublin IRA officer, was interviewed by Detective Hughes of the Special Branch and offered 'many inducements hinting at the restocking of his shop ... if he would give information as to the personel [sic] of the 3rd Batt. [battalion] staff, and the whereabouts of the [arms] dumps'.[11] Hughes had earlier questioned IRA quartermaster Jimmie Brennan and offered him £25 for information on arms dumps in Dublin.[12]

Seán O'Grady of Cork went to his local garda station to apply for a passport and was told by 'Guard Maguire, since promoted to CID ... that unless he handed up a dump for which he would be well paid, a passport could not be granted'. When he refused, the garda suggested that he 'leave a few rusty shotguns on his land ... for which payment would also be made'.[13] At a time when economic necessity was forcing many to emigrate and start a new life in America, this was a particularly persuasive form of coercion.

Mollie Hyland of Cumann na mBan was trailed by a man (possibly Detective Kenny of the Special Branch) who loitered outside her office all day. He told her he knew Frank Kerlin when he was 'in the game' [i.e. before Kerlin's resignation from the IRA in 1927] and that he was trying to 'get in touch' with the IRA again.[14]

One of those suspected of informing was the legendary IRA figure, Seán Hogan of Tipperary, who had been with Dan Breen at Soloheadbeg in January 1919 when two police constables transporting gelignite were ambushed and shot dead. This attack is generally regarded as marking the opening of the Anglo-Irish War. He then went on the run from the police, but came out of hiding to attend a local dance. Arrested at the dance, he was dramatically rescued from police custody on a train by Breen, which resulted in two more dead RIC men. He went on to further distinguish himself by leading a flying column that failed to participate in a single ambush.[15] In December 1926 the IRA chief of staff warned the OC in Tipperary that: 'We have information that Seán Hogan has offered his services to Nelligan [sic] for money. He may, therefore, be used in Tipp. Do not broadcast this. At present all [IRA members] should be told to be discreet, even with people who were prominent in the past.'[16]

Seán Harling, a minor player in the Dublin IRA, was to become its best known informer of the period. Harling was a long-serving republican who had been a courier for the First Dáil and for Éamon de Valera and 'claimed to have worked for Collins'.[17] Though he later referred to himself as an 'ambivalent republican' during the Civil War, he spent most of the war imprisoned by the Free State in the internment camp at the Curragh. After his release he lived with his wife and children in a small gate lodge on the Dartry Road, Dublin. Though he received a small grant of £30 from the IRA, he remained impoverished with no prospect of a job.[18] He eventually approached the gardaí and offered to inform. In the words of David Neligan: 'It was poverty drove Harling into working with us. I felt sorry for the poor wretch.'[19]

In early 1927 Harling was in charge of an IRA arms dump, but when his unit became suspicious of him, it was taken from him. Later he met one of the company's officers, by the name of Garland, and asked him if he now had the dump at his house. Garland, by way of a ruse, told him that 'a girl was minding it'. The IRA's suspicion of Harling was further increased when Michael Clarke, the company OC, was arrested a few months later, and during interrogation the Special Branch told him what they knew about Garland and asked what was the name of the 'girl' in charge of the dump. Based on this, the IRA's Dublin brigade intelligence officer deduced 'Harling is therefore blamed as the cause of the arrests of these men [sic] and the particular line of interrogation.'[20]

Evidence of Harling's treachery continued to be gathered by IRA intelligence. In October 1927 Harling met an IRA man called Ryan, and he 'appeared very indignant over allegations that he was in the CID, and denied he had touch with them'. But the next day he met Ryan again, and made a 'most peculiar statement' withdrawing 'all he had said before, and admitted belonging to the CID'.[21] A few weeks later Harling approached Con Mulligan of Phibsboro, an unemployed ex-member of the Dublin IRA, and offered him £4 10 shillings and 9 pennies as an initial reward for giving information on arms dumps and the names of current officers. Mulligan told the IRA that he refused this offer, though this was doubted.[22]

When Seán Russell and Mick Price were arrested in November 1927 the IRA was informed: 'Seán Harling's pal Jimmie Hayden is suspected of giving Russell and Price away. At least his [the informer's] Christian name is Jimmie and he is a pal of Harlings. On making enquiries Hayden seems the only man who would likely to have done this.'[23] This rather circumstantial evidence, along with the Special Branch seizure of 50,000 rounds of ammunition in a raid on an IRA dump in Glasnevin, sealed Harling's fate. Many years later Moss Twomey also implicated Harling in his arrest in November 1926; however, if true, it's difficult to understand why the IRA took so long to confront Harling.[24]

Meanwhile Harling wisely declined an offer to attend an IRA court martial. Then one evening in January 1928, after he was dropped off close to home by a garda squad car, two men followed him; a shootout ensued and, standing behind one of the pillars of his house, Harling shot one of his assailants in the back of the head, causing the other to flee. The dead man was Tim Coughlan, one of the trio who had shot Kevin O'Higgins. Ironically, Coughlan had been associated with a group of IRA men who had given information to the gardaí leading to the seizure of a large dump in St Enda's college in 1926.[25] David Neligan had Harling and his family packed off to safety in America under the name 'Hurley', at the state's expense. They returned two years later and Harling was fixed up with a clerical job in the Revenue Commissioners. He may have worked out some sort of a deal with the IRA as he was left alone and died aged seventy-five in 1977.[26] His obituary appears to have inflated his rank during the Anglo-Irish War by referring to him as a 'Brigadier-General' of Na Fianna, and failed to mention his subsequent employment by the Special Branch.[27]

Frank Kerlin and the IRA's Intelligence Department
Frank Kerlin, the director of intelligence, was much liked and admired within the organisation and recognised both for his intelligence and sense of humour. He was a Dubliner whose parents had moved to Dublin from

Derry, where they started a decorating business and opened a shop selling paint and wallpaper. He was an outstanding student at the Christian Brothers school in Synge Street and was awarded a university scholarship to study chemistry. Responsibility came early to young Frank as both his parents died when he was eighteen. He and his seventeen-year-old sister, Bridie, took over the shop and reared their three younger siblings. Somehow he managed to juggle his 'parental' responsibilities with his duties in the IRA, and during the Civil War he was appointed the IRA's deputy head of intelligence. In March 1927, he resigned as director of intelligence and in July, following the assassination of Kevin O'Higgins, resigned from the IRA citing 'family and business responsibilities and many serious financial commitments'. His old comrade Seán Lemass persuaded him to join Fianna Fáil and he was elected a TD within a month. He died from TB at an early age in 1932.[28] It is not clear who was appointed in his place though it may have been Staff Captain 'Wilson'.

The Department of Intelligence had a mixed degree of success and failure throughout this period. Kerlin received reports from the more active units around the country, cultivated sources within the police and weeded out IRA informers. His greatest achievement, however, was to maintain contact with IRA prisoners and to help organise a number of successful prison breaks. But all the intelligence in the world wouldn't change the fact that the IRA didn't have sufficient capability to confront the forces of the Free State head on. The most sensitive area of foreign intelligence and espionage remained under the direct control of Moss Twomey and Andy Cooney.

Seán MacSwiney reported from Cork city that: 'The IO [Intelligence Officer] is not doing anything … [and] no IO work is being done in the companies.'[29] Moss Twomey replied that this was a 'great pity', and he hoped 'that the services of every friendly civilian willing to assist are availed of'.[30]

Republican Seán Carroll of Limerick told Kerlin's department that there were 'about 200 tons of explosives at Dunass [sic] House, Clonlara, [County] Clare, for the Shannon work [the hydro-electric scheme under construction]. There is a guard of about 20 minding it. Almost half of the guard are at Castleconnell each night up to 10 o'clock. He thinks it a handy wee job.' Presumably the guard were partaking in libations at Castleconnell in the evenings. Carroll added that he had a nephew, Willie, 'a very good lad, lives at 25 Lower Mount St. [Dublin] and attends some wireless class in Dublin. [He] is not linked up with the [Dublin] brigade. This ought to be seen to at once.'[31]

The brigade adjutant from Mayo wrote to Kerlin, advising him to 'get a friend on [the] Malaranny Bay [*sic*] Hotel staff' as a group of government officials 'travelling incognito went the pace [lived the fast life] there last season'.[32] During the Civil War the Mulranney hotel became a well-known refuge for the IRA. On one memorable occasion the manager, Miss Brosnan of Kerry, allowed them to take the hotel boiler, which they mounted on a truck chassis to make an armoured car, that successfully led the attack on the Free State garrison at Clifden.[33]

Even prisoners helped gather intelligence. The IRA OC in Maryborough prison wrote that Phil Cadden, a fellow prisoner, 'knows of a secret passage [tunnel], running from the military burial ground in Fermoy into the barracks. He is willing to point out where this passage is to anyone who will contact him. We have arranged that the man who'll approach him shall use the word "venus" as a password ... [Cadden] is to be released in a day or two. I know nothing about him except that he is an ex-British soldier and as far as I know him, is alright. He says he stole rifles etc.' The OC was hopeful that the IRA could use the tunnel to enter the barracks and steal weapons.[34]

The IRA's Kildare battalion was entrusted with the responsibility of watching the army barracks at the Curragh.[35] In November 1927 the OC reported that 'revolvers and rifles [were] to be purchased' from the camp and asked Twomey if he would pay for this.[36] Twomey replied that the money was available and added: 'This is very important and if there is any opportunity it must not be missed.'[37]

In May 1926 the chief of staff suggested to Kerlin that an IRA supporter should write to the Special Branch to get a reply on a copy of the 'official paper used by the CID [*sic*]'. He also wanted a Special Branch officer's 'identification disc'.[38] This was a small metal medallion with an ID number carried by plainclothes detectives as a form of identification. Armed with official documents and a disc, IRA men could have impersonated a detective. In 1925 George Gilmore used such a ruse – disguised as a garda and with forged papers he entered Mountjoy prison and rescued nineteen IRA men.[39]

Just as the Special Branch watched the IRA, in turn the IRA kept tabs on the comings and goings of Special Branch officers. The Dublin IRA reported on 'a suspicious looking character who posts himself outside the brown bread shop daily' and decided to 'have his movements watched and [be] followed everywhere' until his identity was uncovered.[40] The IRA observed Detective Kenny as he escorted a 'tall man with a small beard' on his way to board the boat for Glasgow.[41] The North Cork brigade was asked to provide the names of police taking part in raids on the homes of suspected republicans.[42] The chief of military intelligence, Colonel Michael Costello, was seen 'visiting his aunt and uncle-in-law Jerry O'Neill' in Offaly.[43]

A number of contacts were made with gardaí and the Special Branch. The adjutant in Cork recommended that it would be worthwhile contacting Garda Wall, a 'clerk in Superintendent MacMahon's office at the Guard [sic] Depot, Dublin'.[44] Connie Neenan, the IRA representative in America, told Moss Twomey to 'get in touch with Sergeant Leen, Civic Guards, Bandon, County Cork. He is in [the] Superintendent's office, he is fed up with [the] Imperial gang and is going to clear out, possibly emigrate. He is anxious to give information to us. Mention Martin Howard of Listowel, now in New York ... [He sent a letter] to Martin offering to assist. I saw the letter.'[45] The Cork city brigade was promised by a 'dismissed CID man' that he'd provide them with information on suspected informers.[46] In Waterford a garda provided the local IRA with police documents, including information on the recent beating of detained IRA men. He may have already received £100 and the director of intelligence wrote to the local IO: 'A thousand pounds could be well spent on these police people. Be very careful as to how you manage to meet your principal friend there. On no account let anyone know you are meeting him ... Tell him all these documents are useful, but do not pretend they are so valuable as they are; tell him he must get better stuff.'[47]

Cumann na mBan led a campaign from 1927 to intimidate jurors in trials of IRA men. Jurors received leaflets, signed the 'Ghosts', which ranged from an appeal to their patriotism to death threats. The 'success' of this campaign led to the government introducing the Juries Protection Act in 1929.[48] In May 1926 Moss Twomey wrote to Kerlin ordering him to 'find out where [the] panel of jurors is prepared and all details as to how it can be seized a few days before [the] opening of the court'. He also wanted Kerlin to send a 'representative' to 'attend trials [held] under the Treason Act' and to identify the jury if they found the IRA defendant guilty.[49]

In 1927 the IRA expended considerable effort and money in preventing the conviction of Ned O'Reilly for murder. O'Reilly was charged with having shot Garda Hugh Ward during an attack by three men on the garda barracks at Hollyford, County Tipperary as part of the barrack raids of November 1926. He was arrested soon after the raid, while his co-defendant, Jim Ryan, escaped to England. A year later Ryan was captured at a hotel in Penrith, Cumberland, on the border of the Lake District, and returned to Ireland to stand trial with O'Reilly.[50]

Twomey was optimistic that O'Reilly would be found not guilty: 'We have no fears as to [the] result of his case. He has [a] good defence. He was at a priest's house, when [the] raid occurred. [The] priest [was] out [of the house] just at the time, still [he] can swear Ned could not be in [the] raid and come back [to the house]. [The] prosecution is weak.'[51] Strong as the case may have been, the IRA was taking no risks and Twomey wrote to Connie Neenan: 'Send on cash at once ... [Our] last money is exhausted. Had big demands. Ned O'Reilly's defence is costing hundreds.'[52]

The state's main witness was Garda Martin McTigue, who had been in the barracks along with Ward.[53] To prevent McTigue from testifying, the IRA planned to threaten his family, and the director of intelligence asked the IRA adjutant in Claremorris for 'the postal address of Mrs Mac-Tigue [sic], [the] mother of [the] policeman giving evidence against Ned O'Reilly. We intend sending her a few letters anonymously. What influence or pressure can you bring to bear on her or [her] family ...? This [is] urgent. [The] trial may take place this week.'[54] The adjutant replied: 'These people [the McTigue's] are inclined to be in sympathy with us. The brother at home is a very good chap and has always been in our organisation. The man causing the trouble was always a useless kind of chap. Any influence his people may have over him will be used for us.'[55]

The trial finally opened in December 1927, with the two IRA men defended by the barrister, Joseph O'Connor. Seán MacBride (a distinguished lawyer in his own right) later said that O'Connor was 'the best criminal law advocate at the Irish Bar'.[56] Though several of the villagers from Hollyford had witnessed the attack, many of whom were only a few feet or yards away from the perpetrators, none could identify the attackers. The prosecution's case therefore depended on Garda McTigue. McTigue pointed out O'Reilly and Ryan as the two raiders who entered the barracks. O'Connor next cross-examined him and McTigue clarified that O'Reilly pointed a revolver directly at his face. However, when questioned by O'Connor he admitted he had originally said O'Reilly's eyes were brown, which he now knew to be incorrect. O'Connor addressed the jury, arguing that, given McTigue's inability to identify the colour of O'Reilly's eyes, they couldn't rely on the remainder of his evidence. As for Ryan, an acquaintance testified that he was with him the evening in question. With this the foreman of the jury said that they didn't need to hear any more and, to applause in the court, the judge acquitted the two defendants.

Though O'Reilly and Ryan had an excellent barrister, and the state's case was hampered by the lack of evidence and the obvious fear of the witnesses in the village, it's interesting to wonder whether or not the IRA had succeeded in getting at McTigue.[57] O'Reilly later emigrated to America only to return with the onset of the Great Depression in 1930. Not surprisingly the gardaí in Tipperary didn't forget him and after three letters sent to him with a job offer were returned, marked 'not known', he went to the garda station to complain, where he alleged he was 'abused'.[58]

Prisoners

Most IRA prisoners were incarcerated at Mountjoy jail in the centre of Dublin city or Maryborough prison in Portlaoise. Among those in Mountjoy were senior officers such as George Gilmore and Mick Price, serving short sentences or on remand, while the IRA group at Maryborough included a small number of men convicted of serious offences, frequently dating back to the Civil War. The IRA on the outside was able to easily communicate with the Mountjoy men, but those in Maryborough were more isolated and appeared to have endured harsher conditions.

Mountjoy prison

Mountjoy, or the 'Joy' as it's known, is a nineteenth-century prison in Dublin city. The IRA headquarters communicated with the prisoners largely by way of visitors or prison warders.

The IRA was prepared to pay for the services of corrupt warders, such as Bob Glynn, a 'stout dark man, clean shaved, full faced, a native of Ulster'. He already did 'a bit of traffic with the lags [convicts]' in cigarettes, and the IRA proposed to test his reliability by asking him to smuggle in cigarettes to 'a man named Johnson, who could then give them to George [Gilmore] in church'. Another likely recruit was 'warder Bailey, who has or had charge of parcels, this man is always prepared to work for money'.[59] On the other hand, warder Collins, who probably worked for the IRA, was reported by one prisoner to be 'untrustworthy'.[60]

Most warders were, naturally enough, not going to cooperate with the IRA, and Frank Kerlin warned Mick Price and George Gilmore to be careful of a 'warder, pale, thin face and dark complexion, who brings [the] prisoner[s] to [the] visiting boxes, and watches [the] visits, [and] is CID [*sic*]'.[61] Price's brother, Charlie, was cautioned to avoid chatting to warder Folan, as he was a 'CID tout'.[62] Warders who abused or beat up IRA prisoners were liable to be threatened, and in 1928 the IRA shot and wounded the chief warder, Robert Grace.[63]

A Fr Fitzpatrick had contact with George Gilmore in the prison and also knew Charlie Price, which made him of potential value to the IRA. However, Moss Twomey dismissed the idea: 'Fr. Fitzpatrick is just courteous, but could not be depended on much.'[64] One of the IRA's most valuable contacts was a truck driver 'prepared to do anything required', who delivered coal to the prison as part of a regular convoy of four to five lorries. He took in a message to Gilmore, and Kerlin was hopeful that if they could come up with an escape plan he'd assist.[65]

D/I.

DX lo5.

To.
Mr. Campbell.

1½ (243) LSNMU RLEPH PDREG EAHHN GETDL NEKAR AESIS TSJUO RITRN BAUMI
TANTH DRNWT IRAEO AIAGP WTEFG EEDOT UMTAW CADCA IRDAL ITHOE COUWO
VNSHE ADTBW EEOHD EHRGA BESSI TCRAI IGCAN GOEED LINWS ENITO HUGAO
VGESA BIANE RORSA CHHTO LGCGG RGSTT MTHRN TTOIM SIROH MHHMT IPSOO
FAVTE WMHGS KYNEO OSDSA FTLAN MEE.

(81) THGEO UEDTE EIHIN TGUIO GNWTM EWIAE HNCNG RHFUH OLGIR EGMNS
GSOOO OODMA TYYEM ENEOT SIWHE NUIST R.

2. (115) CROFM RKSOY ELDCS RMLWE ESOSP HUTLI AHIAR UHOBR PAEPH UUTWH
LLDNG TMWHA SWTEE HYRHG HYWYI IOCYC EAEOD IAAOR TAOYT HLAHA NPOOC
RDAEI SOONM.

3. Regarding the man mentioned in B5 Para. 1. (227) RWEDS CUIPS
UUMEA TRTTY BTIME NERAA GREAT TMEPO DTNAF HPXOO IWDST ITAOE KUATP
RMWPN SURIH ONRAH ELNEE L MRB WYHEU YIANF TAMCI KMIII IIIWB SSCWI
NHEFY IPSSN RGLKA OELEI SHEUE OIRST ROLHS ADARO NHROY THHFC IEWTL
LVDIA HOSYF TESAB THRAD SKAAD DOEOO HTSLN RUAFO TAEWC HUEUS WE.

4. This information should be acted on at once.

S/CAPT.
for DIRECTOR INTELLIGENCE.

Figure 19. The department of intelligence wrote to 'Mr Campbell' discussing what
prison warders at Mountjoy could be used to smuggle in items for the IRA:

George Gilmore suggests that a warder, named Bob Glynn, who lives in Bucha-
nan St, near Amiens St, would take him some cigarettes, if approached. This
warder is a protestant, and does a bit of traffic with the lags. He could give the
cigarettes to a man named Johnson, who would give them to George in church.
Do not mention to Glynn, that George suggested him. Give him impression
[that] we have no touch [sic] with George.
You may recollect, warder Bailey, who has or had charge of parcels, this
man is always prepared to work for money. You should get in touch with him.
Regarding the man mentioned in Para. 1: You will probably be known to this
warder [Glynn], he is a stout dark man, clean shaved, full faced, a native of Ulster and I think from his appearance an ex-seaman. If he would work, you could
promise him money, if you were satisfied with his trustworthiness. Try him first
with the cigarettes.

The following two sections describe the experiences of George Gilmore
and Michael Price during their imprisonment in Mountjoy

George Gilmore

George was the best known of the three Gilmore brothers, George, Harry
and Charlie, all of whom were in the IRA. They were from Dublin and, un-

like most of their comrades, were of Protestant stock. George was a leading republican socialist and was at one time OC of the Dublin brigade.[66] In November 1925 he organised a jailbreak from Mountjoy, when he entered the prison disguised as a garda sergeant accompanied by five other armed IRA men – two 'policemen' escorting three 'poachers' under arrest. They managed to release nineteen men, including such well-known republicans as Mick Price, Jim Killeen, Michael Carolan and Jim Nugent.[67] Gilmore followed this up three months later with the release of Jack Keogh from Dundrum asylum.[68]

He was finally arrested in November 1926 and sentenced to eighteen months' hard labour for 'taking part in the gallant rescue of 19 political prisoners'. Gilmore refused 'to accept criminal status or wear criminals' clothes' and was confined to a punishment cell in the basement – naked and isolated from the other IRA prisoners.[69] At one point he was forced into prison garb and his hands were restrained in muffs to prevent him from ripping the clothes off, or as *An Phoblacht* wrote, he was in a 'strait jacket'.[70]

Moss Twomey tried to mobilise public support for Gilmore, writing: 'We were all very sorry about G.G. [George Gilmore] and the terrible fight he is up against. We are doing our utmost on the matter of publicity and a special meeting with regard to his case is being arranged ... I am hopeful that from action outside [the prison], George will be transferred [from his current cell].'[71] A mass meeting was held in support of him and the other republican prisoners in Dublin, with de Valera sharing the platform with Art O'Connor of Sinn Féin and Maud Gonne of the Political Prisoners Committee.[72]

Following his transfer from the basement cell, George was seen in the grounds of the prison infirmary by the IRA informant who drove the coal truck. Frank Kerlin gave the truck driver a letter to pass along to Gilmore. Kerlin wrote: 'Leave [a] reply to this despatch at the exact place on [the] ground, where [the] bearer is leaving this note for you, and pin it to a piece of the blue hospital cloth to enable [the] bearer to find it easily. When writing give full details of your location and hours of exercise, also any suggestions re. [regarding an] escape [plan].'[73] Another inmate, Donal O'Donoghue, came up with the bright idea that the IRA could send a man into Mountjoy for a few days to check up on Gilmore. O'Donoghue wrote to Kerlin: '[I] suggest someone be fined for [having] no light [on his bicycle]. Refuse to pay, [and] get seven days [in Mountjoy. He can then] find all about Geo[rge] in B wing. [The person should be a] first offender, [and an] adult.'[74] Moss Twomey replied: 'George Gilmore's brother is to do 4 days [in prison], for not paying [a] fine for [having] no light on [his] bike. He is trying to arrange to be arrested, today or tomorrow. I gave him verbal messages, if he sees you. Be on the lookout.'[75] By January, Gilmore had scored a victory when he was allowed to wear his own clothes, though he continued to agitate for the right to freely associate with the other prisoners.[76]

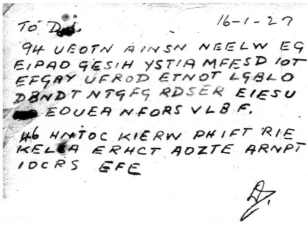

Figure 20. Handwritten note from Donal O'Donoghue in prison to the director of intelligence, Frank Kerlin.

[I] suggest someone be fined for [having] no light [on his bicycle]. Refuse to pay, [and] get seven days [imprisonment, so that he can] find all about George [Gilmore] in B wing. [He should be a] first offender [and an] adult. Charlie Price knows Father Fitzpatrick, see other note.

In May 1927 Moss Twomey sent a letter to George in cipher. The letter, reminiscent of a Christmas letter to a dear friend, is warm and fuzzy with updates on the IRA 'family', but with the addition that there was concern about some unaccounted money. 'Everyone charmed to hear from you, and to hear ... how well you looked. We were all very upset about Xmas time when you were putting up the fight for your clothes, of course all classes of rumours came through. You would be all right now if you had company. I hope you manage to kill the time without being too fed up.' Twomey filled him in as to how his comrades were doing, including '[Seán] MacBride is now running the jam factory', and also explained the IRA's position on the recent negotiations for a republican election pact. Then arose the question of the money: 'At [the] time of your arrest, your accounts were not fixed [up]. There was an apparent deficit of nearly £200 ... [I] am sure, you had not some expenditure written up ... You got £30 from [the] QMG for [a] purchase last October in S[outh] Dublin. [The] man said he [was] not paid. He has been paid now. £30 were [sic] found at your place after your arrest. I presume this was the amount in question ... I do not want to worry you in any way with regard to this as it can quite well wait over until your are out.'[77]

Gilmore seems to have endured his incarceration well and despite all he went through, his mother reported he was 'fine and is well'.[78] This may have been due to his personality, described by one fellow prisoner as 'a withdrawn sort of a man whom you would not intrude on'.[79] He spent time reading Gibbon's *The Decline and Fall of the Roman Empire* from the prison library and was released in early 1928.[80]

Mick Price

Mick Price, another republican socialist, had been OC of the IRA's 1st Eastern division in the Civil War and following that OC of the Dublin brigade.[81] During the Civil War he styled himself as 'Comrade Price'.[82] Todd Andrews described Price unfavourably as Napoleonesque and that he had an expression which represented either 'deep thought or depression'.[83] The veteran republican May Ó Dálaigh was more complimentary: 'Mick Price was the one I like [sic] the best', adding that he was the only IRA leader who helped her wash up the dishes![84] Con Casey, who had served under him during the Civil War, said that Price, was 'very sincere' and was 'constantly in a state of agitation', adding: 'I always thought he was a man under stress, so deeply was he concerned about Ireland and its future.'[85]

In the summer of 1926 following the attacks against moneylenders in Dublin, Price, along with Donal O'Donoghue and Fiona Plunkett, was arrested. After the moneylenders failed to identify the accused in court, the three were remanded in prison. In December Price and O'Donoghue were sentenced to six months in Mountjoy, while Plunkett was released.[86] In jail, Price and O'Donoghue demanded to have freedom of association, the right to wear civilian clothes and other privileges known as political status, and for this they were confined to their cells without exercise privileges.[87]

On 16 December Price wrote to Frank Kerlin that he and O'Donoghue were now allowed to exercise together in the prison yard for two hours each day, but that: 'I am very weak. [I] will send all news of GG [George Gilmore] to Moss [Twomey]. Pick it up on your visits. Do not forget to take [the] girls out [most likely a reference to Kerlin's orphaned sisters]. God bless you in your difficulties. Mick P.'[88] To which Kerlin replied: 'Please send out all [the] news about yourselves [*sic*] and George G[ilmore], as we are making a big push and want as much news as possible. Let me know always [the] exact number of your cells. Let me know [the] names of [the] prison officials against whom action should be taken outside. God bless you.'[89] Around the same time Maud Gonne reported: 'Michael Price is so weak that he collapsed twice at Mass on Sunday.'[90]

Price was becoming deeply depressed in prison, a cause of great concern to Twomey, who wrote: 'My Dear Mick, I need not tell you how sorry I was to see that you were not in good form and it was hard for it to be otherwise after what you had gone through – the close long confinement must have been terrible. I was delighted to hear that the conditions were so changed that you could see your way to go to exercise. I feel sure that in a very short time you will be in good form.' However, as he only had six months to serve, Twomey felt that it wasn't worth the risk to try and rescue either him or O'Donoghue: 'Regarding rescues. I am, and have been, of [the] opinion, it is unwise to rescue men serving short terms, and for [the] sake of [the] men themselves.'[91]

Kerlin asked O'Donoghue if Price's 'condition is bad, or is it merely [a] temporary lapse?'[92] O'Donoghue was reassuring, that though he remained in the prison infirmary, 'Mick [has] improved. [His lapse was] only temporary.' O'Donoghue went on to press for public protests in support of the early release of the prisoners.[93] Twomey countered that he doubted that picketing the prison would be successful, but that 'if it is absolutely essential that Mick be released' quiet diplomacy by approaching 'certain people' would be more productive. Twomey may have been referring to making contact with the Catholic hierarchy by way of intermediaries. Twomey went on to admonish O'Donoghue for under-estimating the severity of Price's condition: 'Miss Delaney visited Mick [a] few days ago. She said he looked very bad and depressed. [I] got [the] impression, she considered him much worse than your report would convey.'[94]

Given the lack of knowledge and understanding of psychiatric illness at the time, it is understandable that O'Donoghue was confused by Price's condition: 'Mick [is] bad now, and then was bad yesterday over [the] special visit [by his brother]. [He was] very bad last week. [I] don't know why, except for this. [He was] normal [the] past three weeks. When [he's] normal, [he's] irritable [and] takes things very seriously. [The] sight of [the] Deputy [governor] and certain warders annoy him, otherwise [he's] sane. [He] needs constant assoc[iation] for cure.' He went on to complain that Price's brother, Charlie, shouldn't ask for special visits as these annoyed him and that Mick disliked Charlie speaking of 'short grass people', a slang term for people (unfortunate enough to come) from Kildare.[95] By requesting special visits Charlie Price was drawing attention to his brother's illness, and this could have been the source of Mick's displeasure. Twomey replied: 'Do your best to prevent him from being moody, and beg him not to be worrying unnecessarily.'

Twomey cautioned O'Donoghue for continuing to demand the right for republican prisoners, both sentenced and those on remand, to have free association. Instead he recommended they should try to improve conditions 'bit by bit' rather than risk confrontation with the prison authorities.[96]

In May 1927, following Price's release, Twomey reported: 'Mick is not well and must take a long rest away, and get good medical treatment', but 'Donal [O'Donoghue] is fine.'[97] However, Price, who was regarded by the gardaí as one of the 'most dangerous' IRA activists of the period, was back in Mountjoy by the end of the year, having been found in possession of a list of three Special Branch car licence plate numbers written on a blank page in a prayer book.[98] Over the course of the 1920s he became increasingly committed to socialism and was eventually 'dismissed with ignominy' from the IRA in 1934, having failed to convince the organisation to support a workers' republic. The following year he joined the Labour party.[99]

Maryborough prison

Maryborough prison, now the maximum security Portlaoise prison in the midlands, was commonly known as 'Maryboro'. The IRA prisoners' OC called the conditions there 'deplorable' and claimed he endured a 'lingering asphyxiation'. The bread was so awful that the baker 'should be in here amongst his compatriots'.[100]

The prisoners included Jack Keogh and members of his 'unit' or 'gang' – Jack Downey, Matt Hughes and Pat Dunleavy. Downey was disliked by some of the others as he was well in with the warders and was allowed special privileges.[101] The person with the most colourful past was the ex-British soldier Jack McPeake, who was serving six years. In August 1922 McPeake was the gunner of Michael Collins' armoured car when they were ambushed by the IRA at Béal na mBláth, County Cork. In a brief firefight, during which McPeake's gun jammed, Collins was shot dead. Two months later McPeake defected to the republican side and brought with him the armoured car. Later he returned to his native Scotland. In 1924 he was arrested and extradited back to Ireland. His presence at Béal na mBláth has generated a legion of unsubstantiated conspiracy theories as to how Collins died. Another prisoner, John Hogan, was serving life for the killing of a soldier during the Civil War and he was probably the prisoners' OC, known as 'S O'S'.

The prisoners were divided among themselves and unable to adopt a coordinated strategy. At one stage during unsuccessful protests to gain 'political treatment', Hogan was left the sole participant. Political treatment was in effect prisoner of war status and included the rights to free association, to wear civilian clothes, and to do 'suitable' prison work, as well as having access to books and newspapers, and to have the 'cells left open until 9 p.m. every night'.[102]

Communication between the IRA and the prisoners in Maryborough was more limited than at Mountjoy. Most despatches went through 'J J' or 'Jack Jones', a senior IRA figure from the midlands, probably Jim Killeen. Killeen was the IRA's adjutant general in 1927. A man called Dray was probably one of the few IRA informants in the prison and may have been a warder or garda. J J wrote to IRA Headquarters: 'Dray is going to [join] the London police, where he will work for you, if [he would be] of any use. Can you do anything by way of reward for his services?'[103]

The life of Jack Keogh serves as an interesting, though unusual, example of a prisoner's experiences.

Jack Keogh

Commandant Keogh was a mid-level IRA officer who led an armed gang in the Ballinasloe area of Galway that attacked unarmed civic guards, frequently stripping them of their uniforms.[104] To the annoyance of the then chief of staff, Frank Aiken, these activities continued even after the end of the Civil War. Keogh was arrested in 1924 and sentenced to ten years' penal servitude.[105] Republicans later argued that the judge actually sentenced him to thirty years, as he recommended the three ten-year sentences were to run consecutively rather than concurrently, though this was disputed by the government.[106]

Keogh was incarcerated in Maryborough, where he spent periods in solitary confinement, on a diet of bread and water.[107] At one stage following a disturbance he was placed in a basement punishment cell. These 'cells were completely dark, and full of cockroaches', with an open sewer outside the cell door.[108] A water pipe burst, flooding his cell and leaving him shivering in two feet of cold water for several hours.[109]

He was one of the Irish prisoners 'adopted' by the Soviet organisa-tion, International Class War Prisoners' Aid, or Red Aid as it was more commonly known. Charlotte Despard was a leading light in the Irish section of Red Aid, which provided financial support to dependants of a small number of prisoners.[110] In March 1926, Red Aid in Smolensk wrote a long letter of support to 'Dear Comrade Jack Keogh', announcing it had been 'given the honour to become the patron of comradely help' to him. Showing a deep knowledge of Irish affairs, it commiserated with his predicament of having been thrown into jail by 'the English bourgeoise', and gave him the hope that he could secure his freedom through martyrdom: 'Right lives also in the tomb, lives and grows until the sides of the coffin shall explode.' In the meantime it would be their 'sacred duty ... to help you as much as possible'.[111]

Whether the letter contributed to it or not, by April Keogh had been certified as insane and was transferred to Dundrum Criminal Lunatic Asylum. Maud Gonne alleged he was 'the sixth victim driven mad in Maryboro' Jail within the last twelve months'. Shortly after his arrival in Dundrum, George Gilmore entered the asylum in a hijacked Clery's department store van and rescued him.

The IRA managed to get him to New York, where Connie Neenan wrote, 'he has cost us a lot of money', and by 'writing home too often [and] giving his address', his presence was detected by the US emigration authorities, who charged him with entering the country 'without [a] passport and being insane'. Given the large community of ex-IRA men in New York – 'there is too much company in New York for him' – Neenan felt that it would be best to send him to Chicago, where an IRA man, Johnny Connors, could get him a job.[112] There he settled for a while and in 1933 Neenan wrote to Twomey: '[I] have no news of Keogh, other than he is alive, working, and possibly giving the wife a run for her money.'[113]

Keogh, his wife Helen and their son and daughter moved in the 1930s to Florida.[114] Around 1940 he returned to Galway where he was employed as a workman. In 1945 at the age of forty-three he went to a chemist shop and purchased a bottle of the aptly named 'Kilcro' – for poisoning crows. A little later his body was found in a field with the empty bottle beside him. At the inquest the coroner stated that it contained sufficient strychnine to poison sixty people.[115] The jury returned a verdict of accidental death.

CHAPTER 6

The IRA in Britain

Do your utmost to carry out sabotage during [the general] strike. Destroy transport petrol supplies. Slash windows to start looting ... derail trains, destroy junctions and signal cabins ... Blacklegs may be ambushed.

IRA chief of staff to an officer in Britain

Things are bad [here in London]. The police [are] very active. Have destroyed most of my stuff and dumped the rest. If I am pinched nothing will be found on me.

Senior IRA officer in Britain to the chief of staff, Moss Twomey

The IRA's units and personnel in Britain were an important arm of the organisation. Weapons and explosives were smuggled across to Ireland, while men on the run from Ireland were given refuge. In the event of renewed conflict with Britain, these units were expected to carry out sabotage and arson attacks. Additionally, the IRA's senior officer, the OC. Britain, worked for Soviet military intelligence and assisted Soviet spies in London.

This chapter discusses IRA activities and organisation in Britain, including much information which hasn't been publicly disclosed before. The organisation's relationship with Soviet intelligence in London is covered in greater detail in Chapter 8.

Background

In the nineteenth century the Irish Republican Brotherhood (IRB) built an underground support network for radical Irish nationalism that stretched from America to Britain. This was later to form the template for much of the IRA's network. In Britain the IRB established itself among sections of the Irish community throughout the country, where its activities included smuggling weapons to Ireland. The IRB was a secretive revolutionary organisation, whose members were commonly known as Fenians and were blamed for a series of bombings in England. These attacks and the resulting police crackdown helped bring about the marginalisation and decline of the organisation. By 1914 there were just 117 members in England and 250 in Scotland.[1]

In 1919 with the outbreak of the Anglo-Irish War, IRA units began to spring up in Britain – these were usually started on local initiative but quickly came under the control of the reorganised IRB and Michael Collins in Dublin. In the words of Art O'Brien, Collins' right hand man in London, 'In so far as London was concerned, IRB and IRA were interchangeable terms.' At its peak there were up to 1,000 men enrolled in the IRA in Britain, though, as in Ireland, only a fraction would have actually reported for 'active duty'. During the Anglo-Irish War the IRA volunteers in Britain were relatively active when compared with many of their comrades in Ireland. The British IRA largely committed acts of arson and sabotage rather than attacks on police officers or soldiers; on one night in November 1920 over a hundred men from Liverpool burned nineteen buildings along the docks. Other actions followed intermittently, and in April 1921 there was a mysterious spate of window-smashing throughout the country. Thousands of windows were broken at night, before the attacks abruptly stopped. Though the culprits were never found, many suspected the IRA of being responsible.[2]

When the IRA split in 1922 (as a result of disagreement over the Anglo-Irish Treaty) the organisation in England largely disintegrated, never to fully recover. In September 1922 during the ensuing Civil War, P. A. Murray was appointed officer commanding (OC.) Britain, and sent to London to reorganise the IRA. Murray was a well-respected operative, whom Seán MacBride referred to as 'a competent Cork man, a pleasant person to work with, silent and efficient'.[3] He found 'the difficulty in England was great but the men were fine' and that 'sources of supply and new contacts and lines had to be built up from zero'.[4] The chief of staff, Liam Lynch, told Murray to lead a bombing campaign, by blowing up buildings and bridges. This, however, was well beyond the resources of the IRA there, and nothing came of it.[5] Instead Murray saw his role as one of supporting and supplying the IRA back in Ireland. In London he made contact with Soviet agents and this may have laid the basis for the later IRA–Soviet agreement.[6] A year after his arrival (and with the ending of the Civil War) Murray returned to Dublin and was appointed IRA adjutant general.[7]

In November 1924 the IRA's adjutant general inspected the units in England and Scotland and reported that none of the units were 'in a healthy condition' and that there was 'great dissatisfaction' among the men.[8]

The key IRA agent in the country was the OC. Britain. The very title 'OC. Britain' speaks to the pretensions of the IRA, and the Soviets found it amusing to think that there was an IRA officer commanding Britain (though in fairness, the IRA did include a full stop between 'OC' and 'Britain').[9] Virtually all significant IRA operations and activities in England were carried out by the OC, either acting alone or with a small group of associates. He smuggled over arms and explosives as well as military manuals, obtained false British passports, oversaw the IRA units in England, assisted escaped prisoners and men on the run from Ireland and gathered technical and military intelligence material for Soviet intelligence. He also forwarded money and despatches to Dublin, which arrived in Britain by way of transatlantic liners from New York. IRA leaders, including Moss Twomey, visited London regularly and met with him, while Seán MacBride came across from Paris. There was also an IRA intelligence system in Britain, though how well it functioned is difficult to say.

The true identity of the OC. Britain in 1926 isn't clear; the only clue I have is that he signed documents with initials, ending in 'M'. By September 1926 'M' was replaced by George. George signed his correspondence as 'HS'. However, in several instances (sometimes in cipher) he was also referred to as George, so this was most likely his real first name. There's evidence that he was George Power from Cork. Power had served in the North Cork brigade along with Moss Twomey during the Anglo-Irish War. In April 1926 Power was in London and Twomey wrote to 'M': 'George Power is in London. He would like to meet you and he may be returning soon. His address is: 6 Lanark Villas, Maida Vale. Call if you can spare time. I enclose a note for him.'[10]

The decline in the fortunes of the IRA in Britain, following its peak during the Anglo-Irish War, occurred as a result of several factors, including: the post-Treaty split and the outbreak of the Civil War in Ireland, the disbanding of the IRB in 1924 by the IRA, the general disillusionment following defeat in the Civil War and the subsequent lack of a coherent strategy. IRA members in Britain were also subjected to intense police scrutiny and officers regularly visited their workplaces, which presented a strong incentive to disassociate from the organisation. In March 1923 the police mounted a massive operation and arrested 110 suspected IRA members and sympathisers, who were then deported and interned in the Free State. Though the regulation under which this was carried out was later found invalid by the courts (allowing the deportees to return), the action significantly weakened the IRA and many of the deportees shied away from the movement.[11]

The IRA organisation in Britain

Aside from the OC. Britain and his assistants in London, the IRA in England was organised into three companies, each of which covered a specific region or area. Number 1 Area comprised London and the home counties, Number 2 Area Manchester, Salford and parts of Yorkshire and Number 3 Area Liverpool and the surrounding region. Additionally, there were small groups of IRA volunteers scattered in a handful of other cities. These units were under the command of the OC. Britain, though in practice he exercised little direct control and showed little interest.[12] There was also an IRA battalion in Scotland which reported directly to headquarters in Dublin.

The three English companies and the Scottish battalion were based in cities – London, Manchester, Liverpool and Glasgow – with major Irish immigrant communities, and which were also centres where the IRB had been strongest in the nineteenth century. While few of the older generation of IRB activists were likely to have remained, there is some indication that a degree of continuity was preserved by a tradition of membership running in families. This link with the past was perhaps strongest in Glasgow. However, there was a high turnover in membership, as many IRA volunteers were transient unskilled or semi-skilled workers, while new immigrants were continually arriving from Ireland.

Aside from petrol for arson, the primary weapon of the IRA in Britain was the revolver – the mainstay of urban guerrilla warfare. And the number of revolvers and volunteers in each centre gives an overview of the IRA's distribution and strength. In March 1926 the IRA reported that in London there were twenty-five 'reliable men', thirty-five revolvers with about 500 rounds of ammunition and no grenades or mines. Liverpool had fifteen to twenty 'good men' (plus some recent IRA immigrants who hadn't formally attached themselves to the company) and thirty revolvers. There were ten to fifteen revolvers in Newcastle, but the number of men there was unknown. There were four men, with five revolvers in Swansea. A small number of IRA volunteers worked at the port of Southampton, where they were able to assist with despatches sent from America, but they were reported to be unarmed, and at Portsmouth there were nine men and four revolvers. There were men with weapons in a few other cities, but they had lost touch with the IRA headquarters.[13]

A report prepared by Seán Russell for the Army Council in 1926 noted that 'for the past few years nobody appeared to have a clear conception of the reasons and objective for maintaining' the IRA in Britain. Russell summed up the situation: 'Without a clear idea and objective, there as elsewhere, it is impossible to rouse interest and get men to work wholeheartedly.' He went on to suggest that the justifications for having the units were primarily twofold: that they would be able to carry out operations in response to British attacks including 'economic warfare' against Ireland ('the Republic') or that they would gather intelligence, supply munitions to the IRA in Ireland and maintain communications with 'foreign countries'. Russell felt that they could 'act as an internal menace to the British Government and try to appear more [a] formidable force than they really are'. The skills needed by these volunteers were 'a good knowledge of engineering, explosives or chemistry and some proficiency in the use of short arms and grenades'.[14]

At the time, the IRA in Britain had only 189 members, and between 1926 and 1927 only ninety-three IRA members emigrating from Ireland requested to be transferred to one of the British companies. The membership was composed of a mixture of 'old timers' and recent IRA immigrants from Ireland; and particularly in Liverpool there was friction between both these groups, which had a serious adverse effect. However, there was a greater degree of support for the IRA among the Irish community in Britain than these figures suggest. Both Sinn Féin and Cumann na mBan had clubs in England, and social functions organised by these and other republican groups were on occasion able to attract large attendances.[15]

During the period 1924 to 1926, the IRA headquarters made an effort to reorganise the units, which cost a 'great deal of money'.[16] Officers who were sent over from Ireland worked with the men and appointed new officers locally. However, Twomey and his colleagues remained consistently dissatisfied, and there is no evidence that any of the British detachments were regarded as capable of effective action. The most that seems to have been expected was that they could have carried out some smuggling and low-level operations such as sabotage.

Seán Russell stated that the IRA in Britain was not worth the 'energy expended and labour involved in maintaining it'. One of the problems was that the IRA was originally conceived in Ireland as the legitimate army of the Irish Republic – with units and a command structure meant to parallel that of the British army – rather than as a secret revolutionary force. This relatively open form of organisation was ill-suited to the situation in Britain, where the members were a tiny minority within a hostile country and pursed by an effective police force. Therefore Russell recommended that 'a smaller force, highly organised and distributed in small groups, in as many cities and large towns as possible would be more effective. That these groups work in secret is essential, and an oath of secrecy might be administered to them. They should avoid as far as possible public connection with Republican civilian organisations and prominent Republicans.' Since many of the IRA's operatives were already known to the police, Russell suggested that the new organisation should be largely composed of volunteers who had emigrated after the Civil War. These recommendations presaged the successful cell structure eventually adopted by the Provisional IRA in the late 1970s.[17] In April 1927, however, Moss Twomey reiterated that the 'efforts to organise' the IRA in Britain had made 'little progress'.[18]

In the spring of 1926 the IRA in London carried out an attack that did little to enhance its reputation. In March the Conservative prime minister, Stanley Baldwin, attended a St Patrick's evening banquet. As 'M' (who was OC. Britain at the time) reported, 'St. Patrick's night operations carried out, but not as successful as desired owing to defective stuff. Two tickets for [the] Hotel Cecil were secured and there four bombs were ignited, but three failed and the other simply spluttered and was ineffective ... The bombs were hopeless and pitiable, considering the risk and expense incurred. One of the two men who went to the Hotel Cecil is detained.'[19] The 'bombs' were actually smoke bombs, making this episode little more than an elaborate schoolboy prank. The arrested volunteer, Hugh Daly, 'acting under official orders ... carried out his instructions to the letter and it was only defective material that rendered ineffective his cool daring. He ignited two "bombs" and throwing one of them quite near, to cover his retreat, he landed the other on the table in front of the prime minister. Had the "bombs" exploded as anticipated this plan would have upset the whole proceedings and in the ensuing confusion Daly would certainly have escaped. However ... owing to faulty mixing of the contents of the "bombs" the asphyxiating gas producing material was untouched and thus rendered abortive the whole operation.' The unfortunate Daly was seized by a Fr Evans and handed over to police.[20]

After his arrest, the police promptly released him 'with a view to the discovery of any colleagues, but [Daly] was rearrested as [he] was about to enter his lodgings'. Notwithstanding the £42 the IRA spent on his defence, he was sentenced to a year in prison.[21] The chief of staff agreed with 'M' that it was a rather expensive failure, though 'if things went as they were planned it would be worth it' and added: 'I hope you will not overlook anything that might be done for him [Daly].'[22] With actions of this calibre it's no wonder that morale amongst the IRA in London was poor!

The next planned attack was of far greater significance, an attempt to cause civil unrest under the cover of the 1926 general strike – the largest industrial dispute ever in British history. The strike grew out of a dispute involving the coal miners. In 1925, with falling prices for coal, the mine owners proposed to cut the miners' wages and increase their work hours. Not surprisingly, the miners resisted and threatened to strike.

Members of the British cabinet and the establishment were concerned that a strike could lead to civil disorder and provide a cover for communist agitation.[23] The *Irish Times* went so far as to say that the strike posed as grave a threat to Britain as did the outbreak of the First World War.[24] This was also a thought that crossed Moss Twomey's mind, and one that he found appealing.

In late April 1926 Twomey asked 'M': 'Do you think there will be a coal strike [sic]? If there is keep an eye on the possibilities arising out of it.'[25] With Stanley Baldwin ostensibly trying to negotiate a settlement, 'M' replied: 'I have it on good authority that both sides are anxious to avoid a strike, especially the miners. If there are any developments I will let you know.'[26]

However, negotiations broke down, and when the miners refused to accept the employers' terms they were locked out. The Trades Union Congress (TUC) reacted swiftly and called a general strike on 3 May – which was initially heeded by up to three million workers throughout Britain. Crowds took to the streets and though largely peaceful there was widespread disruption of basic services and transportation.[27]

On the first day of the strike Moss Twomey wrote to 'M': 'If [the] strike lasts beyond this week you should, if possible carry out sabotage operations in mines, or destroy any forms of transport being used by blacklegs. Power stations or gasworks could be destroyed. If lighting fails, slashing [sic] of windows would bring out the underworld and start looting and consequent suppression. If rioting begins and there are clashes between strikers and police or soldiers, grenades or arms could be used to start shooting. Blacklegs could be ambushed. Only absolutely close and reliable men to be employed, and stress need for care and secrecy. Do your best to do something big. All your other activities to be suspended if necessary.'[28] Two days later Twomey again wrote: 'I was hoping to hear from you saying you could carry out operations if desired ... You need not wait, begin when ready. [I] am disappointed [the] officer from here had not crossed over to [England to] assist you. [I] have sent a special messenger for him today. [I] am wondering if he will be able to cross now [because of the strike]. The QMG [Seán Russell] is in Glasgow. He has been ordered to carry out operations also. I suppose you could not get to him and concert plans. It would be good if you could do so. [I] will be anxious to hear of doings and progress of events generally. What a chance if we had been organised and prepared ... Petrol tin mines would be most destructive and are easily turned out.'[29]

The following day Twomey sent another urgent despatch to an officer with the pseudonym, 'Mr Davis': 'Do your utmost to carry out sabotage during [the] strike. Destroy transport petrol supplies. Slash [*sic*] windows to start looting. Petrol tin mines might be used effectively in many ways. Derail trains, destroy junctions and signal cabins ... Wherever there is [a] good [IRA] section, select the best men for operations. [The] men engaged must be most careful to avoid capture and use arms to get away. Enjoin absolute secrecy. Report progress only in cipher. Chief of staff. Acknowledge receipt at once.'[30] I'm unsure of the true identity of 'Mr Davis' but it's clear he was in contact with an IRA unit in Britain and may have been Seán Russell visiting Glasgow. Twomey wanted to keep any IRA involvement in instigating trouble absolutely secret and therefore the letter to 'Mr Davis' was unsigned, and his title 'chief of staff' was included at the end of the letter but only in cipher. Additionally, to confirm that the despatch had not been captured or intercepted by the police, he asked 'Mr Davis' to promptly report receipt of the letter. Interestingly, four days later there were three railway 'accidents' resulting in four deaths (three of which occurred in Edinburgh) and several injuries. Though *The Irish Times* wrote that: 'It is not suggested in any of the reports that the accidents were in any way due to the action of the men on strike', one must wonder whether the IRA or any other faction had a hand to play in this rather unusual cluster of mishaps.[31]

During the strike there were relatively minor confrontations between the strikers and the police with some stone throwing and window smashing and on occasion the police responded with baton charges – but no major incidents and (officially) no fatalities. The government deployed 80,000 troops which helped guard convoys of food and fuel, arrested thousands of workers, organised volunteers to keep the transportation system going and went on a propaganda offensive, accusing the strikers of trying to wreck the nation. The TUC was credited with helping to maintain order, and made a point of refusing a cheque for several thousand pounds from the All Russian Central Council of Trade Unions. In the face of the government's resolute determination the TUC unconditionally capitulated and called off the strike nine days later on 12 May. The miners were left to carry on the struggle on their own until the winter, when they returned to work on the mine owners' conditions.[32]

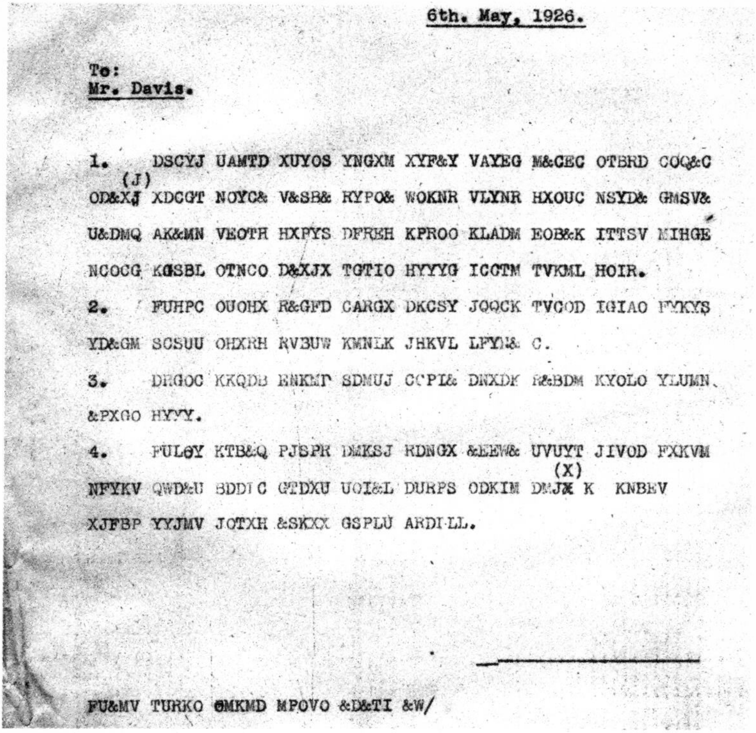

To:
Mr. Davis.

1.   DSCYJ UAMTD XUYOS YNGXM XYF&Y VAYEG M&CEC OTBRD COQ&C
(J)
OD&XJ XDCGT NOYC& V&SB& RYPO& WOKNR VLYNR HXOUC NSYD& GMSV&

U&DMQ AK&MN VEOTH HXPYS DFR&H KPROO KLADM EOB&K ITTSV MIHGE

NCOCG KGSBL OTNCO D&XJX TGTIO HYYYG ICGTM TVKML HOIR.

2.   FUHPC OUOHX R&GFD CARGX DKCSY JOQCK TVCOD IGIAO FYKYS

YD&GM SCSUU OHXRH RV3UW KMNLK JHKVL LFYN& C.

3.   DRGOC KKQDB ENKMT SDMUJ CCPI& DNXDK R&BDM KYOLO YLUMN

&PXGO HYYY.

4.   FULGY KTB&Q PJSPR DMKSJ RDNGX &EEW& UVUYT JIVOD FXKVM
(X)
NFYKV QWD&U BDDIC GTDXU UOI&L DURPS ODKIM DMJK K KNBEV

XJFBP YYJMV JOTXH &SKXX GSPLU ARDI-LL.

FU&MV TURKO OMKMD MPOVO &D&TI &W/

Figure 21. Despatch from the chief of staff to 'Mr Davis' in Britain ordering him to provoke rioting and anarchy under cover of the general strike. This operation was so secret that the author signed his rank in cipher. 'Mr Davis' may have been an alias for Seán Russell.

> Do your utmost to carry out sabotage during [the general] strike. Destroy transport petrol supplies. Slash [sic] windows to start looting. Petrol tin mines might be used effectively, in many ways. Derail trains, destroy junctions and signal cabins.
>   If rioting takes place, arms or grenades can be used, [in order] to start shooting. Blacklegs may be ambushed.
>   Wherever there is [a] good [IRA] section, select [the] best men for operations.
>   Men engaged [in the fighting] must be most careful to avoid capture, and use arms to get away. Enjoin absolute secrecy. Report progress only in cipher.
> Chief of Staff
>   Acknowledge receipt at once

These IRA documents illustrate the organisation's tactics for provoking a breakdown in law and order. It is interesting that there is reference to the smashing of windows, which was a fairly common form of protest at the time, having been employed by suffragettes a few years earlier. This lends credibility to historian Peter Hart's suggestion that the IRA was behind the mysterious campaign of window-smashing that occurred throughout Britain in April 1921.[33] The IRA was clearly unprepared to take advantage of the opportunity presented by the strike, and Moss Twomey was scrambling to put a plan together. If the IRA did indeed mount any attacks —and the railway accidents must be viewed with some suspicion – they weren't officially blamed and they had little effect on the outcome. There's no further mention of the strike in the documents I've seen, though there's a break in the paper trail, with no documents in cipher addressed to or from Britain after 6 May until they resume again in late July 1926.

Intelligence activities

One of the goals of the IRA's reorganisation in Britain was to develop an intelligence network throughout the country. The director of intelligence asked intelligence officers in Ireland to collect the names and addresses of all the volunteers and sympathetic civilians from their districts who had emigrated to Britain. In particular the IRA wanted the names of potential friends in influential professions and in jobs associated with transportation and service, such as members of the clergy, doctors, journalists, civil servants, domestic servants, members of the military and police, waiters, dock workers, seamen, hotel workers and transportation workers.[34]

Along these lines, Twomey wrote to the IRA OC in Cork 1 brigade that: 'There is a detective named O'Reilly in Scotland Yard, a native of Youghal [County Cork] I believe. Quain of Youghal is his uncle, and the officer in charge of [the] Volunteers [is] his cousin ... Quain could be sent to London [to enable us to make contact with O'Reilly] ... This matter is so important I would like you to deal with it yourself.'[35] Meanwhile the IRA in the Irish midlands reported that a person by the name of Dray was going to join the London police and 'will work for you'.[36]

Twomey also reported to the adjutant in north Mayo that: 'In London I met Paul O'Reilly. He said [that] there is a man named Gallagher, a native of Achill, employed in the War Office there. Will you please make inquiries as soon as possible about this man and find out if by any chance he would give information to us. An introduction to or even a personal visit to him by a friend may be necessary ... A Volunteer named 'Ginnelly', also a native of Achill, met Gallagher and Gallagher told him [that] Lavelle – [a] schoolteacher [from] Achill – was a British spy. You should have this person looked up, that is if he has not already come under your notice – P. [Paul O'Reilly] thought he had. Paul is of [the] opinion [that] Gallagher would not work with Ginnelli [*sic*]. As unfortunately the latter proclaimed very openly how his sympathies lay and this would naturally make G. [Gallagher] nervous. Some other link would be necessary.'[37]

The IRA's intelligence officer in Liverpool met a potentially valuable contact when he was serving time in prison: '[The] I.O. [intelligence officer] Liverpool says he met in Maidstone Prison, Todd Sloan [of] 2 Crown Street, Tidal Basin, London E 16 ... [The intelligence officer] alleges he [Sloan] is a communist and has knowledge of government ammunition stocks.' Moss Twomey suggested to George that if 'this man would be useful you would perhaps be able to get an introduction to him through [the] Liverpool officer'.[38] George replied: 'Of course it would be useful in fact very useful but first of all I would want to know how our friend got into touch with him, how long he knew him, how much he knows about him, if he [can] vouch for his genuineness etc. Until I get a more detailed report it would be very indiscreet of me to approach him even with an introduction. This place [London] at the present time is packed with touts, so we will have to be careful.' This exchange shows how conscious George was of security, even more so than Twomey. No further mention was made of Todd Sloan, so it's uncertain as to whether he provided assistance or not.

Todd Sloan was a London dock worker who became a prominent 'radical agitator', fighting for the rights of the unemployed. However, in the 1930s he had a road to Damascus experience and joined the crusading Christian, Oxford Movement, which exhorted people to turn their backs on materialism and prepare 'for a world war against selfishness'. He rejected the divisive class warfare of his past with its 'gospel of hate' and embraced the movement's call for 'God control' of nations to preserve peace in Europe.[39]

In March 1927 Twomey asked George: 'Do you know [the] residences of [the] hangman and [his] assistant? Could these be got if we wanted to? In certain circumstances this may become necessary.'[40]

George replied: 'The following is the hangman's address: 19 Cover-dale Street [*sic*], Hyde Road, Ardwick, Manchester.'[41] Ironically it was on Hyde Road in 1867 that an IRB group rescued a comrade from a prison van, in the process shooting dead a policeman. Based on 'doubtful evidence', three Irishmen were later convicted of the murder and were executed by hanging, becoming thereafter enshrined in the republican pantheon as the 'Manchester Martyrs'.[42]

The IRA in Liverpool reported that it could 'procure from [a] printer's staff, [that are] friendly, [a] copy [of] police reports and CID cards with [an] official stamp'.[43]

Smuggling

From October 1926 to December 1927, George, as OC. Britain, sent across to Ireland shipments of explosives, assorted munitions and a motor-bike – along with military manuals, books and journals. It's quite probable that there were other deliveries which were not listed in these documents. In addition, weapons and explosives were likely smuggled from Liverpool and Glasgow, some of which probably went directly to individual IRA units rather than to Seán Russell in Dublin. The history of a few of these consign-ments illustrates the IRA's *modus operandi* and its smuggling network.

In October 1926 Moss Twomey asked George for gun cotton and potassium chlorate, the latter being the primary ingredient of most of the explosives manufactured by the IRA: '[I'm] asking you to send on the gun cotton at once, if possible ... [and] what about the pot. [potassium] chlorate you were to get?'[44] A few days later Twomey arrived in London to meet with George, where he passed on instructions from Seán Russell detailing how the consignment should be sent and packaged and to whom it should be addressed, and telling him to give Russell two days' notice be-fore the arrival of the explosives at the North Wall at Dublin port.

A little later George sent word to Russell to expect the goods on 25 or 26 October.[45] However, he wasn't actually able to send the case until 29 October and failed to update Russell. Finally, on 1 November George wrote to Twomey that the explosives had been sent, and asked him to confirm receipt by sending a cryptic telegram: 'Joseph Barnes sent a case of goods on [to Dublin] last Friday. [The] delay [was] unavoidable. When it arrives, wire Mrs O'D. just saying 'congratulations' and sign it 'ciss' [sister]. Then I will send [on] the balance.'[46] Meanwhile Russell was furious with George for not adhering to the agreed procedure: '[I] had my man on the docks on the look out as usual, who reported each day he could get no trace, so when I had given up all hope it [finally] arrived' on 2 November – eight days late and 'without the required 2 days notice'. Russell didn't send the cryptic telegram to Mrs O'D, as he didn't want George to send the second half of the consignment to the same address. Due to George's 'bungling', Russell was worried that the address may have been compromised and he had to 'send a new address, which meant completely new arrangements'.[47]

Meanwhile, since George hadn't received the telegram from Dublin he had no way of knowing whether the package had gone through and so wrote to GHQ: 'Could you find out if it did arrive [?] It is a pity that such an important matter received so little attention.'[48] Given Russell's displeasure, this was a rather inopportune remark, and Russell sarcastically retorted: '"It's a pity" says H.S. "that such an important matter received so little attention" – I quite agree.'[49]

In February 1927, Twomey next asked George for a few hundredweight of potassium chlorate, a hundredweight being equivalent to eight stone or fifty kilograms: 'Can you possibly get at once a few cwt [hundredweight] [of] pot. chlorate or as much as you can? Consign it to Messrs O'Connor Cycle Agents, Abbey Street, Dublin as cycle parts. Give [the] QMG a few days notice previous [sic] to despatch. Let me know what you hope to do in this matter.'[50] George replied: 'I can get as much of this stuff as you want, but at the present time I have no place to store or pack [it] in [sic]. If you have any suggestions to make I will be glad to have them or if you could let me have an address where casks could be sent to, it would make it much easier for me.'[51]

If George felt he could send casks of explosives through Dublin port without them being apprehended, he must have doubted the competence of the customs officers or known that they were either sympathetic to or in the pay of the IRA. Even Twomey wasn't completely averse to the idea of sending the explosives in casks rather than disguising them: 'Could [the] stuff be made up so as not to excite [the] suspicion casks would? QMG may be able to arrange to receive casks. So [I] will see him and he will let you know. We require some very soon.'[52]

In the end George bought two hundredweight [100 kilograms] of potassium chlorate for £5 and 10 shillings and, having repacked it with the help of a friend, addressed it to O'Connor's Cycles, from a John Brow in Highgate.[53] The supplier's name, 'John Brow', was probably a non-existent cover invented by George. Three days later, in a cryptic message Twomey acknowledged receipt of the explosives: 'Noted. QMG has full info about this.'[54]

In April Twomey again wrote: 'We will require more pot[assium] chlorate, at least five cwts [hundredweights] and up to half a ton.'[55] There's no further documentation on this batch and presumably it therefore went over without a hitch. In June Twomey requested more 'stuff' or explosives: 'The address to which you will send [the] stuff for [the] QMG is: Mrs Sweeney, Fruiterer and Greengrocer, 5 Harold's Cross, Dublin. Try to make it appear like fruit.'[56] George felt that this would be a challenge and appeared to want to send it over again labelled as bicycle parts: 'It will be hard to make arrangements at this end to fit in with it. Is it not possible to get one similar to the last?'[57] Moss Twomey wrote back that he'd try and get a 'more suitable address'.[58] Most of the correspondence between Twomey and George for the next few months is missing and there's no further mention of smuggling explosives until Twomey reports on a shipment that was captured by the customs in Dublin. As this occurred three months after the last communication regarding 'Mrs Sweeney', it was probably a different consignment.

On 21 September Twomey wrote: '[The] packet you advised [sic] to [the] QMG has not turned up. Can you make inquiries there of [the] railway or [the] carriers? Send me [the name of the railway] station [it was] booked from, [the] route and what you described [the] contents as.'[59] A few days later Twomey updated George: '[The] QMG informs me [that the] packet you sent was opened by customs here and recognised as explosives. He believes he can get it without trouble as he is fixing up with [a] friendly official.' Twomey put the blame on George: 'This occurred through [the] long delay in arrival [as] our agent was not there. Send by return details of contents of [the] consignment. This should always be sent. I hope that this will not upset any of your arrangements there. I shall let you know what the result of the negotiations will be.'[60]

George replied that the shipment 'contained two drums of phosphorus [an incendiary agent], one dozen adaptors for twelve bore shotguns, one galvanometer for testing mine circuits and two tins of aircraft signalling cartridges. The latter I had in stock for a long time'. The container 'was described as cycle parts [and] sent by Saunders from Camden Goods ... to the last address given by [the] QMG. Sorry [I] cannot make enquiries at this end as [the] address given did not exist.' George was hopeful that the customs officer whom Russell was working with would keep quiet about the seizure: 'If the matter is referred to the head-office it will certainly affect my arrangements.'[61] Twomey then asked for some ammunition: 'If [the] stuff held up is received, we will require some .22 ammunition from you, so get it.'[62] The fate of this shipment remains a mystery, as the last mention of it is a sentence from George: 'P.S. I hope you were able to recover that packet.'[63]

In addition to explosives, the IRA were able to easily come by revolvers on the black market. In April 1926 Twomey asked 'M' to 'purchase the sixty Webleys [revolvers] for £30. Keep these for Britain.'[64] 'M' however had some difficulty getting 'silencers for revolvers'.[65] In mid 1926 Jim Killeen, of the IRA's headquarters staff, was arrested trying to smuggle revolvers from England and was sentenced to six months in Pentonville prison, London.[66]

In October George bought half a dozen adaptors for Webley revolvers. An adaptor is a device which allows a weapon to fire bullets of a different calibre.[67] Given the IRA's limited supply of ammunition this was a rather useful accessory. He sent the adaptors over in different consignments. On one occasion an IRA courier was caught by customs in Dublin with three adaptors and confidential IRA despatches; however, only the adaptors were confiscated and she was allowed to go free with the despatches.[68] Around the same time George sent another two adaptors sealed in a box to an IRA safe address and these got through safely.[69]

Twomey wrote to George that: 'Arms and ammunition can be purchased from Horace Soley and Co. 3 Jewin Street, London.'[70] George replied: 'That man [Horace Soley] will not let you or any other person have stuff unless you can produce the necessary papers. Then he would sell as much as he could get hold (at a price).'[71]

One of the more unusual items George sent over was a motorbike that was required by the IRA in Armagh. In April 1926 Twomey wrote to 'M': 'Regarding [the] motorcycle you wished to dispose of, you could send it to: Mr H Magee, Motor and Cycle Agent, Edward Street, Lurgan. Give me notice before sending [it]. Make a good bargain. I presume this can be sent through [to Northern Ireland] direct. Do not send except it is the good value you represented it to be.'[72] The next mention of a motorbike was in January 1927, when Twomey asked George if he had already sent the bike. Presumably this was the same bike that was referred to almost a year earlier. On 7 February, George wrote that he would 'send it some time this week'.[73] A month later the ever efficient George wrote that the bike 'will be sent on Monday the 7th [of March]'.[74] Finally, in mid March, the IRA commander in Armagh reported: 'I received the bike and had £1 3 [shillings] carriage [shipping fee] to pay, had also to get the back stand fixed, it was smashed, had also the get the foot boards and back brake fixed and she isn't going yet. I think she needs overhauled [sic]. I have told the mechanic to put her in going order.' He ended with 'P.S. There was no lamp on the bike either.'[75] Given the state of the bike on its arrival in Armagh, either George was cheated when he bought it, or he got a bargain and pocketed some of the IRA's money for himself.

The OC also sent over a steady supply of military books. These were meant both for Moss Twomey and the headquarters staff, and also for the libraries supposed to be kept by individual IRA units. In March 1926 the chief of staff sent an order for a total of 134 training manuals, ranging from twelve copies each of *Practical Musketry Instructions* and *Machine Gun Training* to one copy of *Smoke Tactics* by Lieutenant Colonel Worrall.[76] Twomey found *The Journal of the Royal United Services Institute for Defence Studies* to be 'quite good' and asked George to send it on to him each quarter.[77] The Royal United Services Institute is a highly influential advisory authority to the Ministry of Defence.[78]

Twomey regularly read books on military strategy and among those he requested were: *The Wilson Diaries* by Field Marshal Sir Henry Wilson and *The Science of War*.[79] Field Marshal Wilson was chief of the imperial general staff in 1918. After the First World War he retired from the military to become a Unionist MP for North Down, only to be assassinated in the streets of London by two members of the IRA in 1922 [who were later hanged].[80] *The Science of War* was a collection of essays by an eminent British military historian, Colonel G. F. Henderson, who argued against the dangers of 'untrained' civilian leaders who 'overruled Generals as they pleased' during time of war.[81] This was a line of argument likely to have found great sympathy among the IRA's leadership!

George may have simply borrowed some of the books from a library, as Twomey once wrote: 'I got those two books you sent me, for which many thanks. Mention if I am to return them to you at once, but I will have them read within a week if this will do.'[82]

George also had some issues of the IRA's paper *An tÓglach* printed in London and then sent over to Dublin for distribution. *An tÓglach* was the official organ of the IRA and contained helpful advice on military tactics. It differed from the more widely available *An Phoblacht*, which was a newspaper meant for the general public. In October 1926 George wrote: 'I sent 1,000 copies of An tOglach [over] during the week. Did ye receive them?'[83] A few months later George sent a 'packet of papers weighing eleven pounds to Parsons' [Newsagents], Baggot Street [Dublin]. Let me know when they arrive and I will send the remainder.'[84]

Passports

One task that the OC. Britain was very successful at was procuring false passports or, to be more accurate, passports in false names. These passports were needed by IRA and Sinn Féin delegates and emissaries travelling abroad and by volunteers emigrating to America who were ineligible for legitimate passports; on occasion the IRA also provided passports to Soviet agents.

The simplest way to create a fake passport was to merely swap out the photograph on a legitimate passport. Seán MacBride did this for Éamon de Valera when he removed the photograph from a priest's passport and substituted one of de Valera dressed in clerical garb.[85]

Another method was to submit a passport application form in a false name to an office of the travel agents, Thomas Cook and Sons, who then forwarded the application to the government's passport office. The address given for the applicant was that of an IRA sympathiser. The application was also signed by a referee, verifying the identity of the applicant. Passport referees were expected to be a designated 'respectable' member of the community such as a priest or medical doctor. On one occasion the IRA forged the name of an alcoholic doctor, Dr Gately, and on other occasions a sympathetic priest signed the form. Presumably the forms were accompanied by a forged birth certificate. When the passport was issued, an IRA agent, giving a false name, collected it at the travel agents.

This was the technique used to get a passport, issued in the name of 'Ethel Chiles', for the Soviet agent Kate Gussfeldt. Gussfeldt was arrested soon after her arrival in Britain and the British secret service or MI5 (who had an informer in the London IRA) were aware of the IRA's involvement. They falsely believed that the passport scheme was a 'private venture', orchestrated by IRA officers in Britain to enrich themselves and wasn't approved by GHQ in Dublin. On her passport application 'Ethel Chiles' gave her address as 62 Rendlesham Road, which also happened to be that of the Woods family, 'whose connection with the Irish Republican Movement is well known'. MI5 reported that Gussfeldt was 'an important agent ... in connection with the Irish Republican Intelligence Service'. After her arrest and brief imprisonment Gussfeldt was deported back to Germany (for further details see the Appendix 2).[86]

One person who acted as a referee for IRA volunteers was Fr Martin McKenna, an Irish Catholic priest in Britain. In 1926, after the police discovered his association with the IRA, he sent a letter to 'M': 'I tried to get into touch [with IRA headquarters] through Bob, but did not succeed. The [British] authorities got at my superiors and ordered me to leave the country. [I'm] barred [from the] USA and [I have] fixed [up] New Zealand. I have booked [passage] for New Zealand via Canada and am going home at once ... It [the trouble] is all about [the] passport I spoke of. Also evidently my name was used extensively for recommendations.'[87] Before leaving for New Zealand Fr McKenna wanted to contact GHQ in Dublin and also 'touched you [OC. Britain] for some cash and stated it was wanted for official purposes'.[88] Twomey wrote directly to the priest: 'Dear Rev. Father, I ... am very sorry indeed to learn what has occurred. I believe you would like to see some of us before you would leave … If you come to Dublin call to 23 Suffolk Street and ask to see Art O'Connor [president of Sinn Féin]. If by any chance he should not be there, call to Miss O'Donel [Peadar O'Donnell's sister-in-law], 24 Eccles Street.'[89]

Twomey wrote to 'M' that the prominent Sinn Féin leader, Fr Michael O'Flanagan, required a passport: 'Fr O'Flanagan may call to O'Donoghue's next week to meet you, regarding a passport. If he wants a camouflaged one proceed to get it, but tell him it may take time. Do not give it to him until you hear from me.'[90] The reference to a 'camouflaged' passport probably refers to one issued in a false name. 'M' replied to Twomey: 'I note your instruction.'[91] On another occasion Twomey asked George for passports for himself and Seán Russell for their proposed trip to Moscow in 1927.

In September 1927 Twomey told George that the 'OC [of the] Dublin Brigade is going to London on holidays. He will be staying at Ernie Noonan's. Go to see him after Sunday. I am giving him a few messages for you.' The Dublin OC was most likely Mick Price, and he was to bring with him photographs of a colleague who needed a passport: 'Get [a] passport for [the] person he has photos of. If you can, keep one photo safely. Get [visas for the] usual countries on [the] passport.'

Welfare

Not surprisingly, given the economic hardships they faced, IRA men in Britain sought financial support from the organisation – while additionally men on the run and escaped prisoners sent over to England had to be cared for until they could find work. The OC. Britain tried to organise accommodation and work for the most deserving cases. Additionally, there were IRA men temporarily in Britain on their way to America. Aside from *bona fide* cases of hardship, there were also the malingerers and chancers.

One of the latter was Dennehy, a veteran who came to England and soon sought charity from the IRA. He was possibly a member of the Dennehy family of Midleton, County Cork, several members of which had been actively involved in the IRA during the Anglo-Irish War.[92] Within days of his arrival in Britain, 'M' had found him bed and board free of charge in Southampton, but he 'became cheeky and not behaving as he ought to, he was compelled to quit' three weeks later. 'M' then got him a job at the seaside resort of Ilfracombe, where he received £1 and 5 shillings a week including accommodation: 'He worked in this job for 3 months and was sacked on being discovered reading the private correspondence of the manager.' 'M' yet again got him a job, this time in a hotel — with a weekly salary of £1, living in. However, 'the chef when calling him one morning pulled the clothes off him and getting out of bed he struck the chef, who called the boss and had him sacked.' Returning penniless to 'M' he received £10.[93] Dennehy sent word of his supposed plight back home and the influential P. A. Murray was enlisted to seek help from Twomey.[94] On hearing 'M's' side of the story Twomey remarked: 'I am sure you are not sorry to be rid of this chap though you may take it for granted he will have a lot of moans — but that doesn't matter.'[95]

Another volunteer who looked to the IRA for support was 'Ted', who was a 'very reliable person' employed full time by the OC. Britain since 1925. His job was probably to assist George in collecting equipment and information on military technology for the Soviets. However, in November 1926 when the Russians decreased their monthly payment he was let go. George felt that 'Ted' had 'been treated very fairly and got a month's notice'. He added: 'Now he does not seem to want work and thinks he is entitled to the £3 [per week] when out of work', 'some months ago he got married and since then he seems to be all out of cash'. A distraught 'Ted' wrote to Moss Twomey complaining that because of his work for the IRA he couldn't get another job; he had no references, no insurance cards, and Scotland Yard detectives had called to places where he had worked previously, leaving word to phone them if he was sighted. He added: 'If I should get a job where they won't bother about a reference, it means the job is no good, that they can't keep a staff. I should get at the most a £1 per week and a pound a week isn't much use to a married man.' He went on to ask Twomey to pay or loan him the passage to America. Twomey wrote to George: 'Do not allow him to pester you. Make very clear to him that you are not to be intimidated.'[96] Twomey wrote a polite and sympathetic letter to 'Ted', but behind his diplomacy the bottom line was that he was on his own: 'I am very sorry to hear of the position in which you find yourself. I assure you that it was sheer financial necessity [that] compelled us to dispense with your services on whole time work. Here at home we were compelled to cut down staff to the barest minimum and we can only afford to maintain a couple of whole time officers for the whole organization. If it were possible I would be very glad to help you out of your difficulties but I regret I am not able to do so now. I assure you we appreciate your services in the past and I hope you will continue to give voluntary [sic] what services you can to the organization.'[97]

A third example was that of an IRA prisoner rescued from Mountjoy who had 'lung trouble', presumably TB. Twomey wrote to 'M' that he 'is now fit to leave hospital [in Ireland] ... Could you fix him up with a friend outside [of] London [in the] south of England if possible. [His] name will be 'Courtney'. Send the arrangements you made. I will be responsible for expenses of upkeep. Get a good place, but as cheap as possible.'[98] Worried about his health, Twomey wanted him looked after in the south of England, where the fresh air and brighter climate was regarded as more therapeutic than the air of the inner cities or the north. 'M' reported back that he was able to find him a 'suitable place'.[99]

Twomey went on to request 'M's' assistance to get 'Courtney' to America, despite being barred from entry, both as an escaped prisoner and as suffering from TB: 'Would there be much difficulty in this man getting a passport for America? [The] doctor says it would now be hard to detect he has lung trouble. It may be as well if you moved to get him one when he arrives [in London].'[100] 'M' replied: 'I don't expect any difficulty [in getting him a passport]',[101] and five months later in October 1926, he reached the US, though the IRA representative in New York, 'Jones', complained that he had to spend $150 for his train fare to the coast, presumably to California, where he could benefit from the hot dry air. 'Jones' went on to grumble that 'in future no man should be sent here officially unless it's absolutely necessary.' Andy Cooney replied from GHQ: 'This is terrible. This man has now cost [us] sufficient to keep the whole thing going for three months, and notwithstanding this, he complains of being badly treated. Make it perfectly clear that outside of the $150 he will not get one cent more. I will have the total cost compiled and sent [to] you in case there are any complaints.'[102]

George helped others, including the veteran whom he gave a loan to, and who later claimed he couldn't repay it as it was stolen from him.[103] George was reluctant to press him, and wrote to Twomey: 'You have no idea how much this man has done for the movement and I assure you that I do not like to have to ask him for the refund of the other money, but I suppose it must be done.'[104] In the end Twomey largely agreed to back down, writing to George: 'We do not wish to unduly press him but I certainly think he should repay the amount of the refund [sic] of the ticket.'[105]

Another man on the run (who was likely Stephen Murphy, an escaped prisoner) had difficulty initially getting a job and Twomey wrote: 'Send Murphy home if he has no job or [an] immediate chance of one.'[106] However, George reported: 'I got him fixed up in a job ... and he has been working every day since. The job is likely to last at least twelve months, if he cares to stick it. The pay is 1/3 [1 shilling 3 pennies] per hour.'[107]

Men on the run had to be constantly vigilant as the gardaí were known to work closely with their colleagues in Britain. The Manchester IRA reported that a 'CID' officer from Enniscorthy was in Britain looking for men on the run, while the IRA's Liverpool intelligence officer wrote that the Free State had agents in the city and in addition had men on board boats looking for evidence of weapons smuggling.[108] The Garda Special Branch monitored the post in Ireland, and 'men on the run in England who have been foolish enough to send photos to their friends in this country [Ireland] have had their photos abstracted and [the] letters arrived without them.'[109]

In May 1927 two IRA volunteers, Hugh Rogers and Frank Boyle, escaped from Belfast prison and Scotland Yard detectives suspected they were in hiding in London, in the Camden Town and Southgate neighbourhood where 'they are known to have associates'.[110] In the Lake District, police arrested Jim Ryan, who was wanted in connection with the killing of Garda Ward during the IRA's barrack raids and was extradited to stand trial in Ireland.[111]

George, IRA Officer Commanding, Britain

George's tenure as OC. Britain was largely marked by disappointments and failures and he had a testy relationship with many back in GHQ. In November 1926 he angered Seán Russell by his failure to follow standard procedure on sending a consignment of explosives to Dublin. The Soviet agent 'James' was critical of the support and information he was getting in London and soon afterwards the Russians decreased their monthly payments, setting off an immediate financial crisis. Andy Cooney rushed to London to meet with 'James'; Cooney was obliged to go as Twomey was serving a short time in prison in Dublin. The Russians however were non-committal to Cooney and refused to either adequately fund the IRA or to formally break off the agreement.

It was in these circumstances that headquarters sent George a letter instructing him to close up his station and report back to Ireland before Christmas. Though unsigned, it was most likely written by Andy Cooney, who took over the running of the IRA during the period of Twomey's imprisonment. Cooney proposed that following George's departure the IRA should continue a smaller operation in London, which was needed to smuggle explosives, get false passports, etc. He recommended to George that: 'A substitute to do odd jobs, that may be necessary, is advisable ... He should be put in touch with [the] method of procuring passports, also with all [the] people useful for getting men away. All available particulars [concerning] resources for procuring stuff [explosives] should be supplied to him. None of the London crowd I met appear to be suitable [as your replacement] with the exception of O'Duffy ... Whether [you're] leaving [London] for good or not, call to Dublin on [your] way home for [the Christmas] Holidays ... Do your utmost to conserve cash, we are in desperate straights just at present ... Some of the stuff you have will be needed here if you are leaving, particularly the camera. You could bring this over with you.'

George replied that he was unable to recommend a replacement: 'I don't think any of the present crowd would do.' He felt that he couldn't introduce his contacts (for getting explosives, etc) to any substitute: 'As you know I was dealing with all my connections as an individual – and all connections were outside the organ ation [the IRA], so you see I could not possibly introduce another to them.' He continued: 'It is not my intention to remain at home [in Ireland]: as you know there is nothing there for me to do. I will have to try and find some sort of employment here; and while here I will be only glad to help in any way I possibly can. Unless

I receive the money due [me, from headquarters] … for books etc. I will not be able to go home at Xmas.'[112]

George visited Ireland at Christmas and met Twomey in Dublin on 29 December (after his release from prison). Twomey told him 'to remain [in London] for the present and until you hear from me'.[113] George promptly returned but Twomey 'was unwell at home for three weeks after Xmas' and failed to send George his monthly allowance.[114] Twomey finally wrote towards the end of January: 'I am rather disappointed I have not had any communication from you for some time … Let me know when writing if you require cash urgently and if so how much.'[115] A frustrated George replied: 'Not having received an acknowledgement of recent communications I thought it better to wait until such time as I knew that you were receiving them.' He added that the Soviets had not made a decision about the relationship but in the interim had given him £150.[116]

Finally George wrote to Twomey: 'I wonder if you know that a communication from your Dept. was sent to me on the 8th of December 1926, instructing me to finish up, to get rid of any whole-time men, offices etc, and to send to Dublin all the books, papers etc relating to me [sic] work here and that I was at liberty to leave when ready to do so. For that month I received no money from GHQ for any purpose, and GHQ did not seem to trouble about any liabilities which I may have had to meet. As a result I had to give notice all round, but as you will understand, this is not a business that you can bring to an end in a few days and I was trying to bring things to a finish when I received your [letter in January] … asking me why I had not reported on certain things. Now the whole thing is so complicated, unbusiness-like and unsatisfactory that I cannot see my way to continue any longer.'[117]

Twomey reminded him that they had met in Dublin subsequent to the letter and that he had also been ill in January, but he was also fed up with George: 'From the attitude you have taken up I am quite agreeable if you wish to square up everything [in London].'[118] However, George got over his anger and continued his work.

In the meantime Twomey asked the IRA's finance and accounts officer to investigate George's finances, writing: 'These accounts appear to be very mixed up.'[119] Confusion was caused by the way George transferred money between his accounts, one he called the General Army account, another the D/I [Department of Intelligence] account.[120] Finally Twomey asked him to 'make out the full [D/I] account' from its inception twelve months previously, and in his quietly persistent way added: 'You need not unduly rush yourself in doing this.'[121]

George was very careful with his personal security and made sure that anyone wishing to contact him should go to the appropriate meeting place or contact address. In February he wrote to Twomey: 'A lady called at my office in ... [word deleted from the text] enquiring for me and called again on the following day and told the liftboy that she was from Ireland and wanted to see me. Can you give me an idea as to who she was?'[122] Another time Twomey told Seán MacBride to call on George, but George felt that the address he gave him shouldn't have been given to MacBride: 'Only one, the Dr [Andy Cooney] can be trusted, all the others are very talkative but ye seem to think differently. It is useless taking precautions if ye insist in doing things like this.'[123]

On 12 May 1927 Scotland Yard raided the All-Russian Cooperative Society, Ltd. (Arcos) headquarters in London, which was the centre for Soviet espionage in Britain. With follow-up police raids occurring across the city, George reported that 'things are bad here' and that he had destroyed incriminating supplies in his possession.[124]

In October Twomey wrote to George that Andy Cooney was going to move temporarily to London to complete his medical studies: 'Mr Smith [Andy Cooney] intends going to London to complete his studies. [He] will probably cross [over] this weekend. He wants you to think of one or two suitable places where he might stay, he will call to Number 8, perhaps he could stay there. Fix nothing definite about digs until he sees you.'[125] George was unhappy with Cooney's presence and felt that headquarters had sent him to oversee his work; in addition, there could already have been animosity between the two arising from the previous letter sent to George telling him to close up his London operation.

George complained to Twomey that Cooney had told him that: 'GHQ are in a better position to know what to do than I am, and [he] wanted to know if I wanted to be a dictator in this business. I told him I could bat anytime I liked. He asked if this was a threat and said the work would get on very well without me. I would like a reply to this ... as soon as possible, and if your opinions are the same as his the sooner you let me know the better. I told you once I would have nothing more to do with 'Smith' and can give many reasons, if you want them. I don't like to be offensive and will reserve a lot more than I have to say. There is one thing I would like you to know; that I have forgotten more about this work than 'Smith' is ever likely to learn.'[126] George was foolish to think he could get Twomey to side with him against Cooney. Twomey replied: 'I have nothing to say to any private quarrel 'Smith' and you may have and I am not interfering. You have no right to demand from me what my opinion is on any views expressed by 'Smith'. No more than on those expressed by any resident in London, say Mr Baldwin [the prime minister]. I am not afraid of dictators as they can be disposed of in a certain way.' Following this unusually aggressive outburst from Twomey, he ended in a more conciliatory fashion in non-crypted text: 'I am very sorry for this friction and I feel that it could be avoided if there were a little "give and take" on both sides.'[127]

George's correspondence ends in January 1928 with what is most likely a reference to Andy Cooney or possibly Seán MacBride. Writing to Moss Twomey he comments: 'Your infallible friend called and gave me your messages. I thought I told you, and I know I told him that he was to get in touch with me through other channels.'[128]

The Merchant

One of the shady characters that George dealt with was an arms dealer named Fitzgerald, whom the IRA referred to as the 'Merchant'.

In 1926, the IRA in London ordered an assortment of equipment from the 'Merchant' and gave him a total of £598 and 4 shillings. This included £200 belonging to 'James', for a 'phone' – presumable some type of military communications wireless or similar device. Of the £398 belonging to the IRA, £36 was for a dozen adaptors for an army service rifle and £12 and 4 shillings for ammunition. When George returned to London following his visit to Ireland at Christmas, he cancelled the IRA's order. However, despite 'continually pressing' Fitzgerald, he received neither his money back nor the 'phone' for the Soviets.[129]

In late January 1927 Twomey wrote to George: 'Did you get back all or any of that £350 [*sic*]? We are in a desperate way for cash.'[130] George replied: 'When I came back [from Ireland] I approached him and he promised [to] let me have some [of the money] but he has not kept his promise ... If I do not get some satisfaction from him soon I will use a little pressure.'[131] Twomey urged him on: 'You must put pressure on your friend for that cash. Tell him plainly you must have it at once. If he refuses what pressure do you propose to put on him?'[132]

George was reluctant to act: 'I don't think the man will refuse to pay. He seems to be playing for time and told me yesterday that he would fix the whole business up early next week, which I doubt. If he refuses I think it is up to you to decide on what kind of pressure we use.'[133] In the interim George was able to sell an 'instrument' he had belonging to the 'Merchant' and recoup £48 of the debt.[134]

Twomey responded: 'As you know this person and I do not, you would be the best judge as to whether moral pressure would do, or if some physical application would be necessary. Has he any property which could be seized and removed? I would not like for the present to threaten exposure.'[135]

George feigned the intention of taking decisive action and wrote in March: 'Unless he fixes this up before the end of next week we will be compelled to take very drastic action. I take it I am at liberty to use any amount of pressure which I may think suitable.'[136]

'Yes, you have full permission to take whatever steps you think necessary to recover the money,' Twomey replied.[137] However, the 'Merchant' called their bluff and in April George merely handed over a letter demanding payment: 'Your attitude at the present moment only confirms our previous suspicions that it has not been your intention at any time to deal with us in an honest and straightforward manner ... Our representative [the OC. Britain] appears to have been entirely deceived by your statement that you had paid the money to the manufacturers as soon as it was handed to you ... We consider this to have been an extremely despicable action on your part and we would inform you that we will be compelled to take very drastic steps to recover the money.'[138]

With nothing happening, Twomey wrote: 'If Fitzgerald has not paid up, can you kidnap him or have him fired at, without wounding him at first? His business place could easily be entered over [the] gate or wall. Have you looked up if any legal action could be taken and a writ issued against him?'[139] Twomey must have had great faith in the British justice system if he thought the IRA could sue an arms dealer who had defrauded them over a highly illegal transaction! George replied: 'Have noted your suggestions',[140] but Twomey continued to prod him: 'There must be no squeamishness in dealing with that man.'[141] George meekly replied: '[The 'Merchant'] stated that at the moment he could not pay back the money. There is, so he says, a lot of money due to him, and as soon as it comes in, he will let us have the amount due, which I doubt very much.'[142] Twomey kept pushing George to physically threaten the 'Merchant', but George may have had no stomach for the job or feared being exposed to the police: 'How do you think I can tackle this business alone?[143] Here I am without a job and money, borrowing all over the place, and having no one to assist in helping me do anything. I know that I am personally responsible, but, please do not expect [me] to do the impossible.'[144] Twomey answered: 'You will recollect when I was speaking to you I stated I realised the difficulty, and offered to send Agents to do so. You replied that you would be able to do so there, and actually mentioned the Agents you would employ to do so. I am prepared to risk expense rather than let him get away with it. If you prepare the business and let me know I am still prepared to do this. I never expected that you yourself should do all the work.'[145]

Whether the 'Merchant' ever paid up or not is not known; however, the issue certainly wasn't settled by October 1927 when Twomey again asked George to 'insist' on Fitzgerald making an immediate payment, and George replied that he had met with him several times to ask for the money.[146]

An interesting question is: who was the 'Merchant'? And the answer leads us on a trail back to the Free State cabinet or Executive Council. What we do know from the documents was that the 'Merchant's' last name was Fitzgerald. And coincidentally there was an arms dealer in London at the time, Francis FitzGerald – with a history of dishonesty – who was known to have dealt with the Free State army and to have had contact with the IRA.[147] Francis W. FitzGerald was also the brother of Desmond FitzGerald, an influential member of the Free State's Executive Council and the Minister for External Affairs.

Francis lived in London where he owned a company, Senior Crozier & Co., which 'professed to be engaged in the sale of chemicals'. Through the business he supplied munitions and explosives, including potassium chloride to the Free State's national army during the Civil War (1922–3). In 1925 the Free State's Committee of Public Accounts reported serious irregularities in these transactions to the Dáil. The committee alleged that FitzGerald sold thirty-two tons of potassium chloride to the army for £56 per ton, even though the deliveries took place over the course of several months when the market price of the chemical fell to only £28 a ton. Additionally, when the explosives were received they were not of the promised quality and were described as 'useless'.

The army also gave him a deposit of £2,250 towards the purchase of 10,000 rifles, which 'disappeared'. FitzGerald claimed that he gave the money to the arms manufacturer Horace Soley as a deposit. However, the weapons were never delivered and the government didn't get the deposit back. FitzGerald was unable to produce a verifiable receipt and prove that he ever handed the money over to Horace Soley. In an interesting parallel, the 'Merchant' had told the IRA that he had handed their money over to an arms manufacturer and was unable to get it back.

FitzGerald additionally agreed to purchase five Hotchkiss machine guns for the army at £750 apiece, but in fact he charged £1,000 each, which the government paid. On top of this there was no record of the machine guns having ever been received. The Public Accounts Committee raised questions about the army's order of 2,500 revolvers. FitzGerald had initially quoted a price of £2 each, but in the end charged £3 5 shillings each.

Eventually the army took legal action against FitzGerald. However, despite the Free State's strong case, the government settled with him on extremely favourable terms. They paid him the £2,250 he claimed to have deposited with Horace Soley for the rifles, and in the event that he recovered the money they agreed to pay his legal costs and let him keep half of the remaining sum. This was despite the fact that they were under no obligation to assume liability. In all FitzGerald received £19,700 from the government. No wonder Tom Johnson, the leader of the parliamentary Labour party, called this 'the most extraordinary settlement that I can conceive' and added: 'Before this settlement took place, there should have been, at least, one resignation from the Executive Council.'

The army's intended use for the rifles in 1922 was also rather murky; it appears that they planned to supply them to joint pro- and anti-Treaty IRA units engaged in a cross-border campaign against the new state of Northern Ireland. This failed campaign was organised in the lead-up to the Civil War with the connivance of Michael Collins, partially with a view to help preserve IRA unity and so prevent Civil War. Ernest Blythe, the Minister for Finance, euphemistically commented: 'After the Treaty not one of these purchases should have taken place', but that at the time 'many people took up an equivocal position'.[148]

In London FitzGerald didn't exactly keep a low profile. P. A. Murray stated that when he was OC. Britain he was 'in touch with Desmond FitzGerald's brother' in London.[149] Later, in January 1925 FitzGerald's gun dealer's licence was revoked and he gave the court an undertaking to return revolvers in his possession to the Free State's high commissioner in Britain.[150] Finally, in 1933 he was described as a works manager from Kensington and was charged with the possession of two automatic pistols, three revolvers and ammunition. He got off rather lightly, being fined £5, and the magistrate ordered the confiscation of the weapons.[151]

Based on this evidence it seems highly probable that the 'Fitzgerald' who defrauded the IRA in 1927 was Francis FitzGerald, the brother of Desmond FitzGerald, the Free State minister.[152]

The IRA in Liverpool

The great port city of Liverpool was home to such a large Irish population that in the early years of the twentieth century the city elected its own Irish Home Rule member of parliament, T. P. O'Connor. In the nineteenth century the IRB organised in the city and established an important arms smuggling route to Ireland. This route was reactivated and developed during the Anglo-Irish War when there was a significant flow of weapons and explosives across the Irish Sea. During the Anglo-Irish War the Liverpool company of the IRA was the most active IRA unit in Britain.

In November 1920 the company successfully mounted a co-ordinated arson attack on warehouses along the docks, but after the subsequent arrests and increased police activity the organisation was 'for all intents and purposes dead'; however, the following year it resumed activity.[153] Between

November 1920 and June 1921 the police had such good intelligence that they were able to arrest four successive captains of the company.[154]

Like the other English units it went into a marked decline following the Civil War. In November 1924 the IRA's adjutant general (AG) inspected the company and reported: 'Nobody was working there ... the whole situation was hopeless.' The veterans of the Anglo-Irish War or 'the old workers', were 'not inclined to work'. On their release from jail these 'old timers' were no longer remaining active and, according to the AG, 'only 5 men are left in Liverpool.' He appointed one of the Fleming brothers – Denis or Patrick – as OC, hoping that he would be able to unify the various factions.

The OC found himself in a frustrating position. The company was badly split between the 'old timers' and the recent IRA immigrants from Ireland, with the former not wishing to associate with the newer arrivals. He also had to spend most of his free time running dances to raise funds for the unit, while there was little help from the other volunteers. The dances were organised in collaboration with the Thomas Ashe Sinn Féin club at the '[Irish National] Forrester's Hall', and the proceeds split 50:50, the other Sinn Féin clubs in the area having refused to help out. The OC spent three nights a week, from 8 to 11 p.m., working at the dances. One dance ended in a free for all after a group of rowdy immigrants from the west of Ireland had to be cautioned over their use of foul language and their 'interruptions'. Finally, in October 1926 he resigned as 'he intended to settle down and get married'.[155]

The company's adjutant suggested another method of fundraising and asked for 'specially printed cards, issued and signed by GHQ' to be sent over so that the company could approach 'friends of the movement who are resident here, with a view to raising funds'.[156]

The 'most important arm of the Organisation [IRA]' in Liverpool was the section covering the docks, also called the Special Service Section, which was staffed by the 'old timers'.[157] As well as smuggling weapons and explosives directly to Ireland they helped transfer munitions from ships arriving from New York and New Jersey onto boats crossing the Irish Sea. The IRA leadership was dissatisfied with the performance and discipline of these men, but at the same time dependent on them. Liam

Pedlar, one of the leading IRA arms agents in New York, remarked in 1924 that 'the last consignment [of weaponry] was taken to and fro a number of times causing much extra expense. I am told that pressure is being exercised to have one by the name of Fleming, put in charge there, and this is given as a reason for the disturbance. If it is the same party as I have had experience of they are N.G. [no good].'[158] Pedlar claimed that during the 'war period' he could get 'nothing done' in Liverpool as Fleming and his comrades wouldn't help him smuggle munitions over from the US, with the result that Pedlar had to send over his own agent to work in Liverpool.[159] The adjutant general wrote to Seán Russell that he would have to give very specific instructions to the Liverpool IRA as to the procedure for receiving contraband from the US, detailing how they should contact the crew on the American boat, who should sign for the goods, etc: 'Unless you put these down in black and white you will have plenty of trouble in Liverpool.' He commented that the Liverpool men needed to be ordered exactly where to send the munitions as they frequently sent them directly to IRA units in Ireland they had connections with and that 'every individual coming from Ireland will get some'.[160]

Notwithstanding their importance, the Liverpool adjutant referred to the Special Service Section as 'absolutely useless'.[161] The men refused to co-operate with the OC; they wanted to elect their own officers and not be mixed in with the recent IRA immigrants to the city. They wouldn't attend parades – though this was probably very reasonable given that they were already well known to the police. The OC reported that the 'old crowd' refused to place their weapons under his control: 'There are a few of the old crowd ... including Tom O'Malley who holds guns and refuses to give them up.' The weapons included four Webley revolvers and a .38 automatic.[162] Twomey initially adopted a non-confrontational attitude and recommended to the OC: 'What I would suggest is that if they refuse to conform to discipline, I would ignore them but would not create any more rows or bickering.' He promised to follow up with the OC and at their next meeting they could decide whether to move the men from active service to the 'reserve' or whether to dismiss them altogether.[163] Twomey wrote to the company's intelligence officer on the same day and was much more intransigent, perhaps because he knew the intelligence officer was in direct contact with the Special Service Section and wanted the tone of his letter passed on: 'It must be clearly understood that if these men will not be subject to Volunteer discipline and if they persist in disobeying orders they must be expelled.'[164]

The local adjutant suggested that the situation could be defused by allowing the men to elect their own officers, a common practice of the IRA early in the Anglo-Irish War.[165] GHQ was against this as the 'old timers' were well known to the police and any officers chosen from amongst them would have difficulty working covertly. Twomey was in prison at the time and so his final decision on the matter is not known.[166]

The dockers also made contact with sailors on Russian merchant ships, and the OC commented: 'It would be an easy matter … to get them [the Russians] to fetch some munitions.'[167] Twomey however didn't want to cut across the existing IRA's agreement with the Soviets, but at the same time wanted to keep his options open and advised the OC: 'These men … may be used later, and you should certainly keep in touch with them and find out exactly how much they are prepared to do.'[168] The Liverpool adjutant even reported that they were in contact with a boat sailing between Buenos Aires and Liverpool: 'We are in touch with a friendly Boat plying this route, if the service is any use?'[169] To which GHQ noncommittally replied: 'I have noted your information.'[170]

In February 1927 Twomey ordered the OC to organise the destruction of arms shipments being sent from Liverpool to Chinese warlords allied with the British, though there's no evidence this was ever complied with (see Chapter 8).[171]

While the Liverpool company may have fallen well short of Twomey's expectations and was incapable of any sustained urban warfare, it at least fulfilled some function for the IRA and far exceeded the capability of the London and Manchester companies.

The IRA in London and Manchester
In London the OC. Britain largely conducted his duties independent of the local company. In late 1924 the adjutant general commented that the unit was no longer holding staff meetings, and he ordered them to meet every two weeks.[172]

In May 1927 Twomey wrote a letter to the London adjutant, furious with him for not carrying out a number of duties, including delivering a package to Dublin: 'It is a very grave matter when the promise and word of a volunteer can no longer be relied on to perform a very simple task.'[173]

By October, Twomey notified George that he had decided to finish with the unit altogether: 'It has been decided to disband [the] unit in London. [The] order for this will be sent [over with the] next messenger. You should now recruit people for special work. If you wish the [IRA] Declaration can be administered to them. You will deal with them as individuals. Report what you will do.'[174] The IRA's declaration of allegiance to the Irish Republic had been substituted for the previous oath of allegiance, in response to the Catholic Church's objection to secular oath-bound societies.[175] Not that this would have mollified the Catholic hierarchy.

In the light of actions such as the pathetic smoke bomb attack at the St Patrick's banquet in 1926, Twomey's decision seems entirely appropriate. He went on to elaborate that: 'No results whatever have been obtained ... the fault lies entirely with the officers, whom they [the Army Council] wish to be severely reprimanded.'[176] There is also evidence in the British secret service files from the period that they had an informer among the IRA in London, though his identity remains unknown.[177]

The Manchester company was the least significant of the main units in Britain and there's little reference to it throughout the documents. In March 1926 a report stated that it had fallen 'out of touch' with Dublin. This appeared to have been somewhat rectified later in the year, as a number of despatches were sent from headquarters and the officers were introduced to the IRA's system of cipher.

In October 1926 Twomey wrote to the company's OC: 'We wanted to get you the stink bombs for [William] Cosgrave's visit, as you were anxious to have them.'[178] Twomey didn't seem to have learned his lesson from the abortive attack on the prime minister the previous March. The same month Twomey arranged for gelignite and detonators to be sent from Glasgow to both Manchester and Liverpool. It's not clear exactly what operation he had in mind for Manchester, though he wanted the Liverpool company to destroy stocks of coal which may have been readied for shipment to British forces and their warlord allies in China (see Chapter 8).[179]

To H/S

Dear Sir,

Unit disbanded

(249) EEAIU TUEAO EEMEE A EUO ISEDD REEUR PIOEC IHD D
TLEOI OINEO RFWIA BEYLS LAODI IDWNG LIRRH AAEUI NRYAD NNOBM OWOGY
DNWTL HIRIN DTRST NUUOO SRERO WISTI ESNEI EEDTS KTTDD WTDEO TCBLR
LXRNP PIHIM TIHIP UHIAO PLTYO EEFEO IOLTV OWBDU OTSSS ELAUC ASEEM
UWLEE AUUO1 MEEIA NOUEI RIEET NNHES HCELW LNTMA AAHD.

Smith going -digs)

(263) EEIIO UTEEI OAMUC ANIEE OUIGD EIBTD UOIEI WNTCH HTSEI
WTHWL SWTOB HTLER LEGBT OTTCS LEENI TERTA RASIE ULMSN LDOSH OFUCM
EOHET TIGEN GOIIY WAHRL ESCEH DFDOI XXEEEX UNEOO SLRET NWPEA LEPTX
FTHRN LMEPO KSKOL HYLIS ANIDE SDOPU RSEYO SAEHT GHYON ISTOO TBAHH
TNTSG IUPOE IEUSA AEEII EEMOR AAIUE IOUAO IHINE SBIEO EAWHL MEURN
ANY.

Yours faithfully.

Figure 22. Moss Twomey wrote to George, the OC in Britain, informing him of the decision to disband the IRA unit in London, and that Andy Cooney ('Mr Smith') was to move to London temporarily.

It has been decided to disband [the] unit in London. Order for this will be sent [over, with the] next messenger. You should now recruit people for special work. If you wish, the [IRA] declaration can be administered to them. You will deal with them as individuals. Report what you will do.

'Mr Smith' intends going to London to complete his studies. [He] will probably cross [over] this weekend. He wants you to think of one or two suitable places where he might stay, he will call to Number 8, perhaps he could stay. Fix nothing definite about digs until he sees you.

In 1927 the police staged raids in the area looking for wanted men, and the intelligence officer had a close shave when they raided his accommodation.[180]

The IRA in Scotland

Scotland, and in particular the industrial heartland of Glasgow and the Clyde, had a long history of IRB and later IRA support and organisation. However, there's very little information available as to what these units actually did and what they planned to do. Though their successes were few, their plans were likely many. One reason for the lack of knowledge is that the Scottish IRA was never fully under the control of headquarters in Dublin. Additionally, unlike the IRA in Ireland, there's very little documentation or memoirs available on the unit.

The situation in Glasgow differed from that in other British cities.

There was a particularly strong history of support for Irish republicans in the city. It was also a stronghold of communism, and this resulted in serious divisions within the local IRA between the supporters and opponents of socialism.

Many of Glasgow's communists and socialists were in turn very supportive of Irish separatism, including the famous John MacLean. Helen Crawford, a leading member of the Soviet-sponsored Workers' International Relief, travelled to Ireland in 1925 as a communist organiser, and was in contact with IRA leaders and supporters there. In 1927 the British secret service (MI5) linked her with the IRA's activities in support of the secret Soviet agent, Kate Gussfeldt and believed she was in contact with the Woods family in London. The Woods were involved with the IRA and had helped Gussfeldt obtain a false passport.

In common with the IRA units south of the border, the Scottish IRA reached peak membership during the Anglo-Irish War, and in August 1920 600 IRA members were reported to be in Scotland. By 1922 this had been reduced to 138.[181] In 1921 an attempt to destroy an oil pipeline along the Forth and Clyde canal failed.[182] And in May of that year the IRA killed a police inspector in a failed attempt to rescue a prisoner from a police van. The aggressive police response, including the arrest of a priest, resulted in rioting – the only case of a serious confrontation between an Irish community and the police in Britain.[183]

In September 1923, following the Civil War, morale among the IRA's supporters in Glasgow was in 'a condition of coma'. In addition to the disillusionment resulting from the Civil War, there was great uncertainty as to what the policy of the republican leaders in Dublin was. There was infighting among pro- and anti-communist supporters in the Scottish IRA and these problems were compounded by the effects of the post-war unemployment and poverty on 'the working class [which] have always been the back bone' of the IRA's support in the city. The Catholic clergy were no longer supportive: 'The clergy who formerly helped a good deal, will not touch us, and in a number of cases have actively worked against us publicly and privately.'[184]

In November 1924 when the adjutant general inspected the Scottish unit he reported that there were 300 members, 200 of whom would turn out for a monthly parade. However, 'there has been nothing done at these parades save to fall men in and give them a few minutes squad drill, [and] collect subscriptions'. The OC was a 'hardworking enthusiastic man a little bit militaristic'. This perhaps was not such a damning criticism in what after all was supposed to be a military organisation! The AG wryly commented: 'On the whole they are the best bunch of officers I ever met in England [sic]. This does not say too much, but they are at least good average men.' He recommended that the unit should henceforth report directly to headquarters in Dublin and not through the OC. Britain in London – something that was a source of much dissatisfaction.

Aside from the size of the unit, it was of importance to the IRA in that it had members and informants working in the factories of the area, many of which manufactured products that had a military application, and also because of the large number of dockers on the Clyde who were Irish. As in Liverpool, IRA support among the dockers enabled the organisation to smuggle weapons and explosives to Ireland. And for this reason Seán Russell was in direct contact with the unit.[185] In 1924, however, the unit appeared not to have any contacts among ships' crew members sailing in and out of Glasgow, and the AG rejected the adjutant's suggestion that they pay men to smuggle for them. The OC however reassured him that he could send anything needed to Dundalk and could get as much gelignite as the IRA required.[186]

Some time after 1924, as part of the IRA's reorganisation, the status of the Scottish brigade was downgraded to that of a battalion. In 1925 divisions in the unit resulted in a violent feud, with allegations of 'vice and corruption prevalent among certain officers', including drunkenness. On one occasion a group of armed men raided a dance hosted by an opposing group and threatened to smash the violin belonging to the musician, who was the widow of an IRA man.[187] A little later one of its most prominent officers, Séamus Reader, was charged before an IRA court martial with misappropriation of funds and, though found not guilty, he was convicted of criminal negligence. However, he disputed the IRA's jurisprudence in the case, arguing that he couldn't be found guilty of negligence as he was never charged with the offence to begin with.[188] Serious allegations were also made against the battalion's OC, who in September 1926 just upped and left Scotland. Twomey reported: 'I was amazed when I returned to find that [the] O/C. Scotland had left there for good and is here in Dublin.'[189]

In February 1927 Twomey wrote to the OC that he was 'very disappointed that you have not reported to GHQ for a long time' and he complained about the 'slackness' of the battalion's intelligence officer.[190] In his apology the OC claimed that the unit had been busy and had placed 200 bombs among coal sent to China. The plan was that after the coal was shovelled into the boilers of Royal Navy patrol vessels in China, the bombs would explode and sink the vessels.[191] This unverifiable claim is further discussed in Chapter 8. Other correspondence with the Scottish brigade mentions attempts to smuggle weapons and to procure a wireless radio.[192]

ASIDE FROM THE SMUGGLING of explosives and the procurement of false passports, there was little that the IRA in Britain could perform with any degree of competence. The members were demoralised, disorganised and undisciplined. The units were also crippled by infighting and even George, the OC. Britain, allowed personal enmity get in the way of efficiently carrying out his job. While some of the blame lies with the members themselves and their local leadership, GHQ was primarily to blame for its failure to develop and communicate a clear strategy and to adequately train, equip and organise the British units.

Moss Twomey appeared impressive when he sent orders for a campaign of sabotage under the cover of the 1926 general strike. But there was no planning, organisation or capability to undertake this, and for these failings he and the rest of the senior leadership in Dublin were also responsible.

As Seán Russell reported, the IRA in Britain needed to be reorganised into small secret highly trained units. It was with this 'cellular' structure and a bombing campaign that targeted primarily economic targets in London that the Provisional IRA was to achieve considerable strategic success almost seventy years later in the 1990s.

CHAPTER 7

The IRA in America

With twenty [tear gas] machines you might be able to take all [of] Dublin without killing non-combatants.

IRA agent in America to the chief of staff, Moss Twomey

We have made wonderful progress in [the] GAA and will be able to control it ... Our policy otherwise is to purify and cleanse the organisation and [the] games. We will succeed.

Connie Neenan, IRA representative in America

America was an important source of funds and weapons for the IRA. The organisation maintained its own agents in New York, who worked closely with the Irish-American organisation Clan na Gael. Aside from smuggling weapons and money, these agents attempted to acquire chemical weapons for use in Ireland, infiltrated the Gaelic Athletic Association in New York and conducted military espionage for the Soviet Union.

Many of these activities are discussed in detail for the first time ever in this chapter. The Soviet connection is covered in Chapter 8.

Historical background

Since the nineteenth century Irish immigrants in America (especially in the major population centres in the north-east) found kinship in a variety of cultural, religious and sporting organisations. These societies, such as the Galway Ladies' Association or the County Cork Men's Benevolent Patriotic and Protective Association, were often based upon the immigrants' county of origin and created a sense of community while allowing immigrants to share information about jobs and housing.[1]

Additionally, the Irish community had their own political organisations which supported Irish separatism, and these political societies tended to be more radical than their counterparts in Ireland. This militancy was the product of a number of factors, including the immigrants' own experience of discrimination and hostility in America from the Protestant 'Anglo-Saxon' establishment and the collective Irish-American folk memory of poverty and 'British atrocities' in Ireland. These factors were compounded by the immigrants' distance and separation from the realities of life back home.[2] The societies had a history of bitter (and sometimes violent) internal feuds. As societies were dissolved, others took their place. Disputes were as much about personality as political differences. The world of radical Irish-American politics was truly Byzantine. However, a basic overview is important to understand the situation in the 1926–7 period.

Clan na Gael (Family of the Irish) was the single most influential Irish-American society whose primary goal was Irish independence. The Clan was a secret society formed in 1867 by a group of Fenians to bring about an Irish Republic by 'physical force'.[3] It made a formal alliance with the Irish Republican Brotherhood (IRB) in Ireland, which it provided with money and some weapons. Internal dissent and fighting bedevilled it throughout its history, and British secret service agents significantly compromised it. The Clan pursued a more violent strategy than the IRB itself, and sent a number of men on bombing missions to England. Most of these disastrous 'Fenian' dynamite teams of the 1880s were either created by British *agents provocateurs* or involved spies who had infiltrated the Clan.[4] In 1900 the warring factions of the Clan were re-united under the veteran Fenian, John Devoy.

With the outbreak of the First World War in 1914, Devoy saw the cause for Irish independence best served by a German victory over Britain and along with many Irish-American activists he took a pro-German stance. In 1916 he helped found the Friends of Irish Freedom (FOIF), which unlike the Clan was an open, mass-based society. Judge Daniel Cohalan, a close ally of Devoy's, led the FOIF. Rather than directly supporting separatists in Ireland he promoted Irish self-determination through propaganda, political activity and fundraising in America.

When the US entered the war alongside Britain in 1917, Devoy and Cohalan were forced to change tack and call for Irish-American patriotic support for the war effort and for the granting of Irish self-determination as part of an eventual peace settlement.[5] However, at the end of the war Britain was able to exclude the independence of Ireland from the settlement and Cohalan went on to divert his energies into successfully lobbying for the United States Senate's rejection of the Treaty of Versailles in

1919. He argued that the Treaty favoured British imperial interests at America's expense.[6]

In 1919, during the Anglo-Irish War, the FOIF inaugurated the Irish Victory Fund, which raised over a million dollars. Cohalan and Devoy envisaged that much of this money would be spent on promoting the Irish cause in America rather than in Ireland.[7] But that summer, when Éamon de Valera, the president of Sinn Féin, arrived in America he clashed with Devoy and Cohalan. Unlike them, de Valera wanted the money sent to Ireland to support the revolution and diverted away from propaganda efforts in the United States, and felt that as leader of the separatists in Ireland he had a leadership role to play among the Irish-American community. The stage was set for an extremely bitter dispute. The Clan split, with the majority of its executive supporting Devoy and Cohalan, and a minority led by Joseph McGarrity siding with de Valera. McGarrity's faction of the Clan was initially called 'Clan na Gael re-organized' but as the section under Devoy's leadership faded, it soon became known simply as 'Clan na Gael'.[8] Devoy and Cohalan retained control of the FOIF and of the paper, the *Gaelic American*, while the single most influential Irish-American paper, the *Irish World*, supported McGarrity and de Valera.[9]

In 1920 de Valera founded the American Association for the Recognition of the Irish Republic (AARIR) as a mass organisation and an alternative to the FOIF.[10] Before leaving the US, he also started a successful bond drive for the Irish Republic.[11]

During the Irish Civil War Devoy and Cohalan, along with the majority of Irish Americans, supported the Free State, while McGarrity and his Clan backed de Valera and the IRA. However, Irish-Americans on the whole were greatly disillusioned by both the Civil War in Ireland and the feuding between the Irish societies in America, resulting in a massive drop off in their involvement and financial contributions. In 1926 an IRA document from America reported: 'There is a general feeling of apathy and inactivity and little or no money coming into the office.'[12]

Clan na Gael

Under Joseph McGarrity, Clan na Gael aligned itself with the IRA and dedicated its resources once again to the achievement of a republic by military means. McGarrity, as chairman of the executive committee, was its dominant figure up until his death in 1940. He was a romantic Irish nationalist, a staunch Catholic, and a militarist who regarded 'political activism as the grave of militant nationalism'.[13] An intermittently successful businessman, he reportedly spent much of his money supporting Irish republicanism. He had a deep attachment and respect for Éamon de Valera, and their friendship even survived de Valera's entry into the Free State Dáil in 1927.

Before November 1925, when the IRA disassociated itself from de Valera's republican 'government', it had been represented in America by the government's 'military attaché', Liam Pedlar – an IRA gunrunner. Money raised by the Clan and others was given to the 'government' and a proportion allocated to the IRA in Ireland. However, following the IRA's parting of ways with de Valera and his supporters, a new arrangement was needed.

In the spring of 1926, Andy Cooney, as chairman of the IRA Army Council, travelled to America. His objectives were to update the Clan on the recent developments in Ireland and clarify the IRA's relationship with de Valera, to negotiate a formal agreement with the Clan and particularly to reach an agreement on the Clan's funding of the IRA. In America Cooney found the IRA's mission to be disorganised and in 'an awful state of affairs'. He wasn't able to communicate with GHQ back in Dublin, Liam Pedlar had forgotten the covering address for telegrams sent from Ireland, and there was no money available to fund his living expenses.[14]

Cooney attended the annual Clan na Gael convention in September, where he reached an agreement with Luke Dillon (representing the Clan) that the Clan would give 'its undivided support, physically morally and financially to the IRA'. The Clan now regarded itself and the IRA 'for all revolutionary purposes ... practically one organization'.[15] In turn the IRA expected the Clan to provide financial support, help smuggle weapons to Ireland and to build support for the IRA in America, particularly among the Irish-American community. However, the Clan had, at the most, only modest success in all three areas.

In October Cooney returned to Ireland, leaving a full-time representative in America to work with Clan na Gael. The representative held the title 'An Timthire', which comes from the Irish *an timtire* meaning 'messenger'. During Cooney's visit the IRA activist 'Mr Jones' was An Timthire, but 'Jones' complained that his IRA-sanctioned espionage work for the Soviet Union prevented him from having the time to devote to An Timthire's administrative and organisational work, and in December 1926 Connie Neenan from Cork was appointed to the position. Neenan's official duties included: representing the Army Council at meetings of the Clan na Gael executive, enrolling IRA veterans in the Clan, sending money back to Ireland, maintaining relations with 'foreign governments and revolutionary organisations' and 'when required' smuggling arms and ammunition back.[16]

Neenan was based in New York where he spent most of his time recruiting and organising IRA veterans, networking among the Irish-American community and raising money. He went on to become a close friend of Joseph McGarrity's and worked 'in perfect harmony' with the Clan.[17] In 1927 he too became involved in the IRA's clandestine activities for the Soviet Union (see Chapter 8).

The Clan na Gael membership, which by 1927 had shrunk to 5,000, was organised into local clubs or camps.[18] In turn the clubs were grouped into districts, which were represented by a district officer. District officers could be elected to the Clan's ruling executive committee, chaired by McGarrity. McGarrity's closest ally on the executive was the secretary, Luke Dillon.

The clubs were predominately in the major Irish centres on the east coast, with a few in other cities with a strong Irish presence, like San Francisco and Chicago. They were frequently identified with particular counties or regions in Ireland, such as the Seán Treacy club with Tipperary.[19] In the mid-1920s the clubs benefited from an influx of IRA veterans fresh from Ireland. The veterans that joined the Clan, though relatively small in number, had an important rejuvenating effect on the existing Clan clubs.[20] These were the men who had actually fought and 'beaten' the British, something that generations of American 'Fenians' had merely dreamed about, and as Connie Neenan wrote: 'The young men are looked up to and respected ... Some of the old organisations [FOIF, Devoy's Clan, etc] are using every means to enrol the new arrivals.'[21] The new members were often unskilled workers, with little money to donate, and the Clan overall lacked the social respectability of other Irish-American societies such as the Ancient Order of Hibernians or even the AARIR. Reflecting the change in membership and the alliance with the IRA, from 1927 on the clubs were renamed 'Clan na Gael and IRA Clubs'.

Naturally enough, the recent IRA immigrants had less immediate impact on the membership of the executive committee, which was composed of long-standing Clan members. Neenan commented: 'We must put a few IRA men on [the] executive at [the] next convention. It is necessary they should be on it.'[22] On the death of Luke Dillon in 1929 Connie Neenan took his place as secretary of the executive.

The Clan's leaders, as exemplified by McGarrity, were socially conservative and staunchly Catholic in their outlook and were uneasy with the socialist rhetoric of some of the IRA's leadership, particularly that of Peadar O'Donnell, as expressed in the pages of *An Phoblacht*. Throughout the second half of the 1920s and in the 1930s McGarrity and his colleagues were concerned that involvement in social issues (to which they were unsympathetic) distracted from the IRA's military goal. It was only natural that McGarrity was to find in Seán Russell a strong ally.

Though the extent of British secret service penetration of the Clan in the late nineteenth century is only now beginning to come to light, the IRA leadership was still aware of the security risk posed by the Clan and was reluctant to share critical information.[23] A secondary consideration was that some members of the executive were supportive of Fianna Fáil. When Neenan sent $5,000 in cash to Ireland, he informed Twomey that 'for obvious reasons I did not tell [the Clan] executive' the means by which the money was sent.[24] George, the OC in Britain, was concerned that the secret agreement with the Russians could be exposed by informers in America: 'Many British secretive [*sic*] service agents are bound to be operating in the States and it is likely that one or two are connected with our people there. It is necessary to be very careful.'[25]

The Clan na Gael and IRA clubs
Following the ending of the Civil War in 1923 and the release of the vast majority of republican prisoners the following year, hundreds, if not

thousands, of IRA veterans emigrated to America and most settled in New York, where they joined 200,000 others of Irish birth. This was a time when the Irish, through control of Democratic Party politics, still 'ruled' New York, and had achieved considerable economic and professional success.[26] The city was an oasis for Irish Catholics, where they were part of the establishment. Here they could live a life insulated to a certain extent from the 'nativist' hostility and discrimination prevalent throughout much of the rest of the United States.

Many IRA veterans were determined to have nothing more to do with Irish politics and stayed well clear of the Clan; others formed groups unaffiliated with the Clan. For those that joined 'the Clan na Gael and IRA Clubs', the clubs became an important part of their lives. They provided members with a valuable network that helped them to get jobs and accommodation and organised social activities where they could find friendship and maybe a suitable Irish Catholic spouse. Some veterans arrived bitter, and in the words of the Cumann na mBan activist Máire Comerford, 'they went with vengeance in their hearts. They and their children are the ones who support the IRA today'.[27]

On New Year's Eve 1926 the clubs held a dance at the Mayo Halls, with two bands and Irish and American dancing, admission 75 cents. Aside from the novelty dances, participants could even engage in 'confetti battles'![28] In 1927 the Clan na Gael and IRA clubs held a St Patrick's night annual ball with step dancing by 'some of the best talent from Ireland' and an invitation to 'come and meet the boys who beat the Tans'.[29] Another popular fundraiser was the semi-annual cruise on the Hudson river. In 1927 Neenan expected to make $1,000 on a twelve-hour 'grand outing and boat ride' on board the SS Pocahontas, with dancing and 'refreshments', tickets $1.50. By 1930 some 3,000 people were enjoying the boat trips with 'a few hours of teeming mirth and pleasure ... a happy release and relaxation from the cramp and care of dull domesticity and the dreary drag of city life'.[30]

Neenan set about organising new clubs, reorganising and reinvigorating existing ones and recruiting recent IRA arrivals. New York was the 'mainstay [of the Clan and] therefore a great deal of attention must be given to it'.[31] Neenan appears to have been possessed with considerable social skill which he used to extend the Clan's influence throughout the Irish community. He professed to be working flat out: 'I have a busy time. I did not have a spare night for months while days are equally busy.'[32] 'Every night means attendance at one or two meetings ... [but] few people are aware of my official capacity.'[33]

In January 1927 he was on the committee organising the Cork Ball.[34] In February he reported that he was reorganising all the clubs in the city: 'We are making big headway, and hope to increase largely to [sic] our numbers inside a few months, by having all IRA men enrolled.' He promised a 'big programme for the coming season', to raise money and improve the organisation.[35] This included the boat rides, dances and Irish sports at Celtic Park.

The clubs' new headquarters in New York was the 'Tara Halls' on 66th Street and Broadway, which Neenan predicted would generate a 'weekly profit'. He noted that IRA men 'arriving in [the] country [were] slow to get in touch' and recommended that they should turn up there on Saturday or Sunday nights. Aside from the weekend dances, with music provided by the likes of 'Seán Hayes and his IRA Radio Orchestra', there were card games during weeknights, a 'republican library' (with works ranging from John Mitchel's *Jail Journal* to Tolstoy's *Anna Karenina*) and copies of *An Phoblacht* were for sale.[36] Given that this was the time of prohibition, another attraction would undoubtedly have been the speakeasy in the basement.[37]

In 1927 in New York there were 'four very good [Clan na Gael and IRA] Clubs, two [of] moderate [quality] and two [poor]. [The auxiliary] women's Clubs [were] good.' Neenan felt that the 'apathy' that had existed in the past had now been 'eradicated' (most likely by the recent influx of IRA men) and that membership and finance was increasing daily. Of the two clubs in Brooklyn, both were doing well and one planned to donate $300 to the IRA. Twomey, however, didn't share his optimism and wrote: 'One would imagine that the organization should be stronger here.'[38]

IRA men intending to emigrate from Ireland were supposed to first get permission to do so from the IRA and then apply to enrol in the organisation's (so called) 'Foreign Reserves'. Lists of the applicants' names along with an American address were forwarded to Neenan, aiding him in his recruitment efforts. He found additional information about the whereabouts of veterans by way of his extensive contacts throughout the community. The 'Foreign Reserves' never had a defined role within the IRA structure and existed largely in name only.[39]

Among the IRA men who wouldn't affiliate was Tom Rogers, an ex-officer from Louth, who admitted he was 'sceptical of [the] Clan'. Rogers had left Ireland against the advice of the IRA. After the gardaí raided his house and found a small quantity of ammunition he went on the run. At the time, Twomey approached him and told him to give himself up and 'take the consequences', as he'd only have received a short prison sentence. However, he disregarded Twomey and left the country, which was regarded as setting a poor example for other IRA members.[40] There were also 'a number of ex-Army [IRA] men from Clare [who] joined Fianna Fáil in preference to Clan [na Gael]. I feel this is [due to] intimidation,' wrote Neenan.[41]

Men applying to join were vetted and if need be their unit back home was contacted to get a reference. An officer in the North Mayo brigade reported to GHQ that 'Lavelle is going to Cleveland and … [he was seeking] a transfer to Republican circles in [the] USA where apart from political or other considerations it would be to his material advantage. His friendship with a member of the Black and Tans brought him into trouble early in 1922.'[42] Twomey also warned Neenan 'to have nothing to do with' Thomas Loughran of County Meath.[43]

Another unwanted veteran was Frank O'Beirne from Sligo. During the Civil War O'Beirne commanded a unit which ambushed a detachment of Free State troops, killing five soldiers and capturing two armoured cars. But following a counter-attack by 400 troops led by General Seán MacEoin, he surrendered along with many of his men.[44] He was imprisoned in Athlone barracks, from where he and eight other republicans escaped. As O'Beirne was scaling the prison wall he somehow lost his shoes and so made a painful exit in his stocking feet.[45] In the meantime he must have fallen out of favour with Moss Twomey. By January 1927 he had arrived in New York and reported to Connie Neenan.[46] But Twomey wrote: '[I] hope O'Beirne is not hanging on. On no account give him cash. If he had not been so utterly useless I would have him court-martialled for disobeying orders.'[47]

Neenan came across other characters in New York: 'Desmond Dowling [a demobilised Free State officer] swanked about here for a time, but has not been seen for [the] past month. Also here are several [other] ex-Free State officers and men. They appear to have no organisation and are not members of Devoy's Clan.'[48]

In May 1927, Neenan gave an overview of the state of the Clan na Gael clubs throughout the country. The situation in New Jersey was 'very poor', despite his 'repeated efforts' to contact the large number of IRA men living there, many of whom were from Mayo.[49]

In Philadelphia (where McGarrity was based) there were 'seventeen men's Clubs [and] one ladies' Club'. The members were mainly long-time 'Fenians' with only a 'few Army [IRA] men'. Neenan talked to them about the IRA's policy and the 'necessity for sending greater assistance home'. Although the recruitment drive was going well, there were a 'number of men in this area lenient towards Fianna Fáil'. Other IRA veterans there were a 'nuisance' – they refused to join and complained that during the Anglo-Irish War 'we never got money from [the] USA and had to pay for [our] own guns. I [Neenan] refuted this personally.'[50]

The situation in Boston was much less favourable; there was considerable support for de Valera and Fianna Fáil, and John O'Sullivan, who had been a district officer and member of the Clan executive was 'definitely Fianna Fáil'. The 'officers are not overly energetic' and they wouldn't help Neenan visit the clubs in the area.[51]

The clubs in Connecticut were doing well and a 1916 Easter Rising commemoration raised '$300 for [the] Army'. Other centres mentioned by Neenan included Detroit 'in fair condition' and California, which was as 'good as ever'.[52]

Twomey wrote to Neenan about 'disquieting reports ... of [the] activities of George Daly, organising [IRA] volunteers in Chicago in an organisation auxiliary to [the] AARIR. Put this down at once.'[53] Neenan agreed: 'George Daly started [an] Army club there to support Fianna Fáil.' An IRA man, Thomas Loftus, was in charge of the men, who 'misunderstood' Daly's position. Neenan reported that he 'instructed our people to stop him' and added that he would also get Anthony Farrell of Mayo to write to Loftus to 'clear up matters'. Overall the situation in Chicago was 'fairly good'. An important function of the Clan was to help members find employment through Irish-American networks and Neenan was able to report that in Chicago 'employment for members [had been] successfully dealt with'.[54]

IRA headquarters also pushed Neenan to persuade veterans to subscribe to *An Phoblacht*, both as a means to keep them in touch with IRA policy and propaganda and as a modest source of income.[55] Cooney wrote to Neenan's predecessor: 'Spare no effort to increase the number of subscribers.'[56] Neenan suggested that if there was an article devoted to America in the 1916 Easter Rising anniversary edition he could 'easily' sell one or two thousand copies and that the article should 'emphasize the point as to the Clan being the only organisation who [*sic*] are now, as in the past, giving material assistance to the Republic'.[57] Neenan professed that: '[I] am doing everything possible for *An Phoblacht*. [I] got [a] special circular sent out, [and] also seek subscribers at each meeting I attend.'[58] It's reasonable to surmise that *An Phoblacht* was primarily of interest only to recent IRA immigrants, rather than long-established Irish-Americans; however (despite Neenan's optimism), sales in the US were poor. In 1930 some 480 copies a week were sent to members of the Clan and by 1932 this had declined to only 100 subscribers in the entire US.[59]

The IRA and the GAA in New York

Complementary to his work in building up the Clan, Connie Neenan planned a covert IRA takeover of the Gaelic Athletic Association (GAA) in New York. In addition he used his influence within the GAA to arrange for the IRA to secretly benefit from the Kerry Gaelic football team's tour of the United States in 1927. By infiltrating and trying to manipulate cultural and sporting organisations Neenan was following in the long tradition of the Irish Republican Brotherhood.

The GAA was arguably the most important Irish fraternal society of the twentieth century. Through its promotion of Gaelic games, primarily football and hurling, it brought the young men (and to a lesser extent the young women) of Ireland together. One of the distinguishing features of the Irish at home and in America has been their strong allegiance to their home county, and the GAA tradition of having teams drawn from individual counties compete against each other played a significant role in the forging of this identity. Nowhere was it more so than in Kerry, which was to produce the greatest Gaelic football teams in the history of the GAA.

The GAA was founded in 1864 by a group of nationalists, some of whom were associated with the IRB. Though the GAA was used by the IRB and later the IRA as a recruiting ground, it became a broadly nationalist organisation without allegiance to any one political party or constituency.[60]

Most of the Irish in America gravitated towards the indigenous sports such as baseball, and the influence of the GAA was largely restricted to centres on the east coast. However, in the New York area the GAA retained a relatively strong following. There it was under the control of the Gaelic Athletic Association of Greater New York – the dominant GAA body in America.[61]

There were several advantages for the IRA and Clan na Gael in having a strong presence within the GAA. First, IRA veterans and non-veterans alike could be recruited through the GAA. Second, IRA men holding elected office within the GAA acquired positions of influence and prestige among the Irish-American community. Third, gate receipts and other monies could be passed on to the IRA. This was either done covertly or occasionally a game could be advertised as being in aid of the IRA or Clan. As Neenan loftily put it, control of the GAA would result in 'enormous gains', including 'purification of [the] games, elevation of [the Irish] race and financial benefits'.[62] Neenan, a member of the New York GAA executive, used this connection as he recruited for the IRA clubs and he reported: 'I am operating [recruiting] with success, using [the] Gaelic Athletic Association for its own and our benefit. [I'm] also paving the way for my appeal for funds.'[63]

Soon after his appointment as An Timthire, he reported: 'I expect to have [a] favourable report of [the] Gaelic Athletic Association in a month or so. I have been working on it for some time.'[64] In January 1927 at the annual convention of the GAA of New York, Neenan was able to make his move. Ninety delegates assembled for what was 'the largest, most successful and most harmonious GAA convention ever held in New York'. Delegates represented their own counties and sports and Neenan attended as a representative for the Cork senior hurlers. At the convention he must have been satisfied to hear that the financial report showed a balance of $3,770. The delegates elected the association's officers and the members of the executive committee.[65] They chose wisely and Neenan reported: 'We have got good representation on [the] governing body [of the] Gaelic [Athletic] Association here. We elected two of our men as: Treasurer [William Magner of Cork] and Vice-President [J. McGuinness of Leitrim] respectively. Had we the necessary material here we could nearly have controlled it. I am on [the] executive committee with a few others [from the IRA].' He clarified: 'Our policy is to purify the games, while using it as a source of revenue. We are trying to run a few field days [games] under different headings if possible for the Army [IRA] funds. With good organisation we should be able to dictate [or gain control] next year.'[66] In another letter he added: 'If some of our fellows were more energetic we could easily control it [the GAA].'[67]

Twomey was disappointed that not enough IRA and Clan na Gael members were participating in the GAA. He wrote to Neenan asking him if he could have it made official Clan policy that members must join the GAA: 'A shame our men will not go into [the] GAA. Could you get their doing so made a policy by the Clan camps [clubs]?'[68]

By February Neenan had made considerable progress in increasing the IRA's influence within the GAA, and the IRA now had a majority among the groups that represented individual Irish counties: 'We have made wonderful progress in [the] GAA and will be able to control it later. [I] have organised each county [group] to gain [an IRA] majority.' He had applied to run several football games, the proceeds of which would benefit the IRA. This was largely done secretly, though one game was openly advertised as an IRA benefit. Neenan was confident that the IRA would succeed in taking control of the GAA – 'we will succeed' – and that at some stage the elected IRA officers and committee members should come out in the open as this would further enhance the respect for the IRA among the members.[69]

Neenan's enthusiasm was somewhat dampened the following month, when he reported: 'We are gaining ground [in the GAA] daily ... the tide is on the turn' but 'some of our fellows are painfully slow'.[70]

The eastern division of the GAA in North America was inaugurated

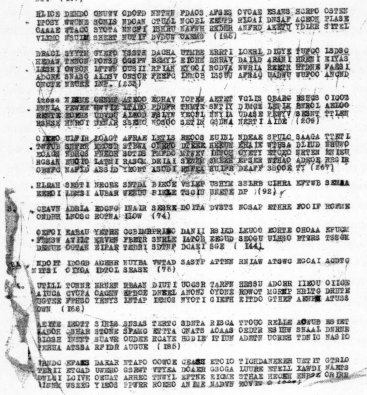

Figure 23. The first page of a three page report from Connie Neenan to Moss Twomey. This is a good example of the amount of cipher in some of the documents sent by the IRA's representatives in America. In the last paragraph Neenan wrote: We have got good representation on [the] governing body [of the] Gaelic [Athletic] Association here. We elected two of our men, as Treasurer and Vice-President respectively. Had we the necessary material here, we could nearly have controlled it. I am on [the] executive, with a few others.

in early 1927, though New York refused to participate. Naturally enough the new organisation attracted Connie Neenan's attention: 'I am anxious we should be strongly represented on it.'[71]

Since Clan membership was secret and Neenan kept quiet about his activities, it's difficult to know the full extent of IRA influence within the GAA in America and for how long it continued. Interestingly, Neenan wrote to Moss Twomey six years later in 1933 about a proposed Kerry football team tour of the US, so he must have retained influence in the GAA at least up until then.[72]

Connie Neenan put his influence in the GAA to use when he helped organise the Kerry football team's tour of the United States in 1927. This
visit was as much the Kerry IRA on tour as it was the Kerry GAA football
team.

The IRA had already planned to benefit from a visiting Irish team
when in the summer of 1926 Tipperary, the all-Ireland hurling champions, toured the United States. On that occasion the IRA's representative made arrangements for Tipperary to play a team drawn from Cork
immigrants at Celtic Park in New York with the proceeds going to the
IRA. The IRA was able to 'square' with the Cork team, though the majority of the players were reported to not be in 'sympathy' with the organisation.[73] However, the IRA's involvement in the Kerry tour was to be on
a far larger scale.

During the Civil War a series of atrocities in Kerry left a legacy of
bitterness unrivalled in the rest of Ireland. In the aftermath of the war,
the GAA was one of the few institutions that could bring together men
from the opposing sides and in this it played a vital role. In 1924 a Kerry
team composed of players who had taken both pro- and anti-Treaty sides
won the All-Ireland Football Championship. And in 1926 the team, captained by John Joe Sheehy, the commander of the IRA's Kerry Number 1
brigade, repeated this feat.

The Kerry GAA now planned an international tour to raise funds for
sports facilities at home and to celebrate their victories. Initially there
was talk of an Australian trip, but the venue was changed to America.

In October 1926, Neenan's predecessor, 'Mr Jones' suggested to Moss
Twomey that the Kerry team should tour the US and Clan na Gael would
'promote the venture'.[74] However, whatever the source of Jones' information, the Clan's executive committee soon told him that they weren't
in favour of supporting the tour. The IRA was now in it alone and 'Jones'
wrote to Twomey: 'If you believe in it get busy. If you disagree [send a]
cable [to me] calling it off.'[75]

In the meantime 'Jones' resigned as An Timthire in favour of Neenan,
who now tried to find a sponsor. Neenan initially proposed that all the
profits of the tour would be handed over to the IRA, which may not have

been a very attractive business proposition for any intending sponsor: 'We failed [to get a sponsor] and the best we can hope for, if they [the Kerry team] come, is to play one match for us.'[76] He put the failure down to 'negligence and circumstances'.[77]

Eventually Ted Sullivan, the leading baseball promoter and entrepreneur, agreed to sponsor the tour. Sullivan (1851–1929) was an Irish-American born in County Clare, and following stints as a baseball player and manager in America he went on to become one of the first major businessmen in the game. He was a pioneer of baseball and made a significant contribution towards transforming it into the national sport. A contemporary newspaper referred to him as 'probably the best known man in base balldom [sic]'. Most famously, he is credited with being the originator of the word 'fan'. Much as Sullivan was honoured in the world of baseball, he couldn't count the IRA and Connie Neenan as among his 'fans'. Neenan regarded Sullivan's support as 'private enterprise where exploitation of [the] champions is indulged in for personal gain' and sent word to the Kerry captain, John Joe Sheehy, that Sullivan 'is not to be trusted'.[78] Neenan added: 'Sullivan pretends to be a martyr to philanthropic motives. I doubt [this] very much.'[79]

Neenan's dislike of Sullivan led him to write: 'Sullivan the promoter is a very shrewd businessman with Jewish habits' who was 'exploiting [the] team for his own ends'.[80] Remarks of this type were common in Ireland and America at the time, and it's actually a credit to the IRA and men like Peadar O'Donnell (who fought against anti-Semitism) that this is the only anti-Semitic comment that we've come across in cipher in the documents.

Neenan wanted Sheehy to ensure that the contract with Sullivan would allow the team to play additional matches to benefit the IRA. Sheehy was told that when the contract was being signed, he should 'expressly reserve freedom of action after [the] matches contracted for, are played'. As Neenan expected to be able to 'arrange to have at least one match in each of the following cities: New York, Boston and Chicago. [The] receipts [would be] for our benefit.'[81] Sheehy felt that most of the team wouldn't object to playing games for the IRA: 'Sheehy states he can get 18 out of the possible 23 players to agree to any of our proposals. The opposition will come from a few individuals here [in America], but I feel we can attend to that question.'[82] It would be interesting to know how exactly Neenan planned to overcome their objections.

Sullivan promised 10 per cent of the proceeds from the gate to the Kerry GAA. Naturally he wanted to maximise the return on his investment and so proposed to take the team to all the major US cities.[83] However, Neenan was more realistic and knew that it would have to be limited to those centres that could actually field a Gaelic football team to play the visitors. He also wanted Sullivan to benefit from as few games as possible; freeing up the team for the IRA games and for the social events in support of Clan na Gael and the IRA. Neenan wrote: 'Sullivan [the] promoter is endeavouring to monopolize the whole situation, but we are going to have a big say in this.'[84] He added: 'I am going to spike him if possible.'[85] He even wanted to start a dispute with Sullivan over his booking the team on an English shipping company, the White Star Line: 'This is an English company ... I am going to cause a row' and he asked Twomey to get Sheehy to stir up trouble in Ireland.[86] If the ships of the White Star Line were good enough for IRA weapons smuggling why weren't they good enough for the Kerry footballers?

Neenan was keenly aware that any public exposure of the IRA's role in the tour could destroy their plans and he warned Twomey: 'I would suggest you keep all reference[s] to [the] GAA and [the] Kerry visit in code, as if you leave [a] message deciphered and [it was] caught in [garda] raids, our plans here would be ruined.'[87]

What about the Kerry players, like Con Brosnan and Paul Russell, who were opposed to the IRA? Twomey wrote that: 'There may be friction as most likely Brosnan and Russell must be taken and these may object to play[ing] for us.'[88] Brosnan was one of the greats of Kerry football. During the Anglo-Irish War he fought with the IRA and in the Civil War was a captain in the national army. Despite all the talk of reconciliation and unity Brosnan was a thorn in Sheehy's side. Sheehy suggested that a threatening letter should be sent to him from America and Neenan wrote: 'Sheehy sent over a message [for someone] to write [to] Brosnan an anonymous letter, informing [the] latter that [the] feeling here is so intensely republican, that it would be safer for him not to come.' However, Neenan added: 'This would not be practical, as Brosnan would publish [the] letter. It would also create a stir here, and when our match is advertised we would be accused of sending threatening letters. Unless Sheehy has other reasons, I would not be in favour of [sending a] letter.'[89] Twomey reported to Neenan that despite Sheehy's best efforts, 'he could not get over having to take [Con] Brosnan and [Paul] Russell and one or two minor [Free] Staters. But outside of these [he] has a team to play. He expects you to do your best to prevent public resentment against those Staters.'[90] Brosnan did indeed go on the tour, but interestingly Russell, who was a garda officer, was reported to have been 'unable to make the trip'.[91]

Neenan also planned to look after the team's social programme which would help with Clan recruitment and with fundraising: 'We can arrange several functions on the social side. On this question I believe we can do immense work for the organisation [the IRA]. I would suggest to Sheehy [that] on his arrival, to leave [the] social side in our hands.'[92] Neenan planned to form a committee to organise the social activities: '[I] am trying to form [a] social committee representing all [of] Ireland, [consisting] of prominent Gaels, to arrange [a] reception for [the] Kerry team. It would be outside [of] Sullivan's programme, while [being] exclusively [drawn from the] Clan.'[93] These activities included 'two boat rides' and a 'big dance'.[94]

Moss Twomey found Sheehy unco-operative and exasperating to deal with. Twomey expected him to help ensure that the team played the fundraising games for the IRA, and that in America he'd use his considerable status as team captain and IRA veteran to help with recruitment for the Clan na Gael and IRA clubs. Twomey wrote: 'Sheehy [is] most unsatisfactory, [I] cannot get him to come to our meetings or give us his views on this business. He has become rather indifferent.'[95] In April, two weeks before the team was due to sail, Twomey reported to Connie Neenan: 'We have succeeded in getting Sheehy to come up here [to Dublin]. We have given him instructions as to [the] work we expect him to do out there. He will go as an accredited representative of the Army Council. He will attend meeting[s] of the Clan executive, Clan reunions or other Clan meetings [if] possible. He will have a week in New York on arrival, before [the] first match. Arrange some work for him, not too much. When you meet, [both of] you can decide your programme ... Sheehy would have [a] good influence with [the IRA] volunteers who have gone there and [would help] to smooth things in clubs, between them and [the] old members.'[96] Before Sheehy's departure, Twomey sent him a written copy of his credentials as the Army Council representative and offered him 'very best wishes for a successful tour'.[97]

One of the final obstacles to the tour was the granting of permission from the GAA's Central Council in Dublin. The GAA's leadership was broadly supportive of the Free State and Neenan warned Sheehy to be 'careful in dealing with matters at home, due to some of the rotten elements existing in various existing GAA councils'.[98] The council can't have been overly enamoured with the overtly republican Kerry team. Additionally, it was concerned about the very real possibility of the players being offered jobs and deciding to emigrate to America; recently six of the Tipperary hurling team had done just that after an American tour. The council met in March 1927 and 'didn't show much enthusiasm' for the tour, with a representative from Cork a vociferous opponent (well if they couldn't beat them on the field maybe they could beat the Kerry team in committee!). However, it was pointed out that the council had already granted permission for the tour in 1926 and so all it could do was add the requirement that the players commit to return to Ireland following the games.[99]

Finally, in May 1927 the players embarked on 'the most historic and talked about trip Kerry footballers had ever undertaken'. Indeed the tour was extremely important to a county badly affected by the trauma of the Civil War, economic recession and endemic poverty. Despite the behind-the-scenes machinations of Connie Neenan and the IRA the trip had an important role to play in drawing people together again and bringing a ray of sunshine and pride into those grey years. Accolades poured in from throughout the Kingdom. Kerry County Council proclaimed: 'By their visit they would bring honour to Ireland and the county which they so ably and successfully represented.' Such was the size and enthusiasm of the crowd that gathered at Tralee railway station to see the team off on their way to the boat at Cobh that some of the players had to be dragged into the compartments of the train through the windows. At Cobh they boarded the *SS Baltic* bound for New York – a ship that featured in many IRA gun-running exploits.

In New York they were greeted by hundreds of supporters, and a police motorcycle escort accompanied the motorcade to City Hall. The highlight of the welcome was a banquet for 1,000 people, including many of the leading luminaries of New York's Irish-American community. Though this was the era of prohibition, during their visit there was 'no shortage of drink to quench the visitors' thirst.

The first game was played against New York at the Polo Grounds before a crowd of 30,000. *The New York Times*, writing about the game, helpfully explained that the sport was a hybrid of soccer and basketball! Unfortunately Kerry were badly beaten 3-11 to 1-7. In the other cities they visited the Kerrymen were victorious. At each stop they received a municipal welcome and in Chicago were given the freedom of the city. In Boston especially, Connie Neenan wanted Sheehy to meet the IRA veterans there to counter the extensive support for Fianna Fáil.

The final game in July was a replay of the contest with New York at Celtic Park. This time, before a smaller crowd of 6,000 and again after a 'gruelling contest', the visitors were beaten 11 to 7. The New Yorkers were accused of rough play and Fr Fitzgerald, who accompanied the Irish team, put their poor showing down to the fact that the pitch was 50 feet shorter than the regulation field in Ireland.[100]

As with all trips, gifts have to be brought to the folks back home. And on the return voyage on the *Baltic* some of the players smuggled Thompson submachine guns in their luggage. These weapons belonged to the IRA and had been under the control of Joe McGarrity in New York.[101]

Con Brosnan had one of the more eventful lives of the players – he went on to win a total of six All Ireland senior football medals and captained the victorious Kerry team in 1931. Politically he was involved in the 'proto-fascist' Army Comrades Association or Blueshirts (which was allied with Cumann na nGaedheal) in the 1930s, until he fell out with them a few years later, following which he broke into the Blueshirts' offices and set fire to copies of their paper, *United Ireland*. In 1933 Neenan again proposed to Twomey a Kerry tour of America, and added that Brosnan wasn't welcome. That same year Twomey wrote to Neenan: 'I wonder if you know that he [Brosnan] has been in Grangegorman [mental] Asylum for the past month. He is a bad case I believe. He felt he was used by Cumann na nGaedheal.' Brosnan passed away in 1975.[102]

Chemical weapons

During the 1920s the IRA made several highly secret attempts in America to obtain intelligence on chemical warfare and weapons. Some of this information was then passed on to Soviet military intelligence (see Chapter 8). The IRA also discussed plans to mount attacks using tear gas, and even mustard gas, in Ireland. This is the story of the IRA and chemical weapons.

There were two principal types of commonly used chemical weapons: poison gases and the non-lethal tear gases, both of which the IRA were interested in.

In the First World War vast quantities of poison gas were used by all the major belligerents. But it failed to have a significant effect on the overall outcome of the war, as armies quickly developed counter-measures and adopted their enemy's technology. By the end of the war, much of the gas was deployed in specially adapted artillery shells, though attacks could also be mounted by releasing the gas from an array of cylinders, or by using crude mortars which fired gas canisters. On occasion gas was sprayed from modified flame-throwers or packed into hand grenades.

Probably the most effective agent used was mustard gas, known as the 'king of gases', which took its name from its faint mustard-like odour. It was primarily a disabling rather than a lethal agent, and was toxic both when inhaled and when it came into direct contact with the skin. The effects of exposure developed slowly over four to eight hours, it irritated the eyes and the lungs, could lead to temporary blindness, and caused blistering and burns of the skin which often took months to heal. A small number of mustard gas shells fired over an area could cause casualties for hours or even days afterwards. It is classified as a persistent gas and, depending on the weather conditions, can linger in the affected area for up to a week or more. Troops had to don both gas masks and special clothing to protect themselves, which severely impaired their fighting ability. The characteristics of mustard gas, especially its persistence, made it particularly suitable as a defensive agent.[103]

Though tear gas is primarily used today by police riot squads, armies used it during the war as an offensive weapon. It had the ability to quickly incapacitate enemy troops or force them to don gas masks, which limited their fighting ability. Tear gas rapidly cleared from the atmosphere, leaving the area again safe for the occupying force. Tear gases (or lachrymators) incapacitate opponents by causing involuntary weeping and temporary blindness. Once exposed to fresh air the victims rapidly recover.[104]

Soon after the war, tear gas weapons were developed for use by the police, particularly in dealing with riots and prison disturbances. Most of these weapons utilised the chemical chloroacetophenone or CN gas, which has more recently been marketed as a personal protective spray under the trade name Mace. CN gas remained the primary tear gas used by law enforcement agencies until replaced by the less toxic CS gas in the 1960s.

The IRA showed considerable interest in tear gas, and given its resources this was a much more practical weapon for the organisation than poison gas. It was particularly interested in tear gas truncheons or billies, among the most commonly produced tear gas weapons in the US, in continuous production from the 1920s through the 1960s. These were primarily used by the police and consisted of a truncheon or billy stick that contained a tear gas cartridge. The firing mechanism and trigger were incorporated into the handle, while the truncheon itself was a metal barrel. To fire the weapon, the trigger in the handle was pressed, resulting in a burst of tear gas emanating from the end of the barrel. There were two basic types of truncheons: spray or blast. The spray type sprayed tear gas vapour for several seconds in the direction the club was pointed, while the blast type instantaneously blasted out a cloud of tear gas, with an effective range of five to fifteen feet. These weapons could be used against one opponent or a small crowd, but tended to have little effect against the rush of a large crowd or in a riot.[105]

In the inter-war years many military experts believed that chemical weapons, specifically agents such as mustard gas, could play a decisive role in the next major conflict.

The first reference I have found connecting the IRA to chemical weapons was an incident from the Anglo-Irish War in 1920 during an attack on the police barracks in Blarney, County Cork. When the IRA failed to blow a breach in the barracks wall with gun cotton, P. A. Murray produced a German bomb, which he 'believed to be a gas bomb'. He was considering using it until someone shouted 'Do it if you want to gas us all' and with that he put it away. Ironically, both Connie Neenan and Dan 'Sandow' Donovan (who was probably the true identity of 'Mr Jones') were among the group with Murray.[106] Since IRA personnel had contact with German arms dealers it's not surprising they may have come across the odd chemical weapon among the stocks left over after the world war. However, at the time there doesn't seem to have been any clear plan or strategy to use these weapons.

In December 1921 during the period of the Anglo-Irish truce, the Royal Irish Constabulary's (RIC) director of intelligence, Brigadier-General Ormonde Winter, feared the IRA would resume hostilities and that 'gas will be used, which is being, I am informed, manufactured in laboratories owned by the Christian Brothers, and other like institutions, some of the chemists so employed having had special training in the manufacture secretly in Germany.'[107] While this report owes more to a fertile imagination (combined with British stereotyping) than the nefarious plans of the Christian Brothers and the IRA, it does raise the question as to whether Winter had information that elements in the IRA were investigating the possibilities of poison gas. Certainly the IRA's munitions and explosives experts, such as Seán Russell, weren't inactive during the time of the truce.

The first reference to chemical weapons in the encrypted documents shows that there was indeed interest in such weapons at GHQ. In April 1925 Frank Aiken asked Liam Pedlar in New York if he had been able to acquire samples of artillery shells containing poison gas. Aiken wrote: 'Artillery gas. Have you succeeded in getting samples of these or is there any hope of it?'[108]

In November 1926, 'Mr Jones' in New York sent a despatch with a 'tear gas formula' to Moss Twomey. The letter went by ocean liner to Southamptom, where George, the OC. Britain, received it, and noted it was 'a formula for the making of some sort of bombs'.[109] He passed it on to a courier, who was later stopped by the customs in Dublin. The customs officers confiscated adaptors for revolvers she was carrying but let her through with the letter and other IRA despatches. GHQ reported back to George that the despatches 'got through safely' and Cooney replied to 'Jones' that he had received the 'chemical formulas'.[110]

That same month Moss Twomey was arrested and briefly imprisoned in Mountjoy along with Mick Price. The ever resourceful 'Mr Jones' felt that tear gas billies could be used to rescue them both. 'Jones' wrote to

Andy Cooney: 'If I can get [in] touch with the right people – I will be able to devote some time to this now – I think there is a chance to get some tear gas here. I was offered six dozen billys and some hundreds of cartridges for $1,500. I refused. If I hang on, I will be able to buy direct from the manufacturer. I am working on this now. I am trying to get about a dozen. If I succeed you might be able to get Price and Moss out.'[111]

With Twomey already released, 'Jones' again sent Cooney a letter that would have also been meant for Moss Twomey: 'Let me know if I should buy machines for releasing gas [and] also [gas] bombs. Billys cost $25 each.'[112] The 'machines for releasing gas' were most likely gas cylinders, while 'bombs' probably referred to gas greanades, which could be thrown by hand or fired by grenade launchers.[113] Twomey was now interested in the idea and replied: 'It would be fine if you succeed in getting some tear gas. Could you there get [sic] a number of men trained in [the] use of this?' Referring to the increased garda activity following the barrack raids, Twomey felt that 'under present conditions' it wouldn't be possible to train IRA men in Ireland in the use of tear gas. He added: 'Let me have more particulars and a sketch or drawing if possible of machines you mention for releasing gas, and bombs. Re [regarding] purchase of billys etc it is chiefly a question of being able to get them sent home [to Ireland]. If you can do this get a small quantity for a trial and to experiment with.'[114]

'Jones' replied with great enthusiasm: 'You ought to be able to make the [tear] gas. I am almost sure I could buy the machines but I have no money. Send an appeal to Clan [na Gael] thru [sic] An Timthire [Connie Neenan] for [the] machines. No training is necessary, all you need to do is turn on a faucet or tap and let it rip. You would need [gas] masks. I think 'Stephen' [the Soviet intelligence officer] could supply them. With twenty machines you might be able to take all [of] Dublin without killing non-combatants. I am sending you a pamphlet, which gives you some idea of it. Expect a price catalogue. I will then have prices. There ought be no difficulty in getting small articles like billys across ... They are very effective I understand.' 'Jones' said he needed $500 to buy the machines.[115] Twomey carefully considered the logistics of a tear gas attack and posed pertinent questions about these machines or cylinders: '[The] principal considerations [are]: amount [of gas] these contain [the] pressure under which [the gas is] released, the power and the radius affected, and [the] atmospheric conditions [needed] for successful employment [sic].'[116] The following month Twomey complained to 'Jones': 'Catalogue and price list for gas apparatus you promised not received yet'.[117]

Twomey told 'Mr Jones' and Connie Neenan that he was 'anxious' to get a few tear gas billies, and he arranged for a sailor, John Hannon, to call on Miss Lagan, an IRA contact in New York. Miss Lagan could introduce Hannon to Neenan or 'Jones' and they should hand over the billies and some 'gun cotton' to Hannon to be smuggled back to Ireland.[118]

In addition to tear gas, Twomey was interested in mustard gas, and he asked 'Jones': 'Try and get formulae for these tear gases and mustard gases, and [an] idea of [the industrial] plant necessary [for manufacturing them].'[119] The Soviet agent 'Stephen' told 'Jones' he would give him the formula for mustard gas, but given the complexity of the production process 'you will not be able to manufacture [it]'. Additionally 'Jones' reminded Twomey that he had already sent him the formulae for tear gas in 1926.[120]

'Jones' clandestinely obtained considerable information on chemical weapons, much of it in the form of reports by the US army's Chemical Warfare Service. This information was passed on to the Soviets, rather than kept for the IRA's own use (see Chapter 8). At one stage he obtained 'the formulae for all the poison gases manufactured here [in the US]. I was very sorry [that] I could not copy this and send it to you [Twomey].'[121]

As things turned out there was no IRA tear gas or poison gas attack in Ireland. However, the questions Moss Twomey asked 'Jones' about deploying tear gas showed he had considered the technical aspects of gas warfare, and had likely talked the issue over with Seán Russell. In these documents two types of attacks were considered.

The first was a limited attack using tear gas firing truncheons to rescue IRA prisoners. Given the right plan, you could probably use any weapon to rescue someone from jail, but the tear gas billy would not be the first choice – though it certainly would have caught the warders and gardaí at Mountjoy by surprise. The warders could have been briefly incapacitated, but the weapon had a short range of only five to fifteen feet and the rescuers, along with the rescued prisoners, would have needed gas masks. Furthermore, if a firefight had broken out, the IRA with their billies would have been badly 'outgunned'.

The second idea, put forward by 'Mr Jones', was for a mass tear gas attack in Dublin, allowing the IRA to take over the capital. This was militarily a ridiculous idea. The IRA would have needed to mount attacks throughout the city, and as to how all the appropriate targets could have been blanketed in tear gas is inconceivable. Releasing such a volume would have required formidable resources and equipment, and on top of that a major limitation would have been the capriciousness of the wind, especially in a city where it is funnelled by the buildings. If all went according to plan, tear gas could have enabled the IRA to take one or two key targets in the city, but they would then have had to deal with a Free State counter-attack and there is nothing to suggest that the IRA had the capability to fight a set piece battle with the better armed, disciplined and trained regular army.

Aside from the military considerations there was the virtual certainty that a large number of civilians would have been exposed to the gas. Children, the elderly and those with lung disease in particular are at increased risk of toxicity and possibly long-term complications. Little is known of the long-term effects following exposure to tear gas, particularly on those with pre-existing medical conditions. [122]

The IRA men would have been operating without proper training in the handling and use of chemical weapons, posing a danger to themselves, their opponents and the civilians of Dublin. Anybody intending to use tear gas needs to be properly trained and aware of its limitations and advantages. At least five deaths have been reported from the inappropriate use of tear gas grenades in confined spaces, and firing a blast type tear gas billy into someone's face can cause permanent blindness. [123]

Twomey showed an interest in mustard gas, one of the most effective of the poison gases. However, producing it was a very complex procedure, requiring an industrial plant far beyond the IRA's capability. Mustard gas could have been loaded into artillery shells and caused havoc among the Free State soldiers, but again the IRA didn't have artillery, or a ready supply of the chemical. If, despite all this, it was somehow possible to deploy

mustard gas, it could have been used in conjunction with tear gas to maximise the effectiveness of the attack. The Free State army, which was unlikely
to have had ready access to gas masks, could have suffered severe casualties. Because of its persistence, mustard gas is a defensive-type gas not well
suited to an attacking force, and the IRA would have had to equip their men
with gas masks and protective clothing. Those exposed to the gas, including
civilians, were liable to develop severe burns, and some would have died
agonising deaths. In the highly unlikely event the IRA could accumulate sufficient supplies, deploy the weapon, and protect its own men, it would then
have had to defend itself from a counter-attack by the Free State army.

The evidence from these documents suggests that there was a pro-
longed discussion at GHQ regarding the IRA's use of chemical weapons. It
was a period of two full years from Aiken's mention of gas artillery shells
to Twomey's request for the weapons from America. And if the RIC's
director of intelligence, Brigadier-General Ormonde Winter, was correct
in his information then the IRA considered their use for over five years.
Throughout this period Seán Russell remained at GHQ, and so the finger
of suspicion must point to his involvement. Considering that the IRA's plan
for seizing power in the Free State depended on swiftly taking control of
Dublin, rather than a set piece war, it seems possible that chemical weapons
figured in this plan. The IRA had no other surprise weapon or tactic.

However, the whole idea of a gas attack on Dublin was far-fetched
and impractical, and it seems inconceivable that many in the IRA leadership, including Moss Twomey, would have actually carried through such
an act and exposed the citizens of Dublin to either tear gas or poison gas
– though they did certainly consider it!

All the major powers in the 1920s possessed chemical weapons expertise and experience, but any attack would have been contrary to the
1925 Geneva Protocol, which banned the use of poisonous and asphyxiating gases (and biological weapons) in war and was soon signed by all the
major powers except the United States and Japan. Ireland, under Cumann
na nGaedheal, acceded to the treaty in 1930 with the reservation that it
would not consider itself bound by the treaty if attacked by a country using
chemical weapons. Although not explicitly stated, the majority of signato-
ries consider that the provisions of the protocol cover tear gas in addition

to poison gas. The United States, however, disputes this.[124] Needless to say the IRA is not a signatory to the protocol! There's a certain irony that Frank Aiken (who was interested in gas artillery shells in 1925) should have been the first signatory to the 1968 Nuclear Proliferation Treaty. This was an honour bestowed on him as Irish Minister for External Affairs for his championing of the cause of nuclear disarmament.

Arms smuggling

During the mid 1920s the IRA smuggled a small quantity of arms and ammunition from America. The smuggling depended on the IRA's ability to purchase weapons in America, support among the longshoremen who loaded and unloaded the ships in New York and New Jersey, sympathetic crew members on the ships or passengers willing to carry the weapons in their luggage, and IRA men at ports in Ireland or Britain able to receive the cargo. As already discussed, this network had originally been developed by the IRB in the nineteenth century and reached its peak during the Anglo-Irish War under the direction of Michael Collins and his agents. But with Collins' support of the Anglo-Irish Treaty, the disbanding of the IRB and the drift of many IRA men away from the movement, it had partially disintegrated.

Following the Irish Civil War, though arms continued to be freely available in America, the IRA was severely constrained by a lack of finance, due to a loss of support from (particularly the wealthier sections of) the Irish-American community.

In New York and New Jersey the IRA had some support among the longshoremen – a key constituency for anyone wanting to smuggle weapons or any other goods. Traditionally the longshoremen had been of Irish stock, and until 1900 about 95 per cent of those on the New York waterfront were Irish. By 1920, however, the Irish were in a minority due to the large influx of Italians, although the workforce at Manhattan's west side docks remained predominately Irish. The longshoremen were organised into a powerful union, the International Longshoremen's Association (ILA), and the Irish were strongly represented among the union's leadership. As the union exercised considerable control over the movement of goods through the docks, it's not surprising that it had links with organised crime.[125]

During the Anglo-Irish War the longshoremen on Manhattan's west side were 'attuned to the struggles of Ireland' and made large donations to Irish relief funds. The men were organised into work gangs which tended to be based upon county of origin in Ireland, and this reinforced their nationalist spirit.[126] In the summer of 1920 some 2,000 longshoremen stayed away from their jobs in support of Irish independence and in protest at the arrest of Terence MacSwiney, the then Sinn Féin mayor of Cork city.[127]

There were several smuggling routes from New York direct to Cobh in Ireland, or to the ports of Liverpool, Glasgow and Southamptom and from there on to ships bound for Ireland. Most of the transatlantic ships were British-flagged vessels, on board which the contraband was transported in the care of a crew member or passenger acting for the IRA.

On arrival at Cobh the weapons were either handed over to dockers working for the IRA or brought to the Rob Roy pub in the town, to be picked up later. Likewise at the British ports there were IRA men working at the docks who would collect the weapons and arrange their transfer to a boat sailing to Ireland.

In addition to weapons, the IRA sent over money by courier, and despatches went back and forth between Ireland and America. The despatches were carried either by a courier or by a sympathetic crew member.

By 1924 the main arms smuggler in New York was Liam Pedlar, who doubled as the 'military attaché' for de Valera's republican 'government'. The smuggling network was probably at a nadir during this period and Pedlar complained to Seán Russell that he had no addresses in Liverpool and Glasgow to 'which stuff [munitions] could be delivered'. Pedlar forwarded several thousand rounds of ammunition to Ireland, mainly for .303 Lee Enfield rifles (the standard British army service rifle of the period), but had to pay men to bring it across. He was able to send IRA despatches to the port of Southampton, but couldn't smuggle weapons there.[128] Pedlar was very disparaging of the IRA section working on the Liverpool docks, writing that 'things seem to be very much mixed up'.[129]

Pedlar sent weapons on the White Star Line's *SS Baltic* and despatches on the British-flagged *Majestic*, *Leviathan* and *Olympic*.[130] He was constantly seeking out crew members who'd work for him. A member of the crew on the *America* agreed to bring over goods, and Pedlar asked Russell to arrange, on the ship's arrival in Cobh, for the IRA to send out a tender to meet the vessel. So that the courier and the local IRA could recognise each other, one of the IRA men would wear a pre-arranged article of clothing which would be similar to a piece worn by the man on the *America*.[131] Around this time the adjutant general also advised that 'it is possible to get men positions as stokers etc. on boats going from London to America'.[132]

Moss Twomey and Andy Cooney set about rebuilding the smuggling network and worked with An Timthire as well as IRA commanders in Britain and Ireland. An Timthire wrote to the chief of staff that a number of crew members could be availed of to bring despatches and 'probably the handling [of] ammunition'. The list included: 'Ed Redmond [the] Second Engineer [on the] *Empress of France*, George McNamara [and] James Murray of Cork [who were] Second Class Deck Stewarts [on the *SS] Baltic*'. The chief of staff told An Timthire that 'communications [despatches] or any stuff [weapons or explosives] which can be sent direct[ly to Cobh] shall be left at [the] Rob Roy [bar],[133] while an IRA man who had emigrated to the US offered his services when he visited Dublin: 'Kevin O'Neill was home from [the] USA, and was willing to take papers or war goods from there if wanted.'[134]

Throughout the 1920s the IRA's attempts to import large shipments of arms and explosives, from either America or the continent, mostly ended in failure and the organisation was defrauded on a number of occasions. The IRA's success was in importing multiple small consignments, which over time added up to a significant quantity of weaponry.[135]

The most spectacular of the large purchases in America was that of 653 Thompson submachine guns in 1921 by a group which included Liam Pedlar. Around fifty guns were promptly sent on board the *SS Baltic* and *Celtic* to Liverpool and from there to Ireland. However, US customs impounded the main cache of 500 weapons, and following a legal tussle they were eventually handed over in November 1925 to the 'owner's agent', Joseph McGarrity, who acted on behalf of the IRA. McGarrity stored the weapons at a warehouse in Manhattan.[136]

Liam Pedlar continued to send a small quantity of those remaining in his possession to Ireland throughout 1923.[137] In February 1925 he wrote to Russell that parts for the guns were at Joe Begley's house in Ireland, but they weren't well cared for and would soon be 'useless'. Begley had been one of the senior arms agents in America, along with Pedlar, during the Anglo-Irish War. Pedlar recommended that Russell could get the guns from Begley by way of an introduction from Kathleen O'Connell (de Valera's long-standing personal secretary).[138]

In 1926, after US Customs returned the 500 guns to McGarrity, 'Mr Jones' attempted to sell the weapons to the Soviets: 'I tried to get "Stephen" [the Soviet intelligence officer in New York] to buy the Thompson guns. I asked [for] $70,000. Whenever they [the Russians] are in doubt they cable home. This is how they treated this offer. I waited patiently for months for an answer. I asked again, and they said that one of their commercial organizations would buy them. I have waited in vain and they can now get someone else to do their dirty work.'[139] In July 1927 John Joe Sheehy and his teammates brought back some of the guns to Kerry on the *Baltic*.[140] By 1936 all the Thompsons had been distributed – most made it back to Ireland, but some fell into the hands of (or were possibly sold to) criminal gangs in America.[141] But the Thompson proved to be of little use to the IRA – it was a short-range, rapid-fire weapon unsuited to the IRA's tactics, and this was compounded by a chronic shortage of ammunition.[142]

One of Connie Neenan's contacts was a man by the name of O'Neill, who worked as crew on the *Victor Emmanuel III*, and Neenan reported to Twomey: '[The] Free State are importing all sizes of ammunition from [the] US. The stuff goes to Dublin direct on Oriel Line [*sic*] boats particularly the *Victor Emmanuel* ... On her last trip she took rifle and artillery ammunition.' Neenan was likely thinking the IRA could seize some of these munitions and he recommended that if Twomey had an informant within the offices of George Bell & Co. (the ship's agents) at Burgh Quay he could get a detailed description of the cargo from the 'bills of lading, a few days before [the] arrival of [the] ship' in Dublin.[143] Interestingly, Neenan mistakenly referred to the shipping line as the 'Oriel Line' rather than the correct 'Oriole Line'. 'Oriel House' was the original headquarters of the CID in Dublin, and the name by which the IRA often called the CID or the Special Branch.

However, the ship's first mate, a Swede by the name of William Dahlgrene, posed a (temporary) obstacle. Neenan described the situation:

'[The] first mate of [the] *Victor Emanuel* [*sic*] is anti-Irish' and had succeeded in removing several Irish men from the crew. 'He is a danger to us and should be dealt with i.e. put in hospital for a few weeks. He would [then] lose [his] ship. He got threatened in Cork before and won't go ashore there. He must be got at over there [in Dublin].'[144] Two months later, before Twomey had a chance 'to meet O'Neill to find out about [the] first mate', Neenan reported that Dahlgrene 'was drowned [*sic*] accidentally during [his] last trip to Dublin. I presume he was drunk.'[145]

On the morning of 29 December, with the *Victor Emanuel* docked in Dublin, Dahlgrene's body was pulled from the water at the North Wall docks. The night before he had visited officers on board another ship with a friend. The friend denied they were drunk, saying: 'We had just one cup of coffee and one drink each.' However, as he was returning to the *Victor Emmanuel* ahead of Dahlgrene he heard a splash. The gardaí determined Dahlgrene had fallen from a gangway which was well lighted and with intact railings. They also reported that when they interviewed the ship's officers who had been with Dahlgrene they were all sober, though this was several hours after the incident. The coroner ruled he had died from drowning but noted a three-inch cut over his left eye which was presumed to have occurred as he fell into the water.

Was Dahlgrene pushed? Did O'Neill or another IRA man do the job? Or was it just a coincidence that he drowned at a time when the IRA wanted him out of the way? Neenan reported that he had previously been threatened in Cork, so Dahlgrene was already a marked man. On the other hand Neenan's warning to Twomey about the first mate wasn't received at GHQ until 19 January 1927, three weeks after the drowning.[146] Dahlgrene's companions denied he was drunk, though if he had been they would have likely denied it anyway. We can only speculate, but there are no clear answers to these questions.

When Twomey was unable to acquire gun cotton in Britain he asked Neenan to try to get it and suggested that O'Neill could bring it over: 'Perhaps [the] man on the *Victor Emmanuel* could bring [a] small lot [over] on each trip. It is urgent.'[147] Two months later Neenan was still trying to acquire some from 'Stephen'.[148]

The picture that emerges of the IRA smuggling operation in the US during the mid 1920s is far from spectacular, but nonetheless it resulted in a steady trickle of weaponry.

De Valera and the IRA

Just as in Ireland, the main threat to the IRA and Clan na Gael in America came from de Valera and Fianna Fáil. IRA veterans in the US retained a great degree of loyalty to de Valera and in 1926 An Timthire wrote that 99 per cent of republican supporters there wouldn't 'stand nasty things to be said of him'.[149] Given this degree of support, Neenan needed to be very careful in criticising or distancing the IRA from de Valera.

De Valera's support organisation in America was the AARIR. However, like all the Irish-American political organisations it went into a decline following the Anglo-Irish Treaty – only it had further to fall than the others. In 1921 its membership was 700,000 and by 1925 this had dropped to 13,870, of whom approximately a quarter were in New York.[150] This was still, however, a larger membership than that of the Clan. Some republicans remained members of both organisations, although overall the AARIR's membership was more affluent and influential than that of the Clan.

In January 1926 Frank Aiken set out on a lecture tour of the US, sponsored by the AARIR.[151] Although no longer chief of staff, he remained an officer attached to the GHQ staff and officially the IRA pronounced that 'he was granted leave of absence to perform work for the Republic abroad.'[152] In reality though de Valera had sent him to raise support and funds for the soon-to-be-founded Fianna Fáil.

On Aiken's arrival the newspapers, including *The New York Times*, inaccurately referred to him as the IRA chief of staff.[153] Aiken didn't correct this error for some time and news of his ouster wasn't commonly known in America. Even Joe McGarrity assumed he was still chief of staff and he was furious when he found out.[154] McGarrity felt that he and the Clan had earned the right to be kept fully informed of developments in Ireland and angrily wrote to Aiken: 'I have failed to learn up to the present time, just what the platform or policy of the party is.'[155] Aiken (and de Valera) were trying to maintain the Clan's support, or at least prevent their condemnation, as they stealthily developed their political policy, and Aiken wrote to McGarrity that 'the Clan na Gael organisation should confine its activities to supporting the Army [IRA] whilst leaving the members free to support their favourite political Republican organisation.'[156]

In the autumn Aiken was suspected of suffering from TB and was sent to recuperate in the dry climate out west. 'Jones' reported: 'He is in California at present under doctor's orders. He was becoming TB [sic].'[157] As instructed by the Army Council, 'Jones' sent him on a copy of General Order 28, which forbade a member of the IRA from standing as a candidate in an election.[158] Aiken continued to be watched by the IRA until his return to Ireland in mid 1927 – still technically a member of the organisation.[159]

Members of the Clan were concerned about what appeared to be another impending split in its ranks; between those who favoured de Valera and those who supported GHQ. In New York the Clan had already been badly affected by the 1920 break with Devoy (when only a minority of the original Clan members aligned themselves with McGarrity's section) and in 1927 members there proposed that Sinn Féin and Fianna Fáil reunite under a 'neutral' leadership. As Neenan reported: 'In the near future, the idea of both republican wings of political organisations [Sinn Féin and Fianna Fáil] becoming united is to be suggested. A convention of each party is to be called when 'Scelig' [J. J. O'Kelly, a Sinn Féin leader] will offer to resign and call on de Valera to do likewise, leaving both conventions to elect a neutral leader. [It is] said [that the] united party will get [the] full support of Devoy's Clan. This is the report, as I got it, and though I see no possibility of it materialising, the New York Clan are very keen on you [Twomey] having this information.'[160] Twomey more realistically replied: 'There is no hope of success for the suggestion ... It would not be entertained I think by any section. They [Sinn Féin and Fianna Fáil] are getting more apart every day.'[161]

A major cause of the dissension within the Clan was a rule passed at the organisation's convention in September 1926, that stipulated that its membership couldn't participate in any political party that was involved in elections in Ireland.[162] The rule was clearly aimed at Fianna Fáil. At the convention Cooney (who was in attendance) had 'advised against passing the rule ... [as he] knew it would lead to friction' and the IRA's leadership in Dublin regarded it as 'unwise'.[163] In February 1927 Neenan reported that the rule had 'driven a lot of old members away, as the latter believe they should be entitled to do as they please. All such members are joining Fianna Fáil. This ... is doing a lot of harm.'[164]

Most republicans in the United States (and Ireland) continued to be unaware of any significant policy differences between Fianna Fáil and the IRA, and were disappointed with Neenan and McGarrity for distancing themselves from de Valera. This was all the more reason for de Valera to remain deliberately ambiguous or misleading in his pronouncements on his plans.

Whatever difficulty the Clan had from Aiken's visit, it was to be nothing compared with the arrival of de Valera himself in March 1927. Ostensibly the purpose of his trip was to give evidence in a court case brought by the Free State to secure possession of the $2.5 million remaining from the $6 million raised for the Irish Republic Bonds. The court's decision in May was a defeat for the Free State and a victory for de Valera's strategy as the judge ruled that the money should be returned to the original subscribers. De Valera hoped that the subscribers would then voluntarily hand over the money to him and Fianna Fáil.[165]

Twomey warned Connie Neenan: 'De Valera is sailing for America tomorrow in connection with [the] Dáil loan litigation and chiefly it is believed to get [a] portion for his party from [the bond] subscribers, in case amounts [sic] are returned [by the court to the] subscribers. You must be active too on this matter. Keep in touch with [the] bond holders' association, and be ready to collect if [the] time comes to do so. You must take it, de Valera will do his utmost to influence and win over influential members of [the] Clan to his party, so be prepared for this ... He must be left in no doubt as to [the] attitude of Clan [na Gael] and no receptions or encouragement to his activities must be given.'[166] A week later Twomey followed this up: 'Keep us informed of de Valera's activities. You will act if he attempts to gain [control] over [the] Clan or prominent members of it. It may be necessary for you and "Jones" to visit various centres [to thwart him].'[167]

De Valera arrived at a difficult time for Neenan, as Joe McGarrity, one of the few people who could have helped him rally the Clan, had left the country. In December 1926 McGarrity resigned as chairman and headed to Colombia in search of needed business opportunities.[168] He was armed with a letter of introduction to the archbishop of Bogota from

Cardinal Dougherty of Philadelphia, who described him as 'an excellent Irish Catholic'.[169] Neenan put the reason for his trip delicately: 'It was not a case of financial difficulties, but he had some idea of improving his accounts.'[170] As it was, McGarrity retuned to the United States in May 1927 and quickly resumed his leadership of the Clan.

Within a month of de Valera's arrival, Neenan reported to Twomey: 'De Valera has done us a lot of damage since his arrival. Through his influence many good members of [the] Clan are actively engaged with Fianna Fáil. His presence had its desired effect as ... certain members [of the Clan] showed their real sympathies. It was the Army [IRA] men that surprises [sic] me. I warned [the] New York [Clan na Gael] Officer Board of the possibilities two months ago, and those who believed I was wrong actually went to meet de Valera ... To avoid [the] Dub. [GHQ] position being misrepresented, I consulted with Art [O'Connor, president of Sinn Féin] and 'Jones'. Later going to meet de Valera and explaining our position and also the good work which the young men had done here, but which could easily be destroyed by his agents. I also told him I disagreed with his policy, so as to avoid a discussion of it.'[171] 'Events at home and de Valera's visit created misunderstanding and apathy [among IRA veterans in the US]. [A] number of Army men who arrived in this country are of no use, some [are] harmful.'[172]

All de Valera had to do was avoid, as far as possible, a confrontation with the IRA and the Clan while steadily winning over their members. And his response to Neenan showed that he was now the master of the situation – a politician who could run rings around the IRA. 'He [de Valera] practically advised us to go on as we were going and stated his desire to bring back the people here to [the] republican idea [sic]. So far he has avoided a full explanation of his policy, so that people cannot locate the weak spots. In personal talk with some individuals he refused to give the important guarantees [such as whether he'd enter the Free State Dáil] which convinced them his policy was wrong.

'He is very well received and getting large sums for elections, even certain Clan members subscribed liberally, who had given insignificant sums to [the] Army [fundraising] appeal. The sooner he returns [to Ireland] the better for us.

'The situation has got so tense that the clause [rule] about [Clan members supporting] outside organisations, [passed] at [the] last [Clan] convention cannot be enforced. As a matter of fact in some districts it has been stated [that Clan] members were free to [do] as they liked. Even some of the Clan executive, favoured the latter course openly in their own areas. At a largely attended reunion in New York, some members wanted the rule enforced: [that] all [Clan] members [who were also members] of constitutional movements be expelled. A very unhealthy discussion arose which lasted a few hours. It did not help the organization in any way. It surprised me the number of Army men who opposed the motion, but their idea was to prevent a split. A certain bunch of old timers would be better out than in.'[173]

Neenan saw the disagreement within the Clan as a threat to its very survival. 'I took up the attitude of preventing a split as it would reduce our numbers to a very small amount. Furthermore it would kill any hope of assisting the Army [IRA]. All our schemes and progress ... would receive a deathblow. Not that members support Fianna Fáil, but they would drop off disheartened and disgusted. It would drive men to become interested elsewhere. My idea is to save the Army men, as in time de Valera's policy will prove its futility. We must retain the Army men united.'[174]

Neenan realised that the Clan rule would be hotly debated at the next convention in the autumn, and he asked Twomey: 'Let me have your views on the matter and what do you suggest as a course of action. We can have it discussed – pros and cons – before [the] Clan convention.'[175] He felt that 'unless [an] amicable arrangement [is] reached trouble will ensue.'[176] 'De Valera's presence has caused all this [sic] question to reappear. If he goes so will all [the] anxiety ... Joe McGarrity is expected back in a month from now. His presence will be helpful.'[177]

The news from around the country was similar to that in New York. 'Boston suffered [the] most from de Valera's visit. Some members wanted to meet him officially, but my [Neenan's] advice was sought [and] I refused to agree. [The] trouble ceased on [my] explanation but still several [men] support Fianna Fáil ... Some members are definitely lost in Boston but we will get on without them.' Neenan also noted support for Fianna Fáil among Clan members in Philadelphia and Chicago.[178]

On 1 May de Valera left Boston to return to Ireland, his visit a success. He had managed to consolidate support in America, while side-stepping any disagreements he had with the IRA. The influential *Irish World* continued to support both de Valera and the Clan. Even *An Phoblacht* in Ireland continued favourable coverage of Fianna Fáil.

Twomey wanted Neenan to keep an eye on the AARIR and report back on their work 'supporting Fianna Fáil' as well as the organisation's 'strength, money raised, activities, nature of [their] propaganda and speeches'. He harboured a hope that IRA supporters within the AARIR would help to split the organisation (just as appeared to be happening to the Clan) and rather wistfully asked Neenan: 'Any organisation being formed by [the] republican [*sic*] minority at [the] AARIR convention?'[179] While Neenan was unable to detect any sign of dissension, he noted that joint branches of the AARIR and Fianna Fáil were being formed and 'It won't be easy to get that lot to work in harmony. The vast majority [of them] are no good.'[180]

While the activities of de Valera threatened the very existence of the Clan, the breach with Devoy was overall of less significance but far more bitter. Neenan made occasional reports back to Ireland on the activities of Devoy, his paper the *Gaelic American* and the FOIF. The *Gaelic American* managed to excel when it came to gutter journalism and its columns reflected Devoy's spite in his old age; de Valera was called a 'dead jew' and the editor of the *Irish World* was accused of having overdosed with a 'chink' in New York's Mott Street. However, the paper was closer to the truth when it accused the AARIR of having more initials in its name than actual members.[181]

At one stage Neenan felt that Devoy might be turning away from supporting the Free State: 'I have it from [a] reliable source that Devoy's Clan and [his] paper are going to constitutionally oppose [the] Free State government at a date not very distant. Latterly they have openly attacked [the] Free State in a series of leading articles. I will report any further news but it is best to leave them carefully to themselves, even though they are most anxious to get a grip on the young [IRA] men [who have recently immigrated].'[182] Twomey told him: '[It's] advisable [that] touch be kept with Devoy's Clan. You should be careful not to get mixed up with them yourself. Perhaps if [the eighty-five-year-old] Devoy died many [members] would come over to us.'[183]

Neenan also reported on the activities of Michael Ryan. Ten years earlier Ryan had been the leader of the United League, the American organisation which supported Irish home rule and John Redmond, but after the collapse of the home rule movement (following the 1916 Rising) he joined Devoy's FOIF.[184] Ryan was a 'notorious bluffer', who even after the war remained strongly pro-German. In February 1927 he attended a function in New York in honour of the visiting retired Admiral Paul Behncke of the German navy at which 'speeches were delivered advocating closer co-operation between Ireland and Germany'.[185]

As it happened there was to be no further split in the Clan, just inexorable decline. It is a remarkable testament to the depth of devotion and admiration Joe McGarrity had for de Valera that their friendship lasted for almost another ten years. The break finally occurred in 1936 with de Valera and Fianna Fáil in government, when an IRA prisoner died in jail – allegedly murdered. De Valera refused an inquest, leading McGarrity to accuse him of 'selling out his former friends and repressing all freedom of thought and action in Ireland with the ruthlessness of a dictator'.[186]

Money

During the Anglo-Irish War, America had been the source of considerable financial support for the IRA and Sinn Féin, and Moss Twomey expected the Clan to continue to provide significant funding for the organisation.

Throughout the Anglo-Irish War (1919–21) the FOIF had raised over a million dollars for the Irish Victory Fund and de Valera's Republican Bonds brought in over six million.[187] Impressive amounts, though admittedly only a fraction ended up in the hands of the IRA. American financial support never again reached such levels, although there were significant amounts raised during and immediately following the Civil War (1922–3).

In early 1923 Joe McGarrity provided $42,000 for Liam Lynch's abortive plan to purchase mountain artillery in Germany.[188] In August of the same year he helped the Clan raise $200,000 to support the Sinn Féin general election campaign, and this effort left the Clan largely broke.[189]

Following this there was a significant drop off in the ability of the Clan to provide money. A 1924 drive to raise $100,000 for by-elections in Ireland was a 'miserable failure'.[190] Altogether between 1923 and September 1926 the Clan alone raised a total of $500,000 for Irish independence.[191]

In January 1925 Liam Pedlar reported to Seán Russell that the Clan had raised '[$]25,000 since July-August last. All efforts in this direction have been made for the election fund.'[192] Russell wanted Pedlar to go to the Clan executive and have the money raised by the Clan directly 'ear-marked' for the IRA instead of going through the 'republican government'. In Pedlar's opinion 'there are a great many in the Clan who would rather subscribe and raise money for the Army than for any political purpose', but he recommended that any changes in the arrangement should be made by the IRA leadership in Dublin in communication with the republican 'government' rather than by him in the US.[193] Frank Aiken angrily wrote to Pedlar complaining about his communicating with 'every conceivable person here [at GHQ]' and to henceforth direct all his correspondence to Seán Lemass, Aiken's partner and the newly appointed 'Minister for Defence'.[194] Aiken was obviously hoping to put an end to this unwanted discussion and keep the Clan on board with de Valera.

However, in August 1925 McGarrity finally declared that henceforth the Clan's money was to be provided for military activities only and not for electioneering.[195] That he didn't pull the plug on the arrangement with the republican 'government' earlier was due to his admiration for de Valera than any abiding faith in the democratic process. This new arrangement with the IRA was cemented by the agreement of September 1926 negotiated by Andy Cooney. When Cooney returned to Ireland in October he brought with him $2,000 from the Clan.[196]

In November 1926 the Soviets cut back on their monthly payments to the IRA, making the IRA almost entirely dependent on funding from the Clan. As a result Andy Cooney wrote to 'Mr Jones' in New York: 'This is intended as an urgent appeal for immediate financial support [from the Clan]. Spare no effort to ensure that money is sent [to] us without delay ... America is our only financial source at present. It is therefore essential that support be sent without delay.'[197] Cooney was so desperate that he even threatened to disband the IRA unless the Clan provided adequate support: 'Owing to [the] non-fulfilment of [the] agreement [by the Soviets] we are absolutely without any money whatever and this at a time when we never needed it more urgently. I have already written [to] you to send on money immediately. If this is not done, we will have no alternative but to close down. Point out to [the] Clann [*sic*] that with them rests the decision as to whether we can maintain our organisation or not.'[198]

An Timthire replied: 'A special appeal for financial help was issued by Clan Headquarters two weeks ago and returns should be completed in another two [weeks]. I attended [a] meeting of [the Clan na Gael] Board of Officers [for] New York and quoted your appeal. As a result each club increased their contribution to [the] appeal by nearly 100%. The Officer Board sanctioned giving at least $300, which should bring [the] total of [the] New York District to $1,000. The Liam Lynch Club [of] New York contributed [the] largest sum, as proof of their repudiation of [the] Cork [IRA] officers [who recently condemned the IRA's killing of a garda officer in the barrack raids].'[199]

In addition the Clan na Gael clubs in San Francisco had already in October 1926 promised to provide $500 monthly – but only a portion of this was ever sent.[200]

Some of the IRA leadership in Dublin suggested that Cooney and Russell visit the US to spearhead an appeal for funds. 'It is suggested here that Seán Russell and myself [Cooney] should go over for a special drive. I am totally against it, particularly at [the] present time when our place is right here. At the same time I would like to know if a special drive would justify itself.'[201] Given the strong support for de Valera among Clan members such a trip would have been potentially divisive, and furthermore, it could have been seen as interfering with the Clan's own authority. Not surprisingly, '[the] executive body of [the] Clan are totally against the proposal of yourself and Seán Russell coming out here. They contend it would not achieve any success, as [the] time and circumstances are unsuitable.'[202]

In mid December Cooney again wrote to 'Jones': 'The situation here is impossible because of lack of finance. We must now have £1,000 immediately. We have kept going by borrowing and our credit is now at zero.' Cooney wanted 'Jones' to give a bank draft for the £1,000 ($5,000) to the IRA courier, Miss O'Connor, who had just brought this despatch to him. So that Cooney could know what boat she was taking on her return to Ireland and when she was leaving, he told 'Jones' to send a cryptic telegram giving the name of the boat and the date the ship set sail from New York. The telegram was to open with the words 'Dorothy sails on the ... ['Jones' was to insert the boat name and date here]'.[203]

The Clan had difficulty raising the money and 'most districts are slow to furnish returns', but finally in January 1927 Connie Neenan (who had recently replaced 'Jones' as An Timthire) sent £1,025 by courier. This was equivalent to $5,000 − $4,000 from the Clan and $1,000 which Neenan had received from supporters in California. He took a number of precautions. The money was sent as cash and not as a bank draft 'as I considered large drafts were suspicious, especially when we had no suitable names for [the] sender or to whom [it was] payable'. Neenan also didn't send a telegram ahead of the courier, as suggested by Cooney: 'I did not cable as to [the] date [the] cash was going over, as I did not want to attract suspicion in any way.'[204]

Neenan expected that when all the returns from the Clan's appeal were in, he'd be able to send on a similar amount again. But even this hoped-for $10,000 (or £2,000) left Twomey 'disappointed that [the] anticipated response will not be higher'.[205]

Twomey explained that while the money from America might be adequate to keep the IRA intact, it was insufficient to carry out the overthrow of the Free State and therefore the IRA was reluctantly forced to continue to work for the Soviets: '[I] am sure you realise how absolutely essential cash is and this necessity alone ... [is the reason for] our anxiety for keeping in with these people [the Soviets]. America will not supply sufficient [finance] for [our] needs except [to keep the] organisation ... this [is] not enough to finance preparations for revolution.'[206]

Twomey was again desperate for cash in April and having to 'exercise rigid economy': 'We have none whatever. We are borrowing against your remittance.'[207] Two weeks later he wrote: 'We are in a deplorable way for lack of cash. Such a state of things never existed ... before. We must know what we can count on from you.'[208]

In May Neenan sent over another $1,250 ($1,000 of which was from the Clan) to Ireland. The cash was sent in an envelope along with other despatches and addressed to the original courier, Miss O'Connor of Leitrim. The sender was given as her father who lived in the US.[209] Later that month the pressure on the IRA eased somewhat when the Russians finally gave them £1,000.

Neenan calculated that the $6,000 raised by the Clan between October 1926 and January 1927 worked out at $1.25 per head, and was 'hopeless, and I have told them so'. He continued: 'Too much money is used for expenses by [the] Clan. This is confidential but as far as I see, it costs too much to run such a small organization. It should be more self-contained.'[210] Twomey was 'keenly disappointed' and added: 'Unless there are hopes of much more support, I doubt if the Clan organisation is worth all the worry, trouble and energy expended by you and some others as well as ourselves on it. Explain to [the Clan] executive [that] we must have £1,000 at once and at least £250 ($1,250) each month.'[211] Neenan agreed that the 'Clan can do a lot more' and that he would discuss the 'exceptionally small' amounts raised with the executive and report back to Twomey.[212] Twomey wanted Neenan to 'put it up to [the Clan] executive that administrative expenses in [the] Clan should be cut down to [a] minimum. Surely a couple of whole-time paid officers should be sufficient, taking [the] strength of [the] organisation into account.'[213]

For all of 1927 the Clan sent over a total of about $20,000 (£4,000), of which $10,000 was sent by McGarrity in November.[214] In 1928 the Clan reported giving $16,000 to Neenan.[215] Overall, small change compared to what had been raised a few years previously.

The amount of money raised by the Clan was limited by the wavering support for the IRA among many of its members, the IRA's lack of military activity, and the socialist rhetoric of some of the leadership at GHQ. The Clan feared that the IRA planned to involve itself with political initiatives, and many members of the Clan were disappointed over its promotion of a republican election pact, all of which diverted attention away from military preparation. Responding to this Twomey took the precaution of writing to Neenan, regarding the pact, that: 'Any proposals we make will specify for the safeguarding of the republican position'.[216] An additional factor was the limited financial resources of many of its members, including Joe

McGarrity, while the difficulty in raising money was compounded by Mc-Garrity's absence in Colombia during the first half of 1927.

Despite the desperate appeals from the IRA, the Clan didn't hold 'mass [public] meetings' to raise money.[217] The barrack raids were the only significant IRA activity of this period and An Timthire reported: 'The recent attacks at home by the Army gave rise to great enthusiasm and admiration amongst all our fellows. We should gain considerably in membership and finance.'[218]

In letters to America Twomey and the leadership exaggerated the military capability of the IRA to encourage donations. An Timthire wrote in 1926 that at a meeting of the New York Clan he 'gave mysterious hints of things that could happen if we had sufficient money. It is necessary to say things here that are not literally correct.'[219] The following year Twomey sent Connie Neenan an impossibly upbeat assessment of the IRA: 'I visited many units recently [and] am very pleased with the situation in most and [it] is generally better (both in numbers and spirit) than I expected. Except [for the] difficulty in openly drilling, things are good.'[220] This after all was a force that wasn't able to competently carry out the garda barrack raids a few months earlier! In a letter to George Gilmore in Ireland around the same time Twomey had used the phrase 'quite pleased' rather than 'very pleased'.[221]

Neenan was careful to ask Twomey to forward receipts to the Clan for all money received: '[The Clan] executive demands receipts for all monies received from them. Send [receipt] when [the] cash arrives.'[222] It was reasonable for the Clan to be cautious, and McGarrity and Luke Dillon had previously accused another IRA emissary, Dan Breen (of Tipperary), of having misappropriated money from the Clan when he was in America, following the Anglo-Irish truce.[223]

Neenan also received money from sources other than the Clan, such as from the running of dances and other fundraisers, and he deducted his personal expenses from these sums. One source was Miss Annie O'Mahoney, who 'was by no means wealthy'. In 1926 she put a dollar a day aside until she was able to hand over $100 to An Timthire and 'under no circumstances would she allow it to be used for any purpose except the Army'. An Timthire wrote to Andy Cooney asking him to send her an official 'note of thanks and

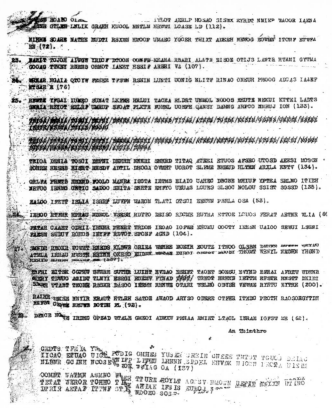

Figure 24. In April 1927 Connie Neenan sent a report to Moss Twomey and Andy Cooney on the republican position in America. He complained about de Valera's success in attracting support from members of the Clan. In this, the fourth page, Neenan commented on fundraising by the Clan and in the postscript named a potential IRA informer within the gardaí:

Paragraph 25: [The] appeal for funds cannot be met for some weeks, [there's] only $1,000 in the [Clan] treasury. Luke [Dillon] put me off until June ... [The Clan has] over 5,000 members. To date their contribution is $6,000 dollars or [$]1.25 per head for nine months. This is hopeless, and I have told them so.

Too much money is used for expenses by Clan. This is confidential, but as far as I see, it costs too much to run such a small organization, it should be more self-contained.

Will write [to] you again, relative to [the] appeal, [and] if possible to send cash.

The final two paragraphs concern the informer in the gardaí:

Get in touch with Sergeant Leen, Civic Guards, Bandon, County Cork. He is in [the] superintendent's office, he is fed up with [the] imperial gang and is going to clear out, possibly emigrate. He is anxious to give information to us. Mention Martin Howard of Listowel, now in New York ... [He sent a letter] to Martin offering to assist.

appreciation', which she would 'treasure'. Unfortunately this despatch was one of those found on Patrick Garland when he was stopped by customs in Cobh and to Miss O'Mahoney's 'embarrassment' was published in the newspapers. A year later she was still subscribing '$20 per month to [the] Army' and had given a '$100 special grant'.[224] This was likely the same 'Miss O'Mahoney' who was a member of the executive committee to welcome de Valera to New York in 1927 and was president of the Irish Republican League in New York. The league was associated with the AARIR.[225]

A significant expense borne by the IRA and the Clan in America was the provision of support for disabled and impoverished veterans and their dependants. The IRA received so many petitions for financial assistance that Frank Aiken said it 'would require at least £10,000 per week to deal fully with every case'.[226] Aiken and later Moss Twomey were adamant that the IRA could only respond to a small proportion of all such requests. By 1923, $250,000 had been raised in the US for the dependants of republican prisoners.[227]

By 1932 the Clan was spending $6,000 annually to support 'disabled' veterans.[228] To cut down on abuse, the policy was for money to be provided to deserving cases by either GHQ or the Clan headquarters and not directly by individual Clan clubs.[229] As Neenan wrote: 'The matter was raised about certain [Clan na Gael and IRA] Clubs assisting destitute cases at home [in Ireland] in their own areas. I refused to sanction sectional drafts [sic] to any area and stated all monies should go through General Headquarters.'[230]

Neenan and 'Jones' were both concerned that too many veterans were dependent on aid from the IRA and the former remarked: 'Too much money has to be expended on such cases ... They are coming here to work and must not expect us to spoon feed them.'[231] Twomey replied: 'In future no money, is on any account, [to be] spent on men going out, even if [they're] on the run, except [for] men sent out in bad health for to be cured, and then only when specific instructions are sent.'[232]

Joseph Blake of Dublin was in San Francisco, under an assumed name, and 'in hospital suffering from TB and his expenses run to $120 a month. A few friends are taking him in charge, still I [Neenan] feel we are being asked to assist, which I am unable to do.'[233] IRA veterans in

San Francisco and New York raised money to bring out Denny Prender-ville from Castleisland, County Kerry, who was ill – probably with TB. Neenan wanted him to enter America by way of Canada as 'he won't be passed by [the United States] Consulate doctor'.[234]

Another republican immigrant whom Twomey wanted Neenan to try and help out was Thomas Curran of Dublin. When in Ireland he 'was em-ployed in one of the railways, did work for us [the IRA] and as a result was imprisoned'. Following his release he was unemployed and forced to emi-grate – leaving a wife and family at home. When he stopped writing home his wife contacted the Dublin brigade: 'His wife states he has no work [in America] and as he cannot send her money she is badly off. Could anything be done for him?' Twomey wanted Neenan to send someone around to his last known address: C/O Mrs Brady, 73 west 88th Street, New York.[235]

IN MAY 1927 'MR Jones' resigned his position as the IRA agent working for Soviet military intelligence in New York and resumed 'civilian employ-ment' (see Chapter 8). Responsibility for this sensitive work was now handed over to Neenan, while Anthony Farrell from Mayo was appointed as his assistant to help him with administrative duties, but not with any responsibility for the clandestine Soviet work.[236]

Neenan continued to work closely with Joe McGarrity, but without a degree of success sufficient to reverse the IRA's misfortunes. The Clan's membership dwindled, and by July 1929 there were only 620 paid up members in New York city.[237] Then in October 1929 the Wall Street Crash marked the beginning of the Great Depression. As unemployment and bankruptcy swept the US, millions were plunged into poverty. Irish immigrants were as badly affected as any other group and many of the Clan's IRA veterans now returned to Ireland. In 1933 Joe McGarrity was expelled from the New York Stock Exchange for 'false book-keeping entries', leaving him almost destitute.

But McGarrity and Neenan were both rescued by the Irish Hospitals Sweepstakes. The sweepstakes was a lottery established in 1930 by the Free State government to finance hospitals and health care in Ireland. At the time lotteries were illegal in America and therefore the two were able to use the IRA and Clan na Gael networks to import, distribute and sell tickets throughout the US. Neenan was soon the sweep's 'principal agent in the United States' and McGarrity was appointed a 'special agent'. In turn McGarrity appointed Moss Twomey in Ireland as a lottery agent. In only five years McGarrity earned a commission of £300,000[238] while Neenan lived a life of affluence, prompting Twomey to write to him: 'We are told you will soon be a millionaire – don't forget us!'[239]

McGarrity, however, continued his involvement in militant republicanism and in 1939 he supported Seán Russell's bombing campaign in Britain, which culminated with an explosion in Coventry killing five people. The unintended civilian casualties occurred when an IRA volunteer panicked and left the bomb he was carrying at a crowded shopping centre. The FBI noted that some of the bombs which the IRA used during the campaign had been smuggled from America and were 'of the type used by [the] police in the United States'.[240] Twomey, no longer chief of staff, was disgusted with the 'senseless demonstrations in a foreign country'.[241]

A year later McGarrity was dead from incurable cancer of the throat and in the 1970s a wealthy Connie Neenan retired to Ireland.[242]

CHAPTER 8

The Soviet Union and China

Wine and women. I am onto the right people now and can produce material of a
high order.

'Jones', an undercover IRA agent in New York

We have been very active, made and placed 200 coal bombs in [the] cargo of
[British] admiralty coal transports for China.

IRA commander in Scotland

In 1927, two men waiting in a café in Amsterdam were joined by a third. A
brief conversation ensued and a package was handed over, before the three
took leave of each other. The first two were representatives of Soviet military intelligence, their guest a member of a revolutionary organisation.

Sounds rather like a clichéd spy novel. Actually it's an accurate representation of a meeting between the IRA and Soviet agents. This is a
relationship that has never before been elaborated upon. A relationship so
secret that IRA men took it to their graves and one that remained largely
unknown to the British secret service and the authorities in America.

Historical background

To understand the clandestine relationship between the IRA and the
Soviets in the 1920s it is necessary to have some familiarity with the circumstances of the time. Given the situation they both found themselves
in, it was almost inevitable that they should have been brought together.

There were two revolutions in Russia in 1917: one a people's revolution in February, which overthrew the Tsar, the other led by Lenin in
October which brought to power a small ruthless clique, the Bolsheviks
or communists. To many Europeans the Russian revolutions represented
a new hope, a move away from the capitalist regimes responsible for
the carnage and destruction of the First World War. Communism was
expected to sweep across Western Europe – poverty, war and injustice
would become things of the past. It may seem strange to us today, but the

Soviet Union was to many educated and intelligent people a beacon of freedom, egalitarianism and prosperity.[1]

After a bloody civil war, during which Britain, France and Japan supported the counter-revolutionaries, the communists established control over most of the former Russian empire, which they renamed the Union of Soviet Socialist Republics (USSR). In 1924 Lenin died and Joseph Stalin began to consolidate power. By November 1927 he had achieved complete control with the expulsion of Leon Trotsky from the Communist Party.

During the mid 1920s the USSR was conscious of the military threat from the capitalist countries. Following years of war and the implementation of disastrous economic policies, the country was almost bankrupt, there was widespread famine, the Red Army's equipment was obsolete, and as a pariah state she had no powerful friends or allies abroad. The major threat was felt to be from an attack in the west led by Poland and Romania. Another possibility, though considered less likely, was an attack across the Chinese border led by Japan. Britain was regarded by the Soviets as their most dangerous enemy, and it was assumed that she would (at the very least) provide material support for any invasion.[2]

In 1927 Soviet concern about the long-term possibility of war was replaced by fear of an imminent invasion. This 'war scare' swept the Soviet Union and was widely promoted both at home and abroad by the government. Recently released documents reveal that the Soviet leadership did not actually believe war was imminent but that the scare was largely a deliberate fabrication, which provided Stalin with the cover to eliminate his rivals.[3]

Meanwhile, the Communist International or Comintern was founded in 1920 as the controlling body of all communist parties around the world. The Comintern was based in Moscow under the control of the Russian Communist Party. Local communist parties were expected to subordinate themselves to Moscow's policies and dictates. But in countries not ripe for communism, strategic alliances between communists and nationalists were approved. Ireland and the IRA fell into this category. To further its cause the Comintern set up front organisations such as International Red Aid (in support of 'political' prisoners) and the League Against Imperialism.[4]

After a series of intelligence disasters, responsibility for foreign espionage was taken from the Comintern in 1924 and handed over to Red Army intelligence or *Razvedupr* (RU).[5] Little is known about the RU and yet it was the 'most important intelligence agency of the Soviet Union', reporting directly to the ruling Politiburo of the Communist Party. Compared with the thugs who ran the *Cheka* or secret police, its members were often highly educated and sophisticated, and frequently non-communist. This facilitated their covert activities and ability to penetrate foreign governments and society.[6]

RU operatives, who were identified by a false first name, ran clandestine networks of agents in the west, often on a massive scale. They frequently operated under the cover of Soviet trade missions, such as Arcos in London and Amtorg in New York. The RU gathered information about military, scientific and industrial developments, in addition to political intelligence. Informants were handed a document, known as a questionnaire, which listed the precise technical information required.[7]

The items on the questionnaire were tailored to the priorities of the Soviet Union, such as technical information on chemical warfare. In the First World War the Russian army had been unable to adequately respond to German poison gas attacks, and Russian fatalities of 56,000 accounted for over half the total number of deaths from gas on all fronts throughout the war.[8] During the Civil War the British reportedly used mustard gas against Soviet troops in Siberia.[9] In the inter-war years many in the west as well as Russia continued to believe that poison gas would play a decisive role in future wars, and the Soviets devoted considerable energy to developing chemical warfare capability. Mustard gas was regarded as one of the most promising agents.

The Soviets were also interested in acquiring data on mechanised warfare (particularly tanks), airplane engines and military communications equipment.

The Soviet Union and Ireland, 1917 to 1925

The overthrow of the Russian Tsar was greeted by many in Ireland with great enthusiasm. People were able to relate to the toppling of a monarchy that was perceived by many to be foreign and that exploited an impoverished people. They were delighted when the communists called for an end to the First World War and for national self-determination. In February 1918 some 10,000 people attended a rally at Dublin's Mansion House in support of the revolution.[10] Later, in the Ireland of the 1920s, while only a small number of people were enthusiasts for the Soviet Union, there remained a tolerance of communism in many sections of society. This acceptance disappeared in 1930 when the Catholic Church took a strong stance against the USSR and its militant atheism.[11]

The Comintern's attempts to build a mass Irish communist party were failures and the first Communist Party of Ireland was dissolved in 1924 with fewer than fifty members.[12] Jim Larkin (the hero of the 1913 Dublin Lockout) was the only Marxist in Ireland with a large base of popular support. However, Larkin refused to be subservient to Moscow or anyone else; he proved extremely difficult to work with, and can be described as unpredictable, egocentric, paranoid, litigious, intolerant and with a history of misappropriating funds. By 1927 the Russians were beginning to look elsewhere, until he finally broke with them in 1929.[13]

For a period of time in the mid and late 1920s the IRA was to be the most promising ally for the Soviets in Ireland – combining, as it did, popular support together with communists in leadership positions. IRA members actively participated in Comintern front organisations – Mick Fitzpatrick was on the presidium of the International Friends of Soviet Russia, Donal O'Donoghue and Frank Ryan attended the Congress of Oppressed Nationalities and Peadar O'Donnell, as editor of *An Phoblacht*, provided the Soviets with a public outlet for their propaganda. In 1926 the paper enthusiastically reported that, in Russia, 'miners have a 6 hour [work day] ... which seems wonderful'. So good that the miners themselves didn't know it! When the republican and socialist activist Charlotte Despard visited the Soviet Union she observed: 'There were no locked doors in the prisons, the prisoners managing their own affairs.'[14] Communist cadres were recruited from amongst the IRA's ranks and O'Donnell's close friend Seán Murray was to become general secretary of the second Communist Party of Ireland in 1933.[15] However, despite their disproportionate representation on the Army Council, the vast majority of IRA members had little sympathy or interest in communism.

Irish republicans had a long history of attempting to negotiate an alliance with the Soviet Union. Beginning in 1919, an IRA emissary, Harry Boland, made contact with Soviet representatives in America. In 1921 de Valera sent a representative to Moscow to conclude a recognition treaty and secure arms and ammunition, but the Soviets, having just signed an Anglo-Russian trade agreement, backed out.[16] In August 1922 the British Communist Party sent two representatives to Dublin who met with leaders of the IRA (possibly including Ernie O'Malley) and an agreement was reached that the Soviets would supply weapons to the republicans.[17] However, there is no evidence for any substantial transfer of weapons to the IRA during the Irish Civil War period. In January 1923, the Free State's representative in Geneva reported that de Valera had sent a message to the Soviet foreign commissar asking for money.[18]

However, contacts of some sort must have continued, since Frank Aiken wrote to Liam Pedlar, the republican 'Military Attaché' in America, in April 1925: 'Touch with Russians [sic]. We have definitely decided to drop this – hopeless bunglers, in any case as far as we can see, and not very eager to help.'[19]

In the summer of 1925 the IRA sent a small delegation to Moscow, led by P. A. Murray of the headquarters staff. Murray had had contacts with the Soviets in 1923 when he was IRA OC in Britain. Also included were Seán Russell, Mick Fitzpatrick a leading IRA communist, and the Sinn Féin TD Gerry Boland. Boland was a close confidant of de Valera's and was probably sent by him to keep an eye on the other three.

Stalin met privately with Murray, with just an interpreter present, and told the Irishman 'your revolution has not gone far enough' – which I suppose could be taken as a compliment. He wanted to find out from Murray to what extent the IRA with their widespread contacts throughout the Irish diaspora could assist Moscow. Murray later claimed that no agreement was reached, as Stalin was concerned that any weapons supplied might be traced back to the Soviets by the British, and that Ireland was too remote to be of interest to the Russians.[20] This version is supported by comments later made by General Krivitsky of Red Army Intelligence to MI5 (British secret service) following his defection to the West: 'The Polit Bureau [sic] refused assistance because of their anxiety not to offend the British Government as well as the impossibility of supporting the nationalistic aspirations of the IRA at the same time as the international activities of the Irish Communist Party.'[21]

But in fact some sort of an agreement was reached, either at this time or shortly afterwards, and Russell returned to Dublin via Berlin, where he met a Soviet agent, 'Mr X', to formalise the arrangements for lines of communications with the Soviets. 'Mr X' then came to London where Russell introduced him to the IRA OC in Britain.[22] Two later statements confirm that an agreement was reached around this time. In 1926 Andy Cooney said that there was 'a definite agreement made [by the Soviets] with [the] late C.S. [chief of staff, Frank Aiken]'. This had to be before Aiken was deposed as chief of staff in November 1925.[23] And in March 1927 Moss Twomey referred to an 'agreement made in Lond. [London]' before May 1926 with the Soviets.[24]

The apparent contradiction between the statements of General Krivitsky and Moss Twomey and Andy Cooney may be one of semantics. Krivitsky states that there was no agreement with the IRA 'as a political body' but he states that 'individual members [of the IRA] may have been recruited as intelligence agents for special purposes'.[25] Thus what the IRA took to be an 'agreement', the Soviets may have regarded more as an arrangement with individual IRA members. As far as P. A. Murray's denial is concerned (it's reasonable to expect that), just like the remainder of the IRA leadership, he would continue to deny any agreement with the Soviets. When he and other veterans gave interviews and reminisced about their IRA years in later life, their narrative was one of heroic ambushes in the Anglo-Irish War and not cloak-and-dagger with the Russians.

The IRA agreed to spy for the Russians in Britain.[26] In turn the Soviets promised to pay for the information, though they were evasive about whether they'd supply weapons.

Thanks to the success of the IRA in the Anglo-Irish War and its resultant sterling revolutionary credentials, the Soviets likely over-estimated its capability and didn't fully comprehend the extent to which the organisation had declined. There were many ways in which the IRA could be of value to the Soviets: 1. Conduct military espionage in Britain and America. 2. Assist Soviet agents by providing false passports and other forms of cover. 3. In the event of war between Russia and Britain, attack

British merchant shipping and launch diversionary attacks in England. 4. Promote Comintern fronts and Soviet propaganda in Ireland. 5. Enable the Soviets to recruit among IRA members, to build a communist base in Ireland. 6. Provide the Soviets with contacts throughout the Irish diaspora in America and Europe. 7. Provide propaganda and material help to nationalists in China, who were a key Soviet ally. 8. In the unlikely event of the IRA seizing power in the Free State and the subsequent Irish withdrawal from the British Commonwealth, the integrity of the British empire could be threatened. On all but the last of these key points the IRA either delivered or planned to do so.

The risk for the Russians was that discovery of the relationship would bring down on them the wrath of Britain, an important trading partner and their most feared military threat.

The IRA had little to lose from an alliance with the Soviets. They stood to gain money, arms and military training. Furthermore, just as the First World War had provided the IRA in the past with a crucial advantage, an Anglo-Soviet war could provide the IRA with the opportunity to attempt to seize power in Ireland and encourage the Soviets to provide them with significant military aid. The only risks were that the Russians wouldn't deliver the money and arms, and that communist efforts and propaganda would encourage IRA members to prioritise social revolution over the national revolution. Indeed the latter was to happen in the 1930s as many leading republicans left the IRA for radical or communist politics.

The Soviet—IRA agreement

By 1926 the IRA and Red Army intelligence had a fully operational and clandestine relationship. The cornerstone of this was the supply of information on military technology (much of it gained by espionage) in return for Russian money. The IRA was in contact with the Russians in London, Paris, Amsterdam and New York. The Soviets had a history of dealing with subservient communist parties, but this was a relationship of mutual distrust with both parties trying to exploit the other.

From November 1925 on, Moss Twomey and Andy Cooney oversaw the agreement on the Irish side, and along with Seán Russell they were intensely suspicious of the Russians, to whom they had no ideological commitment. For their part, the Soviets handed over as little money as possible, and did their best to avoid providing weapons. General Walter Krivitsky, was later to admit 'he worked with them [the IRA] purely as intelligence agents and for a time got quite useful information out of them, at the same time experiencing difficulty in evading attempts to interest him in the terrorist activities of their organisation.'[27] Twomey wrote: 'These people [the Russians] are so shifty...they are out to exploit us and use for their ends' and 'except for our urgent need of cash, I would not be so keen on this [agreement], but am very much so [enthusiastic] on this account',[28] while Cooney called them 'people in whom we cannot place much confidence'.[29] Somewhat ironically, 'Jones' in New York referred to the Soviets as 'absolutely unscrupulous'.[30]

Right from the start the IRA tried to prevent the Soviets from using their men as paid agents rather than representatives of the 'Irish Republic'. Russell in September 1925 was concerned that 'Mr X' was trying to use the OC. Britain as an individual agent.[31] Seán Lemass, the republican 'Minister for Defence', replied: 'We must be on terms of absolute equality with X's Government or there can be no liaison.' Later Connie Neenan echoed this concern when he wrote to Twomey: 'At the moment we are just paid servants.'[32]

To maintain secrecy, the IRA was very cautious in making any references to the Soviets. Aside from two documents from the autumn of 1925, any significant information that James Gillogly and I have discovered has been in cipher. There are some references, which are not in cipher, but it would be impossible to deduce their meaning without already being familiar with the encrypted text. It's also possible that information could have been written in secret ink and no longer available. Even within the coded documents the IRA tended to be indirect and cryptic. For instance there was only one direct mention of 'Moscow' and agents were virtually always referred to by their pseudonyms. The IRA agent in America, 'Mr Jones', cautioned Twomey: 'I am [of] the opinion that you should not write any despatches relative to 'Stephen' [the Soviet intelligence officer in the US] on official paper even in cipher.'[33]

The IRA agents in London and America performed a range of services for the Russians and with differing degrees of success.

In London the IRA supplied the Soviets with information on military technology and with false passports for spies. They also collected money from the Soviets for the work done in both Britain and America. The quality and quantity of information supplied by the IRA in Britain failed to match that obtained in the US.

The principal agents in London were the IRA OC. Britain and his Red Army intelligence (RU) contact 'James'. For the first part of 1926 the OC. Britain can only be identified by the last letter of his initials, 'M'. In September 1926 'M' was replaced by George (also known as 'HS'). 'James' was the RU officer in contact with the IRA in London, and he may have been the same person as 'Mr X' whose cryptonym was no longer mentioned after 1925. Also involved with the London connection was Seán MacBride (or 'Mr Ambrose'), who at the time lived in Paris.

George's information was acquired by various methods and through a wide range of contacts: visits to the Patent Office, purchases of items (often from shady sources), journal subscriptions under false names, the existing IRA network in Britain, informants in factories supplying military equipment and a small number of informants in the military or police.

In the latter part of 1925 the OC. Britain supplied the Soviets with information on ships, drawings of a specified airplane engine, a sample of a gas mask, and drawings of airplane navigational equipment that had been obtained from the Patent Office. Later George wrote to Twomey asking him to send on specifications of aircraft engines manufactured at the Beardmore engineering company in Glasgow, where the IRA had an informant. He was particularly interested in two powerful engines suitable for air force bombers, the Typhoon and the 1,100 horsepower Simoon: 'They [Beardmores] make the best aero engine on the market. Could you get me particulars about their Typhoon one, also their Simoon one? All information should be reliable.'[34] Twomey even contacted the IRA in Cork and asked them the feasibility of getting 'working drawings of [the] latest designs of tractors out of Fords [car factory]'.[35]

At the time the royal navy had the most advanced sonar system (called ASDIC) for detecting submarines and information about this would have been invaluable to the Russians. In the autumn of 1926 Seán MacBride travelled from Paris to London, where he met with both George and Moss Twomey. MacBride asked George for 'particulars of [a] submarine detector [system]'[36] and received back 'a brief specification and a complete drawing'.[37]

'James' also handed over £200 to George for a piece of telecommunications equipment or wireless (referred to as the 'phone'). However, George's middleman, Fitzgerald, took the money and reneged on the deal, leaving 'James' out of pocket.[38]

George spent considerable time and effort buying military manuals, books and journals for both 'James' and the IRA's own use, among them *The Journal of the Royal United Services Institute for Defence Studies*.[39]

The IRA was able to help out the Soviets with false passports, and in March 1927, when a communist agent Kate Gussfeldt was arrested with a passport in a false name, the British secret service, MI5, traced it back to the IRA.[40] In April 1927, when the Russians planned to send an agent, 'John' on undercover work to Romania, 'James' approached George for help. George wrote to Twomey: 'J [James] told me that "John" is going to Roumania [*sic*] and J would like if you could make him a representative of some woollen mills for that part of the world, if this is possible. Send papers etc. to my covering address and send [textile] samples to [the] address I gave you when [you were] here. He will need everything a representative of a firm is supposed to have ... I would be very glad if you would give it your immediate attention as it's extremely urgent.' George typed the name and the address of the false business on a piece of paper and handed it to an IRA volunteer 'Reynolds' to bring to Twomey.[41] But 'Reynolds' then re-wrote the name in pencil and brought this note with him. When he arrived in Dublin, neither he nor Twomey could read the name.[42] In the meantime, George, 'thinking ye [Twomey] had the matter on hand', destroyed his own copy of the name and address, and so five weeks later the IRA still hadn't helped James out.[43]

Then there's the strange case of E. Donnelly, a military police officer who was convicted by court martial for stealing secret codebooks. MI5 intercepted a letter addressed to him in prison, which was purported to be from 'Dr Gately', the same name the IRA had forged as a referee on the passport application for Kate Gussfeldt.[44] In April 1927 Twomey wrote to George: 'Donnelly has got two years' hard labour. [He] was tried by court martial. Can you get [the] evidence against him and how he was caught?'[45] George replied: 'I had a letter from him after his arrest saying he was suspected of knowing something about things that were missing. I think myself that he must have been caught in the act.'[46] These oblique comments paint a picture of an IRA agent caught stealing secret code or cipher books, which were to be passed on to the Soviets.

On one occasion 'James' offered to write for the IRA journal, *An tÓglach*: 'James and his friend, who have had great experience in street fighting and guerrilla tactics could be got to write for our paper.'[47] Twomey realised the potential instructional value of these articles: 'Independent of printing James' articles in *An tÓglach*, we would like to get them. [We] would print some of them.'[48]

Russian money

The primary reason the IRA worked for the Russians was for the money that was handed over in London and later in Amsterdam. Twomey estimated that it cost about £400 per month to maintain the IRA, with additional money required for any significant operation.[49] The two main sources of income were Clan na Gael and the Soviets. Support from the Clan was steadily decreasing and Twomey summed up the situation: 'Were it not we are in such desperate need of cash and that [the] assistance from Clan [na Gael] is so very disappointing, I would not be so keen on this business [the agreement with the Soviets]. To me the maintenance of this [connection] ... appears indispensable to our carrying on the Army here.'[50] Later he wrote that the IRA 'could not carry on' without Soviet financing.[51]

Of even greater value than money to the IRA would have been Soviet-supplied weaponry. 'Stephen' promised 'Jones' that the Soviets 'would give us all the material [weapons] we would need'. 'Jones' didn't believe 'Stephen' and he told Twomey to 'test them' on this promise.[52] Twomey pushed 'Jones' to 'ask "Stephen" to be more explicit as to [the] offer of material. Where will he give delivery and ... what facilities will he give to get it into Ireland?'[53] It's probable that Stephen's promise was unauthorised and merely given so as to encourage 'Jones' to continue to supply him with intelligence. On another occasion 'James' obliquely hinted that 'when our work together comes off better we can help you more and in different ways.'[54] Despite these statements the Soviets likely had no intention of ever providing the IRA with weapons, short of war breaking out between them and Britain.

Initially the Soviets agreed to pay over a monthly stipend but they decreased the amount on a number of occasions and sometimes paid nothing for months. Ultimately they were manoeuvring to pay only the IRA's expenses for acquiring the information and equipment. It seems likely that this was a deliberate Russian ploy, but there was also a financial crisis in Russia, caused by a combination of internal economic woes and the expenditure of large amounts of money on foreign adventures, particularly support for the Chinese nationalists and their communist allies.

One way to generate money is to print it and this the Russians did. In October 1926, Seán MacBride reported from Paris: 'Several bad £50 Bank of England notes have been passed here lately. These are said to emanate from Russia.'[55] Later in 1929 the Soviets are known to have printed counterfeit American $100 bills.[56]

Other than to say that Soviet cash was crucial to the IRA, it is hard to know exactly how much was handed over. The amount of money provided was continually changing. In January 1926 the OC. Britain received £200 from 'James'.[57] Later in the summer 'James' complained bitterly about the work the IRA was doing in London: 'The expected progress has not been fulfilled', the IRA had not sent over sufficient men to do the required work, had not provided information the Soviets wanted about Ireland and little material had been purchased and even that was slow in coming. At this time the stipend was temporarily cut in half (due to 'the economic crisis in our country'), leaving £250 for the IRA.[58] This suggests that the full stipend was £500 monthly, and is supported by George's communication in November 1926 stating that he was owed £1,000 for October and November, of which 'James' had paid £350. However, at the same time the Russians also announced that henceforth the amount was being reduced to £100.[59]

This threw the IRA into a financial crisis, and with Twomey temporarily imprisoned in Mountjoy, George requested Andy Cooney: 'Come or send someone over to deal with the matter immediately.'[60] Cooney met with 'James' on 26 November and 'James' said that 'he was very anxious that we should continue to work for them, but [he] could not give any money, outside of minor expenses'. Cooney replied that the relationship was terminated and 'James' agreed to write to Moscow 'for further instructions'. Cooney was furious with the Russians: 'They let us down at a most critical time [their London] agent failed to carry out a definite agreement made with [the] late CS [Frank Aiken].'[61] In Cooney's opinion: 'He ['James'] may be replaced by another man, a thing we should encourage.'[62] But despite Cooney's attitude the IRA continued to gather material for the Russians.

In America 'Mr Jones' asked 'Stephen' what the situation was from his perspective. 'Stephen' responded that he was 'very enthusiastic re. [regarding] our relations. He said that his people were very doubtful when the thing first started, but now they decided that they were very pleased, not only to work with us, but that they would like to consolidate relations. That they further decided that they would also give us all the material [weapons] we needed, also the financial end of it would be satisfactory to us.'[63]

By February 1927 the agreement was in a state of limbo, and aside from £150 that 'James' had handed over the previous December, the IRA had not received 'a penny of [the] monthly amount guaranteed'.[64] Twomey added: '[It's] difficult to understand these people, [with] 'Stephen' desiring to continue and [the] London man [wanting] to break off, if [they're] working under [the] same superior direction. It may be [that] they do not consider [the] London business very important, or [that it] justifies [their] expenditure. If it is finally decided to discontinue [the] London end, we can probably make a special arrangement about America. We will not continue or incur risks for nothing.'[65]

Meanwhile, the Irish trade unionist and socialist leader, Jim Larkin went to Moscow in November 1926 to attend a meeting called by the Comintern to inquire into why an Irish Communist Party hadn't been founded to replace that dissolved in 1924.[66] Twomey mistook the visit as evidence of Larkin's continued influence in Moscow, and suspected that this was an explanation for the withdrawal of Soviet support: 'We have evidence that recently certain so called extremist and revolutionary labour groups in Ireland have cut across us ... we would endeavour to squelch these people. We could prove they are not national[ist] and are really counter-revolutionary.'[67] Twomey added: 'Larkin is not a revolutionary [figure] now, except in speech, and outside of [a] section in Dublin, has no influence whatever.' Desperate to find a culprit, Twomey even added Fianna Fáil to the mix: 'We have strong suspicion Fianna Fáil have made touch also lately, and both this party and Larkin have cut us out.'[68] Blaming Fianna Fáil was not as bizarre as it now seems. At the time there were a number of left-wing members of Fianna Fáil, including P. J. Rutledge, the vice-president, who supported land reform in Ireland. Furthermore, in the subsequent September 1927 general election Larkin called on voters to support Fianna Fáil,[69] while in 1928 de Valera visited the League Against Imperialism's Berlin office.[70]

Finally, in March 1927, at Jones' own urging, Twomey told him to stop working for 'Stephen' until £5,000 was handed over and a new agreement made. To confirm this, he sent Jones a cryptic cable: 'Suspend deliveries immediately without cancelling contract'.

Twomey now decided that 'the only satisfactory way to fix things properly is to send a delegation to Stephen's HQ [Moscow]. If we can get enough cash for expenses and arrange about passports we will do this.' He proposed that he and Russell travel to the 'fountainhead'. [71]

Twomey visited London to meet 'James' and to make arrangements for the trip. This time he came away believing that 'James' genuinely wanted to help. 'James' had explained that the problem for the Soviets was that 'all resources are behind the Cantonese [the Chinese nationalists]'. Ironically 'James' also told him that the IRA could have dealt more cleverly with the Russians by charging for each item delivered, rather than depending on 'grants at pleasure'.[72]

Acquiring two false passports with visas for Russia posed problems; George could only secure passports with visas for western Europe: 'I can only get passports for the continent, after that ye would require assistance from 'James' or the [Communist] Party, otherwise it would be impossible to get there without coming out in the open.'[73] 'James' suggested that Twomey and Russell travel to France on British passports and then use American passports to either travel directly to Russia or go to Germany first, from where the Soviets could get them to Russia. Twomey reported 'James' 'can arrange visas from Germany from his people' and he forwarded a photograph of himself and Seán Russell to Connie Neenan asking him to arrange for two American passports in false names. He suggested the passports could be sent over to Ireland by courier on a transatlantic liner to Mick Burke in Cobh, or posted separately, one to John Williams and the other to Henry Irwin of Thomas Cook and Son, Grafton Street, Dublin.[74] Neenan replied via a cryptic cable: 'Suggestions for deliveries unacceptable', indicating that he couldn't get the passports,[75] while George told Twomey that if he wanted a passport he'd need to go to London in person.[76]

In view of the support 'James' and 'Stephen' gave to the proposed trip, Twomey wanted 'Jones' to continue supplying items to 'Stephen' but 'you could slack off and let stuff accumulate. Just give a little.'[77]

Constrained by a lack of cash for the trip and the difficulties in getting passports, Twomey sent one final plea for cash to 'James' on 25 April. The dubious premise of the letter was that £5,000 from the Soviets would fund the republican electoral alliance, leading to victory in the general election in June 1927. Once in power, the new republican government would renege on the Anglo-Irish Treaty, and withdraw from the British Commonwealth, which in turn would threaten the stability of the empire:

My dear friend James, When speaking to you last, I explained how essential it is that we put forward revolutionary candidates at the forthcoming general election. To do this money is indispensable. I hope that you have represented the situation and its possibilities to your people and that they appreciate them.

[I] believe [that] if we can finance enough candidates, a majority of republicans can be secured. Having a majority, a situation will be created in which England must either attack us or submit to the repudiation of the Treaty, under which the Free State was set up, and [with] the acceptance of a Republic here, you can appreciate the effect of this, especially on the Dominions [of] the British Empire and in fact the whole world.

If we got £5,000 pounds at once we could put up our candidates. The time before the election is very short to conduct the campaign. We would appreciate this amount now, with such an opportunity to exploit a situation, [rather] than a greater amount after the opportunity might have been allowed to pass.

We feel [that] you should stand by us financially. We have done our best for you and I am sure you will agree we are entitled to the amount requested. It is due almost as arrears on the agreement with you, apart from consideration of services rendered elsewhere.

Please inform George without delay if we can have the money. With assurances of my regards. Your friend. Chairman [Moss Twomey].[78]

The fall of the British empire for a mere £5,000 certainly seemed like good value!

Two weeks later George 'had a letter from "James". He is in Moscow. He told me to inform you [Moss Twomey] that everything would be fixed up and he is anxious that you cable this decision to our representative in America ... He will be back in less than two weeks.'[79] A few days later Twomey sent word to America to resume the work, but 'until money is actually paid, however, do not give everything.'[80] By mid-May the prospects of a republican election pact had ended in failure and Twomey was worried that 'James' could find out. He wrote to George: 'Do not mention anything about this to "James" should you see him.'[81]

On 27 May George sent a cryptic message to Twomey notifying him that 'James' was ready to hand over £1,000.[82] After Twomey collected the money in London he wrote to Connie Neenan, summing up the extent of the financial crisis. He reported that the IRA were in debt to the tune of £300 to 'friends' and that none of the full-time officers at GHQ 'had got a penny for a few months'.[83] Twomey was also critical of the way 'James' had treated George, including ordering equipment costing £40 and then becoming uncontactable: 'It was cool on [the] part of "James" to put you in such a position'.[84]

Two weeks before the Russians handed over the money to Twomey, they suffered a major setback in London. For quite some time MI5 had been aware that the Soviet trade office, known as Arcos, was the headquarters for Red Army intelligence in Britain. Acting on the pretext of a stolen obsolete Royal Air Force training manual, the Special Branch carried out a raid on the Arcos offices on 12 May. When the Russians refused to hand over the keys to two massive safes the police brought in pneumatic drills and oxyacetylene torches and carried off piles of incriminating documents. The haul provided evidence of a huge Soviet intelligence and subversion effort and on 26 May Britain severed diplomatic relations with the USSR. Following this the RU declared Britain a 'denied area', meaning that espionage against it had to be carried out from adjacent countries and the base for intelligence operations against Great Britain was moved to Amsterdam, with only a few 'deep cover' networks left in the country.[85] With the Special Branch active throughout the city, George

Ref. No. HS/33.

To/
   C/S.   16th., May, 1924.

1. (144) SⲰAMF. ⲰNWNV. LGNI Ⲱ. ⲰUTPN. DUIID. CTMMF. OFAUS.
SRⲰⲰS. NⲰHLⲰ. ATCBY. ⲰODTD. BⲰYⲰO. ILVYT. DMINF.
YMⲰRD. TDSⲰL. BTTRA. ASFUI. NⲰCOR. STPTR. YPITO.
RSCHO. IOSⲰA. HUⲰAU. AVVOA. RCIMH. ⲰAGCH. DFHIG.
OLNN. Keep in touch with your private address.

Best wishes.

Figure 25. George, the OC in Britain, reported to Moss Twomey on the increased police activity in London following Scotland Yard's raid on the headquarters of the Soviet trading offices (Arcos):

Things are bad. Police [are] very active. Have destroyed most of my stuff and dumped the rest. If I am pinched nothing will be found on me. Be careful what you say in letters coming across.

---

reported to Twomey on 16 May: 'Things are bad. Police very active. Have destroyed most of my stuff and dumped the rest. If I am pinched nothing will be found on me. Be careful what you say in letters coming across.'[86] For some reason Twomey felt that George should be OK: 'I do not think there is any cause for undue anxiety.' Twomey also realised that the raid would make the Soviets more dependent on the IRA: 'This business may result to our advantage.'[87]

Not surprisingly, 'James' dropped out of sight, and George wrote in June: 'I have not heard from "James" or his friend. I thought I gave you to understand that I had made definite arrangements, as to how we were to pick up again when they are in a position to do so. He has [a] covering address and calling addresses for getting in touch here.'[88]

Though George continued to send books and journals to the Soviets, they were no longer covering his expenses: 'Funds are getting very low. [The] book account has taken nearly all the cash in hand. Subscriptions overdue for many journals. If you can, will you please send me a little [money]. If we are to maintain the connection I think it is essential that we keep on sending the books etc.'[89] By the beginning of October they had told him they would cover his expenses for book purchases.

Taking advantage of this, Twomey asked for *The Science of War*, 'provided you do not have to spend our money'.[90]

'James' contacted George again in September: '[I] received another letter from [our] friend [James]. He is in Amsterdam. He wants to see 'Ambrose' [Seán MacBride] immediately. [He] gives [the] name of a café where he can be met in. [He] says he has a present which he is anxious to get rid of.'[91]

However, with Seán MacBride in jail (falsely accused of the killing of Kevin O'Higgins) Twomey replied that George's request was 'rather awkward and impossible to fulfil at the present' and asked if 'James' could send on the 'present'.[92] Whatever the 'present' was, subsequent letters reveal that it doesn't appear to have been money. George pressed Twomey to go to Amsterdam himself: 'I have received another letter from [James'] representative and he mentions that he and another man are still waiting in Holland for the chairman [of the Army Council] or some officer, who will be in a position to settle some big questions. Would it be possible for you to come here this weekend?'[93] Walter Krivitsky of the RU later claimed he met with three IRA officers in Holland in 1927.[94]

It's here in the autumn of 1927 that our information on the Soviet connection with the IRA in Britain ends. Given the degree of secrecy accorded the relationship, it would be conjecture to make any statements as to how the association continued, or indeed if it did. However, there is evidence to suggest it may have ended soon afterwards. Or did it just go deeper or was the centre of the relationship moved to America?

The refusal of the Russians for much of 1927 to pay the IRA was, aside from financial constraints, likely a deliberate ploy. Stalin had committed himself to 'socialism in one country' and the duty of the RU was to help strengthen the revolution at home, not entangle the Soviet Union in the dreams and plans of the IRA, which on discovery would have been detrimental to Soviet interests. Walter Krivitsky said that the Russian politburo 'temporarily forbade any dealings with the Irish to avoid possible prejudice to their attempts to obtain credits in London'.[95] In addition, it was natural for the Soviets to try and get as much from the IRA for as little expenditure as possible, and to continually endeavour to run their IRA contacts as individual agents. The RU was prepared to give a little money

262

No. 57.

20th. Sept.,1924.

My dear Sir,

(180), DTIAEAEVCC. SPCOD.EEOOD.
OELEE.EHTAE.ETFHE.TOTAW.EHEIO.CHRER.TSEMH.MENSG.
IRMSA.SIYOR.TAWNT.OAIEE.AEEIO.UAEWI.NENSA.BISFN.
YEHSF.ATEMW.MDEAA.ARHUO.EEAOE.IEAAU.OIAEE.VLFIM.
EMGFE.ISHXR.EERNH.EMIAH.NAIII.RORDT.NRANE.ESSET.

Yours very sincerely,

Figure 26. The OC. Britain, George, reported to Moss Twomey that 'James', the Soviet intelligence officer, wanted to meet Seán MacBride ('Ambrose') in Amsterdam. This letter was written in September 1927, and not 1924:

> Received another letter from [our] friend ['James']. He is in Amsterdam. He want[s] to see 'Ambrose' immediately. [He] gives [the] name of a café where he can be met in, says he has a present, which he is anxious to get rid of.

to the IRA in return for useful intelligence, but not to provide significant financing or weapons.

Krivitsky said that when he renewed contact with IRA personnel, he worked with them until they presented him with 'definite suggestions for collaboration in a terrorist plan', and, judging the risk too great, he again terminated the contacts.[96] He also said that when Soviet intelligence wanted to recruit an agent 'their first recruiting ground is the Communist Party: if that fails they invariably try and seek out an Irishman.'[97]

Was Walter Krivitsky 'James'? Krivitsky was a senior RU agent stationed in Berlin and from his own admission (following defection to the west) had contacts with the IRA over a period of time. 'Mr X' we know was stationed in Berlin, and this was probably another name for 'James'. While 'James' usually met with George in London he did not have to be based there, and could have regularly travelled from Berlin under the guise of a Soviet diplomat or trade representative.

Another RU agent, Ignace Poretsky, alias 'Ludwik', was stationed in Holland from 1928 to 1929 and had contacts with the IRA but found them 'to be of little use' as 'they were convinced that their own problems were the world's most important'. After he was observed by British intelligence meeting with IRA representatives, sketches of him were published in English newspapers, forcing his reassignment.[98]

The IRA and Russians in America

It was 'Mr Jones' in New York who provided the Russians with the most important intelligence. 'Jones' was a highly colourful character: aggressive and arrogant, outrageous and confident. In a typical exchange with Twomey, after an IRA officer from Clare complained that he couldn't make contact with 'Jones' in New York, 'Jones' told Moss Twomey: 'When I see him he won't write home any more.'[99]

Initially 'Jones' was both An Timthire (the IRA's chief representative in the US) and the IRA's intelligence agent assigned to work with 'Stephen' of Red Army intelligence. In the autumn of 1926 'Stephen' asked him to devote himself full time to intelligence work and that this would 'necessitate very long journeys'. 'Jones' therefore wrote to Andy Cooney in October, stating in his own inimitable way: 'If you don't send over a man at once [to take over An Timthire's duties], I will appoint one myself, as it will be impossible to carry on the two jobs after next week.'[100] By the end of the year, Cooney and Twomey had appointed Connie Neenan to replace him as An Timthire. 'Jones' and Neenan worked well together and Neenan appears to have been the only other person in the US fully aware of what 'Jones' was up to.

In November, 'Jones' was working flat out for 'Stephen', spending up to five days a week outside of New York. 'My job is getting very hard ... wine and women. I am onto the right people now and can produce material of a high order but I have to bring good whiskey along and stay up all night drinking with whores and the people who give me the stuff. 'Stephen' is satisfied and offered me a raise in pay. I refused, as I don't want him to think I am doing it for the money. I may not last long at this pace. If you hear of me being mixed up in a scandal, you will understand.'[101] He added: 'I may have to put up in swank hotels in future [and] to do this I must have good clothes. I intend to ask him to furnish these if necessary as I couldn't afford to buy them.'[102] Twomey reasonably replied: 'Expenses of clothes and extra hotel expenses should be borne by Stephen.'[103]

IN THE US THE Russians were principally interested in information on the armed forces and the defence industries – intelligence on chemical weapons being a particular priority.[104] The United States army's Chemical Warfare Service, under the command of General Amos Fries, had responsibility for all aspects of chemical warfare including research and development. The service had extensive experience in the refinement and production of mustard gas, which was regarded as the most effective gas used in the First World War. In addition, towards the end of the war an American officer, Captain Lewis, had developed the highly toxic Lewisite, which like mustard gas was potentially fatal when absorbed either through the skin or inhaled. In the 1920s and 1930s the Russians devoted considerable resources to the production and deployment of these two gases. The US had also developed advanced gas masks borrowing on British and French designs.

'Jones' provided 'Stephen' with a wide array of information, covering areas such as chemical warfare, official reports from the army, navy and air service and airplane engine testing. In the field of chemical warfare he supplied copies of the journal, *Chemical Warfare* for the years 1922, 1923 and 1924. This was a journal produced by the Chemical Warfare Service, which Connie Neenan described as of 'wonderful value' to the Russians. There was also 'a complete book of various army gases', which probably refers to the book, *Chemical Warfare* written by General Fries as a 'labor of patriotism'. This was published by McGraw Hill in 1921 and though available in bookshops at the time was a most macabre production, containing detailed information and formulae of the poison gases of the First World War. In addition 'Jones' handed over the 1926 annual report of the Chemical Weapons Service and two gas masks, one of which was developed for army of-

Despatch No.4.

Dear Mr. Browne:-

I. To acknowledge ~~~~ despatch No.I5. received here 3d.inst.

2. The reason I did not ack. despatch No.I4. dated 8th.Sept,not 2nd. Sept.,was Smith was in this country that time,and handled all home communications. I may have been asked to ack.,if I was I didn't remember. Iwas asked to ask questions of certain men re Par.I7. Of those men I only met Whooly,and he says that he has only one article,and he refuses to disclose where that is. I will get Murphy's in a few days. I don't expect to locate Collins. Will you please be a little more discreet when using my name.

3. Did you reveivean important message dated IIth. October.
    VNFTU SIEPG ATRIH ETOGO AUHTT ASWMN TASAA WMRII O. (4I)

4. NEUII ATBER CCMAG ESEHO KLNHN REOCO ETFVF FEOCL OR. (42) When I see him he won't write home any more. I also wrote other men of that group and got no reply.

5. Re para.5. I will look up those men ,but don't expect any results.

6. re your para.6.Noted.
    STMNH ENMDO UG LMU SRTGE IMRMA TITIC SSNRL IOAOO RDPRE SAOY. (49)
    If not there must be something wrong with your end.
    GPEUP DTNPI AUMOE TIENS OHEYE IHEON SNERE RLIHE TECVA SOBRE
    MRAYN FMNTO ARBGE KIBH. (69)

7. ONTMKWYUDI DEWAT LSCTO CMIFI AEEDO IOOPT LFNIO TTMMO IUHEN
    CSOOL NOKTN SENEOTNSWU A. (7I)

8. Re para. 4. of my despatch No.3.
    KUBTA LEOHV ICFTA YTDCR OLURN EISIY BVOUE SLNTE YEOXT IEFAF EFISE
    XXXXXXX GIVOG IACNI NOLUF FIREA REBGI. (80)

9. My job is getting very hard I was asked to concenterate and give results. I have,but it means :-
    OEOGHHOGNW TIWAT CEROS TDHOT NOIRO UHLAI AHUEI AMGVW NGTEE NOENI
    EREYI RLEWH NUAIO NLGDG FIHDT OMINT WEEIM PARDBKAROP HNGNA HEHDH
    HPNDT EDFTG OLNNO FENOP ARIYU NEESA TPRLB NAPKS WTMRW EIADA IIHV.
    (I64)

    SOSEH DESSE ADTIE ARFAI MAFIA MIEIM INIFI DISTM NIRPI OGTFD YOHTT
    ENSTN NNAUN ACPEE RTNOH DAEWK RSFED IOY. (88)

    APCDY TINFE ALOHE IDETO MPUNA AONCU ISREL SOIBN IMGYI SLLEE IWDTI
    AXAHY TUGAN NTHMN DSAPU OA. (77)

    ENNOM UNROL SEPOI EPWUF OCNOH WSHFE NTOEM DEESJ EKHTM AESOG TCDOV
    REMRO NTYNI ETIR FSEEB DOMEC BBNEC HAOMO TEINT IUTFA APISM WTGTE
    IWEOS SITPL HDOWO EOAEM ANEAV IIO-E TPOIG STANLOWLEI LFNTPINGSS
    OBCGD ATVOT EYUYN RON. (I83)

Figure 27. The IRA's agent in New York, 'Mr Jones', reported to Moss Twomey on the success of his espionage activities for 'Stephen', the Soviet intelligence officer.

In paragraph 9 'Jones' wrote: 'My job is getting very hard I was asked to concentrate [*sic*] and give results. I have, but it means:- wine and women. I am on to the right people now, and can produce material of a high order, but I have to bring good whiskey along, and stay up all night drinking with whores and the people who give me the stuff. "Stephen" is satisfied and offered me a raise in pay. I refused as I don't want him to think I am doing it for money. I may not last long at this pace. If you hear of me being mixed up in a scandal, you will understand.'

ficers so as to allow the wearer to use a field telephone or wireless.[105]

Other items supplied included: a technical drawing of the Browning .50 calibre anti-aircraft machine gun, the 1926 annual reports of the chief officers commanding the artillery and the infantry, 'important technical notes [from the] Navy Construction Yard' and information on a naval torpedo.[106]

Regarding airplane technology and the air service, 'Jones' gave the Russians documents on tests of two Packard airplane engines – one the 520 horsepower 1500 engine, the other the 2500 engine. Neenan claimed that: 'This saved Stephen's people $250,000 as they intend[ed] to buy one prior to getting [the] test [results].' There were also Air Service 'tests, photos and drawings', 'Specifications issued by [the] Officer in Charge [of the United States Army] Air Service' and '[flight] manuals [from the Air Service's flight training school at] Kelly Flying Field [in Texas]'. In addition there were 'aero technical bulletins', and 'technical notes' and memoranda for the years 1924 through to 1927.[107]

In 1926 'Jones' engaged in negotiations for items that cost up to $500,000. He hoped that 'Stephen' would purchase them through him and so preserve a connection that could be later exploited by the IRA for their own purposes, as well as landing him a hefty 'commission'. 'I ['Jones'] built my connection thru [sic] people who were helping me in the hope that I would buy stuff, the price of which might run up to $500,000. I discovered that our friend ['Stephen'] was buying the stuff. I asked him to give me the buying of some of it and I would be in a position to give very valuable information. He refused. This puts me in a hole and I may lose good connections. He knows this and it's his lookout. It will mean hard work to work it up again. There is a big commission going with this.' It is intriguing to wonder what this highly expensive equipment was. 'Jones' refers to it as 'stuff' and this was a term used by the IRA for munitions, specifically explosives.[108]

'Jones' didn't specify who his sources were, though he mentioned one particularly valuable 'connection' who was not Irish. He also clarified that he had multiple sources and additional potential informants whom he hadn't 'tapped', due to the refusal of the Soviets to adequately fund the IRA.[109] Given that much of the intelligence consisted of up-to-date military reports, it is reasonable to assume that at least some of his informants were serving military personnel. Why did they spy for the Russians? American communists could have informed out of a sense of idealism. But it was unlikely that 'Jones' had much contact with communists, aside from possible contacts among Irish-American socialists and trade unionists sympathetic to the IRA. Some Irish-Americans would have been open to supplying information to the IRA if they felt it was in support of the 'struggle' against Britain, and it is highly unlikely that 'Jones' would have explained that the information was being passed on to the Soviets. Money was also a likely motivating force for informants, particularly those with alcohol or other problems. I've found no evidence to suggest that the FBI or other US agencies were aware that the IRA was spying for the Soviet Union. In 1940 the FBI director, J. Edgar Hoover, wrote: 'The Bureau has not been greatly concerned in the past with the activities of the Irish Republican Army except on specific occasions.' The words 'specific occasions' are most likely a reference to IRA contacts with Germany during the First World War, which the federal authorities investigated at the time.[110]

Towards the end of 1926 'Stephen' brought up the issue of the Soviet 'war scare' with 'Jones' and proposed that when Britain and the Soviet Union went to war, the IRA would help sink British merchant ships sailing from ports on the east coast. 'Jones' reported: 'They [the Soviets] are going to go to war with our friends [Britain]. Not at once, probably next Fall [sic]. When that time came I would go home so I would have to train a man to take my place [in America], as we will have to work for him during [the] war period. We would have to destroy all our friend's shipping. He will supply all the necessary material. I would have to organise the men etc.'[111] Twomey replied: 'Regarding destruction of shipping, it is a most delicate matter. Doing so may involve [the] United States in war; not by England in declaring war on [the] USA, but by [the] USA against others.' He was probably inferring that the US would declare war on the USSR if it found out about the Soviet involvement. Twomey, however, was not dismissing the idea of sabotage: 'Destruction may be feasible, if it could be done secretly and without capture of our agents. Could you ensure this?'[112] However, 'Jones' cautioned: 'Under the excitement of war conditions, we would get almost all our men to do anything, but could not give any guarantee that we could avoid casualties in killed and captures [sic] ... I am sure if war broke out, 'Stephen' would try to use us in every way possible.'[113] By March, 'Stephen' reported that 'there was no immediate danger of war from their [the Soviet] end'.[114] In early May 1927, a week before the British raid on the Arcos offices, Twomey noted ominous signs: 'Word from Glasgow that there is great activity in Nobel's factory making bomb plates and fuses. Working overtime, aeroplanes being constructed by Beardmores on the Clyde'. 'Our friend ['James'] in London has left and his successor is absent at the moment. We have a feeling [that] big international events and probably war on Russia are impending' and added 'lately a French newspaper published what purported to be plans for a joint attack by England and Japan on Russia.' Twomey asked Connie Nennan to update him on 'possible happenings in such [a] direction'.[115] In November at the IRA army convention the delegates passed a motion pledging IRA support for the Soviets in the event of war.[116]

Contrary to actual Soviet policy at the time, 'Stephen' professed that the Russians should be glad to have the IRA as allies: 'Owing to the strained relations with England he was of the opinion that they [the Soviets] would make friends with anyone under the circumstances.'[117]

Unlike 'James' in London, 'Stephen' seemed to have been genuinely very concerned about the possibility of a break with the IRA. In February 1927 Twomey wrote to 'Jones' that: 'we may have to break off, even temporarily, to let them see they cannot dupe us or treat us as they wish' and when 'Jones' told 'Stephen' that the connection was to be broken, the latter was 'mad'. He summoned 'Jones' to a meeting where they talked about this for three hours. 'Stephen' was 'wildly excited over the matter, and will do anything to keep us on his hands'. Jones had already slacked off on his work for 'Stephen', reporting: 'I notified my connections that I would not see them for a few weeks. I also had told Stephen during argument that I had not tapped certain sources, which would give results, because I felt they had no intention of being straight with us. He said that he believed this. Of course there is a certain amount of truth and bull in it, as I did not work hard on the job for some time past, but I gave satisfactory results just the same. It will take ten weeks to get an answer from his HQ and he thinks I am treating him bad in not supplying him with stuff in the meantime. From his attitude I think everything will be alright, as he is more or less helpless without us, all you have to do is use the strong hand.

The chief cause of the trouble is his HQ have no idea who supplies the material. He [is] getting all the credit. As far as I can gather, he never reports in detail how or where he gets the stuff etc.' 'Stephen' offered to pay the expenses for an IRA delegation to go to Moscow to try and get the Soviets to resume funding, provided that 'Jones' would either continue working for him or hand over control of a particularly valuable informant. 'Jones' refused. 'Stephen' claimed to be making this offer on his own bat, without sanction from Moscow, and he told 'Jones' 'not to report the matter to his HQ'. The two 'parted very good friends'.[118]

'Jones' was not a person overburdened with modesty and believed he was the main intelligence source for the Soviets in America: 'They almost depend on us solely to do their work here.'[119] This was unlikely, however, given the presence of RU networks among American communists. He added: 'I have been very successful in my work. When the last man [Soviet agent] was leaving, he was lavish in his praise of my work. They [*sic*] told me that when I got time for a vacation that they would send me to their capital and that they would teach me their language etc. This of course is all bull, which I pretended to swallow. I am of [the] opinion it is with a view to getting me to work for them independently. Later on this morning, I told him I was expecting a cable ordering me to cease working [for the Russians]. He was very much upset [and] he asked me what I would do. I only laughed thinking he would ask me to work direct[ly for him] and compromise himself, [but] he is too wise.'[120] 'Jones' continued to put pressure on 'Stephen', who was said to be in a 'state of despair'.[121] He felt that the IRA had been exploited by the Soviets, and in an interesting choice of words wrote: 'Believe me these people [the Russians] are getting away with murder, but they will not do so [for] much longer as I am going to resign next month.'[122]

'Jones' was 'determined to get back to civilian employment'.[123] In March Twomey wrote to Neenan: 'Prevent 'Jones' [from] resigning ... he may need cash which you can give him. He is too hasty and almost unreasonable.'[124] But 'Jones' was adamant: 'I will not work whole time again. Not even for one day.'[125] By early May 'Jones' had 'definitely given up'. Twomey felt let 'down badly' and wrote him a final letter asking him to reconsider: 'You appreciate I am sure the delicate nature of this work, how very few suitable persons there are to do it. A person who may be capable may not be close or reliable enough. We can have nobody who does not fulfil the last conditions.'[126]

Twomey wrote to Neenan recommending that he should take Jones' position and get someone else to perform the administrative and organisational duties of An Timthire: 'The work is so delicate and needs such secrecy it may be advisable [that] you take it on yourself and get someone else as An Timthire.' In the meantime, to maintain the relationship 'Jones' introduced Neenan to 'Stephen'.[127]

Since the agreement with the Soviets dated from 1925 it was to be expected that a number of Irish republicans in America would have known about it, though not in detail. Neenan contradicted himself somewhat when he said that: no one 'is aware of his [Jones'] work, but all believe he is working for [the] Army [IRA]', and then he suggested that the IRA take advantage of Jones' resignation to discretely get the word out that the agreement had been terminated: 'We could tell those who know that [the] connection with 'Stephen' [has been] broken off.'[128] Twomey added that Neenan should officially retain the title An Timthire so as not to arouse suspicion.[129]

Twomey advised Neenan: 'You should be free to devote a good deal of your time to "Stephen". This work may cease at any time, and if it does you will be able to resume [your duties as] An Timthire ... Pretend to "Stephen" you must travel on his work, charge expenses to him and in this way keep in touch with [the] distant camps [IRA-Clan na Gael clubs] of ours.'[130]

Who was 'Mr Jones'?

'Mr Jones' is one of the most colourful and intriguing characters of these encrypted documents, a maverick with a blend of toughness, bluster and intelligence. Piecing together clues from the documents, we can get evidence as to his probable identity.

Firstly, 'Mr Jones' signed his name either 'Jones' or 'JB'. What did the 'B' stand for? In May 1927 Twomey wrote a letter to an IRA officer travelling to America: 'I am anxious to hear from An Timthire if Mr Byrne has given up wholetime [sic] work?'[131] As this was at the time when 'Jones' resigned and given that there would have been very few full-time IRA officers in America, it is reasonable to assume that 'Mr Byrne' was the name by which 'Mr Jones' was known in public. Then what was Byrne's first name? Twomey wrote to Neenan, telling him that a courier would call looking for 'you or Dan Byrne' and that he was to be given explosives or samples of tear gas.[132] Given the sensitivity of this matter, it's clear that 'Dan Byrne' was working closely with Neenan. In addition, throughout Neenan's despatches in cipher there's only one other IRA man whom he names as being in his confidence and that was 'Dan'. For example, when Neenan sent $5,000 to the IRA in Ireland he remarked that the method for transferring the money was so secret that he hadn't told the Clan but 'Dan and myself [apart from the couriers] ... were the only persons who knew the means by which the money was sent.'[133] As the name 'Dan' is frequently written in cipher it's reasonable to assume that this is really Byrne's and hence Jones' first name. 'Dan' was also probably from Cork – as was Connie Neenan and Moss Twomey. This is suggested in Neenan's letter to Twomey when he recommended that the newly appointed An Timthire 'must not be from Cork. Note this. I feel others thought Cork were running [the] whole outfit.'[134]

I'm unaware of any senior IRA officer of the time in either America or Ireland called Dan Byrne, never mind one who would have been entrusted with such an important mission. It's therefore likely that the last name 'Byrne' was a false name, particularly if 'Jones' was in America illegally or on the run from the gardaí in Ireland. Interestingly, Connie Neenan himself said he travelled to Boston in 1930 under an assumed name.[135]

Connie Neenan had an older brother, Dan, in America, but by the time Neenan arrived in 1926 he was already seriously ill and was soon to pass away.[136] A dying Dan Neenan, who was not a prominent IRA figure (even if he had been an IRA volunteer) doesn't fit the description of 'Jones'.

There were a number of senior IRA officers in America at the time, such as Con Lehane from Cork who had led the IRA's attacks from Donegal into Northern Ireland in 1922. But there's only one whose first name is 'Dan' – Dan 'Sandow' Donovan.

Sandow was one of the toughest IRA gunmen, not just in Cork, but in Ireland – a hard man.[137] During the Anglo-Irish War he fought in Cork city alongside Connie Neenan. In 1920 he personally shot police divisional commissioner Smyth at the County Club in Cork.[138] Smyth was the most senior police officer killed in the conflict. In the lead-up to the Civil War in 1922 Sandow masterminded the capture at sea of the British arms ship the *Upnor*. The IRA operatives seized so much arms and ammunition that they're reported to have needed 200 lorries to cart it all away.[139] A small incident that occurred during the Anglo-Irish War serves as a colourful illustration of Sandow's personality and ingenuity. At that time in Cork, much to the annoyance of the IRA, there was a priest who regularly spoke out against the organisation during sermons at mass. This presented it with the dilemma: how to stop him but without harming him — as it was inconceivable to shoot or rough up a priest. Therefore Sandow walked up to the priest in the street, drew his gun and pointed it at him: 'I was ordered to do it Father, but I can't. But there are others who are not as particular as I am.' It's reported that the priest kept quiet after that.[140]

In March 1924 Sandow took part in an attack on British soldiers and civilians as they were leaving the British base at Spike Island in Cork harbour. Spike Island was one of the naval bases allotted to the royal navy under the terms of the Anglo-Irish Treaty. The IRA men were disguised as Free State soldiers and the operation was a failed attempt to destabilise the government. The gardaí immediately suspected Sandow and the IRA had to whisk him off to America.[141] As a wanted man, Sandow couldn't have entered the US legally and so must have been there under an assumed name. He did eventually return to Cork, the date of which I'm uncertain, though it may have been during the Depression when many IRA exiles returned home.

Therefore when one looks at factors such as name, personality and stature within the IRA there's very strong circumstantial evidence to suggest that 'Mr Jones' was Dan 'Sandow' Donovan. A true Irish James Bond!

The IRA and China

One of the more bizarre plans of the IRA was to provide political and military support to Chinese nationalists under Chiang Kai-shek.

By 1926 China was divided into fiefdoms controlled by warlords, while many of the key ports and cities were controlled by foreign powers. Within these treaty ports and their 'concessions' foreigners could trade and engage in economic activity protected by unfair treaties forced upon the Chinese. The foreigners thrived on the absence of a strong central Chinese government and were protected by a large army and naval presence. Warships of many nations, including the royal navy, patrolled the seas around China and the great Yangtze river. Britain, followed by Japan, was the largest foreign investor in China and together these two countries accounted for over 50 per cent of foreign investment.[142] To protect her interest Britain supported the powerful northern warlord Marshal Wu Peifu.[143] America, with a smaller stake in China, adopted a more neutral stance.[144]

The city of Canton in the south of the country was the Chinese nationalists' stronghold. Chiang Kai-shek was the leader of the nationalist party, the Kuomintang, which was allied to the tiny Chinese Communist Party. The Russians believed that a nationalist victory resulting in the defeat of the foreign 'imperialists' and their Chinese allies would trigger similar uprisings throughout Asia, including India, and ultimately lead to the collapse of the British empire.[145] In addition, victory by the communist–nationalist alliance would help secure the border with Russia and displace the more threatening Japanese. To build up Chiang's National Revolutionary Army the Soviets provided massive resources and a host of military advisors. The fate of China also played an important role in the struggle for power in Russia, with Stalin supporting the communist alliance with the Kuomintang, while Trotsky called for Soviet support of the communists exclusively.[146]

In July 1926 the National Revolutionary Army launched a major campaign to reunify China, called the Northern Expedition. Following a string of military victories by the nationalists, in late 1926 the British began to consider recognising the Kuomintang government.[147] The following March the nationalists took the key city of Shanghai, and around the same time the already-strained relations between the communists and nationalists disintegrated into fighting, leading ultimately to the rout of the communists and the Russians by December.[148]

So where does the IRA fit into this? There are a number of reasons (none of them very good) why the IRA should have considered supporting the Kuomintang and Chiang Kai-shek. First, any war that threatened Britain and her empire was in the IRA's interests. Second, it was an opportunity to stir up anti-British propaganda by labelling Britain's involvement as imperialist. Third, and perhaps most importantly, this was a further service it could perform for the Soviets and particularly Stalin. IRA support consisted of a combination of propaganda and military assistance. However, the Russians may have overestimated the degree of assistance the IRA could have provided the Chinese. In particular the IRA and their partners, Clan na Gael, retained little ability to mobilise American public support – as by 1927 they represented only a small minority within the Irish-American community. This was in stark contrast to Daniel Cohalan's and the Friends of Irish Freedom's successful campaign against US senate ratification of the Treaty of Versailles only eight years previously.

An Phoblacht and the Irish-American newspapers were able to spin the Chinese struggle as a war against British imperialism. In September 1926 the 'Wanshien massacre' was given prominent coverage. This incident occurred when troops belonging to Britain's ally, Marshal Peifu, attempted to commandeer British merchant vessels at the river port of Wanhsien, to cross the Yangtze river. The British took evasive action during which a sampan capsized and several Chinese soldiers were reportedly drowned. Wu's local commander retaliated by seizing two merchant ships and their crews. A tense standoff ensued as the British brought up their gunboats; finally the royal navy made a surprise attack to retake the boats. The attackers were beaten back but with the loss of several hundred Chinese, including civilians, and seven British fatalities.[149] In New York the *Irish World* proclaimed 'British butcher 5,000 Chinamen', who died 'mostly by British bombardment of the city'.[150] In January 1927 *An Phoblacht* reported: 'Nationalist China is fighting to drive British brigands and thugs from her shores.'[151]

Twomey wrote to Connie Neenan telling him to mobilise Irish-American opinion in support of the Chinese, as it 'is [a] good opportunity for [the] display of anti-British feeling'. He wanted Neenan to get in touch with 'agents of the Cantonese [nationalist] government' and to 'arrange demonstrations'.[152] Neenan contacted the Clan Executive who said they would 'endeavour to help' but were limited as they no longer had their own newspaper.[153] He also 'went to [the] *Irish World* ... to give all possible publicity to the Chinese fight for independence. They promised [to support the Chinese] and are getting copy [supplied text] from [the] Chinese representative here.' Neenan felt that, though 'labour' unions and 'some Irish-American newspapers are pro-Cantonese', the papers were otherwise 'completely imperialistic'. There was, however, a shift in the spring as he noticed calls for foreign withdrawal from China.[154] In April Neenan was able to report 'pro-Chinese demonstrations held in Philadelphia [were] well attended'.[155] Philadelphia was the hometown of Joe McGarrity and this demonstration was likely the product of McGarrity and Neenan's efforts. In May the *Irish World* reported that a demonstration was held outside the British embassy in Washington by the (well-known civil rights group) 'Hands-off China Conference of Philadelphia'.[156]

But the IRA was (on the surface at least) endeavouring to mobilise more than public opinion in support of the Kuomintang. Around January 1927 Mr Tang, an 'important Chinese representative', visited Ireland at the invitation of the IRA. Tang was a writer, resident in London, who was associated with the British Independent Labour party (a left-wing group affiliated with the more moderate Labour party) and acted as a Kuomintang representative. In Ireland Tang attended a 'good pro-Chinese demonstration' and met with Twomey, Cooney and O'Donnell, who found him 'a fine type'. Following this meeting Twomey reported that the Chinese 'would welcome any [IRA] men we may send out. Of course we have none suitable. If any [men] there [in America are] anxious to go they should be encouraged.'[157] In February the Army Council passed a resolution that 'the principle of Volunteers going to China was approved, provided conditions of service, cost of travelling were satisfactory'.[158] Whether this was serious or not is difficult to determine; it's possible it was merely a sop to the Russians and some of the left-wing IRA members such as Peadar O'Donnell. However, at the behest of the Council, O'Donnell prepared a report on the feasibility of this venture which the OC in Britain, George, delivered to Tang.

In the meantime, the British police suspected Tang of seeking weapons and set up a crude sting operation. He received a phone call to discuss an 'interesting proposition' and to attend a meeting with a 'mysterious man' in Twickenham. Suspecting an attempt to entrap him, he first sent a registered letter to Scotland Yard stating that he suspected that the man he was going to see 'was seeking to involve peaceable citizens in illegal action' and that he was attending the meeting with a witness solely to 'expose the undesirable nature of the transaction'. Arriving at the house the man said: 'I represent a syndicate which has any amount of stuff and is prepared to sell to these Chinese boys. We can give you submarines, field artillery, tanks, rifles, ammunition – anything you want.'

'What about aeroplanes?' asked Tang.

'Yes, we can supply you with about thirty of them.' The man finished: 'My people want to help the boys who are fighting for their freedom against the British. I'll fight for any country that's against the damned British. I've got a crowd of Irish willing to fight now, if your people will get them to China.'[159] This police trap is reminiscent of the more successful Special Branch schemes against the Fenians in the previous century. It would appear that Scotland Yard had some limited information on Tang to act on; perhaps they were just aware of his trip to Ireland, but were unfamiliar with the extent of his contacts with the IRA. Tang already knew how the IRA made contact and who were their representatives, and so this is another example of how the British intelligence forces weren't well informed on IRA work for the Soviets.

February was definitely China Month for the IRA, as they undertook two other projects in support of the Chinese nationalists. The OC of the Scottish battalion reported to Twomey: 'China situation we have been very active, made and placed 200 coal bombs in cargo of [British] admiralty coal transports for China'. Coal bombs are devices made of a chunk of metal, with a hollow centre containing explosives. They are made to resemble coal by coating the surface in a mixture of tar and coal dust. The bombs are placed among a pile of coal, and when fed into the boiler of a ship are supposed to explode. A Confederate secret service officer, who originally came from Belfast, invented the coal bomb during the American Civil War. The Fenians could have learned about the bomb either from ex-Confederate soldiers who joined them or from an anonymous letter published in *The Times* in 1875, which gave a full description of the bomb. In turn the Scottish IRA was descended from a long Fenian tradition. The IRA plan was that bombs would arrive among the coal in China and be unwittingly shovelled into the boiler of a royal navy ship, most likely one patrolling the Yangtze. Whether the bombs were even placed by the Scottish unit is unlikely and I have found no evidence that one actually exploded. The Scottish OC wasn't guilty of an overstatement when he said: 'This job [making the bombs] is a bit dangerous and requires a lot of time to construct.'[160] Twomey was 'glad you took advantage of [the] coal' but wanted attacks on British ships bringing supplies and weapons to China: 'Could a ship or ships for China be burned or destroyed by scuttling or other means? Do your utmost on this.'[161]

Twomey was now on a roll and he sent a message to the IRA in Liverpool, marked 'destroy when read': 'Your IO [intelligence officer] reports shipments from there to China. If you can do your utmost to destroy any ammunition or other armament or stores being sent. Could you get some time mines or incendiary bombs put on ships or put ships on fire with petrol or other inflammables? Keep this absolutely secret. Do not discuss it. Either carry out the operations or say nothing about it.'[162]

This is the extent of our information on IRA support for Chiang Kai shek and his nationalist party. Probably the only effect it could have had was to encourage American support for Chinese self-determination, and even on this it probably had a negligible effect. The Americans, not burdened with an imperial past, were already more favourably disposed to China than the European powers and in 1928 signed a trade treaty, returning to China control over her trade with America.[163]

THIS IS A SNAPSHOT of the IRA's relationship with the Soviet Union and her allies in 1926 and 1927. Little of this clandestine association has been suspected, let alone described. The degree of secrecy the IRA maintained is impressive given that many of the participants later resigned from the IRA and in later life frequently talked extensively about their experiences. This may be partially due to the degree of disapproval which association with the Soviets engendered in Ireland from the 1930s on. On the other hand, many in the IRA remained life-long socialists and continued to publicly support the USSR.

The relationship was controlled by military men in the IRA such as Twomey and Russell and was not driven by ideological interests. Republican socialists in the IRA who would have been sympathetic to the Soviet Union were kept in the background.

The actual value of the information the IRA acquired for the Soviets is difficult to assess. What is undeniable is that the organisation supplied a steady stream of technical and tactical information from America and Britain to Red Army intelligence. 'James', however, was critical of what he received in London: 'We have got only very few valuable material [*sic*].'[164] This may have been his honest assessment, although in espionage it's standard to push agents to get better and better information by criticising what's already been done. General Krivitsky of Red Army intelligence said that 'for a time he got quite useful information' from his IRA agents.[165]

On the other hand, the IRA believed that it was 'Mr Jones' in America that acquired the most important intelligence for the Soviets and not the IRA in Britain. This was information that 'James' and Krivitsky probably weren't privy to.

'Jones' passed on Fries' book, *Chemical Warfare*, which was a freely available publication, but the other military reports he acquired were restricted and would be expected to have been of greater value to the Russians. At the time the Soviets had a covert chemical warfare programme with the Germans, but information on American chemical weapons procedures, including production techniques, would have been complementary. In particular the Americans had expertise with mustard gas and lewisite, two of the gases which the Russians felt were of the most military value. America had also made advances in the development of gas masks. The technical information on airplane engines, machine guns and submarine detection sonar (and even the tractors made by Ford – if it was ever handed over) fit in with the pattern of improvement in Russian military technology and armament which occurred during the inter-war years. And though no one item or report may have been crucial, all in all it may have helped to make Soviet technology and weaponry the formidable resource it was to become.

Although information on specific and operational details may have been kept to an inner circle, a relatively large number of officers must have known about the alliance. For instance, the agreement was originally made under the leadership of Frank Aiken, and he and Seán Lemass would have been familiar with it, as presumably was de Valera. Members of the IRA headquarters staff and the Army Council should also have known, given the many passing comments that Twomey made in the papers and to officers, including George Gilmore and Frank Kerlin.

I have found no evidence that the intelligence agencies in Britain, America and the Irish Free State were aware either of the full extent of the IRA's clandestine and espionage activity or that the IRA and the Soviet Union had a formal agreement. It was fortunate for Britain that the Soviets exercised restraint in not providing significant military support to the IRA.

As the agreement was so secret it's difficult to know for certain whether it was ended in the late 1920s or whether it continued maybe in a more limited form. At some time (possibly the late 1920s or early 1930s) George Gilmore and Dave Fitzgerald of the IRA went to Moscow to attend a military training course but returned home when British intelligence found out. In 1930 Seán MacBride met with the leadership of Clan na Gael to tell them of a proposed agreement with the Soviet Union which promised 'substantial' aid and the opportunity for twenty-five to thirty IRA officers to train in Russia.[166]

One cannot but suspect that there may also be another chapter to be written about the Provisional IRA and the USSR.

Conclusion

The decryption of these documents gives a fresh insight into the IRA. It provides an opportunity to make an assessment that is independent of both the narratives prepared by the IRA and its veterans for public consumption and those of third-party observers or historians on the outside looking in.

In writing this, James and I were led by the evidence without knowing where exactly it would lead us. There were many surprises; the extent of the relationship with the Soviet Union and the ability of de Valera to consistently outmanoeuvre the organisation being two examples. The IRA that emerged was divided and ill-disciplined, lacking a unifying ideology or strategy. Though there was no lack of talent in the leadership, there was a complete failure of leadership. Overall this is a picture of incompetence. Having said that, some of the IRA's security procedures and ability to engage in espionage were truly impressive.

The papers also reveal an organisation that was largely the sum of its dominant personalities. The prison letters in particular have a very humanising effect and demonstrate the commitment and sincerity of many of its leaders. This is the story of individuals as much as it is of an organisation: of Garda Ward who was pointlessly shot and killed, of the newsboy who was attacked by Fr Barrett, of Jack Keogh the bully who died a miserable death, of Annie O'Mahoney who put a dollar a day aside for the IRA, and of countless others.

There was no one point at which the 'old IRA' of the Anglo-Irish War became what's regarded as the 'bad IRA' of recent times. The tactics used during the struggle with the British were not terribly different to those the IRA tried to use against the Irish Free State. The leaders from the Anglo-Irish War left not so much because of moral indignation but because they were tired of defeat and realised the organisation had no achievable plan. The killing of unarmed gardaí just seemed so pointless and a waste of human life.

Overall, men like Moss Twomey and Andy Cooney were a restraining force in the organisation. Though the IRA considered using chemical warfare, in practice it didn't resort to it (nor did it realistically have the capability to do so), and if it had, was it any more to blame that the nations that used it in the First World War?

This is one of the first (if not the first) attempts to present a picture of a revolutionary group through the decryption of its internal correspondence, in the process giving a more nuanced and fuller picture. It raises ethical and moral questions with no easy answers and shows that Irish society can't easily distance or separate itself from the IRA. The IRA had a formative influence on Irish society and additionally had supporters and sympathisers throughout all sections of the community.

In international terms the IRA at the time was an important and highly advanced revolutionary group. Only a few years earlier it had prevented the British forces from defeating it, and had led one of the first successful modern anti-colonial struggles, a struggle that combined military and political strategies in a way that set the pattern for the remainder of the twentieth century.

Epilogue

In the years following 1927 the IRA continued to decline. There was little in the way of coordinated military activity and the organisation failed to develop a political programme with popular appeal. As the leadership drifted further to the left, it helped found the radical (and short-lived) socialist organisation Saor Éire (Free Ireland) in 1931.[1]

That year there was an upsurge in activity, with shootings – including the killing of a garda superintendent in Tipperary – intimidation of juries and reports of widespread drilling.[2] In the run-up to the general election of March 1932 Frank Aiken approached Moss Twomey with a proposal that the IRA merge with Fianna Fáil, which Twomey rejected.[3] The IRA supported Fianna Fáil in the election campaign, and with the party's victory and formation of a government the IRA was on a crest of a wave. Membership increased to around 10,000 and the organisation openly recruited and paraded in public.[4] Many in the IRA thought that the organisation and Fianna Fáil would work together to bring about a republic. However, the excitement was short-lived and Fianna Fáil continued to attract members and support from the IRA.

At the same time, with the Catholic Church in the vanguard, the mood in the country became stridently anti-communist and the socialists in the IRA came under increasing attack from within the movement.[5] This led in 1934 to the departure of most of the leading socialist republicans – including Peader O'Donnell, Michael Price and George Gilmore.[6]

Two years later two brutal killings shocked the country. Henry Boyle Sommerville, an elderly retired British admiral, accused of encouraging local men to join the British navy, was shot at his home in Cork. And in Waterford a local volunteer, John Egan, was killed after it was alleged he had cooperated with the gardaí's investigation of illegal drilling in the county. This resulted in de Valera's government banning the IRA in June.[7] Moss Twomey was arrested and sentenced to three years in jail and was replaced by a rapid succession of chiefs of staff including Seán MacBride.[8] In 1938 Seán Russell, allied with IRA members from the north and Joe

McGarrity of Clan na Gael, became chief of staff in what was virtually a *coup d'etat*. Russell committed the organisation to a disastrous bombing campaign in Britain and an ill-chosen alliance with Nazi Germany. In 1940 he died on board a German u-boat on his way to Ireland.[9]

Under Russell's leadership the IRA was reduced to fewer than 2,000 members in the Free State,[10] and during this time Moss Twomey, Tom Barry, Seán MacBride and Donal O'Donoghue left the organisation.[11] The IRA was never again to be a force to be reckoned with in the south of Ireland. Fifteen years after the 1925 army convention, Frank Aiken and Éamon de Valera were in government and the IRA was largely irrelevant.

What was the legacy of the IRA from the time of Moss Twomey's leadership? As with anything, it depends on one's perspective. In military and moral terms it was a failure, epitomised by Russell's sordid death. However, it also produced men (as it rejected the participation of women) who made an important contribution to the new state. Peadar O'Donnell, Mick Price and others continued to campaign on behalf of the disadvantaged during a time of awful poverty. Somewhat ironically, Seán MacBride achieved an international reputation as a champion of human rights. He was a founder of Amnesty International and a co-recipient of the 1974 Nobel Peace prize. Presumably when he visited Moscow in 1977 to receive the Lenin Peace prize he travelled on a legitimate government-issued passport![12]

Fianna Fáil grew directly out of the IRA and must be considered part of the IRA's legacy. It took with it the IRA's tradition of egalitarianism and of active participation (and dissent) by its membership. While Cumann na nGaedheal founded the democratic institutions of the state and assured the rule of law, Fianna Fáil became the state's first mass political party and ensured public participation and full support for the state. It was de Valera who realised Michael Collins' dream of using the Treaty as the stepping stone to a republic. And it was the gunmen of Fianna Fáil who finally helped marginalise the IRA and the men of violence in the south, just as the gunmen of Sinn Féin were to do so in the north sixty years later.

APPENDIX I

Organisations, groups and technical terms

American Association for the Recognition of the Irish Republic (AARIR): Irish-American organisation that supported Fianna Fáil and Éamon de Valera.

An Timthire: title of the full-time IRA representative in America. In December 1926 Connie Nennan succeeded 'Mr Jones' in this position.

Army, the: informal term for the IRA, used by its membership.

Army convention: held every few years and attended by delegates from units throughout Ireland. When in session it was the IRA's 'supreme authority'. It elected the Army Executive, which in turn elected the Army Council.

Army Council: the seven-member committee, which was the governing body of the IRA, except when an army convention was in session. Decided on IRA policy and strategy.

Army Executive: an IRA committee which elected the Army Council. Following the Civil War it lost most of its other powers and was largely by-passed by the Army Council and chief of staff.

Cable: telegram.

Call house: a house or business where a caller could be put in contact with the IRA or make a delivery for the IRA.

Chief of staff: commander of the IRA – supreme in all military matters. In command of GHQ and usually chaired the Army Council.

CID (Criminal Investigation Department): derogatory term used by the IRA for the Garda Special Branch. The term originated with a notorious Free State 'police' division disbanded in 1923.

Cipher: a system for concealing plain text, by replacing the letters of the text with assigned letters and/or rearranging the letters

Clan na Gael: secret and militant Irish-American organisation in alliance with the IRA.

Clan na Gael and IRA clubs: local clubs in America that formed the base of Clan na Gael. Members included IRA veterans.

Code: a method for concealing plain text, by replacing it with new complete words, phrases or sentences.

Covering address: an address to which communications, books and other media were sent to and from here forwarded to the intended recipient – either an IRA member or unit. Most covering addresses received letters, while others were designated for telegrams, magazines or newspapers etc.

Dump: also arms dump. Secret and secure storage place for arms, explosives or confidential documents. IRA quartermasters had overall responsibility for the storage of munitions.

Fenian: popular (but inaccurate and sometimes derogatory) name for members of Clan na Gael and the Irish Republican Brotherhood. Derived from the 'Fenian Brotherhood', a radical Irish-American organisation of the 1860s.

Fianna Fáil: political party founded by Éamon de Valera in 1926. Most of the leadership had been senior officers in the IRA and its establishment badly split the IRA.

Friends of Irish Freedom (FOIF): Irish-American organisation, led by Judge Daniel Cohalan, and allied with John Devoy. By 1922 it opposed both the IRA and Éamon de Valera.

General Headquarters (GHQ): the IRA's headquarters in Dublin, overseen by the chief of staff and responsible for the day-to-day running of the IRA.

Hand delivery: despatches or money were often carried by an IRA courier rather than risking the postal system.

IRA units: in order of descending size: brigade, battalion and company.

Irish Republican Brotherhood (IRB): secret revolutionary organisation which helped found the IRA. IRB members formed an elite within the IRA. In 1924 the IRA disbanded the organisation due to the number of Free State supporters among the IRB's leadership.

Keyword or keyphrase (key): a word or phrase shared between the sender and recipient of a cipher and used as part of the encryption and decryption processes.

MI5: British secret service, responsible for protecting the UK's national security.

Officer commanding or OC: commander of an IRA unit. The OC of a brigade was known as a brigadier-general, while the OC of a company was a captain.

Officer commanding Britain (OC. Britain): the senior IRA officer in Britain. Based in London and in contact with Soviet agents. 'M' held this position in the first half of 1926. 'HS' or George succeeded him.

Plain text: a message that isn't encrypted.

Potassium chlorate: the main ingredient in most explosives manufactured by the IRA.

Précis: a plain text summary of a message written in cipher or code. Usually it's very difficult to understand the full meaning of this summary without prior knowledge of the original ciphered document.

RU: Razvedupr, Red Army intelligence. The IRA provided intelligence to two of its agents: 'Stephen' and 'James'.

Safe house: a house or business where the IRA could meet, store documents and supplies or where a volunteer could safely spend the night.

Sinn Féin: the dominant republican political party in the Free State, until the resignation of its president Éamon de Valera in 1926. From then on it became increasingly marginalised and had a strained relationship with the IRA.

Special Branch: armed detective section of the gardaí, responsible for combating the IRA.

Stuff: cryptic term used by the IRA. Usually meant 'explosives', occasionally arms and ammunition or other equipment.

Volunteer: term for a member of the IRA. It usually referred to the equivalent of a 'private', but could also be used to include officers.

Appendix 2

The Mystery Woman

MYSTERY WOMAN AT OLD BAILEY.

Revealed As A Spy From Germany.

YARD CHIEF'S STORY.

Forged Passport: Gaol And Deportation.

SIR WYNDHAM CHILDS, the head of the Secret Service Department at Scotland Yard, revealed at the Old Bailey this afternoon the history behind the prosecution of "Ethel Chiles," a woman who landed at Dover with a forged British passport.

The woman had been found guilty by the jury, and Mr. Justice Finlay sentenced her to two months' imprisonment in the second division with a recommendation for deportation.

She had pleaded not guilty to five counts in connection with the possession of the passport. The plea was her only contribution to the conduct of the case.

No evidence was offered on her behalf.

Sir Wyndham Childs revealed that she

Cutting from a British newpaper on the case of the Soviet spy, Kate Gussfeldt (alias Ethel Chiles) for whom the IRA obtained an illegal passport. The article was filed among Moss Twomey's papers at GHQ, but without any accompanying comments or explanation.

One of the more intriguing stories in the documents is that of the 'mystery woman'. In the Twomey papers there's an undated newspaper clipping with the headline: 'Mystery woman at the Old Bailey'. There's no direct reference to her in the other papers. Just two short sentences which appear to be indirect references.

Who was she? What was her connection to the IRA? Some of the clues can be found in British secret service (MI5) files which were recently made public. [1]

Kate Gussfeldt was a 28-year-old German communist, who first came to the attention of the British authorities in the winter of 1924 in Cologne, which was then under British military occupation following the war. She was found in the company of a British soldier in a café and arrested by the 'British Morality Police' as a suspected prostitute.

In 1924 the secret service observed her as she made three trips to Britain to attend and address meetings of the Comintern front organisation, the Workers' International Relief Committee or WIR. On her second visit she stayed in Glasgow and met with the well known activist, Helen Crawford. They travelled together to a communist women's conference in Manchester, and realising that she was being tailed, she swapped clothes with Crawford, allowing her to elude the police and return to the continent using a German passport in a false name. Helen Crawford had spent time in Ireland as a communist organiser in 1925 and remained in close contact with the IRA supporter Charlotte Despard.

In 1925 Gussfeldt travelled to New York, returning to Europe in January 1927. That year she attended the League Against Imperialism meeting in Brussels, acting as an interpreter at secret meetings.

In March 1927 MI5 sent details to customs with instructions to arrest a woman with a British passport in the name of 'Ethel Chiles' on her arrival in the country. Gussfeldt, was observed arriving at Dover by boat from Calais and was followed to London, where Scotland Yard detectives arrested her at Victoria Station. She gave her name as 'Ethel Chiles' of Clapton and refused to give further information or make a statement. The following day she was charged with entering the UK on an 'irregular passport' and refusing to answer questions as to her identity and nationality. However, as the passport was found to have been issued by the British Foreign Office, the charge was dropped and a new charge of 'conspiring with some person or persons unknown to obtain by false pretences a British passport' was substituted. British intelligence suspected her of arriving in Britain 'in order to get in touch with a certain suspect group in London'.

While under arrest she sent a message to Helen Crawford. Meanwhile MI5 went through her belongings in fine detail. Labels on her suitcases showed that she was travelling from Berlin to Britain. All the other labels had been removed so as to prevent tracing her movements – except for one: a small torn piece of a label indicating that she had recently been to New York. Among her luggage were 'a vast number of pieces of soap and bottles of scent' which were chemically analysed, but turned up nothing. There was also a deflated rugby ball, which posed a challenge to the secret service: 'So far no one has been able to offer any solution as to this!' A first aid kit contained two small tubes of potassium permanganate, which was an antiseptic but could also be used as both an invisible ink and developer.

There were three notebooks. One included rather mediocre poetry written in German. Another was a diary, which contained information written in secret ink concerning three American ex-Air Service officers. The first was Lieutenant Herbert O'Fahy, who had spent five years in the Air Service but was dismissed in 1923 for 'flying very low over a Lincoln Memorial meeting while President Harding was speaking'. He was currently employed 'sky writing' and dropping pamphlets on race meetings, etc. Next was Frank, a pilot who wanted to serve in the Soviet Air Force. And lastly, George, a member of the American Communist Party, was a research engineer with Western Electric, specialising in radios.

With the aid of an 'informant' within the London IRA, MI5 was able to trace the origin of her passport. The passport, issued by the London Passport Office, was obtained through Thomas Cook and Sons and posted to Kate Gussfeldt in Germany. An 'Englishman' Frank Mathews had brought the application form to the Thomas Cook office and the referee on the application was a Dr Gately. British intelligence tracked the doctor down and described him as 'a doctor addicted to low habits and a tippler'. They agreed with him that his signature had been forged. MI5 noted another coincidence; the letter sent to Donnelly, a British military policeman imprisoned for stealing government codebooks, was also signed in the name 'Dr Gately'. 'Ethel Chiles' gave her address as 62 Rendlesham Road, which also happened to be that of the Woods family 'whose connection with the Irish Republican Movement is well known'. One of the young men of the family had been deported from Britain in 1923 due to his suspected IRA links.

After Gussfeldt's arrest the police interviewed Mrs Woods, but she remained unaware of the purpose of their visit, until she read later in the paper of the arrest of 'Ethel Chiles'. She then sent a message to an IRA man 'O'Neill' that she needed to meet him urgently. 'O'Neill' told her to 'say she knew nothing' if asked about the passport. At the same time MI5 were watching the short personal notices (commonly placed in newspapers at the time) for any cryptic message that could be connected with the case. They puzzled over messages such as: 'Can I have lumble? Tumble. Wumbles' – which was carefully cut out of *The Times* by an agent and pasted into the Ethel Chiles file. But the message that caught their attention was one which Helen Crawford was suspected of having inserted:

'W.- Thanks for message. Longing 2 c u 2. –M. Received. Be more cautious. Not settled yet'.

At the same time as Kate Gussfeldt's arrest George reported to Moss Twomey: 'Things are very hot at present'.[2] Twomey replied: 'Have you any fears for [the] connection on account of [the] matter about which you sent [the] newspaper cuttings?'[3] To which George added: 'I don't think there is the slightest danger, but you never know what they may come across. I took all the precautions I could'.[4]

The informer inaccurately reported to MI5: 'that this type of work is not being conducted with the knowledge or sanction of the heads of the IRA in Ireland and their funds do not benefit by any money received. It is a private venture on the part of one or two senior IRA officers here who have got in touch with the Russian and German agents and are pocketing the proceeds. They are making use of people like the Woods and Donnelly in a pretence that the work is being done for the Irish cause'.

MI5's opinion was that Gussfeldt 'was acting as an important agent, not only in connection with the Irish Republican Intelligence Service' and that 'she had come over for the purpose of working with the German agent [sic] and in his absence taking charge of the business here'. MI5 suspected that both the Russian and German intelligence agencies could have been involved.

So MI5 was on to something but they hadn't quite got to the bottom of it. It's clear from the communications sent to Twomey that GHQ authorised the passport scheme. Who was the IRA informant? Maybe a disaffected or laid off officer? Gussfeldt was a Soviet spy and was involved with military espionage in America. Whether she was going to work with the IRA in Britain or not is not clear. Was 'James' the 'German agent'? There are so many threads to this story: Helen Crawford, Donnelly, the 'German agent', etc.

After a few months detention Kate Gussfeldt was deported back to Germany.

Notes

Abbreviations used in footnotes

Adjt: adjutant
AG: adjutant general
CS: chief of staff
DI: Director of Intelligence
MD: Minister of Defence
MTUCDA: Moss Twomey Papers University College Dublin Archives
OC: officer commanding
QMG: quartermaster general

INTRODUCTION
1 CS to OC No. 3 Area Britain, 24 February 1924 [1927], in MTUCDA P69/48 (242).
2 Friedman, W and Callimahos, L. *Military Cryptanalytics* (originally published by the National Security Agency, re-published by Aegean Park Press, Laguna Hills, 1985), Part 1, Vol. 1, p. 12.
3 'The National Security Agency', *Wikipedia*, reviewed 1 May 2008.
4 S to Mr Jones, 10 November 1926, in MTUCDA P69/183 (173–4); chairman to An Timthire, 3 February 1927, in MTUCDA P69/183 (121–2 and 123–5).
5 JB to Mr Brown, 26 November 1926, in MTUCDA P69/183 (168–9); [JB] to Mr Browne [*sic*] 26 December 1926 [the date marked on the letter is '26 November' but this appears to be in error], in MTUCDA P69/183 (155, 156); chairman to Mr Jones, 3 February 1927, in MTUCDA P69/183 (115, 116–18).
6 Hanley, B., *The IRA, 1926–1936* (Four Courts Press, Dublin, 2002), p. 193.
7 Adjt Dundalk batt to director of intelligence, 11 [August] 1927, in MTUCDA P69/196 (105).
8 Merriam – *Webster on Line*, entry titled 'call house', reviewed 2 May 2008.
9 CS to OC Scotland, 24 February 1924 [1927], in MTUCDA P69/48 (296).
10 1st Staff Officer [Offaly] to CS, 5 December 1923 [1926], in MTUCDA P69/41 (248).
11 Hanley, *The IRA, 1926–1936*, p. 200.

CHAPTER 1: THE IRA'S COMMUNICATIONS SECURITY
1 Definitions of some cryptographic terms may be found at the end of this chapter.
2 The American Cryptogram Association may be contacted through their website http://www.cryptogram.org.
3 D'Imperio, M., *The Voynich Manuscript: An Elegant Enigma* (National Security Agency, Fort George G. Meade, Maryland, 1978)
4 Kahn, D., *The Codebreakers* (The Macmillan Company, New York, 1967).
5 Pelling, N., *The Curse of the Voynich* (Compelling Press, Surbiton, Surrey, 2006).
6 C/S to [no name], No. 84, 16 June 1927, in MTUCDA P69/48(3).
7 Friedman, W.F. and Callimahos, L.D., *Military Cryptanalytics Part I Volume 1*, p. 12.

8 Suetonius Tranquillus, G., *The Lives of the Twelve Caesars* (Gutenberg.org document 6400, 2006); (1) Gaius Julius Caesar, para. LVI.

9 [no name] to H.S., Ref S/83, 2 June 1927, in MTUCDA P69/48(12).

10 Chief of staff to OC South Dublin batt. C:12, 5 April 1927, in MTUCDA P69/48(78).

11 M.D. to H.S., 23 June 1927, in MTUCDA P69/48(1).

12 Smith to Browne, 2 December 1926, in MTUCDA P69/183(165).

13 H.S. to M.D., 20 June 1924 (1927), in MTUCDA P69/48(2).

14 M to D/Intelligence, A/155, 26 December 1927, in MTUCDA P69/196(14).

15 To C/S, 20 May 1923 (1926), in P69/47(174).

16 J.B. to Mr Brown, Despatch No. 5, 26 November 1926, in MTUCDA P69/183(168).

17 To George, Ref. MD 10, 2 May 1927, in MTUCDA P69/148(75).

18 OC No. 3 Area, Britain to adj. general GHQ, 4 October 1926, in MTUCDA P69/171(3).

19 To adjt. No.3. Area Britain, 16 November 1926, MTUCDA P69/47(58).

20 Chief of staff to OC South Dublin batt. C:12, 5 April 1927, in MTUCDA P69/48(78).

21 Internet website http://www.gutenberg.org.

22 *Web 1T 5-gram Version 1*, Linguistic Data Consortium, University of Pennsylvania, 2006.

23 LS for D/Intelligence to C/S, 5/5/26, in MTUCDA P69/44(66).

24 'Pages from a Communications Log Book', in MTUCDA P69/195.

25 D/I to C/S, 6/2/25, in MTUCDA P69/137(13).

26 Chairman Army Council to An Timthire, 2 March 1927 in MTUCDA P69/ 183 (88).

27 Chairman of Army Council to An Timthire, 24 February 1927 in MTUCDA P69/ 183 (106).

28 To Mr Jones, 14 December 1926 in MTUCDA P69/183(161).

29 Jude Patterson to James Gillogly, private message, 26 November 2007.

30 Chairman to An Timthire, 6 May 1927, in MTUCDA P69/183(56).

31 C/S to D/Intelligence, CD/7, 4 May 1923 (1926), in MTUCDA P69/44(62).

32 Communications logbook entries, undated, in MTUCDA P69/195.

33 Kahn, *The Codebreakers*, pp. 145–9.

34 Dodgson, C. L. (as Lewis Carroll), 'The Alphabet-Cipher', in *The Complete Works of Lewis Carroll* (Modern Library, New York, 1936), pp. 1283–4.

35 Kahn, *The Codebreakers*, pp. 216ff.

36 *Ibid.*, pp. 77–8.

37 C/S to D/Intelligence, CD/7, 4 May 1923 (1926) in MTUCDA P69/44(62).

38 To QMG, F/A 52, 3 Deire Foghmhair 1925, in MTUCDA P69/208(6).

39 See Chapter 11 for a more complete exposition of the context of this message.

40 D/I to C/S, 6/2/25, in MTUCDA P69/137(13).

41 Callimahos, Lambros D., *Traffic Analysis and the Zendian Problem* (National Security Agency, 1959. Reprinted by Aegean Park Press, 1989).

CHAPTER 2: THE IRA'S SYSTEM OF COMMUNICATIONS

1 Earl Long was a populist politician from Louisiana and brother of the well-known Huey Long. The above quote is a paraphrase, the full version being: don't write anything you can phone. Don't phone anything you can talk. Don't talk anything

you can whisper. Don't whisper anything you can smile. Don't smile anything you can nod. Don't nod anything you can wink. *Wikipedia* website, 'Earl Long', reviewed 27 February 2008. *Brainyquote.com*, 'Earl Long quotes', 8 May 2008.

2 Director of Intelligence to IO Waterford, 27 May 1924 [1927], in MTUCDA P69/196 (163).

3 An Timthire to [unaddressed], 18 March 1927, in MTUCDA P69/183 (80).

4 McMahon P., 'British intelligence and the Anglo-Irish truce, 1921', *Irish Historical Studies*, Vol. XXXV, No. 140 (November 2007), pp. 519–40.

5 A note which is unsigned and unaddressed, no date, in MTUCDA P69/48 (25); probably accompanied HS to CS, 12 May 1924 [1927], in MTUCDA P69/48 (24); MD to HS, 18 May 1927 in MTUCDA P69/48 (21).

6 HS to CS, 27 May 1927, in MTUCDA P69/48 (16).

7 MD to HS, 29 May 1927, in MTUCDA P69/48 (15); HS to CS, 1 June 1924 [1927], in MTUCDA P69/48 (10).

8 MacEoin, U., *The IRA in the Twilight Years, 1923–1948* (Argenta Publications, Dublin, 1997), p. 118.

9 Tarpey M., *The Role of Joseph McGarrity in the Struggle for Irish Independence* (Arno Press, New York, 1976) p. 43.

10 Borgonovo, J., *Florence and Josephine O'Donoghue's War of Independence* (Irish Academic Press, Dublin, 2006), p. 76.

11 List of IRA keywords, no date, in MTUCDA P69/47 (114); Aire Cosanta to QMG, 3 October 1925, in MTUCDA P69/208 (6).

12 O'Halpin, E., *Defending Ireland: The Irish Free State and its Enemies since 1922* (Oxford University Press, Oxford, 2000), pp. 56–7.

13 Twomey spelled obscure as 'obsecure'; chairman to An Timthire, 27 May 1927, in MTUCDA P69/183 (25).

14 HS to CS, 6 May 1927, in MTUCDA P69/48 (27).

15 HS to MD, 20 June 1924 [1927], in MTUCDA P69/48 (2).

16 MD to HS, 23 June 1927, in MTUCDA P69/48 (1).

17 DI to adjt. general, 13 January 1925, in MTUCDA P69/137 (16–17).

18 In the original document 'never' is spelled 'neven'. CS to Assistant adjt Cork 1, 3 May 1926, in MTUCDA P69/44 (87–8).

19 CS to OC Scotland, 12 October 1926, in MTUCDA P69/41 (43).

20 Adj. Liverpool to adjt general, 28 October 1926, in MTUCDA P69/47 (57).

21 In the original decryption 'no.' was used as an abbreviation for 'number'; DI to [no name], 10 December 1926, in MTUCDA P69/193 (62).

22 In the original decryption 'rec'd' was used as an abbreviation for 'received' and 'ack' for 'acknowledge'. Unsigned to DI, 23 January 1927, in MTUCDA P69/41 (10).

23 Unsigned to Mr Jones, 18 March 1927, in MTUCDA P69/183 (81 and 82–3).

24 From An Timthire, unaddressed, 10 May 1927, in MTUCDA P69/183 (29–30).

25 MacEoin, *The IRA in the Twilight Years*, p. 841.

26 MD to HS, 29 May 1927, in MTUCDA P69/48 (15).

27 Unsigned to Mr Jones, 18 March 1927, in MTUCDA P69/183 (81, 82-83).

28 Ambrose to DI, 15 September 1926, in MTUCDA P69/193 (120).

29 This letter is addressed to Mr Smith or Andy Cooney. However, Moss Twomey acknowledged receipt of it on 11 May 1927, in MTUCDA P69/183 (53) and he appears to have been the intended recipient; Jones to Mr Smith, 20 April 1927, in MTUCDA P69/183 (54).

30 Chairman to Mr Jones, 11 May 1927, in MTUCDA P69/183 (53).

31 E-mail communication from Seamus Helferty, 9 May 2008.

32 Unsigned [from DI] to George G, 10 December 1926, in MTUCDA P69/193 (63).

33 *Ibid.*

34 Experiment carried out in the Mahon/Chin household with an unfolded paperclip, 4 May 2008; not verified under conditions of incarceration.

35 Unsigned [from DI] to George G, 10 December 1926, in MTUCDA P69/193 (63); DI to Mick P, 10 December 1926 in MTUCDA P69/193 (66).

36 Chairman to An Timthire, 3 February 1927, in MTUCDA P69/183 (123–5).

37 Communications log book, no date, circa September 1926, in MTUCDA P69/195.

38 *Ibid.*

39 Between 1924 and 1926 two IRA veterans who emigrated to New Zealand planned to keep in touch with the organisation by enrolling in its 'foreign reserves, in Hanley, B., *The IRA, 1926–1936* (Four Courts Press, Dublin, 2002), p. 162; JB to Mr Brown, 26 November 1926, in MTUCDA P69/183 (168-169).

40 Cowan was spelled 'cowman'; Unsigned to Mr Jones, 14 December 1926, in MTUCDA P69/183 (161–2).

41 JB to Mr Browne, 25 October 1926, in MTUCDA P69/183 (180).

42 'To make it worse addressee left here and had no relatives locally to see after her correspondence', unsigned to adjt general, 1 November 1924 [1927], in MTUCDA P69/149 (108–10).

43 Chairman to [unaddressed], 12 April 1927, in MTUCDA P69/183 (71–72).

44 *Ibid.*

45 *Ibid.*

46 In Twomey's reference to 'the Sweetman brothers' it is unclear which of the Sweetmans exactly he was referring to; McGee, O., *The IRB: The Irish Republican Brotherhood from the Land League to Sinn Féin* (Four Courts Press, Dublin, 2005) p. 316; MacEoin, U. *Survivors* (Argenta Publications, Dublin, 1987), pp. 38, 41 and 525; MacEoin, *The IRA in the Twilight Years*, pp. 312 and 210, *Wikipedia*, entry on John Sweetman, reviewed September 2006.

47 Borgonovo, *Florence and Josephine O'Donoghue's War of Independence*, p. 148.

48 Andrews, C. S., *Dublin Made Me* (Mercier Press, Dublin and Cork, 1979), p. 245.

49 *Irish Times*, 1 May 1926.

50 Unsigned to Mr Jones, 14 December 1926, in MTUCDA P69/183 (161–2).

51 CS to IO Number 3 Area (Liverpool), 12 October 1926, in MTUCDA P69/47 (61).

52 'Re sending [of] messages via Cove [Cobh]. Of course they could be given to Mick Burke through Rob Roy', chairman to An Timthire, 3 February 1927, in MTUCDA P69/183 (123–5).

53 CS to Comdt S, 7 [or possibly 6] September 1926, in MTUCDA P69/47 (133).

54 Maryborough was the pre-independence name for Portlaoise, and the IRA frequently misspelled or abbreviated it to Maryboro; DI to Jack Jones, 18 August 1927, in MTUCDA P69/197 (97).

55 JJ to DI, 28 August 1927, in MTUCDA P69/197 (93).

56 DI to Jack Jones, 21 December 1927, in MTUCDA P69/197 (54).

57 HS to CS, 8 March 1924 [1927], in MTUCDA P69/48 (258).

58 CS to HS, 6 April 1927, in MTUCDA P69/48 (143).

59 HS to CS, 1 June 1924 [1927], in MTUCDA P69/48 (10).

60 Communications log book, no date, circa September 1926, in MTUCDA P69/195.

61 JB to Mr Brown, 26 November 1926, in MTUCDA P69/183 (168–9).

62 An Timthire to Mr Smith, 20 April 1927, in MTUCDA P69/183 (48–51).

63 Cowan is spelled 'Cowman'. Unsigned to Mr Jones, 14 December 1926, in MTUCDA P69/183 (161–2).

64 OC South Connemara battalion to CS, 28 September 1926, in MTUCDA P69/47 (124).

65 HS to MD, 25th Nov. 1925 [1927] in MTUCDA P69/150 (16).

66 Adjt. Liverpool to adjt. gen, 5 November 1926, in MTUCDA P69/47 (56).

67 Communications log book, no date, circa September 1926, in MTUCDA P69/195.

68 Chairman to [no name], 12 April 1927, in MTUCDA P69/183 (71–2).

69 Una is spelled 'Uma' in the first letter. Chairman to An Timthire, 8 April 1927, in MTUCDA P69/183 (74–5). Chairman to [no name], 12 April 1927, in MTUCDA P69/183 (71–2).

70 Communications log book, no date, circa September 1926, in MTUCDA P69/195.

71 An Timthire to Mr Smith, 20 April 1927, in MTUCDA P69/183 (48–51).

72 Chairman to An Timthire, 3 February 1927, in MTUCDA P69/183 (121–5).

73 Communications log book, no date, circa September 1926, in MTUCDA P69/195.

74 HS to 'Dear Sir', 27 December 1927, in MTUCDA P69/150 (5).

75 Communications log book, no date, circa September 1926, in MTUCDA P69/195.

76 For DI to Jack Jones, 2 June 1924 [1927], in MTUCDA P69/197 (153).

77 Adjt. Midland batt to adjt. gen, 18 January 1928, in MTUCDA P69/149 (68).

78 Bessborough spelled as 'Bessboro', MD to HS, 19 May 1927, in MTUCDA P69/48 (19).

79 HS to CS, 20 April 1927, in MTUCDA P69/48 (61).

80 Chairman to [no name], 12 April 1927, in MTUCDA P69/183 (71–2).

81 Acting adjt. N Wexford to D. Comms, 23 January 1928, in MTUCDA P69/149 (40).

82 Communications log book, no date, circa September 1926, in MTUCDA P69/195.

83 MD to HS, 29 May 1927, in MTUCDA P69/48 (15).

84 Unsigned to HS, 2 June 1927, in MTUCDA P69/48 (12).

85 Communications log book, no date, circa Sept. 1926 in MTUCDA P69/195.

86 Chairman to [no name], 12 April 1927, in MTUCDA P69/183 (71–2).

87 An Timthire to Mr Smith, 20 April 1927, in MTUCDA P69/183 (48–51).

88 Capt. W to CS, 4 May [1926] in MTUCDA P69/44 (8-9).

89 An Timthire to Mr Smith, 20 April 1927, in MTUCDA P69/183 (48–51).

90 CS to OC Scotland, 12 October 1926, in MTUCDA P69/41 (43).

91 Communications log book, no date, circa Sept. 1926 in MTUCDA P69/195.

92 DI to Jack Jones, 21 December 1927, in MTUCDA P69/197 (54); chairman to An Timthire, 18 March 1927, in MTUCDA P69/183 (77–8).

93 An Timthire to Mr Smith, 20 April 1927, in MTUCDA P69/183 (48–51).

94 McCarthy spelled as 'McCardhy'; chairman to An Timthire, 18 March 1927, in MTUCDA P69/183 (77–8).

95 Chairman to An Timthire, 18 March 1927, in MTUCDA P69/183 (77–8).

96 CS to OC. Britain, 23 April 1926, in MTUCDA P69/44 (81).

97 CS to Comdt. S, 7 [or possibly 6] September 1926, in MTUCDA P69/47 (133).

98 Chairman to [no name], 12 April 1927, in MTUCDA P69/183 (71–2).

99 Chairman to An Timthire, 3 February 1927, in MTUCDA P69/183 (123–5).

100 CS to HS, 16 June 1927, in MTUCDA P69/48 (3).

101 Sth Galway to CS, 7 March 1923 [?1927], in MTUCDA P69/48 (253).

102 S O'S to J Jones, 8 May 1926 [or 1927] in MTUCDA P69/197 (163). S O'S to DI, 17 May 1927 in MTUCDA P69/197 (160-161).

103 CS to OC Cork 1 Brigade, 26 April 1926 in MTUCDA P69/44 (95). CS to DI and QMG, 26 April 1926 in MTUCDA P69/44 (173).

104 CS to OC South Kilkenny, 20 September [year missing, 1926?], in MTUCDA P69/ 47 (129).

105 Chairman to Mr Jones, 14 April 1927, in MTUCDA P69/183 (61–2).

106 Communications log book, no date, circa September 1926, in MTUCDA P69/ 195.

107 Ballymackey was spelled 'Ballymachney' in cipher; Unaddressed and unsigned note, 19 April 1926, in MTUCDA P69/44 (187); OC. Britain to CS, 21 April 1926, in MTUCDA P69/44 (186).

108 CS to DI and QMG, 26 April 1926 in MTUCDA P69/44 (173).

109 Name spelled 'O'Sdea'; HS to CS, 26 May 1927, in MTUCDA P69/48 (11 and 14).

110 His name was spelled 'Shanaghan' in the despatch, 'for Chairman' to An Timthire, 20 Oct. 1926 in MTUCDA P69/183 (184-185).

111 CS to HS, 24 February 1924 [1927], in MTUCDA P69/48 (297–8).

112 IO Dublin Brigade to DI, 2 September 1927, in MTUCDA P69/196 (86–7).

CHAPTER 3: A NEW LEADERSHIP: 1926–1927

1 Lynch was a well-respected and successful commander during the Anglo-Irish War in Cork. However, this contrasted with his role in the Civil War; Hopkinson, M., *Green Against Green: The Irish Civil War* (Gill & Macmillan, Dublin, 1988), p. 257.

2 I was unable to obtain a reliable estimate of IRA deaths; based on Hopkinson, they may have been approximately 1,000 or so; Hopkinson, *Green Against Green*, pp. 268, 273.

3 Hegarty P., *Peadar O'Donnell* (Mercier Press, Cork, 1999), p. 162.

4 CS to Military Attache, USA, 15 April 1925, in MTUCDA P69/37 (221–3).

5 Pax Ó Faoláin in MacEoin, U., *The IRA in the Twilight Years, 1923–1948* (Argenta Publications, Dublin, 1997), p. 147.

6 Connie Neenan in MacEoin, U., *The IRA in the Twilight Years, 1923–1948* (Argenta Publications, Dublin, 1997), p. 249.

7 CS to Military Attache, USA, 15 April 1925 in MTUCDA P69/37 (221–3).

8 Hanley, B. *The IRA, 1926-1936* (Four Courts Press, Dublin, 2002), p. 161.

9 Figures for the period 1924 to 1926; Hanley, *The IRA, 1926–1936*, p. 162.

10 Minutes of meeting of Army Executive, 27 April 1927, in MTUCDA P69/48 (104–5); the officer was identified as 'TD', and therefore was likely Tom Derrig, who was elected to the Executive in November 1925. Less than two months later he had been elected a TD for Fianna Fáil. However, it's possible that he had already been replaced on the committee. Another prominent officer with similar initials was Tom Daly, who unlike Derrig remained active in the IRA; Hanley, *The IRA, 1926-1936*, p. 209.

11 At the Army Executive meeting in August 1924, sixteen of the members present, three of those absent and at least two of the headquarters staff were described as being generals; Army Executive meeting minutes, 10 to 11 August 1924, in MTUCDA P69/179 (84); in March 1925 the OC of the Dublin brigade gave his rank as brigadier-general, 1 March [1925], MTUCDA P69/48 (275); Michael McLoughlin, the OC of the Carrick-on-Shannon brigade, in his application for transfer to the foreign reserves stated his rank to be brigadier-general, 1925 in MTUCDA P69/169 (4); based on the roll call from 9 April 1927, meeting of officers, there were thirteen brigades, in MTUCDA P69/48 (152).

12 CS to Military Attache, USA, 15 April 1925, in MTUCDA P69/37 (221–3).

13 Hanley, *The IRA, 1926–1936*, p. 11.

14 CS to IO Tipperary brigade, 2 October 1925, in MTUCDA P69/206 (12).

15 CS to Military Attache, USA, 15 April 1925, in MTUCDA P69/37 (221–3).

16 CS to Comdt. LP, 15 October 1924, in MTUCDA P 69/37 (116).

17 MacEoin, U., *Survivors* (Argenta Publications, Dublin, 1987), pp. 456–7.

18 Regan, J., *The Irish Counter-Revolution: 1921–1936* (Gill & Macmillan, Dublin, 1999), pp. 75–6.

19 English, R., *Radicals and the Republic: Socialist Republicanism in the Irish Free State, 1925–1937* (Clarendon Press, Oxford, 1994), p. 7.

20 Communication from Seamus Helferty. CS to Military Attache, USA, 15 April 1925 in MTUCDA P69/37 (221–3); Lawlor, C., *Seán MacBride, That Day's Struggle: A Memoir 1904–1951* (Currach Press, Blackrock, 2005), p. 85.

21 Bowyer Bell, J., *The Secret Army: The IRA 1916–1970* (The John Day Company, New York, 1971), p. 52.

22 *Ibid.*, p. 51.

23 CS to Military Attache, USA, 15 April 1925, in MTUCDA P69/37 (221–3).

24 *Ibid.*

25 References for the 1925 army convention; English, *Radicals and the Republic*, pp. 66–70; Bowyer Bell, *The Secret Army*, pp. 52–3; Hanley, *The IRA, 1926–1936*, p. 207.

26 English, *Radicals and the Republic*, p. 66.

27 Unsigned to chairman of the Army Council, 18 November 1925, in MTUCDA P69/181 (74–6).

28 Hanley, *The IRA, 1926–1936*, p. 19.

29 Bowyer Bell, The Secret Army, p. 57; Hanley, *The IRA, 1926–1936*, pp. 19, 193.

30 MacEoin, *The IRA in the Twilight Years*, p. 116; Hanley, *The IRA, 1926–1936*, p. 20.

31 'Wilson', who was attempting to type, appears to be Staff Captain Wilson and not a female typist; A 'S/Capt W.' is listed as a member of the GHQ staff in the roll call for the officers meeting on 9 April 1927, in MTUCDA P69/48 (157–8, 152, 160); Mick Price also approved 'Wilson' to act as his proxy on the Army Council on 16 December 1926, in MTUCDA P69/193 (59); there is in addition a reference to a 'Miss Wilson' who worked for Moss Twomey, see 1 March 1924 [1927], in MTUCDA P69/48 (277); however, Twomey by convention ordinarily referred to women either by their first name or used the titles 'Miss' or 'Mrs'; all of this suggests that 'Wilson' was Captain Wilson and not Miss Wilson; Unsigned to George [Gilmore], 2 May 1927 in MTUCDA P69/48 (75).

32 Moss Twomey was under arrest on this date, and the letter was likely written by Andy Cooney; CS to HS, 8 December 1926, in MTUCDA P69/47 (10–11).

33 CS to Finance and Accounts Officer, 1 March 1927, in MTUCDA P69/48 (277).

34 CS to OC Dublin Brigade, 3 March 1924 [1927], in MTUCDA P69/48 (267).

35 Andrews, C. S., *Dublin Made Me* (Mercier Press, Dublin and Cork, 1979), pp. 154, 205, 218–19; MacEoin, *Survivors*, p. 375; Hanley, *The IRA, 1926–1936*, p. 207.

36 Con Casey in MacEoin, *Survivors* (Argenta Publications, Dublin, 1987), pp. 27, 375; MacEoin, *The IRA in the Twilight Years*, p. 853; Andrews, *Dublin Made Me*, p. 227.

37 Army Council minutes April 1926, in MTUCDA P 69/181 (46); MacEoin, *The IRA in the Twilight Years*, p. 34; Bowyer Bell, *The Secret Army*, p. 57.

38 Bowyer Bell, *The Secret Army*, pp. 64–5.

39 Minutes of the Army Council meeting, January 1927, in MTUCDA P 69/181 (3).

40 Chairman to An Timthire, 3 February 1927, in MTUCDA P69/183 (123–5).

41 The following letter implies that 'Mr Smith' or Andy Cooney was in the United States by 4 June; to Mr O'Sullivan from Mr O'Connor, 18 June 1926, in MTUCDA P69/182 (31).

42 To chairman of Army Council from chief of staff, 12 April 1926, in MTUCDA P69/181 (48).

43 Quote from a captured IRA despatch, *The Irish Times,* 1 May 1926.

44 The minutes of the Army Council, on 18 November 1925 record that 'A appointed C/S', in MTUCDA P 69/183 (69); Army Council minutes from April 1926, report: 'A announced he had decided to visit the US and this was approved', in MTUCDA P 69/181 (46).

45 Hanley, *The IRA, 1926–1936*, p. 19.

46 CS to adjt North Mayo brigade, 26 October 1923 [1926], in MTUCDA P69/39 (107).

47 MacEoin, *Survivors*, p. 851

48 Hanley, *The IRA, 1926–1936*, p. 19.

49 MacEoin, *The IRA in the Twilight Years*, p. 843.

50 Hanley, *The IRA, 1926–1936*, p. 19.

51 Bowyer Bell quoted in MacEoin, *The IRA in the Twilight Years*, p.853; see also English, *Radicals and the Republic*, p. 115 and MacEoin, *The IRA in the Twilight Years*, p. 851.

52 Twomey received two volumes on Stonewall Jackson from OC. Britain and also requested Field Marshal Wilson's diaries and *The Science of War* by Colonel Henderson; MD to HS, 25 April 1927, in MTUCDA P69/48 (59); MD to HS, 17 October 1927, in MTUCDA P69/150 (20).

53 CS to OC No. 2 Area, 14 October 1923 [1926], in MTUCDA P69/47 (98).

54 Document titled 'Publicity' and signed by 'C' [which was the designation assigned to Twomey in Army Council documents] 20 February 1926, in MTUCDA P69/181 (52–3).

55 MacEoin, *The IRA in the Twilight Years*, p. 842; reference to Lynch and the uniforms is from Todd Andrews in the O'Malley notebooks, UCD Archives.

56 The handwriting in the O'Malley notebooks is notoriously difficult to read, and the distinguished historian Peter Hart appears to have misread this quote. Hart wrote in *The IRA at War 1916–1923* that Twomey 'was a good staff officer who had a sense of reality'. I have carefully read the document and reviewed my interpretation with UCD Archivist Seamus Helferty, and feel that the correct interpretation is as I've quoted in my text; P.A. Murray in the O'Malley notebooks, UCD Archives, P17/b, 88. Hart P., *The IRA at War 1916–1923* (Oxford University Press, Oxford, 2003), pp. 163–4.

57 OC Number 3 Area to CS, 8 October 1926, in MTUCDA P69/47 (66–9).

58 CS to OC Number 3 Area, 12 October 1923 [1926], in MTUCDA P69/47 (63–64).

59 Chairman to An Timthire, 11 May 1927, in MTUCDA P69/183 (41–3).

60 HS to CS, 27 April 1924 [1927], in MTUCDA P69/48 (57).

61 CS to OC South Dublin batt, 29 April 1927, in MTUCDA P69/48 (77).

62 MD to HS, 6 May 1927, in MTUCDA P69/48 (50).

63 MacEoin, *Survivors*, p. 24.

64 Hanley, *The IRA, 1926–1936*, p. 195.

65 MacEoin, *Survivors*, p. 21.

66 English, *Radicals and the Republic*, pp. 72–3; MacEoin, *Survivors*, p. 24.

67 Hanley, *The IRA, 1926-1936*, p. 195.

68 Officially the montion was proposed by the Tirconaill (Donegal) battalion of the IRA; English, *Radicals and the Republic*, p. 68.

69 English, *Radicals and the Republic*, p. 69.

70 Hegarty P. *Peadar O'Donnell*, p. 211.

71 *Ibid.*, p. 8.

72 *Ibid.*, p. 10.

73 English, *Radicals and the Republic*, p. 71; English, R., *Armed Struggle: The History of the IRA* (Macmillan, London, 2003), p. 44.

74 O'Connor, E. *Reds and the Green: Ireland, Russia and the Communist Internationals 1919–43* (UCD Press, Dublin, 2004), pp. 105, 142.

75 Bowyer Bell, *The Secret Army*, p. 59; MacEoin, *Survivors*, p. 33; English, *Radicals and the Republic*, p. 102.

76 Lee, J J. *Ireland 1912–1985: Politics and Society* (Cambridge University Press, Cambridge, 1989), p. 105.

77 There are at least four biographies on O'Donnell: Ó Drisceoil, D., *Peadar O'Donnell* (Cork University Press, Cork, 2001); Hegarty, P., *Peadar O'Donnell* (Mercier Press, Cork, 1999); Freyer, G., *Peadar O'Donnell* (Bucknell University Press, Lewisburg, 1973); McInerney, M., *Peadar O'Donnell: Irish Social Rebel* (O'Brien Press, Dublin, 1976).

78 English, *Radicals and the Republic*, p. 109.

79 *Ibid.*, p. 91; Bowyer Bell, *The Secret Army*, p. 58.

80 O'Drisceoil D., *Peadar O'Donnell* (Cork University Press, Cork, 2001), p. 41.

81 Mrs Patsy O'Hagan in MacEoin, *Survivors*, p. 170.

82 Tom Maguire in MacEoin, *Survivors*, pp. 300–1.

83 Lawlor, *Seán MacBride, That Day's Struggle*, p. 111.

84 MacEoin, *Survivors*, p. 252.

85 Seán MacBride in MacEoin, *Survivors*, p. 122.

86 Tony Woods in MacEoin, *Survivors*, p. 318.

87 Ernie O'Malley in *On Another Man's Wound* quoted in English, *Radicals and the Republic*, p. 36.

88 Minutes of Army Council meeting and notes on constitution for proposed Revolutionary Organisation, 17 February 1927 in MTUCDA P69/48 (117–20, 312 and 315–16).

89 MacEoin, *Survivors*, p. 32.

90 Minutes of Army Council Meeting, 27 January 1927, in MTUCDA P69/181 (3); notes for Constitution for Revolutionary Organisation, 17 February 1927 in MTUCDA P69/48 (312).

91 Army Council Meeting Minutes, 17 February 1927, in MTUCDA P69/48 (117–

20); CS to HS, 18 February 1924 [1927], in MTUCDA P69/48 (300).

92 Joint Meeting of Representative Members of Fianna Fáil and of representatives of the Army Council, 15 April 1927, in MTUCDA P69/48 (115); meeting of Representative Individuals of Republican Bodies, 26 April 1927, in MTUCDA P69/48 (107).

93 Seán Russell quoted in the 'Discussion on [the] Memo' at the IRA officers meeting, 9 April 1927, in MTUCDA P69/48 (161–2).

94 Hanley, *The IRA, 1926–1936*, p. 195.

95 Pax O'Faolain in MacEoin, *Survivors*, p. 148.

96 Tony Woods in MacEoin, *Survivors*, p. 328.

97 MacEoin, *The IRA in the Twilight Years*, p. 843.

98 MacEoin, *Survivors*, p. 571.

99 Unsigned to HS, 26 September 1927, in MTUCDA P 69/150 (28)

100 E, member of Army Council, Memorandum to members of Army Council on our future policy in Britain, 11 Feb. 1926 in MTUCDA P69/181 (67-68).

101 Minutes of Army Council meeting, 27 Jan. 1927 in MTUCDA P69/181 (3).

102 Hanley, *The IRA, 1926–1936*, p. 196.

103 *Ibid.*

104 *Ibid.*

105 HS to CS, 1 November 1926, in MTUCDA P69/41 (30).

106 The text literally reads: '1,000 rds of .45 amm'; Ambrose to DI, 15 September 1926, in MTUCDA P69/193 (120).

107 'For Chief of Staff' to HS, 8 Nov. 1926 in MTUCDA P69/41 (29). Unsigned to 'A Chara Dhil, 25 Nov. 1926 in MTUCDA P69/47 (52).

108 Lawlor, *Seán MacBride, That Day's Struggle*, pp. 100–5.

109 Tony Woods in MacEoin, *Survivors*, p. 320; Lawlor, *Seán MacBride, That Day's Struggle*, p. 107.

110 Moss Twomey quoted in MacEoin, *The IRA in the Twilight Years*, p. 843.

111 Ambrose to CS and DI, 9 October 1926, in MTUCDA P 69/41 (264).

112 Lawlor, *Seán MacBride, That Day's Struggle*, pp. 95–7.

113 Ambrose to CS, 18 February 1926, in MTUCDA P 69/80 (2).

114 MacBride in his memoirs wrote that he and his wife lived in a small flat in the Rue d'Annonciation in Passy. In the communications log book, the following contact addresses are given for 'Ambrose'. Telegrams were to be sent to: Elie, 4 Rue de la Terrasse, Paris 17 and letters to: Lynch, 20 Rue de la Paix. The letter was to be placed inside a second envelope, with the name 'Ambrose' written on the outside. It was standard IRA security to send letters and telegrams to addresses different than where the IRA operative actually lived; Lawlor, *Seán MacBride, That Day's Struggle*, p. 100; communications log book, no date in MTUCDA P69/195.

115 HS to 'Dear Sir', 13 September 1924 [1927], in MTUCDA P69/150 (24), unsigned to HS, 22 September 1927 in MTUCDA P69/150 (31); document of the Political Prisoners Committee, approximately October 1927, in MTUCDA P 69/197 (75).

116 Tarpey, M., *The Role of Joseph McGarrity in the Struggle for Irish Independence* (Arno Press, New York, 1976), pp. 175–6.

117 O'Connor, *Reds and the Green*, p. 105.

118 Hanley, *The IRA, 1926–1936*, pp. 99–101.

119 *Ibid.*, pp. 97–8.

120 In 1935 O'Donoghue married the very capable Cumann na mBan activist Sighle

Humphreys; Hanley, *The IRA, 1926–1936*, p. 195; D to DI, [1]6 January 1927, in MTUCDA P69/41 (14).

121 Hanley, *The IRA, 1926–1936*, p. 104; Mulvihill, M., *Charlotte Despard: A Biography* (Pandora Press, London, 1989), p. 143.

122 Hanley, *The IRA, 1926–1936*, p. 104.

123 Linklater, A., *An Unhusbanded Life, Charlotte Despard: Suffragette, Socialist and Sinn Féiner* (Hutchinson, London, 1980), p. 226; Mulvihill, *Charlotte Despard*, p. 138.

124 William Butler Yeats, *He Wishes for the Cloths of Heaven*.

125 Tom Heavey in MacEoin, *Survivors*, p. 454.

126 CS to OC Cork 1, 15 February 1924 [1927], in MTUCDA P69/48 (281–2).

127 Mulvihill, *Charlotte Despard*, pp. 4–5, 9, 51, 130.

128 *Ibid.*, p. 116; website: www.Spartacus.schoolnet.co.uk, reviewed 28 April 2006.

129 Mulvihill, *Charlotte Despard*, p. 38; Linklater, *An Unhusbanded Life*, p. 224.

130 Linklater, *An Unhusbanded Life*, p. 227.

131 *Ibid.*

132 *Ibid.*, pp. 227, 234.

133 Unsigned to Mr Jones, 14 December 1926, in MTUCDA P69/183 (161–2).

134 Linklater, *An Unhusbanded Life*, p. 230; Mulvihill, *Charlotte Despard*, pp. 154–5.

135 Mulvihill, *Charlotte Despard*, p. 150; Linklater, *An Unhusbanded Life*, p. 234.

136 Mulvihill, *Charlotte Despard*, pp. 179, 183, 192.

137 HS to CS or CAC, 9 December 1926, in MTUCDA P69/47 (24).

138 Name spelled 'O'Sdea'. HS to CS, 26 May 1927, in MTUCDA P69/48 (11, 14).

139 HS to 'Dear Sir', 27 December 1927, in MTUCDA P69/150 (5); HS to MD, 5 January 1924 [1928], in MTUCDA P69/150 (3).

140 Hanley, *The IRA, 1926–1936*, pp. 71–4.

141 *Ibid*, p. 74; MacEoin, *The IRA in the Twilight Years*, p. 37.

142 Hanley, *The IRA, 1926–1936*, pp. 71–4.

143 CS to DI, 14 May 192[6], in MTUCDA P69/12 (59).

144 English, *Radicals and the Republic*, p. 67.

145 Notes for constitution proposed for revolutionary organisation by C. 17 February 1927, in MTUCDA P69/48 (315–16).

146 An Timthire to Mr Smith, 20 April 1927 in MTUCDA P69/183 (48–51); CS to 'A Chara', 6 May 1927, in MTUCDA P69/183 (63).

147 Brigade adjutant to CS, 27 April 1927, in MTUCDA P69/48 (38).

148 The archbishop of Tuam in 1930; letter from Tuam Sinn Féin cumann in 1924; Paseta, S., 'Censorship and its Critics in the Irish Free State 1922–1932', *Past & Present*, 181 (November 2003), pp. 193–218.

149 Paseta, 'Censorship and its Critics', pp. 193–218.

150 Moss Twomey was under arrest at the time and therefore was unlikely to have been the author of the letter, who was probably the adjutant general; CS to OC Dublin brigade, 21 November 1923 [1926], in MTUCDA P69/41 (249).

151 CS to OC Limerick, 3 March 1924 [1927], in MTUCDA P69/48 (263); CS to OC Dublin brigade, 3 March 1924 [1927], in MTUCDA P69/48 (267); CS to OC Waterford battn, 3 March 1924 [1927], in MTUCDA P69/48 (269); CS to OC Cork 1 brigade, 3 March 1924 [1927], in MTUCDA P69/48 (176).

152 *Irish Times*, 14 March 1927.

153 *Irish World*, 19 March 1927 and 2 April 1927.

154 This letter is signed 'CG' and, given that Charles Gilmore was a senior and militant member of the South Dublin battalion, I've made the presumption that he was the

author; CG to CS, 28 March 1927, in MTUCDA P69/48 (79).

155 S Capt. for CS to OC South Dublin battn. 30 March 1924 [1927], in MTUCDA P69/48 (80).

156 *Irish Times*, 21 March 1927.

157 CS to OC Dublin brigade, 5 April 1927, in MTUCDA P69/48 (169).

158 *Irish Times*, 21 March 1927.

159 *Ibid.*, 16 and 21 March 1927.

160 *Ibid.*, 16 March 1927.

161 Paseta, 'Censorship and its Critics', pp. 193–218.

162 MacEoin, *The IRA in the Twilight Years*, p. 122.

163 *New York Times*, 18 March 1929 and an undated paragraph discussing the film, by Hal Erickson, Reviewed on the *New York Times* website, Movies section, 2 April 2008.

164 CS to OC Dublin brigade, 26 February 1927, in MTUCDA P69/48 (291).

165 CS to OC Tipperary brigade, 18 March 1924 [1927], in MTUCDA P69/48 (224); CS to OC Cork 1 brigade, 18 March 1924 [1927] in MTUCDA P69/48 (223).

166 OC Dublin 1 brigade to the proprietor of the Corinthian cinema, 1 March 1927, in MTUCDA P69/48 (275).

167 *Irish Times*, 12 March 1927.

168 Hanley, *The IRA, 1926–1936*, p. 74.

169 Kramer, A, *Dynamic of Destruction* (Oxford University Press, Oxford, 2007), p. 76.

170 CS to OC. Britain, 16 April 1926, in MTUCDA P69/44 (182).

171 OC. Britain to CS, 24 April 1926, in MTUCDA P69/44 (80).

172 MacEoin, *The IRA in the Twilight Years*, p. 153; Hanley, *The IRA, 1926–1936*, pp. 74, 234; Hanley reports that the gardaí believed in 1929 that the IRA planned to bomb Elverys.

173 Hanley, *The IRA, 1926–1936*, p. 71.

174 *Ibid.*, p. 73.

175 *Ibid.*, pp. 72–3, 233.

176 Unsigned to HS, 3 October 1927, in MTUCDA P69/150 (25).

177 QMG to CS, 4 May 1924 [1927], in MTUCDA P69/48 (47).

178 MacEoin, *The IRA in the Twilight Years*, pp. 154–5.

179 Coogan T. P., *The IRA: A History* (Roberts Rinehart Publishers, Niwot, Colorado, 1993), p. 36.

180 CS to OC Dublin brigade, 6 May 1927, in MTUCDA P69/48 (48).

181 Hanley, *The IRA, 1926–1936*, pp. 75–6, 234.

182 MacEoin, *The IRA in the Twilight Years*, p. 840.

183 Hanley, *The IRA, 1926–1936*, pp. 75–6. *Irish World*, 25 September 1926; *An Phoblacht*, 5 November 1926.

184 Agreement was made with 'D'; as already discussed, this most probably was Peadar O'Donnell. While 'D' in the Army Council minutes appears to be O'Donnell, the 'D' in the second document was Donal O'Donoghue who was still in jail; minutes of Army Council meeting, 27 January 1927, in MTUCDA P69/181 (3); CS to D [Donal O'Donoghue in prison], 28 January 1924 [1927], in MTUCDA P69/41 (9).

185 CS to D [Donal O'Donoghue in prison], 28 January 1924 [1927], in MTUCDA P69/41 (9).

186 CS to D, 28 January 1924 [1927], in MTUCDA P69/41 (9).

187 Andrews, *Dublin Made Me*, p. 307.

188 *Ibid.* p. 225.

189 Doorley M. *Irish-America Diaspora Nationalism: The Friends of Irish Freedom, 1916–1935* (Four Courts Press, Dublin, 2005), p. 133.

190 Briscoe R. *For the Life of Me* (Little Brown and Company, Boston, 1958), p. 224.

191 English, *Radicals and the Republic*, p. 100; Regan, *The Irish-Counter Revolution*, p. 148.

192 Ó Drisceoil, *Peadar O'Donnell*, p. 43; Coogan, *The IRA*, p. 40.

193 Coogan, *The IRA*, p. 40.

194 *Ibid.*

195 *Ibid.*

196 English, *Radicals and the Republic*, pp. 12, 96, 98.

197 *Ibid*, p. 10. Notes for constitution for revolutionary organisation, 17 February 1927, in MTUCDA P69/48 (117); notes for constitution proposed for revolutionary organisation by 'C', 17 February 1927, in MTUCDA P69/48 (315–16).

198 This may be a reference to a prisoner by the name of James Kavanagh; DI to Jack Jones, 21 December 1927, in MTUCDA P69/197 (54).

199 Notes of statement by CS, 9 April 1927, in MTUCDA P69/48 (154–5); Hanley, *The IRA, 1926–1936*, pp. 207, 209.

200 Hanley, *The IRA, 1926–1936*, p. 113.

201 Patterson, H., *The Politics of Illusion: A Political History of the IRA* (Serif, London, 1997), p. 37.

202 Hanley, *The IRA, 1926–1936*, p. 115.

203 Lawlor, *Seán MacBride, That Day's Struggle*, p. 124.

204 MacEoin, *The IRA in the Twilight Years*, p. 856.

205 *Ibid.*, p. 842.

206 IO Number 2 Area to DI, 6 November 1927, in MTUCDA P69/196 (2).

207 English, *Radicals and the Republic*, p. 102; MacEoin, *Survivors*, p. 32.

208 MacEoin, *Survivors*, p. 568.

209 Chairman of Army Council to An Timthire, 24 February 1927, in MTUCDA P69/183 (106–7).

210 Máire Comerford in MacEoin, *Survivors*, p. 53.

211 Hanley, *The IRA, 1926–1936*, p. 93.

212 *New York Times*, 1 May 1926 and 22 June 1926; CS to A. adjt. Cork 1, 3 May 1926, in MTUCDA P69/44 (87–8); MacEoin, *The IRA in the Twilight Years*, p. 128; it can be deduced that Seán MacSwiney was the assistant adjutant of Cork 1 brigade from the following two documents: S MacS to CS, 23 April 1926, in MTUCDA P69/44 (96–100) and CS to OC Cork 1, 28 April 1926, in MTUCDA P69/44 (93-94); *Irish Times*, 27 and 28 April, 1 May and 22 June 1926.

213 Bowyer Bell, *The Secret Army*, p. 57.

214 MacEoin, *The IRA in the Twilight Years*, p. 840.

215 *An Phoblacht*, 5 November 1926; *Irish Times*, 3 November 1926.

216 MacEoin, *The IRA in the Twilight Years*, p. 840.

217 DI to MP [Mick Price], 17 December 192,6 in MTUCDA P69/193 (55).

218 MacEoin, *The IRA in the Twilight Years*, p. 129; Hanley, *The IRA, 1926–1936*, p. 79.

219 Bowyer Bell, *The Secret Army*, p. 58.

220 Unsigned to 'A Chara Dhil [Dear Friend]', 25 November 1926, in MTUCDA P69/47 (52); though unsigned this letter is from Cooney as the author states that he was going to travel to London to meet with the Soviet agent 'James', and Cooney was

the person who in fact made this trip. The recipient is uncertain, though it may have been Seán Russell.

221 Unsigned to 'A Chara Dhil [Dear Friend]', 25 November 1926, in MTUCDA P69 /47 (52).

222 'J' to CS, 18 November 1923 [1926], in MTUCDA P69/41 (251–2).

223 CS to S Officer Offaly brigade, 23 November 1923 [1926], in MTUCDA P69/41 (250).

224 CS to OC Tipp. brigade, 4 December 1923 [1926], in MTUCDA P69/47 (40); this letter may have been written by Cooney standing in for Twomey; alternatively the adjutant general could have also been temporarily appointed chief of staff.

225 Hanley, *The IRA, 1926–1936*, p. 79. *New York Times*, 22 November 1926. *Irish Times*, 18 December 1926.

226 *New York Times*, 22 November 1926.

227 Unsigned to 'A Chara Dhil [Dear Friend]', 25 November 1926, in MTUCDA P69 /47 (52).

228 MacEoin, *The IRA in the Twilight Years*, p. 129; *New York Times*, 22 November 1926.

229 Unsigned to Jones, 7 December 1926, in MTUCDA P69/183 (163-164); unsigned to 'A Chara Dhil [Dear Friend]', 25 November 1926, in MTUCDA P69/47 (52).

230 Unsigned to An Timthire, 25 November 1923 [1926], in MTUCDA P69/183 (171).

231 In MTUCDA P69/196 (41–3).

232 Unsigned to 'A Chara Dhil [Dear Friend]', 25 November 1926, in MTUCDA P69/47 (52).

233 *Cork Examiner*, 29 November and 5 December 1926; in MTUCDA P69/196 (41–3).

234 Acting secretary executive to M. Murphy, 8 December [1926], in MTUCDA P69/48 (318).

235 Unsigned to An Timthire, 25 November 1923 [1926], in MTUCDA P69/183 (171).

236 *Ibid*.

237 Unsigned to Mr Jones, 7 December 1926, in MTUCDA P69/183 (163–4).

238 Unsigned to Mr Browne, 26 December 1926, in MTUCDA P69/183 (156); date on the document is incorrectly given as 26 November 1926 but this is corrected elsewhere.

239 Unaddressed from An Timthire, 21 December 1926, in MTUCDA P69/183 (159–60).

240 *Ibid*.

241 HS to CS or chairman, 17 November 1926 in MTUCDA P69/41 (27), unsigned to 'A Chara Dhil [Dear Friend]', 25 November 1926, in MTUCDA P69/47 (52).

242 Unsigned to Jones, 7 December 1926, in MTUCDA P69/183 (163–4).

243 CS to HS, 8 December 1926, in MTUCDA P69/47 (10–11).

244 *An Phoblacht*, 17 December 1926.

245 DI to MP [Mick Price], 17 December 1926, in MTUCDA P69/193 (55).

246 Unsigned to MP, 17 December 1926, in MTUCDA P69/47 (7).

247 OC 4th battalion, Dublin to CS, 3 December 1926, in MTUCDA P69/47 (22–3).

248 An Timthire to unaddressed, 21 December 1926, in MTUCDA P69/183 (159–60).

249 *Irish World*, 27 November 1926.

250 Unsigned to MP, 17 December 1926, in MTUCDA P69/47 (7).

251 Unsigned to 'A Chara Dhil [Dear Friend]', 25 November 1926, in MTUCDA P69/ 47 (52).

252 Unsigned to MP, 17 December 1926, in MTUCDA P69/47 (7).

253 QMG to CS, 4 May 1924 [1927], in MTUCDA P69/48 (47).

254 Chairman to An Timthire, 3 February 1927, in MTUCDA P69/183 (123–5).

255 Minutes of meeting of the Army Executive, 27 April 1927, in MTUCDA P69/48 (104–5).

256 Bowyer Bell, *The Secret Army*, p. 58.

257 CS to OC Cork 1 brigade, 10 February 1924 [1927], in MTUCDA P69/48 (338).

258 DI to 'unaddressed', 10 December 1926, in MTUCDA P69/193 (62).

259 Regan, *The Irish Counter-Revolution*, pp. 251–6; Bowyer Bell, *The Secret Army*, p. 60.

260 Chairman to An Timthire, 18 March 1927, in MTUCDA P69/183 (77–8); Hanley, *The IRA, 1926–1936*, p. 115.

261 Hanley, *The IRA, 1926–1936*, p. 115.

262 Unsigned to George, 2 May 1927, in MTUCDA P69/48 (75).

263 MacEoin, *The IRA in the Twilight Years*, p. 134.

264 Chairman to An Timthire, 8 April 1927, in MTUCDA P69/183 (74–5).

265 Chairman to unaddressed, 12 April 1927, in MTUCDA P69/183 (71–2).

266 Minutes of Army Council meeting, 5 April 1927, in MTUCDA P69/48 (112).

267 Jones to Browne, 28 February 1927, in MTUCDA P69/183 (102–4).

268 Meeting of officers regarding republican co-ordination in the general election and memorandum of suggested basis of co-ordination between republican bodies, 9 April 1927, in MTUCDA P69 48 (35–6, 152, 154–6 and 157–62).

269 Minutes of meeting of Army Council, 11 April 1927, in MTUCDA P69/48 (108).

270 Chairman to unaddressed, 12 April 1927, in MTUCDA P69/183 (71–2).

271 Chairman to An Timthire, 8 April 1927, in MTUCDA P69/183 (74–5).

272 MD to HS, 19 May 1927, in MTUCDA P69/48 (19).

273 Chairman to Mr Jones, An Timthire, 14 April 1927, in MTUCDA P69/183 (61–2).

274 Joint meeting of representative members of Fianna Fáil and of representatives of the Army Council, 15 April 1927, in MTUCDA P69/48 (115).

275 Unsigned to George [Gilmore], 2 May 1927, in MTUCDA P69/48 (75).

276 Seán Lemass and Gerald Boland to secretary Army Council, 29 April 1927, in MTUCDA P69/48 (33). Minutes of Army Council, 28 April 1927, in MTUCDA P69/48 (114).

277 Chairman to An Timthire, 29 April 1927, in MTUCDA P69/183 (58–9).

278 Unsigned to George, 2 May 1927, in MTUCDA P69/48 (75).

279 Secretary of Army Council to E. de Valera, 11 May 1927, in MTUCDA P69/48 (30).

280 E. de Valera to secretary of Army Council, 13 May 1927, in MTUCDA P69/48 (29).

281 Hanley, *The IRA, 1926–1936*, p. 208.

282 Unsigned to George, 2 May 1927, in MTUCDA P69/48 (75).

283 Regan, *The Irish Counter-Revolution*, pp. 270–1; Hanley, *The IRA, 1926–1936*, p. 209.

284 Coogan, *The IRA*, p. 40.

285 Mr Ambrose, Outline of the present movement, July 1927, in MTUCDA P69/72 (14), quoted in Hanley, *The IRA, 1926–1936*, p. 246.

286 Lawlor, *Seán MacBride, That Day's Struggle*, p. 106.

287 Regan, *The Irish Counter-Revolution*, pp. 273, 421.

288 MacEoin, *The IRA in the Twilight Years*, p. 136; Bowyer Bell, *The Secret Army*, p. 61.

289 MacEoin, *The IRA in the Twilight Years*, p. 136.

290 Bowyer Bell, *The Secret Army*, p. 61–2.

291 Dublin brigade IO to DI, 23 July [1927], in MTUCDA P69/196 (142–3); Christly Quearney in MacEoin, *The IRA in the Twilight Years*, p. 768.

292 Dublin brigade IO to DI, 23 July [1927], in MTUCDA P69/196 (142–3).

293 Dublin brigade IO to DI, 27 July [1927], in MTUCDA P69/196 (133–4).

294 *Ibid.*

295 Bowyer Bell, *The Secret Army*, p. 62. Regan, *The Irish Counter-Revolution*, p. 273.

296 DI to OC Waterford battalion OC, 6 September 1927, in MTUCDA P69/196 (74).

297 Lawlor, *Seán MacBride, That Day's Struggle*, p. 107.

298 *Irish World*, 10 September 1927.

299 HS to 'Dear Sir', 1 November 192[7], in MTUCDA P69/150 (18).

300 IO Dublin brigade to DI, 12 December 1927 in MTUCDA P69/196 (19).

301 Bowyer Bell, *The Secret Army*, p. 62; Regan, *The Irish Counter-Revolution*, p. 274.

302 Regan, *The Irish Counter-Revolution*, pp. 274–6.

303 Kramer, *Dynamic of Destruction*, p. 238-239.

304 Unsigned to chairman of Army Council, 18 November 1925, in MTUCDA P69/181 (74–6).

CHAPTER 4: : THE IRA's LOCAL UNITS

1 Hanley, B. *The IRA, 1926–1936* (Four Courts Press, Dublin, 2002), pp. 206–7. The IRA may also have been responsible for the mysterious death of William Dahlgrene, first mate on the *Victor Emmanuel II* (see Chapter 7). Additionally four people died in Britain in railway, accidents, that occurred in May 1926 during the general strike. This was at a time when the IRA wanted to disrupt the railway system and 'derail trains' (see Chapter 6).

2 *Ibid.*, p. 12. O'Donoghue, F., *No Other Law* (Anvil Books, Dublin, 1986), p. 219.

3 Hanley, *The IRA, 1926–1936*, pp. 12–13.

4 *Ibid.*, p. 30.

5 *Ibid.*, pp. 200–1.

6 The St Enda's dump was captured on 1 February 1926; Hanley, *The IRA, 1926–1936*, p. 47; MacEoin, U., *The IRA in the Twilight Years, 1923–1948* (Argenta Publications, Dublin, 1997), p. 125.

7 Coogan, T. P., *The IRA: A History* (Roberts Rinehart Publishers, Niwot, Colorado, 1993), p. 72.

8 An Timthire to Mr Smith, 20 April 1927, in MTUCDA P69/183 (48–51).

9 Hanley, *The IRA, 1926–1936*, p. 49.

10 MacEoin, *The IRA in the Twilight Years*, pp. 129–30.

11 In his report to the Army Executive Twomey used the word 'pleased' and to Gilmore he stated he was 'quite pleased'; minutes of Army Executive meeting, 27 April 1927, in MTUCDA P69/48 (104–5); unsigned to George [Gilmore], 2 May 1927, in MTUCDA P69/48 (75).

12 Hanley, *The IRA, 1926–1936*, p. 12.

13 *Irish Times*, 26 October 1926.

14 CS to OC Dublin brigade, 26 October 1926, in MTUCDA P69/41 (45).

15 *Irish Times*, 28 and 29 March 1927.

16 Chairman of Army Council to An Timthire, 8 April 1927, in MTUCDA P69/183 (74–5).

17 Some of this account is taken from a newspaper cutting in the Twomey papers. The title of the paper and the date aren't included in the cutting, though 'April 1926' is written in by hand, MTUCDA P69/44 (39). The eight defendants were listed as: Christopher Brennan, Thomas Gerrard, Patrick and Michael Hogan, Charles Rann, Denis and Thomas Corr and John Cherubine. Named in court, but not on trial, were Arthur and William Kelly. In Ernie O'Malley's memoir of the Civil War, *The Singing Flame* (Anvil Books, Dublin, 1992, p. 295) Thomas Gerrard is named as a medical orderly at Portobello barracks who smuggled out a letter for the badly wounded O'Malley. Arthur Kelly of Hanover Street West, Dublin was arrested in October 1924 in connection with the killing of a British soldier in Cobh, though members of the Cork 1 brigade had actually carried out the attack. Reference: MacEoin, *The IRA in the Twilight Years*, p. 108; *Irish Times*, 1 March, 17 April, 24 April, 4 May, 8 May, 20 May and 29 June 1927.

18 'Almost one-third of the 1,545 members of the Crown Forces who were killed or seriously wounded by the IRA between January 1920 and the Truce occurred in Co. Cork'; quoted from: Augusteijn, J., *From Public Defiance to Guerilla Warfare* (Irish Academic Press, Dublin, 1996), p. 18.

19 Hanley, *The IRA, 1926–1936*, p. 20.

20 *Ibid.*, p. 12.

21 Seán MacSwiney is described as assistant adjutant in a despatch, CS to OC Cork 1 brigade, 28 April1926, in MTUCDA P69/44 (93–4) which cross references S MacS to CS, 23 April 1926, in MTUCDA P69/44 (96–100).

22 Fallon, C., *Soul of Fire: A Biography of Mary MacSwiney* (Mercier Press, Cork, 1986), pp. 132–3.

23 S MacS to CS, 23 April 1926, in MTUCDA P69/44 (96–100).

24 CS to OC Cork 1 brigade, 12 April 1926, in MTUCDA P69/44 (102).

25 CS to OC Cork 1 brigade, 15 February 1924 [1927], in MTUCDA P69/48 (281–2).

26 Meeting of officers regarding republican co-ordination in the general election, 9 April 1927; roll call, in MTUCDA P69/48 (157–8, 152, 160); discussion on memo in MTUCDA P69/48 (161–2).

27 Brigade adjutant Limerick brigade to CS, 27 April 1927, in MTUCDA P69/48 (38); Hanley, *The IRA, 1926–1936*, p. 12

28 Unsigned note, likely from the Limerick brigade adjutant, to CS, 27 April 1927, in MTUCDA P69/48 (40); S Commdt for D. of Intelligence to CS, 25 May 1926, in MTUCDA P69/12 (47).

29 Hopkinson, M., *Green Against Green: The Irish Civil War* (Gill & Macmillan, Dublin, 1988) p. 210.

30 S Commdt. for D. of Intelligence to CS, 25 May 1926, in MTUCDA P69/12 (47).

31 CS to OC Waterford batt. 6 September 1927, in MTUCDA P69/50 (26).

32 Hopkinson, M., *The Irish War of Independence* (Gill & Macmillan,Dublin, 2002), p. 146.

33 Hanley, *The IRA, 1926–1936*, p. 12

34 Meeting of officers regarding republican co-ordination in the general election, 9 April 1927; discussion on memo in MTUCDA P69/48 (161–2).

35 [1st staff officer] Offaly to CS, 18 November 1923 [1926], in MTUCDA P69/41 (251–2).

36 1st staff officer to CS, 5 December 1923 [1926], in MTUCDA P69/41 (248); references to General Prout in Hopkinson, *Green Against Green*, pp. 136, 154, 168, 209–10, 225, 246.

37 This letter is signed 'chief of staff'; however, Moss Twomey was imprisoned at the time, and so it was likely written by Andy Cooney; CS to S Officer Offaly brigade, 23 November 1923 [1926], in MTUCDA P69/41 (250).

38 Twomey remained in prison at the time of this letter. CS to 1st staff officer, 13 December 1923 [1926], in MTUCDA P69/41 (247)

39 Hanley, *The IRA, 1926–1936*, pp. 12–13.

40 OC battalion Connemara South to CS, 28 September 1926, in MTUCDA P69/47 (124).

41 S Galway to CS, 7 March 1923 [the date the document was received was 9 March 1924, and thus the actual year was likely 1927], in MTUCDA P69/48 (253).

42 Dáil Éireann, Volume 124, 15 March 1951. Committee on Finance, adjournment debate, appointment of paymasters; Reviewed on www.oireachtas.ie on 15 March 2008.

43 Hanley, *The IRA, 1926–1936*, p. 12.

44 *Ibid.*, p. 209.

45 Unsigned, N Mayo brigade to adjt. general, 1 November 1924 [1927], in MTUCDA P69/149 (108–10).

46 In this despatch the service of 'J Barret' were also offered; 'M' to adjutant general, 8 September 1924 [1927], in MTUCDA P69/149 (121–2).

47 Canfield, B., 'The three-inch Stokes mortar', excerpted from 'US Infantry Weapons of the First World War'. Reviewed on the website www.worldwar1.com, 28 April 2008.

48 Based on the numbers presented by Brian Hanley, 511 of the IRA's members were from Northern Ireland units in 1930. Hanley, *The IRA, 1926–1936*, pp. 12–13.

49 CS to S Capt W, 3 May 1926, in MTUCDA P69/44 (11–12).

50 The relevant despatch was sent by the intelligence officer of the Armagh battalion to the director of intelligence in Dublin: '1. Enquires have been sent to Armagh police barracks, re Tommy Donnelly, who is working in Fianna Fáil interests in 2. Sergt Rowe (RUC) Markethill has been transferred to Dromitee (South Armagh) and Sergt Browne (RUC) has been transferred from the latter Station to Markethill'; IO Number 2 Area to DI, 6 November 1927 in MTUCDA P69/196 (29).

51 There is considerable evidence that the IRA's organiser in the north, 'Captain W', was 'Staff Captain Wilson'; documents from the north are signed 'W Capt GHQ'; a Staff Captain W attended the IRA officers' meeting in Dublin, 9 April 1927, P69/48 (157–8, 152, 160); there is a reference to 'Wilson' working at GHQ, Unsigned to George [Gilmore], 2 May 1927, in MTUCDA P69/48 (75); Mick Price also approved 'Wilson' to act as his proxy on the Army Council on 16 December 1926, in MTUCDA P69/193 (59).

52 Captain W to CS, 4 May [1926], in MTUCDA P69/44 (8–9); Captain W to CS, 20 May 1923 [1926], in MTUCDA P69/47 (173–6).

53 Captain W to CS, 20 May 1923 [1926], in MTUCDA P69/47 (173–6).

54 This document is dated 23 May 1926 and signed by the chief of staff; given Cooney's departure for America by late May it was likely written by Twomey; CS to Staff Captain W, 26 May 1923 [1926], in MTUCDA P69/47 (172).

55 Brian Hanley writes that the information on Turley's torture was found in letters he wrote to his family while banished to Britain, and that these were uncovered

in a police raid on the family home in 1945. Hanley also quotes another Belfast IRA veteran of the period referring to the battalion's use of 'brutal methods' to discipline members; Hanley, *The IRA, 1926–1936*, pp. 48–9 and 225; Coogan, *The IRA*, pp. 175–6; MacEoin, *The IRA in the Twilight Years*, p. 845; also personal communication from Brian Hanley, 29 April 2008.

56 Captain W to CS, 20 May 1923 [1926], in MTUCDA P69/47 (173–6).

57 Communications log book, no date [circa September 1926], in MTUCDA P69/195.

58 Captain W to CS, 4 May [1926], in MTUCDA P69/44 (8–9).

59 O'Connor, E., *Reds and the Green: Ireland, Russia and the Communist Internationals 1919–43* (UCD Press, Dublin, 2004), p. 229 and a photograph of Tommy Watters, between pages 84 and 85.

60 Communications log book, no date [circa September 1926], in MTUCDA P69/195.

61 This document is dated 23 May 1926 and signed by the chief of staff. Given Cooney's departure for America by late May it was likely written by Twomey; when this paragraph was decrypted, the chief of staff's spelling of *An Phoblacht* was 'An Poblact'. CS to Staff Captain W, 26 May 1923 [1926], in MTUCDA P69/47 (172).

62 MacEoin, *The IRA in the Twilight Years*, p. 179.

63 CS to S Capt. W, 16 April 1926, in MTUCDA P69/44 (19).

64 Note that Jones uses American spelling in this despatch. Six counties, a term for the six out of the nine counties of Ulster which constituted the state of Northern Ireland. JB or Jones to Mr Browne [Twomey], 21 October 1926, in MTUCDA P69/183 (183).

65 S [Smith] to Mr Jones, 10 November 1926, in MTUCDA P69/183 (173–4).

CHAPTER 5: INTELLIGENCE

1 McMahon, P., 'British Intelligence and the Anglo-Irish truce, July–December 1921', *IHS*, Vol. xxxv, No. 140 (November 2007).

2 Hopkinson, M., *The Irish War of Independence* (Gill & Macmillan, Dublin, 2002), p. 69.

3 Hopkinson, *The Irish War of Independence*, p. 88

4 O'Halpin, E., *Defending Ireland: The Irish Free State and its Enemies since 1922* (Oxford University Press, Oxford, 2000), pp. 3–4.

5 *Ibid.*, pp. 11–14.

6 *Ibid.*, p. 55.

7 *Ibid.*, p. 65.

8 MacEoin, U., *The IRA in the Twilight Years, 1923–1948*, p. 118.

9 MacEoin, U., *Survivors* (Argenta Publications, Dublin, 1987), p. 458.

10 Adjt Dundalk batt to DI, 23 Aug. 1927, in MTUCDA, P69/196 (105).

11 Intelligence officer Dublin 1 brigade to DI, 27 October 1927, in MTUCDA, P69/196 (37–9).

12 IO Dublin brigade to DI, 23 July [1927], in MTUCDA, P69/196 (142–3) and IO Dublin brigade to DI, 26 July 1927, in MTUCDA, P69/196 (135–6).

13 From OC Cork 1 brigade, 20 [March] 1927, in MTUCDA, P69/48 (199).

14 IO Dublin brigade to DI, 27 October 1927, in MTUCDA, P69/196 (37–9).

15 Hopkinson, *The Irish War of Independence*, pp. 26, 117, 122.

16 CS to OC Tipperary brigade, 4 December 1923 [1926], in MTUCDA, P 69/47 (40); Moss Twomey was in Mountjoy prison on this date, therefore the author is uncertain.

17 MacEoin, *The IRA in the Twilight Years*, p. 146; O'Halpin, *Defending Ireland*, p. 67.

18 Debtors who have made no payments, 10 September 1923 [1926], in MTUCDA P69/48 (301).

19 Griffith, K. and O'Grady, T. *Ireland's Unfinished Revolution* (Roberts Rinehardt, Colorado, 1999), pp. 337–9.

20 IO Dublin brigade to DI, 27 July [1927], in MTUCDA, P69/196 (133–4).

21 IO Dublin brigade to DI, 27 Oct 1927, in MTUCDA, P69/196 (37–9).

22 IO Dublin brigade to DI, 12 Dec 1927, in MTUCDA, P69/196 (19).

23 J to DI, 13 December 1927, in MTUCDA, P69/196 (18).

24 MacEoin, *The IRA in the Twilight Years*, p. 840; DI to MP, 17 December 1926, in MTUCDA P69/193 (55).

25 Hanley, B. *The IRA, 1926–1936* (Four Courts Press, Dublin, 2002), p. 48. MacEoin, *The IRA in the Twilight Years*, p. 125.

26 Griffith and O'Grady, *Ireland's Unfinished Revolution*, pp. 338–41; MacEoin, *The IRA in the Twilight Years*, pp. 35, 146. O'Halpin, *Defending Ireland*, p. 67; *Irish Times*, 23 August 1977.

27 *Irish Times*, 23 August 1977.

28 Andrews, C. S., *Dublin Made Me* (Mercier Press, Dublin and Cork, 1979), pp. 193–5; Hanley, *The IRA, 1926–1936*, pp. 114, 246. 'J O'Neill' to CS, 28 July 1927, in MTUCDA P69/49 (8).

29 S MacS to CS, 23 April 1926, in MTUCDA, P69/44 (96–100).

30 CS to OC Cork 1 brigade, 28 April 1926, in MTUCDA, P69/44 (93–4).

31 To CS from S/Commdt for DI,   May 1926, in MTUCDA, P69/12 (47).

32 Brigade adjutant Mayo to DI, 23 December 1923 [1926], in MTUCDA, P69/193 (47–8).

33 MacEoin, *Survivors*, pp. 471–3.

34 S O'S to J Jones, 8 May 1926, in MTUCDA, P69/197 (163), S O'S to DI, 17 May 1927, in MTUCDA, P69/197 (160–1).

35 Hanley, *The IRA, 1926–1936*, p. 46.

36 OC Kildare batt to CS, 29 November 1927, in MTUCDA, P69/50 (6).

37 CS to OC Kildare batt, 5 December 1927, in MTUCDA, P69/50 (5).

38 CS to DI, 4 May 1923 [1926], in MTUCDA P69/44 (62–3).

39 MacEoin, *Survivors*, p. 122.

40 Staff commandant for DI, to IO Dublin brigade, 23 November 1926, in MTUCDA P69/193 (96).

41 Dublin brigade IO to DI, 2 September 1927, in MTUCDA P69/196 (86–7).

42 AG to adjutant Cork 2 brigade, 1 February 1924 [1927], in MTUCDA P69/171 (15).

43 CO Offaly to DI, 21 October 1927, in MTUCDA P69/196 (26).

44 Adjt Cork 1 brigade to DI, 26 December 1927, in MTUCDA P69/196 (14).

45 This paragraph concerning Sergeant Leen of the gardaí was very difficult to decipher due to the poor quality of the original document and to errors made in the original encryption by Connie Neenan. In our copy it was difficult to make out the original letters in cipher. James Gillogly and I are very grateful to Seamus Helferty for reviewing the original and sending us clarification on the cipher text.

The uncorrected decryption is as follows: 'get in touch with sergt leen civic guards bardon county conk [*sic*] he is in superintendents office he is fed up gitn imperial wan[-?c?o?] and is going to clear out possibly emigrate. he is anxious to give information to us mention martin howard of iistowel now in new york sent iou also about a letter he sent to martin offering to assist i saw the letter.

James Gillogly wrote that: the N in 'conk' comes from the N in group RNIFP, line 2 group 4. The G in 'gitn' (which obviously should be 'with') and the W in 'wan-' are both from line 2 group 10, NIGWN, which is clear enough. The N in 'gitn' and the [-C?O?] letter in 'wanc[-c?o?]' are the first and second letters of line 3 group 3 NCCSE. The latter looks more like a C to me because of the serif on top. The clear G in 'gitn' is right above the W in 'wan-', so I think what has happened is that the W and G were interchanged on the worksheet, making 'witn' and 'gan-'. The N of 'witn' is right below the H in 'office he is', and again could have been a transcription error. Bottom line: I think it should read 'Imperial gang', and the difficulty comes from the coder not getting enough sleep!

'Mention martin howard': The next word becomes 'ofiistowel'. The 'of' must introduce his residence, but 'iistowel' doesn't trigger any connections with me, therefore likely 'Listowel'. — We have seen the L on this typewriter offset to the right before. The first I comes from NIORI, the second from UTINO (end of line 2), the S from the last letter of IFSIS, line 2 group 6, the T from OOMNT (line 1 group 1), the O from HOYLT (line 1 group 6), the W from WOSER (line 1 group 4), the E from WEROR (line 2 group 2), and the L from TIALK (line 2 group 4).

An Timthire to Mr Smith, 20 April 1927, in MTUCDA P69/183 (48–51).

46 S MacS to CS, 23 April 1926, in MTUCDA P69/44 (96-100).

47 DI to IO Waterford, 27 May 1924 [1927], in MTUCDA P69/196 (163).

48 Hanley, *The IRA, 1926–1936*, pp. 99–100.

49 CS to DI, 14 May 192[6], in MTUCDA P69/12 (59).

50 DI to adjt. Tipperary brigade, 16 November 1927, in MTUCDA P69/197 (66). MacEoin, *Survivors*, pp. 471–3.

51 To George, 2 May 1927, in MTUCDA P69/48 (75).

52 To An Timthire from chairman, 18 March 1927, in MTUCDA P69/183 (77–8).

53 *Irish Independent*, 19 November 1927.

54 DI to adjt. Claremorris brigade, 21 June 1924 [1927], in MTUCDA P69/196 (168).

55 Adjt. Claremorris brigade to DI, 27 June 1924 [1927], in MTUCDA P69/196 (167).

56 Lawlor, *Seán MacBride, That Day's Struggle*, pp. 124–5.

57 *Irish Times*, 6 December 1927.

58 MacEoin, *Survivors*, p. 188.

59 S/Capt to Mr Campbell, 21 July 1927, in MTUCDA P69/196 (149).

60 IO Dublin brigade to DI, 7 September 1927, in MTUCDA P69/196 (85).

61 DI to Mick P, 10 December 1926, in MTUCDA P69/193 (66); to George G, 10 December 1926, in MTUCDA P69/193 (63).

62 To DI from D, 23 January 1927, in MTUCDA P69/41 (10).

63 MacEoin, *The IRA in the Twilight Years*, p. 145.

64 D to DI, [1]6 January 1927, in MTUCDA P69/41 (14); D to DI, 16 January 1927, in MTUCDA P69/41 (13); CS to D, 4 February 1927, in MTUCDA P69/41 (4).

65 DI to George G, 7 January 1927, in MTUCDA P69/193 (29); DI to D, 14 January 1927, in MTUCDA P69/193 (6).

66 Hanley, *The IRA, 1926–1936*, pp. 192–3.

67 MacEoin, *The IRA in the Twilight Years*, p. 122; MacEoin, *Survivors*, pp. 564–5.

68 MacEoin, *Survivors*, p. 565.

69 *Irish World*, 15 January 1927; *Irish Times*, 11 December 1926.

70 Cronin, S., *The McGarrity Papers* (Anvil Books, Tralee, 1972), p. 146; *An Phoblacht*, 24 December 1926.

71 To Mick Price from Twomey, 17 December 1926, in MTUCDA P69/47 (7).

72 MacEoin, *The IRA in the Twilight Years*, p. 130.

73 DI to George G, 7 January 1927, in MTUCDA P69/193 (29).

74 D to DI, 16 January 1927, in MTUCDA P69/41 (13).

75 CS to D, 28 January 1924 [1927].

76 *Irish World*, 15 January 1927.

77 To George from Twomey, 2 May 1927, in MTUCDA P69/48 (75).

78 CS to D, 4 February 1927, in MTUCDA P69/41 (4).

79 MacEoin, *Survivors*, p. 377.

80 *Ibid.*, p. 565. MacEoin, *The IRA in the Twilight Years*, p. 149.

81 Hanley, *The IRA, 1926–1936*, pp. 196–7.

82 MacEoin, *Survivors*, p. 375.

83 Andrews, *Dublin Made Me*, p. 223.

84 MacEoin, *Survivors*, p. 369.

85 *Ibid.*, p. 375.

86 MacEoin, *The IRA in the Twilight Years*, p. 128; *An Phoblacht*, 17 December 1926.

87 *Irish World*, 15 January 1927.

88 Mick P to DI, 16 December 1926, in MTUCDA P69/193 (59).

89 DI to MP, 17 December 1926, in MTUCDA P69/193 (55).

90 *Irish World*, 15 January 1927.

91 Twomey to Mick, 17 December 1926, in MTUCDA P69/47 (7).

92 DI to D, 14 January 1927, in MTUCDA P69/193 (6).

93 D to DI, [1]6 January 1927, in MTUCDA P69/41 (14).

94 CS to D, 28 January 1927, in MTUCDA P69/41 (9).

95 D to CS, 30 January 1927, in MTUCDA P69/no number, grouped with file 41.

96 CS to D, 4 February 1927, in MTUCDA P69/41 (4).

97 CS to George, 2 May 1927, in MTUCDA P69/48 (75).

98 MacEoin, *The IRA in the Twilight Years*, p. 141; Hanley, *The IRA, 1926–1936*, pp. 196–7; *Irish Times*, 8 November 1927.

99 MacEoin, *The IRA in the Twilight Years*, pp. 279–80; Hanley, *The IRA, 1926–1936*, pp. 196–7.

100 S O'S to J J, 8 May 1926 [?], in MTUCDA P69/197 (163).

101 S O'S to DI, 17 May 1927, in MTUCDA P69/197 (160–1).

102 S O'S to DI, 17 May 1927, in MTUCDA P69/197 (160–1).

103 From J J, 1 December 1927, in MTUCDA P69/197 (60).

104 *Connacht Tribune*, 17 May 1924.

105 MacEoin, *The IRA in the Twilight Years*, p. 125.

106 *Irish Independent*, 23 April 1926.

107 *Ibid.*

108 S O'S to DI, 17 May 1927, in MTUCDA P69/197 (160–1).

109 *Irish Independent*, 23 April 1926; *An Phoblacht*, 19 February 1926.

110 O'Connor, E., *Reds and the Green: Ireland, Russia and the Communist Internationals 1919–43* (UCD Press, Dublin, 2004), pp. 105,109.

111 Letter received by Mrs Despard, 16 March 1926, in MTUCDA P69/193 (124).

112 MD to Mr Brown, 15 January 1927, in MTUCDA P69/132–3.

113 Neenan to Twomey, 1933, in MTUCDA P69/135 (51).

114 Mac Con Uladh, D., *Jack Keogh – Ballinasloe IRA* (www.Ballinasloe.org, 2005–2007).

115 *Connacht Tribune*, 12 May 1945.

CHAPTER 6: THE IRA IN BRITAIN

1 Hart, P., *The IRA at War 1916–1923* (Oxford University Press, Oxford, 2003), p. 145.

2 *Ibid.*, pp. 142–59.

3 Lawlor, C, *Sean MacBride, That Day's Struggle*.

4 Murray in the O'Malley notebooks, UCDA, P17b/88.

5 *Ibid.*

6 MacEoin, U., *The IRA in the Twilight Years, 1923–1948*, p. 116.

7 O'Malley, C. and Dolan, A., *'No Surrender here!' The Civil War Papers of Ernie O'Malley 1922–1924* (Lilliput Press, Dublin, 2007).

8 AG, report on Britain, 17 November 1924, in MTUCDA P69/44 (366–9).

9 General W. Krivitsky's MI5 file; CAB 126/250 from the National Archives, Kew.

10 CS to OC. Britain, 16 April 1926, in MTUCDA P69/44 (182).

11 Hart, *The IRA at War*, pp. 174–5.

12 Hanley, *The IRA, 1926–1936*, pp. 170–1.

13 March 1926, in MTUCDA P69/12 (61).

14 'E', Memorandum to members of Army Council on our future policy in Britain, 21 February 1926, in MTUCDA P69/183 (65–6).

15 Hanley, *The IRA, 1926–1936*, p. 171.

16 CS to OC No 2 Area, 14 October 1923 [1926], in MTUCDA P69/47 (98).

17 Memorandum to members of Army Council on our future policy in Britain, 21 February 1926, in MTUCDA P69/181 (65).

18 Minutes of meeting of the Army Executive, 27 April 1927, in MTUCDA P69/48 (104–5).

19 OC. Britain to CS, 19 March 1926, in MTUCDA P69/44 (262).

20 OC. Britain to CS, 27 April 1927, in MTUCDA P69/44 (78).

21 OC. Britain to CS, 27 April 1927, in MTUCDA P69/44 (78).

22 CS to OC. Britain, 3 May 1926, in MTUCDA P69/44 (73–4).

23 Taylor, R., 'The General Strike', Centre for Economic Performance at the London School of Economics, ESRC website: www.esrc.ac.uk, reviewed 28 February 2008.

24 *Irish Times*, 4 May 1926.

25 CS to OC. Britain, 23 April 1926, in MTUCDA P69/44 (183). In this discussion of the general strike of 1926 Moss Twomey, rather than Andy Cooney, is credited as being the author of letters signed 'chief of staff'. Based on evidence discussed in Chapter 2 it seems likely that Twomey took over the role of chief of staff in April 1926.

26 OC. Britain to CS, 27 April 1926, in MTUCDA P69/44 (79).

27 *Encyclopaedia Britannica*, United Kingdom, 'The Baldwin era and General Strike'; *Wikipedia*, 'UK General Strike of 1926', reviewed 21 May 2007; Taylor, 'The General Strike', *www.esrc.ac.uk*, reviewed 28 February 2008; Cunliffe, B., Bartlett, R., *et al*, *The Penguin Atlas of British and Irish History* (Penguin Books, London, 2001), pp. 236–8.

28 CS to OC. Britain, 3 May 1926, in MTUCDA P69/44 (72).

29 CS to OC. Britain, 5 May 1926, in MTUCDA P69/44 (29).

30 CS to 'Mr Davis', 6 May 1926, in MTUCDA P69/44 (26).

31 *Irish Times*, 11 May 1926.

32 *Irish Times*, 10 May 1926; *Encyclopaedia Britannica*, United Kingdom, 'The Baldwin era and General Strike'; *Wikipedia*, 'UK General Strike of 1926', reviewed 21 May 2007.

33 Hart, *The IRA at War*, pp. 158–9.

34 DI to IO's All Units, 12 April 1923 (the year may actually be 1926), in MTUCDA P69/12 (64–5).

35 CS to OC Cork 1 brigade, 20 September [probably 1926], in MTUCDA P69/41 (26).

36 JJ to 'A Cara', 1 December 1927, in MTUCDA P69/197 (60).

37 CS to adjt. North Mayo, 26 October 1923 [1926] in P69/39 (107).

38 CS to HS, 24 February 1924 [1927], in MTUCDA P69/48 (297–8).

39 *New York Times*, 8 September 1938. *Time*, 19 September 1938.

40 CS to HS, 2 March 1927, in MTUCDA P69/48 (272–3).

41 The street address is given as Coverdale Street, but this probably should have been Coverdale Crescent; HS to CS, 14 March 1924 [1927], in MTUCDA P69/48 (246).

42 'Eyewitness in Manchester', from www.manchesteronline.co.uk website, reviewed 1 March 2008; McGee, O., *The IRB: The Irish Republican Brotherhood from the Land League to Sinn Féin* (Four Courts Press, Dublin, 2005), pp. 36–7.

43 Adjt to AG, 5 November 1926, in MTUCDA P69/47 (56).

44 CS to HS, 14 October 1926, in MTUCDA P69/47 (76).

45 QMG to CS, 18 November 1926, in MTUCDA P69/41 (18).

46 HS to CS, 1 November 1926, in MTUCDA P69/41 (30).

47 QMG to CS, 18 November 1926, in MTUCDA P69/41 (18).

48 HS to CS, 10 November 1926, in MTUCDA P69/41 (28).

49 QMG to CS, 18 November 1926, in MTUCDA P69/41 (18).

50 CS to HS, 18 February 1924 [1927], in MTUCDA P69/48 (300).

51 HS to CS, 25 February 1927, in MTUCDA P69/48 (293–4).

52 CS to HS, 2 March 1927, in MTUCDA P69/48 (272–3).

53 HS to CS, 5 March 1927, in MTUCDA P69/48 (260–1); In this letter HS wrote that he 'may be able to get a friend to assist in this matter', i.e. repacking the explosives from their original casks; HS to CS, 14 March 1924 [1927], in MTUCDA P69/48 (246); HS to CS, 18 March 1924 [1927], in MTUCDA P69/48 (210).

54 Unsigned to HS, 21 March 1927, in MTUCDA P69/48 (209).

55 CS to HS, 6 April 1927, in MTUCDA P69/48 (143).

56 CS to 'Dear Sir', 16 June 1927, in MTUCDA P69/48 (3).

57 HS to MD, 20 June 1924 [1927], in MTUCDA P69/48 (2).

58 MD to HS, 23 June 1927, in MTUCDA P69/48 (1).

59 Unsigned to HS, 21 September 1927, in MTUCDA P69/150 (33).

60 Unsigned to HS, 26 September 1927, in MTUCDA P69/150 (28).

61 HS to MD, 26 September 1924 [1927], in MTUCDA P69/150 (29); HS to MD, 29 September 1924 [1927], in MTUCDA P69/150 (27).

62 Unsigned to HS, 3 October 1927, in MTUCDA P69/150 (25).

63 HS to MD, 14 October 1924 [1927], in MTUCDA P69/150 (21).

64 CS to OC. Britain, 8 April 1926, in MTUCDA P69/44 (218).

65 CS to OC. Britain, 23 April 1926, in MTUCDA P69/44 (81); OC. Britain to CS, 27 April 1926, in MTUCDA P69/44 (79).

66 Hanley, *The IRA, 1926–1936*, pp. 33, 220. MacEoin, *The IRA in the Twilight Years*, p. 129; MacEoin writes that Killeen served three months, while Hanley states six months.

67 HS to CS, 6 October 1926, in MTUCDA P69/47 (80).

68 'For CS' to HS, 8 November 1926, in MTUCDA P69/41 (29) Act; CS to HS, 13 November 1926 in P69/41 (20).

69 Act. CS to HS, 13 November 1926 in P69/41 (20). HS to CS, 10 November 1926, in MTUCDA P69/41 (28).

70 CS to HS, 14 October 1923 [1926], in MTUCDA P69/47 (76).

71 HS to CS, 17 October 1926, in MTUCDA P69/41 (32).

72 CS to OC. Britain, 23 April 1926, in MTUCDA P69/44 (81); CS to S. Capt W, 30 April 1923 [1926], in MTUCDA P69/44 (16).

73 Unsigned to CS, 7 February 1927, in MTUCDA P69/48 (310).

74 Unsigned to CS, 5 March 1927, in MTUCDA P69/48 (260–1).

75 OC No 2 Area to CS, 18 March 1927, in MTUCDA P69/48 (191).

76 CS to QMG, 12 March 1923 [1926], in MTUCDA P69/44 (320).

77 CS to HS, 14 October 1923 [1926], in MTUCDA P69/47 (76); HS to CS 17 October 1926, in MTUCDA P69/41 (32)

78 www.guardian.com website, 22 December 2005.

79 MD to HS, 17 October 1927, in MTUCDA P69/150 (20).

80 Hart, The IRA at War, pp. 194–220; Wikipedia, 'Henry Hughes Wilson', www.wikipedia.org, reviewed 21 February 2008.

81 New York Times, 7 October 1905.

82 CS to HS, 28 January 1924 [1927], in MTUCDA P69/48 (311).

83 HS to CS, 6 October 1926, in MTUCDA P69/47 (80).

84 Parsons' shop was a well known Dublin landmark and at the time was a general store and newsagents owned by Benjamin Parsons. During the Anglo-Irish War, a printer was installed in the basement to produce a republican newssheet. In 1949 the family sold the shop; see: Lynch, B., Parsons Bookshop (The Liffey Press, Dublin, 2006), p. 3; HS to CS, 27 March 1927, in MTUCDA P69/48 (186).

85 Lawlor, Seán MacBride, That Day's Struggle, pp. 86–7.

86 Newspaper cutting, no date, P69/48 (52-53). File on Ethel Chiles, National Archives, Kew, KV 2/591. HS to CS, 18 March 1924 [1927] in MTUCDA P69/48 (210). MD to HS, 6 May 1927 in MTUCDA P69/48 (50). HS to CS, 14 May 1924 [1927] in MTUCDA P69/48 (23).

87 Martin to [no name], 19 April 1926, in MTUCDA P69/44 (187).

88 OC. Britain to CS, 21 April 1926, in MTUCDA P69/44 (186); CS to OC. Britain, 3 May 1926, in MTUCDA P69/44 (73–4).

89 Unsigned to Rev. McKenna, 27 April 1926, in MTUCDA P69/44 (176).

90 CS to OC. Britain, 23 April 1926, in MTUCDA P69/44 (82).

91 OC. Britain to CS, 27 April 1926, in MTUCDA P69/44 (79).

92 O'Farrell, P., Who's Who in the Irish War of Independence and Civil War, 1916–1923 (Lilliput Press, Dublin, 1997), p.26.

93 OC. Britain to CS, 24 April 1926, in MTUCDA P69/44 (80).

94 CS to OC. Britain, 17 April 1926, in MTUCDA P69/44 (195).

95 CS to OC. Britain, 3 May 1926, in MTUCDA P69/44 (73–4).

96 Ted to CS, 14 May 1927, in MTUCDA P69/48 (5–6); HS to CS, 17 May 1924 [1927], in MTUCDA P69/48 (20). MD to HS, 28 May 1927, in MTUCDA P69/48 (17).

97 CS to Ted, 16 June 1927, in MTUCDA P69/48 (4).

98 CS to OC. Britain, 23 April 1926, in MTUCDA P69/44 (82).

99 OC. Britain to CS, 27 April 1926, in MTUCDA P69/44 (79).

100 CS to OC. Britain, 23 April 1926, in MTUCDA P69/44 (82).

101 OC. Britain to CS, 27 April 1926, in MTUCDA P69/44 (79).

102 S to Mr Jones, 10 November 1926, in MTUCDA P69/183 (173–4).

103 CS to HS, 9 February 1924 [1927], in MTUCDA P69/48 (308).

104 Unsigned to CS, 5 March 1927, in MTUCDA P69/48 (260–1).

105 CS to HS, 10 March 1927, in MTUCDA P69/48 (250).

106 CS to HS, 14 October 1923 [1926] in MUCDA P69/47 (76).

107 HS to CS, 17 October 1926, in MTUCDA P69/41 (32).

108 MTUCDA P 69/196 (50); IO Number 3 Area to DI, 9 December 1926, in MTUCDA P69/193 (67).

109 Letter from the Midland battalion, in MTUCDA P69/193 (8).

110 Newspaper cutting, 25 December 1927, in MTUCDA, no reference number.

111 Newspaper cutting, no date, attached to a document from the DI to the adjt. Tipperary brigade, 16 November 1927, in MTUCDA P69/197 (66).

112 HS to CS, 14 Dec 1926, in MTUCDA P69/47 (9).

113 CS to HS, 24 February 1924 [1927], in MTUCDA P69/48 (297–8).

114 CS to HS, 28 January 1924 [1927], in MTUCDA P69/48 (311); CS to HS, 24 February 1924 [1927], in MTUCDA P69/48 (297–8).

115 CS to HS, 28 January 1924 [1927], in MTUCDA P69/48 (311).

116 Unsigned to CS, 7 February 1927, in MTUCDA P69/48 (310).

117 Unsigned to CS, 18 February 1927, in MTUCDA P69/48 (308).

118 CS to HS, 24 February 1924 [1927], in MTUCDA P69/48 (297–8).

119 CS to F. and Accts Officer, 1 March 1924 [1927], in MTUCDA P69/48 (277).

120 CS to F. and Accts Officer, 1 March 1924 [1927], in MTUCDA P69/48 (277).

121 CS to HS, 10 March 1927, in MTUCDA P69/48 (250).

122 HS to CS, 25 February 1927, in MTUCDA P69/48 (293–4).

123 HS to MD, 1 December 1924 [1927], in MTUCDA P69/150 (9).

124 HS to CS, 16 May 1924 [1927], in MTUCDA P69/48 (22).

125 Unsigned to HS, 3 October 1927, in MTUCDA P69/150 (22).

126 HS to MD, 1 December 1924 [1927], in MTUCDA P69/150 (9).

127 Unsigned to HS, 5 December 1927, in MTUCDA P69/150 (8).

128 HS to MD, 5 January 1924 [1928], in MTUCDA P69/150 (3).

129 HS to CS, 25 February 1927, in MTUCDA P69/48 (293–4).

130 CS to HS, 28 January 1924 [1927], in MTUCDA P69/48 (311).

131 Unsigned to CS, 7 February 1927, in MTUCDA P69/48 (310).

132 CS to HS, 9 February 1924 [1927], in MTUCDA P69/48 (309).

133 Unsigned to CS, 18 February 1927, in MTUCDA P69/48 (308).

134 HS to CS, 25 February 1927, in MTUCDA P69/48 (293–4).

135 CS to HS, 24 February 1924 [1927], in MTUCDA P69/48 (297–8).

136 Unsigned to CS, 5 March 1927, in MTUCDA P69/48 (260–1).

137 CS to HS, 10 March 1927, in MTUCDA P69/48 (250).

138 Unsigned and unaddressed letter, 29 March 1927, in MTUCDA P69/48 (183). HS to CS, 3 April 1924 [1927], in MTUCDA P69/48 (182).

139 MD to HS, 25 April 1927, in MTUCDA P69/48 (59).

140 HS to CS, 27 April 1924 [1927], in MTUCDA P69/48 (57).

141 MD to HS, 6 May 1927, in MTUCDA P69/48 (50).

142 HS to CS, 14 May 1924 [1927], in MTUCDA P69/48 (23).

143 MD to HS, 18 May 1927, in MTUCDA P69/48 (21).

144 HS to CS, 24 May 1924 [1927], in MTUCDA P69/48 (18).

145 MD to HS, 28 May 1927, in MTUCDA P69/48 (17).

146 MD to HS, 17 October 1927, in MTUCDA P69/150 (20); HS to MD, 20 October 1924 [1927], in MTUCDA P69/150 (19).

147 In this chapter the name 'Fitzgerald' is presented in this format when it is taken from decrypted cipher or other IRA correspondence. In the cipher there is no distinction make between capitals and lower case letters and therefore it would be presumptuous of James or myself to write it as (the less common) 'FitzGerald'. However, the arms merchant, Francis FitzGerald's family are known to have written their name with a capital 'G'. Therefore for the purposes of accuracy I've used both formats, depending on whether the text came from IRA documents or referred directly to Francis FitzGerald or his brother, Desmond.

148 Dáil in Committee – Reports of the Committee of Public Accounts. Dáil Éireann, Vol. 12, 7 July 1925; *Irish Times*, 12 September 1927.

149 P. A. Murray in the O'Malley Notes, P17b/88.

150 MacEoin, *The IRA in the Twilight Years*, p. 238.

151 *Ibid.*, p. 238.

152 Dr Garret FitzGerald is of the opinion that the 'Merchant' was not the same person as Francis W FitzGerald. At the time I contacted Dr FitzGerald I had made the mistaken assumption that the Merchant's name was 'T. F. Fitzgerald'. This was based on a misreading of the text of P69/48 (59), 25 April 1927. Originally James Gillogly and I thought that the decryption of Paragraph 7 (130) should read: 'T F Fitzgerald has not paid up ... '. However, we went back to double check our copy of the document and realised that we had mistaken an 'I' as a 'T' and thus the first two words of the decryption should instead be 'If Fitzgerald ... ' Due to the font used on the typewriter by the IRA at the time it is relatively easy to mistake these two letters. Therefore I gave the wrong initials for Fitzgerald aka the 'Merchant' when in communication with Dr Garret Fitzgerald.

153 Hart, *The IRA at War*, pp. 153–4.

154 *Ibid.*, pp. 170–1.

155 The Irish National Foresters was a moderate nationalist organisation which was primarily a benevolent and fraternal society. A small number of branches are still in existence. OC No. 3 Area to CS, 11 Oct 1923 [1926], in MTUCDA P69/47 (66–9); CS to IO No. 3 Area Britain, 16 October 1923 [1926], in MTUCDA P69/47 (96).

156 Adjt to AG, 13 November [1926], in MTUCDA P69/47 (53).

157 Adjt to AG, 28 October 1926, in MTUCDA P69/47 (57).

158 MA to QMG, 21 November 1924, in MTUCDA P69/37 (226).

159 MA to QMG, 16 February 1925, in MTUCDA P69/37 (227–8).

160 AG to QMG, 17 November 1924, in MTUCDA P69/138 (12–13).

161 Adjt to AG, 28 October 1926, in MTUCDA P69/47 (57).

162 In the documents it's clear that the unit that was refusing to co-operate was the Special Services Section based on the docks, and though it's not directly stated, Tom O'Malley would appear to be a member of that section, though it's possible he could have been an 'old timer' member of another section of the Liverpool Company. OC No. 3 Area to CS, 8 October 1926, in MTUCDA P69/47 (66–9); IO Liverpool to CS, 27 October 1926, in MTUCDA P69/47 (29–33).

163 CS to OC No. 3 Area, 12 October 1923 [1926], in MTUCDA P69/47 (63–4).

164 CS to IO No. 3 Area, 12 October 1926, in MTUCDA P69/47 (61).

165 Adjt. to AG, 5 November 1926, in MTUCDA P69/47 (56).

166 For AG to adjt. No. 3 Area, 16 November 1926, in MTUCDA P69/47 (58).

167 OC No. 3 Area to CS, 8 October 1926, in MTUCDA P69/47 (66–9).

168 CS to OC No. 3 Area, 12 October 1923 [1926], in MTUCDA P69/47 (63–4).

169 Adjt to AG, 28 October 1926, in MTUCDA P 69/47 (57).

170 For AG to adjt No. 3 Area, 16 November 1926, in MTUCDA P69/47 (58).

171 CS to OC No. 3 Area, 18 February 1924 [1927], in MTUCDA P69/48 (242).

172 Report on Britain, 17 November 1924, in MTUCDA P69/44 (366–9).

173 CS to adjt. No. 1 Area, 6 May 1927, in MTUCDA P69/48 (45).

174 Unsigned to HS, 3 October 1927, in MTUCDA P69/150 (22).

175 Coogan, T. P., *The IRA: A History* (Roberts Rinehart Publishers, Niwot, Colorado, 1993), p. 33.

176 CS to OC No. 1 Area, 11 October 1927, in MTUCDA P69/150 (15).

177 KV 2/591 National Archives, Kew.

178 CS to OC No. 2 Area, 14 October 1923 [1926], in MTUCDA P69/47 (98).

179 CS to OC No. 3 Area, 12 October 1926, in MTUCDA P69/47 (108). Adjt No. 3 Area to AG, 13 November [1926], in MTUCDA P69/47 (53).

180 Commandant No 2 Area to DI, 30 Aug. 1927, in MTUCDA P69/196 (83).

181 Hart, *The IRA at War*, p. 144.

182 *Ibid.*, p. 170.

183 *Ibid.*, p. 157.

184 Organiser's report on Irish republican organisation in Scotland, 20 September 1923, in MTUCDA P69/44 (373–4); report on position of republican organisation in Scotland, 20 September 1923, in MTUCDA P69/44 (371–2).

185 Report on Britain, 17 November 1924, in MTUCDA P69/44 (366–9).

186 AG to QMG 17 November 1924, in MTUCDA P69/138 (12–13).

187 Hanley, *The IRA, 1926–1936*, p. 172; Pete Hughes to Frances Carty, 8 May 1925, in MTUCDA P69/62 (17–18).

188 CS to OC. Britain, 23 July 1926, in MTUCDA P69/47 (144).

189 CS to Comdt. S, 7 [or possibly 6] September 1926, in MTUCDA P69/47 (133).

190 CS to OC Scotland, 9 February 1927, in MTUCDA P69/48 (322). CS to OC Scotland, 24 Feb. 1924 [1927] in MTUCDA P69/48 (296).

191 OC Scottish batt [*sic*] to CS, 13 February 1927, in MTUCDA P69/48 (320).

192 CS to QM Scotland, 19 October 1926, in MTUCDA P69/41 (44).

CHAPTER 7: THE IRA IN AMERICA

1 Bayor, R. and Meagher, T., *The New York Irish* (John Hopkins University Press, Baltimore, 1996), p. 485.

2 Doorley, M., *Irish-American Diaspora Nationalism: The Friends of Irish Freedom, 1916–1935* (Four Courts Press, Dublin, 2005), p. 160.

3 *Ibid.*, pp. 17–18.

4 McGee, O., *The IRB: The Irish Republican Brotherhood from the Land League to Sinn Féin* (Four Courts Press, Dublin, 2005), p. 133.

5 Doorley, *Irish-American Diaspora Nationalism*, p. 85.

6 *Ibid.*, p. 96.

7 *Ibid.*, p. 92.

8 *Ibid.*, p. 134.

9 Hanley, B., 'Irish Republicans in interwar New York', unpublished paper, p. 2.

10 Doorley, *Irish-American Diaspora Nationalism*, p. 134.

11 Tarpey, M., *The Role of Joseph McGarrity in the Struggle for Irish Independence* (Arno Press, New York, 1976), p. 224.

12 Quoted from an IRA document found on the arrested courier, Patrick Garland, *New York Times*, 1 May 1926.

13 Hanley, 'Irish Republicans in interwar New York', p. 165.

14 To Mr O'Sullivan from M O'Connor, 18 June 1926, in MTUCDA P69/182 (31).

15 Report of the foreign relations committee, no date, in MTUCDA P69/183 (136).

16 Chairman to An Timthire, 9 February 1927, in MTUCDA P69/183 (113–14).

17 An Timthire to [no name], 1 February 1927, in MTUCDA P69/183 (129–31).

18 An Timthire to Mr Smith, 20 April 1927 in P69/183 (48–51).

19 Hanley, 'Irish Republicans in interwar New York', p. 11.

20 Ibid., pp. 7–8.

21 An Timthire to [no name], 28 February 1927, in MTUCDA P69/183 (98–9).

22 An Timthire to [no name], 1 February 1927, in MTUCDA P69/183 (129–31).

23 McGee, The IRB.

24 An Timthire to [no name], 1 February 1927, in MTUCDA P69/183 (129–31).

25 HS to MD, 20 June 1924 [1927], in MTUCDA P69/48 (2).

26 Bayor and Meagher, The New York Irish, pp.337, 396.

27 MacEoin, U., Survivors (Argenta Publications, Dublin, 1987), p. 52.

28 The Advocate, 1 January 1927.

29 The Advocate, 19 March 1927.

30 Hanley, B., The IRA: 1926–1936 (Four Courts Press, Dublin, 2002), p. 163; Irish World, 28 May 1927. Hanley, 'Irish Republicans in interwar New York', p. 12; An Timthire to Mr Smith, 20 April 1927 in P69/183 (48–51).

31 An Timthire to [no name], 18 May 1927, in MTUCDA P69/183 (38–40).

32 An Timthire to Mr Smith, 20 April 1927 in P69/183 (48–51).

33 An Timthire to [no name], 18 May 1927, in MTUCDA P69/183 (38–40).

34 The Advocate, 15 January 1927.

35 An Timthire to [no name], 28 February 1927, in MTUCDA P69/183 (98–9).

36 An Timthire to [no name], 18 May 1927, in MTUCDA P69/183 (38–40); Hanley, 'Irish Republicans in interwar New York', p. 11.

37 Hanley, 'Irish Republicans in interwar New York', p. 12.

38 Chairman to An Timthire, 3 June 1927, in MTUCDA P69/183 (3–4).

39 Hanley, The IRA, 1926–1936, p. 162.

40 An Timthire to [no name], 18 May 1927, in MTUCDA P69/183 (38–40); chairman to An Timthire, 3 June 1927, in MTUCDA P69/183 (3–4).

41 An Timthire to Mr Smith, 20 April 1927 in P69/183 (48–51).

42 Bde adj North Mayo brigade to DI, 23 December 1923 [1926], in MTUCDA P69/193 (47–8).

43 Chairman to An Timthire, 8 April 1927, in MTUCDA P69/183 (74–5).

44 Hopkinson, M., Green Against Green: The Irish Civil War (Gill & Macmillan, Dublin, 1988), p. 159.

45 MacEoin, Survivors, pp. 446–7.

46 MD to Mr Brown, 15 January 1927 in P69/183 (132–3).

47 Chairman to An Timthire, 3 February 1927, in MTUCDA P69/183 (123–5).

48 An Timthire to [no name], 28 February 1927, in MTUCDA P69/183 (98–9); An Timthire to [no name], 21 December 1926 in P69/183 (159–60).

49 An Timthire, 3 June 1927, in MTUCDA P69/183 (3–4); An Timthire to [no name], 18 May 1927, in MTUCDA P69/183 (38–40).

50 An Timthire to [no name], 18 May 1927, in MTUCDA P69/183 (38–40).

51 Ibid.

52 Ibid.

53 Chairman to An Timthire, 24 February 1927, in MTUCDA P69/183 (106–7).

54 An Timthire to [no name], 18 May 1927, in MTUCDA P69/183 (38–40); An Timthire to [no name], 28 February 1927, in MTUCDA P69/183 (98–9).

55 An Timthire to [no name] 13 January 1927, in MTUCDA P69/183 (129–31).

56 S to Mr Jones, 10 November 1926, in MTUCDA P69/183 (173–4).

57 Neenan frequently uses American-style spelling, such as 'emphasize' here; An Timthire to [no name], 28 February 1927, in MTUCDA P69/183 (98–9).

58 An Timthire to Mr Smith, 20 April 1927, in MTUCDA P69/183 (48–51).

59 Hanley, *The IRA: 1926–1936*, p. 164.

60 McGee, *The IRB*, p. 119.

61 Lee, J. and Casey, M., *Making the Irish American* (New York University Press, New York, 2006), p. 468.

62 An Timthire to [no name], 18 May 1927, in MTUCDA P69/183 (38–40).

63 An Timthire to Mr Smith, 20 April 1927 in P69/183 (48–51).

64 Unsigned to Mr Browne, 2 December 1926, in MTUCDA P69/183 (165).

65 *The Advocate*, 15 January 1927.

66 An Timthire to [no name], 1 February 1927, in MTUCDA P69/183 (129–31); *The Advocate*, 15 January 1927.

67 MD [*sic*] to Mr Brown, 15 January 1927, in MTUCDA P69/183 (132–3).

68 Chairman to An Timthire, 3 February 1927, in MTUCDA P69/183 (123–5).

69 An Timthire to [no name], 28 February 1927, in MTUCDA P69/183 (98–9).

70 An Timthire to [no name], 18 March 1927, in MTUCDA P69/183 (80).

71 An Timthire to [no name], 28 February 1927, in MTUCDA P69/183 (98–9).

72 Neenan to Twomey, 1933, in MTUCDA P69/185 (51).

73 *Irish Times*, 1 May 1926.

74 JB to Mr Browne, 25 October 1926, in MTUCDA P69/183 (180).

75 JB to Mr Browne, 8 November 1926, in MTUCDA P69/183 (178–9).

76 MD to Mr Brown, 15 January 1927, in MTUCDA P69/183 (132–3).

77 An Timthire to [no name], 1 February 1927, in MTUCDA P69/183 (129–31).

78 *Ibid*.

79 An Timthire to [no name], 28 February 1927, in MTUCDA P69/183 (98–9).

80 *Ibid*. An Timthire to [no name], 18 March 1927, in MTUCDA P69/183 (80).

81 An Timthire to [no name], 1 February 1927, in MTUCDA P69/183 (129–31); CS to OC Kerry 1 Bde, 25 February 1924 [1927], in MTUCDA P69/48 (295).

82 An Timthire to [no name], 1 February 1927, in MTUCDA P69/183 (129–31).

83 *The Advocate*, 2 April 1927.

84 An Timthire to [no name], 11 March 1927, in MTUCDA P69/183 (84–5).

85 An Timthire to [no name], 18 March 1927, in MTUCDA P69/183 (80).

86 *Ibid*.

87 An Timthire to [no name], 28 February 1927, in MTUCDA P69/183 (98–9).

88 Chairman to An Timthire, 3 February 1927, in MTUCDA P69/183 (123–5).

89 An Timthire to [no name], 28 February 1927, in MTUCDA P69/183 (98–9).

90 Chairman to An Timthire, 29 April 1927, in MTUCDA P69/183 (58–9).

91 Terrace *Talk Ireland* website, 'Kerry's First American Tour of 1927', reviewed 30 Aug. 2006.

92 An Timthire to [no name], 1 February 1927, in MTUCDA P69/183 (129–31).

93 An Timthire to [no name], 28 February 1927, in MTUCDA P69/183 (98–9).

94 An Timthire to]no name], 18 May 1927, in MTUCDA P69/183 (38-40).

95 Chairman to An Timthire, 8 April 1927, in MTUCDA P69/183 (74–5).

96 Chairman to An Timthire, 29 April 1927, in MTUCDA P69/183 (58–9).

97 CS to 'A Chara', 6 May 1927, in MTUCDA P69/183 (63).

98 An Timthire to [no name], 1 February 1927, in MTUCDA P69/183 (129–31).

99 *The Advocate*, 2 April 1927.

100 Information on the 1927 tour. Terrace *Talk Ireland* website, 'Kerry's First American Tour of 1927', reviewed 30 August 2006. *New York Times*, 30 May 1927, 5 July 1927 and 18 July 1927. *Irish World*, 17 July 1927 and 23 July 1927; An Timthire to [no name], 18 May 1927, in MTUCDA P69/183 (38–40).

101 Coogan, *The IRA*, p. 73.

102 Twomey to Neenan, 1933, in MTUCDA P69/185 (24). Neenan to Twomey, 1933, in MTUCDA P69/185 (51). MacEoin, U., *The IRA in the Twilight Years, 1923–1948* (Argenta Publications, Dublin, 1997), p. 238.

103 Amos, F. and West, C., *Chemical Warfare* (McGraw Hill, New York, 1921), pp. 18, 19, 22, 80, 150, 163, 168, 175, 176, 380.

104 *Ibid.*, pp. 15, 137, 143, 390, 137.

105 Swearengen, T., *Tear Gas Munitions* (Charles C. Thomas, Springfield, Illinois, 1966), pp. 4, 5, 12, 20, 22, 23, 53, 103–11.

106 Borgonovo, J., *Florence and Josephine O'Donoghue's War of Independence* (Irish Academic Press, Dublin, 2006), pp. 102–3, 109.

107 McMahon, P., 'British intelligence and the Anglo-Irish truce, 1921', *Irish Historical Studies*, Vol. XXXV, No. 140 (November 2007), pp. 519–40.

108 CS to Military Attache, 15 April 1925, in MTUCDA P69/37 (221–3).

109 JB to Mr Browne, 8 November 1926, in MTUCDA P69/183 (178–9); HS to CS, 10 November 1926, in MTUCDA P69/41 (28).

110 Act. CS to HS, 13 November 1926, in MTUCDA P69/41 (20); [No name] to Mr Jones, 10 November 1926, in MTUCDA P69/183 (173–4).

111 JB to Mr Brown [in this case the letter is for Cooney and not Twomey], 26 November 1926, in MTUCDA P69/183 (168–9).

112 No name to Mr Browne (this letter is in reply to letters from Cooney, and was most likely read by both Cooney and Twomey), 26 December 1926, in MTUCDA P69/183 (156).

113 Kramer A. *Dynamic of Destruction*, p. 54

114 Chairman to Mr Jones, 3 February 1927, in MTUCDA P69/183 (116–18).

115 Jones to Browne, 28 February 1927, in MTUCDA P69/183 (102–4).

116 [No name] to Mr Jones, 18 March 1927, in MTUCDA P69/183 (82–3).

117 Chairman to Mr Jones, 29 April 1927, in MTUCDA P69/183 (66).

118 Chairman to An Timthire, 18 March 1927, in MTUCDA P69/183 (77–8); [No name] to Mr Jones, 18 March 1927, in MTUCDA P69/183 (82–3); chairman to An Timthire, 8 April 1927, in MTUCDA P69/183 (74–5). There's a reference in cipher in this last document to 'mace and billys' and also in an unencrypted document P69/48 (340), 7 February 1924 [1927]. This could not be referring to the trade name 'Mace' for CN gas which was developed in 1962 , but might be a reference to the billy or truncheon as a 'mace'. As the phrase is both in cipher and plain text, it verifies the accuracy of the decryption; in P69/183 (80) Twomey mentions a 'Dan Byrne' and, as discussed in Chapter 11, this is most likely another name for 'Mr Jones'.

119 [No name] to Mr Jones, 18 March 1927, in MTUCDA P69/183 (82–3).

120 Jones to Mr Smith, 8 April 1927, in MTUCDA P69/183 (68).

121 Jones to Browne, 28 February 1927, in MTUCDA P69/183 (102–4).

122 Hu, H. *et al.*, 'Tear Gas – Harassing Agent or Toxic Chemical Weapon?' *Journal of the*

American Medical Association, Vol. 262, No. 5 (4 August 1989).

123 Swearengen, *Tear Gas Munitions*, p.105. Hu, *et al.*, 'Tear Gas – Harassing Agent or Toxic Chemical Weapon?'

124 'Protocol for the Prohibition of the Use in War of Asphyxiating, Poisonous or Other Gases, and of Bacteriological Methods of Warfare', US Department of State website, reviewed 2 February 2008; 'High contracting Parties to the Geneva Protocol', Stockholm International Peace Research Institute website (*www.sipri. org*), reviewed 2 February 2008.

125 Durney, J., *The Mob: The History of Irish Gangsters in America*.

126 Bayor, R. and Meagher, T., *The New York Irish*, p. 366.

127 *Ibid.*, p. 370.

128 MA to QMG, 21 November 1924, in MTUCDA P69/37 (226); MA to QMG, 16 February 1925, in MTUCDA P69/37 (227–8).

129 MA to QMG, 21 November 1924, in MTUCDA P69/37 (226).

130 *Ibid.*

131 MA to QMG, 16 February 1925, in MTUCDA P69/37 (227–8).

132 AG to QMG, 17 Nov. 1924, in MTUCDA P69/138 (12–13).

133 CS to OC Cork 1, 26 April 1926, in MTUCDA P69/44 (95).

134 Note, unsigned and unaddressed, no date. Stamped: IRA 23 Aug. 1927, in MTUCDA P69/196 (104).

135 Hart, P., *The IRA at War 1916–1923*, p. 183.

136 *Ibid.*, p. 184–91.

137 *Ibid.*, p. 189.

138 MA to QMG, 16 February 1925, in MTUCDA P69/37 (227–8).

139 Jones to Mr Browne, 28 February 1927, in MTUCDA P69/183 (102–4).

140 Coogan, T. P., *The IRA: A History* (Roberts Rinehart Publishers, Niwot, Colorado, 1993), p. 73.

141 Hart, *The IRA at War*, pp. 190–1.

142 *Ibid.*, pp. 189–91.

143 An Timthire to [no name], 21 December 1926, in MTUCDA P69/183 (159–60). *Irish Times*, 9 November 1926.

144 An Timthire to [no name], 21 December 1926, in MTUCDA P69/183 (159–60).

145 An Timthire to [no name], 28 February 1927, in MTUCDA P69/183 (98–9); Chairman to An Timthire, 3 February 1927, in MTUCDA P69/183 (123–5).

146 Chairman to An Timthire, 2 February 1927, in MTUCDA P69/183 (123–5).

147 In cipher both Twomey and Neenan spelled the ships name as the *Victor Emanuel*, leaving out the second 'n'; chairman to An Timthire, 9 February 1927, in MTUCDA P69/183 (111–12).

148 An Timthire to Mr Smith, 20 April 1927, in MTUCDA P69/183 (48–51).

149 *Irish Times*, 1 May 1926.

150 Hanley, 'Irish Republicans in interwar New York', p. 3.

151 *New York Times*, 17 January 1926.

152 Minutes of meeting of Army Executive, 27 April 1927, in MTUCDA P69/48 (104–5).

153 *New York Times*, 17 January 1926.

154 Coogan, *The IRA*, pp. 80–1.

155 Tarpey, *The Role of Joseph McGarrity*, p. 232.

156 Cronin, S., *The McGarrity Papers* (Anvil Books, Tralee, 1972), p. 144.

157 JB to Mr Browne, 8 November 1926, in MTUCDA P69/183 (178–9).

158 JB to Mr Brown, 5 November 1926, in MTUCDA P69/183 (168–9).

159 Chairman to An Timthire, 9 February 1927, in MTUCDA P69/183 (111–12).

160 An Timthire to [no name], 1 February 1927 in P79/183 (129–31).

161 Chairman to An Timthire, 2 March 1927, in MTUCDA P69/183 (88–9).

162 Report of the foreign relations committee, no date, in MTUCDA P69/183 (136).

163 Chairman to An Timthire, 2 March 1927, in MTUCDA P69/183 (88–9); chairman to An Timthire, 11 May 1927, in MTUCDA P69/183 (41–3).

164 An Timthire to [no name], 1 February 1927 in P69/183 (129–31).

165 Tarpey, *The Role of Joseph McGarrity*, pp. 224–5.

166 Chairman to An Timthire, 24 February 1927, in MTUCDA P69/183 (106–7).

167 Chairman to An Timthire, 2 March 1927, in MTUCDA P69/183 (88–9).

168 MD to Mr Brown, 15 January 1927, in MTUCDA P69/183 (132–3).

169 Letter of introduction from Cardinal Dougherty, 13 December 1926 in McGarrity papers, MS 17553 NLI.

170 An Timthire to [no name], 28 February 1927, in MTUCDA P69/183 (98–9).

171 An Timthire to Mr Smith, 20 April 1927, in MTUCDA P69/183 (48–51).

172 An Timthire to [no name], 18 May 1927, in MTUCDA P69/183 (38–40).

173 An Timthire to Mr Smith, 20 April 1927, in MTUCDA P69/183 (48–51).

174 *Ibid.*

175 *Ibid.*

176 An Timthire to [no name], 18 May 1927, in MTUCDA P69/183 (38–40).

177 An Timthire to Mr Smith, 20 April 1927, in MTUCDA P69/183 (48–51).

178 An Timthire to [no name], 18 May 1927, in MTUCDA P69/183 (38–40).

179 Chairman to An Timthire, 9 February 1927 in P69/183 (111–12).

180 An Timthire to Mr Smith, 20 April 1927 in P69/183 (48–51).

181 Hanley, 'Irish Republicans in interwar New York', pp. 4–5.

182 An Timthire to [no name], 1 February 1927 in P69/183 (129–31).

183 Chairman to An Timthire, 2 March 1927 in P69/183 (88–9).

184 Doorley, *Irish-American Diaspora Nationalism*, pp. 34, 64, 89.

185 An Timthire to [no name], 28 February 1927, in MTUCDA P69/183 (98–9); *New York Times*, 24 February 1927.

186 Tarpey, *The Role of Joseph McGarrity*, pp. 305–6.

187 Doorley, *Irish-American Diaspora Nationalism*, p. 193.

188 Tarpey, *The Role of Joseph McGarrity*, p. 200.

189 *Ibid.*, pp. 210–11.

190 *Ibid.*, pp. 218.

191 *Ibid.*, p. 231.

192 MA to QMG, 9 January 1925, in MTUCDA P 69/37 (225); the currency for the amount of 25,000 is not given, but is more likely to be US dollars than £ sterling.

193 MA to MD, 21 January 1925, in MTUCDA P69/37 (229–30); MA to QMG, 9 January 1925, in MTUCDA P 69/37 (225).

194 CS to MA, 15 April 1925, in MTUCDA P69/37 (221–3).

195 Tarpey, *The Role of Joseph McGarrity*, p. 221.

196 An Timthire to [no name], 18 May 1927, in MTUCDA P69/183 (34).

197 Unsigned to An Timthire, 25 November 1923 [1926], in MTUCDA P69/183 (171).

198 Unsigned to Jones, 7 December 1926, in MTUCDA P69/183 (163–4); though this letter is unsigned there is considerable evidence that it was written by Andy Cooney rather than Moss Twomey. Firstly, Twomey was still imprisoned. Secondly, the

writer states that he had 'just' met the Soviet agent 'James' in London and Cooney had met with 'James' less than two weeks earlier – see: unsigned to 'A Chara Dhil', 25 November 1926, in MTUCDA P69/47 (52). Third, the author refers to his 'leaving' the US, and Cooney had returned to Ireland in the autumn of 1926, whereas Twomey hadn't recently been in the US, if ever.

199 An Timthire to [no name], 21 December 1926, in MTUCDA P69/183 (159–60); most likely from Connie Neenan rather than 'Mr Jones'; Neenan accepted the position of An Timthire on 2 December.

200 JB to Mr Browne, 21 October 1926, in MTUCDA P69/183 (183); chairman to An Timthire, 3 June 1927, in MTUCDA P69/183 (3–4).

201 Unsigned to Jones, 7 December 1926, in MTUCDA P69/183 (163–4).

202 MD to Mr Brown, 15 January 1927, in MTUCDA P69/183 (132–3).

203 Unsigned to Mr Jones, 14 December 1926, in MTUCDA P69/183 (161–2); An Timthire to [no name], 10 May 1927, in MTUCDA P69/183 (29–30).

204 An Timthire to [no name], 1 February 1927, in MTUCDA P69/183 (129–31).

205 Chairman to [no name], 2 March 1927, in MTUCDA P69/183 (88–9).

206 Instead of 'except' the actual decryption is 'expect' which I have taken to be an error by the document's author; unsigned to Mr Jones, 18 March 1927, in MTUCDA P69/183 (82–3).

207 Chairman to An Timthire, 29 April 1927, in MTUCDA P69/183 (58–9); chairman to An Timthire, 8 April, in MTUCDA P69/183 (74–5).

208 Chairman to An Timthire, 11 May 1927, in MTUCDA P69/183 (41–3).

209 An Timthire to [no name], 10 May 1927, in MTUCDA P69/183 (29–30); O'Connor's title is given as both 'Miss' and 'Mrs'.

210 An Timthire to Mr Smith, 20 April 1927, in MTUCDA P69/183 (48–51).

211 Chairman to An Timthire, 11 May 1927, in MTUCDA P69/183 (41–3).

212 An Timthire to [no name], 18 May 1927, in MTUCDA P69/183 (34).

213 Chairman to An Timthire, 3 June 1927, in MTUCDA P69/183 (3–4).

214 Tarpey, *The Role of Joseph McGarrity*, p. 243.

215 *Ibid.*, p. 246.

216 Chairman of Army Council to An Timthire, 8 April 1927, in MTUCDA P69/183 (74–75).

217 Unsigned to Mr Browne, 26 December 1926, in MTUCDA P69/183 (156); unsigned to Jones, 7 December 1926, in MTUCDA P69/183 (163–4).

218 An Timthire to [no name], 21 December 1926, in MTUCDA P69/183 (159–60).

219 An Timthire quoted in a document captured from the IRA courier, Patrick Garland, and published in the Irish papers; *Irish Times*, 1 May 1926.

220 Chairman of Army Council to An Timthire, 8 April 1927, in MTUCDA P69/183 (74–5).

221 Unsigned to George [Gilmore], 2 May 1927, in MTUCDA P69/48 (75).

222 MD to Mr Brown, 15 January 1927, in MTUCDA P69/183 (132–3).

223 Ambrose, J., *Dan Breen and the IRA* (Mercier Press, Cork, 2007).

224 Miss Annie O'Mahoney's address was given as: 431 W. 24th Street, New York; An Timthire to [no name], 28 February 1927, in MTUCDA P69/183 (98–99). *Irish Times*, 1 May 1926.

225 *An Phoblacht*, 10 December 1926; *The Advocate*, 23 April 1927.

226 CS to military attache, 15 April 1925, in MTUCDA P69/37 (221–3).

227 Tarpey, *The Role of Joseph McGarrity*, p. 213.

228 Hanley, *The IRA: 1926–1936*, p. 164.

229 Chairman to An Timthire, 2 March 1927, in MTUCDA P69/183 (88–9).

230 An Timthire to [no name], 1 February 1927, in MTUCDA P69/183 (129–31).

231 MD to Mr Brown, 15 January 1927, in MTUCDA P69/183 (132–3).

232 Chairman to An Timthire, 3 February 1927, in MTUCDA P69/183 (123–5).

233 An Timthire to [no name], 1 February 1927, in MTUCDA P69/183 (129–31).

234 An Timthire to [no name], 18 March 1927, in MTUCDA P69/183 (80).

235 Chairman to An Timthire, 24 February 1927, in MTUCDA P69/183 (106–7); chairman to An Timthire, 20 May 1927, in MTUCDA P69/183 (32).

236 Chairman to An Timthire, 3 June 1927, in MTUCDA P69/183 (6).

237 Hanley, 'Irish Republicans in interwar New York', p. 3.

238 Coleman, M., 'The Irish Hospitals Sweepstake in the United States of America, 1930–39', *HIS*, Vol. xxxv, No. 138 (November 2006), pp. 220–37.

239 Twomey to Neenan, 3 March 1933, in MTUCDA P69/185 (78–9).

240 FBI file on IRA, no date, referred to the bombing dated 28 May 1939, file number 61–555.

241 Tarpey, *The Role of Joseph McGarrity*, p. 339.

242 *Ibid.*, pp. 330–40

CHAPTER 8: THE SOVIET UNION AND CHINA

1 I use the terms 'Russia' and 'Soviet' interchangeably, as the Soviet Union was in reality the Russian Empire in another guise. The independence of the constituent republics of the USSR was largely fictitious and control was centralised in Moscow.

2 Leonard, R., *Secret Soldiers of the Revolution: Soviet Military Intelligence 1918–1931* (Greenwood Press, Westport, Connecticut, 1999), pp. 171–2.

3 *Ibid.*, pp. 86–7.

4 O'Connor, E., *Reds and the Green: Ireland, Russia and the Communist Internationals 1919–43* (UCD Press, Dublin, 2004), pp. 6–7.

5 In 1941 the RU was renamed the more familiar GRU; Leonard, *Secret Soldiers of the Revolution*, p. 17.

6 Leonard, *Secret Soldiers of the Revolution*, pp. XII–XIII.

7 *Ibid.*, pp. 57, 71.

8 Tucker, J., *War of Nerves: Chemical Warfare from World War 1 to Al-Quaeda* (Pantheon Books, New York, 2006), p. 20.

9 Conversation in 2007 with Jeffrey Smart, Chief Historian, Aberdeen Proving Ground, Maryland.

10 O'Connor, *Reds and the Green*, p. 15.

11 *Ibid.*, pp. 2–3.

12 *Ibid.*, p. 89.

13 *Ibid.*, pp. 93, 127; MacEoin, U., *The IRA in the Twilight Years, 1923–1948* (Argenta Publications, Dublin, 1997), pp. 116–17.

14 *An Phoblacht*, 22 January 1926; O'Connor, *Reds and the Green*, pp. 128, 170.

15 O'Connor, *Reds and the Green*, pp. 165, 187–8.

16 *Ibid.*, pp. 45, 47.

17 *Ibid.*, p. 1.

18 *Ibid.*, p. 74.

19 CS to military attaché, 15 April 1925, in MTUCDA P69/37 (221–3).

20 O'Connor, *Reds and the Green*, p. 112.

21 I am very grateful to Emmet O'Connor for sending me a copy of Krivitsky's M.I.5 file; CAB 126/250 from the National Archives, Kew.

22 S to MD, 30 September 1925, in MTUCDA P69/208 (7).

23 Unsigned to Jones, December 1926, in MTUCDA P69/183 (163–4).

24 Unsigned to Mr Jones, 18 March 1927, in MTUCDA P69/183 (82–3).

25 I am very grateful to Emmet O'Connor for sending me a copy of Krivitsky's M.I.5 file; CAB 126/250 from the National Archives, Kew.

26 S to MD, 30 September 1925, in MTUCDA P69/208 (7).

27 O'Connor, *Reds and the Green*, p. 113.

28 Chairman to Jones, 3 February 1927, in MTUCDA P69/183 (116–18); chairman to An Timthire, 11 May 1927, in MTUCDA P69/183 (41–3).

29 Unsigned to Jones, 7 December 1926, in MTUCDA P69/183 (163–4).

30 Jones to Mr Browne, 28 Feb. 1927, in MTUCDA P69/183 (102-104).

31 S to MD, 30 September 1925, in MTUCDA P69/208 (7).

32 An Timthire to [no name] 11 March 1926, in MTUCDA P69/183 (84–5).

33 Jones to Mr Browne, 28 February 1927 in P69/183 (102–4).

34 HS to CS, 14 May 1924 [1925], in MTUCDA P69/48 (23); notes on Beardmore engines in *Wikipedia*, 'Avro Aldershot and Blackburn Cubaroo', 19 January 2008.

35 CS to acting adjt Cork 1, 3 May 1926, in MTUCDA P69/44 (87–8).

36 CS to HS, 28 October 1926, in MTUCDA P69/41 (31).

37 HS to CS, 1 November 1926, in MTUCDA P69/41 (30).

38 To CS from HS, 7 February 1927, in MTUCDA P69/48 (310); HS to CS, 17 February 1927, in MTUCDA P69/48 (293–4).

39 CS to HS, 14 October 1923 [1926], in MTUCDA P69/47 (76); HS to CS 17 October 1926, in MTUCDA P69/41 (32).

40 KV 2/591 National Archives, Kew.

41 HS to CS, 20 April 1927, in MTUCDA P69/48 (61).

42 MD to HS, 28 May 1927, in MTUCDA P69/48 (17).

43 HS to CS, 24 May 1924 [1927], in MTUCDA P69/48 (18).

44 KV 2/591 National Archives, Kew.

45 MD to HS, 25 April 1927, in MTUCDA P69/48 (59).

46 HS to CS, 27 April 1927, in MTUCDA P69/48 (57).

47 M to CS, 3 April 1926, in MTUCDA P69/44 (219).

48 CS to OC. Britain, 8 April 1926, in MTUCDA P69/44 (218).

49 Chairman to An Timthire, 3 June 1927, in MTUCDA P69/183 (3–4).

50 Chairman to Mr Jones, 11 May 1927, in MTUCDA P69/183 (53).

51 Chairman to An Timthire, 3 June 1927, in MTUCDA P69/183 (3–4).

52 JB to Brown, 26 November 1926, in MTUCDA P69/183 (168–9).

53 Chairman to Jones, 3 February 1927, in MTUCDA P69/183 (116–18).

54 James to 'Dear Friend', 12 August 1926, in MTUCDA P69/181 (16–17).

55 Ambrose to CS and DI, 9 October 1926, in MTUCDA P69/41 (264).

56 Leonard, *Secret Soldiers of the Revolution*, p. 113.

57 OC. Britain to CS, 27 April 1926, in MTUCDA P69/44 (78).

58 To the Director from James, 28 July 1926, in MTUCDA P69/181 (19); to 'Dear Friend' from James, 12 August 1926, in MTUCDA P69/181 (16–17).

59 HS to CS or Chairman, 17 November 1926, in MTUCDA P69/41 (27).

60 HS to CS or Chairman, 17 November 1926, in MTUCDA P69/41 (27).

61 CS to HS, 8 December 1926, in MTUCDA P69/47 (10–11); unsigned to Mr Jones, 7 December 1926, in MTUCDA P69/183 (163–4); unsigned to 'A Chara Dhil', 25 November 1926, in MTUCDA P69/47 (52).

62 CS to HS, 8 December 1926, in MTUCDA P69/47 (10–11).

63 Unsigned to Mr Browne, 26 December 1926, in MTUCDA P69/183 (156).

64 HS to CS or CAC, 9 December 1926, in MTUCDA P69/47 (24).

65 Chairman to Mr Jones, 3 Feb 1927, in MTUCDA P69/183 (116–18).

66 O'Connor, *Reds and the Green*, p. 122–123.

67 To Mr Jones from Chairman, 3 February 1927, in MTUCDA P69/183 (116–18).

68 Unsigned to Mr Jones, 18 March 1927, in MTUCDA P69/183 (82–3).

69 O'Connor, *Reds and the Green*, p. 129.

70 *Ibid.*, p. 142.

71 Unsigned to Mr Jones, 18 March 1927, in MTUCDA P69/183 (82–3).

72 Chairman to Mr Jones, An Timthire 14 April 1927, in MTUCDA P69/183 (61–2).

73 HS to CS, 25 March 1924 [1927], in MTUCDA P69/48 (188).

74 Chairman to Mr Jones, An Timthire 14 April 1927, in MTUCDA P69/183 (61–2).

75 Chairman to An Timthire, 6 May 1927, in MTUCDA P69/183 (56).

76 HS to CS, 27 April 1924 [1927].

77 Chairman to Mr Jones, An Timthire 14 April 1927, in MTUCDA P69/183 (61–2).

78 Chairman to George, 25 April 1927, in MTUCDA P69/48 (60).

79 HS to CS, 6 May 1927, in MTUCDA P69/48 (27).

80 Chairman to An Timthire, 11 May 1927, in MTUCDA P69/183 (41–3).

81 MD to HS, 19 May 1927, in MTUCDA P69/48 (19).

82 HS to CS, 27 May 1927, in MTUCDA P69/48 (16).

83 Chairman to An Timthire, 3 June 1927 P69/183 (3–4).

84 Unsigned to HS, 31 May 1924 [1927], in MTUCDA P69/48 (13); HS to CS, 26 May 1927, in MTUCDA P69/48 (11 and 14); George wrote that he needed £40 to £50 after he made the purchases for 'James'.

85 Leonard, *Secret Soldiers of the Revolution*, pp. 74–7. *New York Times*, 13 May 1927.

86 HS to CS, 16 Mayy 1924 [1927], in MTUCDA P69/48 (22).

87 MD to HS, 18 May 1927, in MTUCDA P69/48 (21).

88 HS to MD, 20 June 1924 [1927], in MTUCDA P69/48 (2).

89 HS to 'Dear Sir', 27 September 1924 [1927], in MTUCDA P69/150 (26).

90 HS to 'Dear Sir', 1 October 1924 [1927], in MTUCDA P69/150 (12); MD to HS, 17 October 1927, in MTUCDA P69/150 (20).

91 'Friend' may refer to a Soviet agent other than 'James'; HS to 'Dear Sir', 20 September 1924 [1927], in MTUCDA P69/150 (32).

92 Unsigned to HS, 22 September 1927, in MTUCDA P69/150 (31).

93 HS to MD, 20 October 1924 [1927], in MTUCDA P69/150 (19).

94 O'Connor, *Reds and the Green*, p. 113.

95 *Ibid.*, p. 113.

96 *Ibid*.

97 *Ibid.*, pp. 129–30.

98 Poretsky, E., *Our Own People* (The University of Michigan Press, Ann Arbor, 1970), p. 84.

99 For chairman to An Timthire, 20 October 1926, in MTUCDA P69/183 (184–5); JB to Mr Browne, 8 November 1926, in MTUCDA P69/183 (178–9).

100 JB to Smith, 5 October 1926, in MTUCDA P69/183 (186).

101 JB to Browne, 8 November 1926, in MTUCDA P69/183 (178–9).

102 JB to Brown, 26 November 1926, in MTUCDA P69/183 (168–9).

103 Chairman to Jones, 3 February 1927, in MTUCDA P69/183 (116–18).

104 Jacob Monsess, National Archives, Kew, KV 2/982.

105 An Timthire to [no name], 10 May 1927, in MTUCDA P69/183 (29–30); Fries, A. and West, C., *Chemical Warfare* (McGraw Hill, New York, 1921).

106 An Timthire to [no name], 10 May 1927, in MTUCDA P69/183 (29–30).

107 An Timthire to [no name], 10 May 1927, in MTUCDA P69/183 (29–30).

108 JB to Mr Brown, a corrected paragraph, 26 November 1926, in MTUCDA P69/183 (167).

109 Jones to Smith, 20 April 1927, in MTUCDA P69/183 (54).

110 FBI files on IRA. 3 July 1940, 61–7550.

111 JB to Brown, 26 November 1926, in MTUCDA P69/183 (168–9).

112 Chairman to Jones, 3 February 1927, in MTUCDA P69/183 (116–18).

113 Jones to Browne, 28 February 1927, in MTUCDA P69/183 (102–4).

114 Jones and An Timthire to no name [chairman], 11 March 1927, in MTUCDA P69/183 (84–5).

115 MD to HS, 6 May 1927, in MTUCDA P69/48 (50); chairman to An Timthire, 6 May 1927, in MTUCDA P69/183 (56).

116 O'Halpin, E., *Defending Ireland: The Irish Free State and its Enemies since 1922* (Oxford University Press, Oxford, 2000), p. 73.

117 Jones to Mr Browne, 28 February 1927, in MTUCDA P69/183 (102–4).

118 Chairman to Mr Jones, 3 Feb. 1927, in MTUCDA P69/183 (116–118); Jones to Mr Smith, 8 April 1927, in MTUCDA P69/183 (68); Jones to Mr Smith, 20 April 1927, in MTUCDA P69/183 (54).

119 Jones and An Timthire to no name [chairman], 11 March 1927, in MTUCDA P69/183 (84–5).

120 Jones to Browne, 28 February 1927, in MTUCDA P69/183 (102–4).

121 An Timthire to Mr Smith, 20 April 1927, in MTUCDA P69/183 (48–51).

122 Jones to Mr Browne, 28 February 1927, in MTUCDA P69/183 (102–4).

123 An Timthire to Mr Smith, 20 April 1927, in MTUCDA P69/183 (48–51).

124 Chairman to An Timthire, 18 March 1927, in MTUCDA P69/183 (77–8).

125 Jones to Smith, 20 April 1927, in MTUCDA P69/183 (54).

126 Chairman to An Timthire, 11 May 1927, in MTUCDA P69/183 (41–4); chairman to Jones, 11 May 1927, in MTUCDA P69/183 (53).

127 An Timthire to [no name], 10 May 1927, in MTUCDA P69/183 (29–30); chairman to An Timthire, 11 May 1927, in MTUCDA P69/183 (41–4).

128 An Timthire to [no name], 10 May 1927, in MTUCDA P69/183 (29–30).

129 An Timthire to Mr Smith, 20 April 1927, in MTUCDA P69/183 (48–51); chairman to An Timthire, 11 May 1927, in MTUCDA P69/183 (41–4).

130 Chairman to An Timthire, 3 June 1927, in MTUCDA P69/183 (6).

131 CS to 'A Chara', 5 June 1927, in MTUCDA P69/183 (63).

132 Chairman to An Timthire, 8 April 1927, in MTUCDA P69/183 (74–5).

133 An Timthire to [no name], 1 February 1927, in MTUCDA P69/183 (129–31).

134 An Timthire to [no name], 10 May 1927, in MTUCDA P69/183 (29–30).

135 MacEoin, U., *Survivors* (Argenta Publications, Dublin, 1987), p. 252.

136 *Ibid.*, p. 250.

137 Twohig, P. and Ó Maoileoin, S., *Blood on the Flag* (Tower Books, Ballincollig, 1996), p. 92.

138 MacEoin, *Survivors*, p. 255.

139 Hopkinson, M., *Green Against Green* (Gill & MacMillan, Dublin, 1988), pp. 73–4.

140 Twohig and Ó Maoileoin, *Blood on the Flag*, p.101.

141 MacEoin, *The IRA in the Twilight Years*, p. 141.

142 Spence, J. *The Search for Modern China* (W. W. Norton and Company, New York, 1990), p. 382.

143 *Ibid.*, pp. 348–9.

144 *Ibid.*, p. 381.

145 Leonard, *Secret Soldiers of the Revolution*, p. 38.

146 *Ibid.*

147 Spence, *The Search for Modern China*, pp. 345–9.

148 *Ibid.*, p. 353; Leonard, *Secret Soldiers of the Revolution*, pp. 38–42.

149 'The Wanhsien Incident', on the website: *www.hmsfalcon.com*, 2 January 2006.

150 *Irish World*, 25 September 1926.

151 *An Phoblacht*, 28 January 1927.

152 Chairman to An Timthire, 3 Feb 1927, in MTUCDA P69/183 (123–5); chairman to An Timthier, 9 February 1927, in MTUCDA P69/183 (111–12).

153 An Timthire to [no name], 28 February 1927, in MTUCDA P69/183 (98–9).

154 An Timthire to Mr Smith, 20 April 1927, in MTUCDA P69/183 (48–51).

155 *Ibid.*

156 *Irish World*, 28 May 1927.

157 Chairman to An Timthire, 3 February 1927, in MTUCDA P69/183 (123–5).

158 Minutes of Army Council meeting, 17 February 1927, in MTUCDA P69/48 (117); CS to HS, 18 February 1927, in MTUCDA P69/48 (300).

159 Newspaper cutting in the Twomey papers in UCD; no number, no date.

160 OC Scottish batt to CS, 13 February 1927, in MTUCDA P69/48 (208).

161 CS to OC Scotland, 24 February 1927, in MTUCDA P69/48 (296).

162 CS to OC Number 2 Area Britain, 24 February 1927, in MTUCDA P69/48 (242).

163 Spence, *The Search for Modern China*, p. 381.

164 James to 'Dear Friend', 12 August 1926, in MTUCDA P69/181 (16–17 and 11–12).

165 I am very grateful to Emmet O'Connor for sending me a copy of Krivitsky's M.I.5 file; CAB 126/250 from the National Archives, Kew.

166 Cronin, S., *The McGarrity Papers* (Anvil Books, Tralee, copyright 1972), pp. 161, 181; Tarpey, M., *The Role of Joseph McGarrity in the Struggle for Irish Independence* (Arno Press, New York, 1976), p. 265.

EPILOGUE

1 Coogan, T. P., *The IRA: A History* (Roberts Rinehart Publishers, Niwot, Colorado, 1993), p. 200.

2 *Ibid.*, p. 37. MacEoin, U., *The IRA in the Twilight Years, 1923–1948*, pp. 190, 195.

3 Hanley, B., *The IRA, 1926–1936* (Four Courts Press, Dublin, 2002), p. 14.

4 *Ibid.*, pp. 14–17.

5 *Ibid.*, p. 17.

6 MacEoin, *The IRA in the Twilight Years*, pp. 279–80.

7 Hanley, *The IRA, 1926–1936*, pp. 18, 144, 206; Coogan, *The IRA*, p. 68.

8 Hanley, *The IRA, 1926–1936*, pp. 18, 194.

9 *Ibid.*, pp. 197–8.

10 *Ibid.*, p. 18.

11 *Ibid.*, pp. 191, 194, 196, 199.

12 *Ibid.*, p. 194.

<small>APPENDIX</small> 2

1 Newspaper cutting, no date, P69/48 (52-53). File on Ethel Chiles, National Archives, Kew, KV 2/591.

2 HS to CS, 18 March 1924 [1927] in MTUCDA P69/48 (210)

3 MD to HS, 6 May 1927 in MTUCDA P69/48 (50)

4 HS to CS, 14 May 1924 [1927] in MTUCDA P69/48 (23)

Bibliography

Manuscripts
University College Dublin Archives
Moss Twomey Papers.
Ernie O'Malley Notebooks

National Library of Ireland
Joseph McGarrity Papers

The National Archives, Kew.
Security Service Files: KV 2/591, Ethel Chiles a.k.a. Kate Gussfeldt.
  KV 2/805, General W. Krivitsky.
  KV 2/982, Jacob Monsess

FBI files on the IRA
1939 and 1940

Contemporary newspapers
An Phoblacht, reviewed at the National Library of Ireland
Connacht Tribune, on-line access.
Irish World, reviewed at the National Library of Ireland
The Advocate, reviewed at the New York Public Library
The Irish Independent, on-line access
The Irish Times, on-line access
The New York Times, on-line access

Published works
Andrews, C. S. *Dublin Made Me* (Mercier Press, Dublin and Cork, 1979)
Augusteijn, J. *From Public Defiance to Guerrilla Warfare* (Irish Academic Press, County Dublin, 1996)
Bayor, R. and Meagher T. *The New York Irish* (Johns Hopkins University Press, Baltimore, 1996)
Borgonovo, J. *Florence and Josephine O'Donoghue's War of Independence* (Irish Academic Press, Dublin, 2006)
Bowyer Bell, J. *The Secret Army: The IRA 1916-1970* (The John Day Company, New York, 1971)
Briscoe, R. *For the Life of Me* (Little Brown and Company, Boston, 1958)
Callimahos, L. *Traffic Analysis and the Zendian Problem* (Aegean Park Press, Walnut Creek, California, 1989)
Coogan, T. P. *The IRA: A History* (Roberts Rinehart Publishers, Niwot, Colorado, 1993)
Cronin, S. *The McGarrity Papers* (Anvil Books, Tralee, 1972)
Cunliffe, B., Bartlett R. *et al*, *The Penguin Atlas of British and Irish History* (Penguin Books, London, 2001)
D'Imperio, Mary, *The Voynich Manuscript: An Elegant Enigma* (National Security Agency, Fort George G. Meade, Maryland, 1978).

Dodgson, Charles L. (as Lewis Carroll), 'The Alphabet-Cipher', *The Complete Works of Lewis Carroll* (Modern Library, New York, 1936)

Doorley, M. *Irish-American Diaspora Nationalism: The Friends of Irish Freedom, 1916–1935* (Four Courts Press, Dublin, 2005)

Durney, J. The Mob: The History of Irish Gangsters in America

English, R. *Armed Struggle: The History of the IRA* (Macmillan, London, 2003)

— *Radicals and the Republic: Socialist Republicanism in the Irish Free State, 1925–1937* (Clarendon Press, Oxford, 1994)

Fallon, C. *Soul of Fire: A Biography of Mary MacSwiney* (Mercier Press, Cork, 1986)

Friedman, W. F. and Callimahos, L. D. *Military Cryptanalytics*, Part I, Volume 1 (Aegean Park Press, Laguna Hills, 1985)

Fries, A. and West, C. *Chemical Warfare* (McGraw Hill, New York, 1921)

Griffith, K. and O'Grady, T. *Ireland's Unfinished Revolution* (Roberts Rinehardt, Colorado, 1999)

Hanley, B. *The IRA, 1926–1936* (Four Courts Press, Dublin, 2002)

Hart, P. *The IRA at War 1916–1923* (Oxford University Press, Oxford, 2003) pp. 163-64.

Hegarty, P. *Peadar O'Donnell* (Mercier Press, Cork, 1999).

Hopkinson, M. *Green Against Green: The Irish Civil War* (Gill and Macmillan, Dublin, 1988)

Hopkinson, M. *The Irish War of Independence* (Gill and Macmillan, Dublin, 2002)

Kahn, David, *The Codebreakers* (The Macmillan Company, New York, 1967)

Kramer, A. *Dynamic of Destruction* (Oxford University Press, Oxford, 2007)

Lawlor, C. *Seán MacBride, That Day's Struggle: A Memoir 1904-1951* (Currach Press, Dublin, 2005)

Lee, J. J. *Ireland 1912–1985: Politics and Society* (Cambridge University Press, Cambridge, 1989)

Lee, J. and Casey, M. *Making the Irish American* (New York University Press, New York, 2006)

Leonard, R. *Secret Soldiers of the Revolution: Soviet Military Intelligence 1918–1931* (Greenwood Press, Westport, Connecticut, 1999)

Linklater, A. *An Unhusbanded Life, Charlotte Despard: Suffragette, Socialist and Sinn Féiner* (Hutchinson, London, 1980)

Lynch, B. *Parsons Bookshop* (The Liffey Press, Dublin, 2006)

MacEoin, U. *Survivors* (Argenta Publications, Dublin, 1987)

— *The IRA in the Twilight Years, 1923-1948* (Argenta Publications, Dublin, 1997)

McGee, O. *The IRB: The Irish Republican Brotherhood from the Land League to Sinn Féin* (Four Courts Press, Dublin, 2005).

Mulvihill, M. *Charlotte Despard: A Biography* (Pandora Press, London, 1989)

O'Connor, E. *Reds and the Green: Ireland, Russia and the Communist Internationals 1919–43* (UCD Press, Dublin, 2004)

O'Donoghue, F. *No Other Law* (Anvil Books, Dublin, 1986)

Ó Drisceoil, D. *Peadar O'Donnell* (Cork University Press, Cork, 2001)

O'Farrell, P. *Who's Who in the Irish War of Independence and Civil War, 1916–1923* (Lilliput Press, Dublin, 1997)

O'Halpin, E. *Defending Ireland: The Irish Free State and its Enemies since 1922* (Oxford University Press, Oxford, 2000)

O'Malley, C. and Dolan A. *'No Surrender here!' The Civil War Papers of Ernie O'Malley 1922–1924* (Lilliput Press, Dublin, 2007).

Patterson, H. *The Politics of Illusion: A Political History of the IRA* (Serif, London, 1997).

Pelling, Nicholas, *The Curse of the Voynich* (Compelling Press, Surbiton, Surrey, 2006).

Poretsky, E. *Our Own People* (The University of Michigan Press, Ann Arbor, 1970).

Regan, J. *The Irish Counter-Revolution: 1921–1936* (Gill & Macmillan, Dublin, 1999)

Spence, J. *The Search for Modern China* (W W Norton and Company, New York, 1990)

Suetonius Tranquillus, Gaius, *The Lives of the Twelve Caesars* (Gutenberg.org document 6400, 2006), (1) Gaius Julius Caesar, para. LVI.

Swearengen, T. *Tear Gas Munitions* (Charles C. Thomas, Springfield, Illinois, 1966)

Tarpey, M. *The Role of Joseph McGarrity in the Struggle for Irish Independence* (Arno Press, New York, 1976)

The Concise Oxford Dictionary (Clarendon Press, Oxford, 1979), sixth edition

Tucker, J. *War of Nerves: Chemical Warfare from World War 1 to Al-Qaeda* (Pantheon Books, New York, 2006)

Twohig, P. and O Maoileoin, S. *Blood on the Flag* (Tower Books, Ballincollig, 1996)

Journals

Coleman, M. *The Irish Hospitals Sweepstake in the United States of America, 1930 – 39.* Irish Historical Studies, xxxv, no. 138 (Nov. 2006), pp. 220-237.

Hanley, B. *Irish Republicans in interwar New York,* unpublished paper

Hu H. *et al. Tear Gas – Harassing Agent or Toxic Chemical Weapon?* Journal of the American Medical Association, 4 Aug. 1989, Volume 262, number 5

McMahon, P. *British intelligence and the Anglo-Irish truce, 1921*, Irish Historical Studies, XXXV, No. 140 (Nov. 2007), pp. 519–540.

Paseta, S. *Censorship and its Critics in the Irish Free State 1922–1932.* Past & Present, 181, Nov. 2003, pp. 193–218.

Websites

Note: Due to the possibility of inaccuracy of on-line sources, they were only occasionally used as a source. When referenced, we made extensive efforts to independently verify and cross-reference the information and the material was used for peripheral topics or non-critical information.

Ballinasloe.org

Brainyquote.com

http://www.gutenberg.org.

esrc.ac.uk. Centre for Economic Performance at the London School of Economics

guardian.com

home.rochester.rr.com/thatchetree/index.html

hmsfalcon.com.

Manchesteronline.co.uk

Merriam-Webster online

www. Spartacus.schoolnet.co.uk

Web 1T 5-gram Version 1, Linguistic Data Consortium, University of Pennsylvania, 2006.

Oireachtas.ie (Irish parliament or Dáil)

sipri.org, Stockholm International Peace Research Institute website.

Terrace Talk Ireland

US Department of State website

Wikipedia

Worldwar1.com

Acknowledgements

There were two aspects of this project that made it most memorable: one was the documents themselves, which revealed a world of intrigue reminiscent of a John le Carre spy novel. The other was the many wonderful and interesting people I met during the last four years.

It has been a delight working with James Gillogly whose expertise fascinated me at every stage of this work. I'm very grateful for Jim and his wife Marrietta's sage advice and hospitality. Marrietta's editing and review of the manuscript was of enormous value.

The encrypted documents came from the Moss Twomey papers at University College Dublin Archives. I'm extremely grateful to Seamus Helferty, the principal archivist, for his tremendous assistance, encouragement and patience in answering my many queries. I'm also grateful to the ever helpful archivists: Lisa Collins, Kate Manning and Orna Somerville.

Brian Hanley was most generous of his time and provided me with much information including an unpublished paper on the IRA in America. Emmet O'Connor was also of great help and sent me relevant portions of the MI5 file of General Walter Krivitsky. Tim Pat Coogan shared his insights on the IRA and was unfailingly hospitable. Dr Garret FitzGerald was most gracious to give of his time and to respond to my queries.

In Dublin I'm indebted to the advice and assistance of Peter O'Leary, Des Mahon and Joe Allen. Thanks to Mike and Caroline Allen, Francis Devine, Sean O'Mahony and Michael MacEvilly. In Cork I'd like to thank Deirdre and Maeve Crofts. With fond memories of Dominic Crofts and Helen O'Donovan. I'd like to take this opportunity to also thank Tony Duggan who went out of his way to provide me with tremendous help on a still unfinished research project. Meda Ryan from Clare was particularly helpful and gracious. Thanks to Ann Horan in Offaly and Yvonne Murphy of the Linen Hall Library in Belfast. Many thanks to the staff at the National Library of Ireland and the Military Archives, Dublin – particularly Commandant Victor Lang.

Thanks to Mark Ellis and Arthur McIvor in Glasgow and to Graham Stevenson and the staff at the National Archives in England.

In Hawaii I'd like to thank Oren and Fran Schlieman, William Bagasol, Joy Yamashiro and Joe Solem. While in Moanalua Valley I'm extremely grateful to Dan Henshaw, Natalie Lindsey, Jeanne Munson, Colleen Kelley and Cha Smith for their encouragement and support.

On mainland America I'm very grateful to William Colbert, Dave Smith and the American Cryptogram Association, Aedin Clements, Michael Short, Raymond Leonard, David Chuber, Robert Walk, Peter McDermott, Jonathan Tucker, Marilynn Johnson, Kevin Kenny, Pat Noone-Bonner, Maureen Depoortere, Barbara Horn, Cathy O'Brien, Julia Eichhorst, John P McCarthy, Dan Lyons, Bente Polites and the staff at the New York Public Library.

I'm particularly grateful to the folks at Mercier Press especially Mary Feehan, Eoin Purcell, Patrick Crowley and Lisa Daly who designed the book cover.

The information required for this book was very specific and I was unable to avail of the knowledge of many of those who offered to help. To these people I'm very grateful.

To all whose assistance I've failed to mention, I apologise.

While much of the IRA's secret correspondence in this book concerns official policy, some of it – particularly the prison correspondence of Mick Price and George Gilmore – is personal and of this I'm deeply respectful and admire their sense of duty and sacrifice. Though many IRA actions and plans during this period are concerning from a moral perspective, I was also touched by the dedication and commitment of many volunteers and the women who acted as couriers and provided safe houses and covering addresses. Jim and I acknowledge the suffering of those who crossed the IRA – some for merely attempting to give evidence in a court of law.

My son Tommy (age 10) has been a source of great inspiration, fun and (frankly) great ideas. Thanks Tommy! My wife, Sui Lan, has been of tremendous support and encouragement, without which I couldn't have worked on this for the past four years.

If you, the reader, have any information on the characters or incidents mentioned in this book, James and I would love to hear from you. Maybe you noticed the name of a grandparent or a great-aunt. Maybe you know something more about 'Mr Jones' or George the IRA commander in Britain. We'd like to include any verifiable information in a future edition. You can write to us: Tom Mahon or James Gillogly, c/o Mercier Press, Unit 3, Oak House, Bessboro Road, Blackrock, Cork, Ireland.

Tom Mahon, Honolulu, Hawaii

I would like to thank my wife Marrietta Gillogly for her constant support, for providing a sounding board as I developed new attacks, for helping read some of the messages with difficult handwriting and faint typing, and for reading and helping tune the entire manuscript. David L. Smith, William K. Mason, Eleanor Joyner and Jude Patterson, members of the American Cryptogram Association, each provided valuable advice and assistance in the decryption process. Thanks also go to the American Cryptogram Association for thirty-five years of training and experience in tackling unknown ciphers.

James J. Gillogly, Long Beach, California

Index

DAYS OF FEAR

Diary
of a
1920s
Hunger Striker

FRANK GALLAGHER

TANS, TERROR AND TROUBLES

KERRY'S REAL FIGHTING STORY 1913–23

T. RYLE DWYER

THE
SQUAD

and the

intelligence operations of

Michael Collins

T. RYLE DWYER

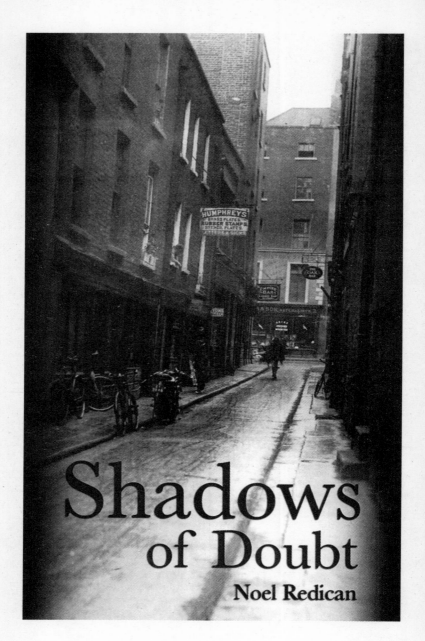

Shadows
of Doubt

Noel Redican